DAUGHTERS OF THE KING:

WOMEN AND THE SYNAGOGUE

A Survey of
History, Halakhah, and
Contemporary Realities

EDITED BY

Susan Grossman
Rivka Haut

DAUGHTERS OF THE KING

WOMEN AND THE SYNAGOGUE

THE JEWISH PUBLICATION SOCIETY

Philadelphia · *New York* · *Jerusalem*

5752/1992

The English renderings of passages from the Hebrew Bible conform generally to
Tanakh: The Holy Scriptures (JPS, 1985). In some cases, however, an alternative
translation has been used by the author.

Library of Congress Cataloging-in-Publication Data
Daughters of the King : women and the synagogue : a survey of history,
    halakhah, and contemporary realities / edited by Susan Grossman and
    Rivka Haut. — 1st ed.
        p.   cm.
    Includes bibliographical references and index.
    ISBN 0-8276-0395-9
    1. Women in synagogues.   2. Women, Jewish—Religious life.
3. Women—Legal status, laws, etc. (Jewish law).   4. Prayer—Judaism.
5. Women, Jewish—Biography.   I. Grossman, Susan, 1955- .
II. Haut, Rivka, 1942- .
BM726.D37   1992
296.6'5'082—dc20   91-31430
                                                                  CIP

Design: Adrianne Onderdonk Dudden

וִיהַלְלוּהָ בַשְּׁעָרִים מַעֲשֶׂיהָ

And let her works praise her in the gates
Proverbs 31:31

This volume is dedicated in loving memory of

GOLDIE S. COHEN

(1 9 0 2 – 1 9 9 0)

by her family:

her husband, Dr. Abram Cohen;

her children,

Betty A. Cohen, Josephine Cohen, D. Walter Cohen;

her grandchildren,

Jane E. Millner, Martin S. Millner,

Amy S. Cohen, Joanne L. Cohen;

and her great-grandchildren,

Rachel E. Millner, Lauren R. Millner,

Michael S. Millner.

To the memory of our grandmothers
Shaindel and Chaikie, Rose, and Shirley
and to the honor of our mothers
Esta and Adaline

CONTENTS

TWO
HALAKHAH

Contents

ACKNOWLEDGMENTS

This book grew out of a shared spiritual journey and intellectual dialogue over the course of several years between the two of us, individuals of disparate backgrounds and philosophies. Rivka was raised and educated in an Orthodox neighborhood in Brooklyn. She and her husband, an attorney who is an ordained Orthodox rabbi, raised their two daughters to be modern Orthodox. Susan, born into an assimilated second-generation American family, first began learning about Judaism as a college senior. She is now one of the first women rabbis in the Conservative Movement. She and her caterer/composer husband are partners in an egalitarian marriage, sharing in the rearing of their young son.

Although we lived within a few blocks of each other, we probably would never have met except that, in a neighborhood full of synagogues, our paths crossed while seeking a religious community in which we could feel comfortable. We each found our way to a newly formed, nontraditional Orthodox synagogue that was dedicated to involving women to the fullest extent possible under Orthodox Jewish law.

After several years of working to increase our involvement in the ritual of the synagogue, we found that, unfortunately, even this synagogue could not fulfill our needs as women. We realized then that there are inherent limitations for women who wish to actively participate in services in a traditional Orthodox setting. At this point, our paths parted: Rivka went on to help organize the Flatbush Women's Davening Group. Susan helped found a local Ḥavurah group and later entered rabbinical school. Since then, although representing different constituencies, we have joined with others to assert the legal and halakhic rights of women to pray together at the Western Wall in Jerusalem and throughout Israel. The dialogue between us has continued because our shared experiences as Jewish women overrode any differences we had concerning movement affiliation or religious philosophy.

We have met many other women who face similar frustrations. These women represent all aspects of the Jewish community: Orthodox, Conservative, Reform, and Reconstructionist; those raised to be observant, the newly religious "returnees" (*baᶜalot teshuvah*), and converts; and rabbis, cantors, and other Jewish professionals. All across the Jewish world, we found that women are seeking to redefine their role *vis-à-vis* Judaism in general and the synagogue in particular.

We realized that for all these women, and the men who support their efforts, the courage to challenge accepted norms has been fueled by knowledge. Knowledge of the past serves as a beacon to the future. However, one must be wary of the pitfalls of revisionism on the one hand and apologetics on the other, which have marred some works on women and Judaism. In light of these considerations, we decided to write this book as a resource for those who seek to create new realities and as a record of their achievements.

It has been our pleasure to work with many talented and committed individuals in the course of completing this volume. While we cannot possibly name all those people and institutions that have been supportive of this project, we would like to acknowledge some that have been particularly helpful. Among these are the assistance we received from the Library of the Jewish Theological Seminary of America, particularly from Yael Penkower, the reference librarian, whose vast knowledge of Judaica we relied upon constantly. We are also very grateful to Shulamith Berger, archivist at Yeshiva University, and to Nan Bases for her sage counsel and legal advice. In addition, we would like to mention these individuals for their special input: Monty Penkower, Paula Hyman, Rela Monson, Blu Greenberg, Larry Kohler, Annelise Orleck, and Donna Swift. Our editors at The Jewish Publication Society have been thoughtful and enthusiastic throughout the project. We particularly wish to thank Diane W. Zucker-man, managing editor, Gloria Klaiman, copy editor, Michael A. Monson, executive vice president, and, especially, Sheila F. Segal, former consult-ing editor.

In one respect, the verse, "The King's daughter is all glorious within," is applicable to the beauty and support we both found within our fami-lies. Our husbands, Irwin Haut and David Boder, both read various drafts of the book. Their gifts of time, encouragement, and insight have been invaluable. Rivka's daughters Sheryl and Tamara, and sons-in-law, David Rosenberg and Seth Weissman, were always supportive and helpful. Susan's son, Yonatan, arrived during the completion of this volume, high-lighting the fact that what we are working for on this project is not only for ourselves, but for our children as well. We pray that somehow this book will have a positive effect on their lives and the lives of their children.

Susan Grossman and Rivka Haut
13 December 1989
15 Kislev 5750

NOTE ON TRANSLITERATION

The editors have adopted a popular system for transliteration of Hebrew, except for the following letters, which have no English equivalent:
    ʾ = alef
    ʿ = ayin
    ḥ = ḥet (pronounced as the guttural "ch" in German)
   kh = khaf (pronounced as the guttural "ch" in German)

ABBREVIATIONS

Adv. Jud.	Aduersus Iudeos	Hor.	Horiyot
Ant.	Antiquities	Hos.	Hosea
Ar.	Arkhin	Hul.	Hullin
Av. Zar.	Avodah Zarah	Isa.	Isaiah
BARev.	Biblical Archeology Review	IM	Igrot Moshe
		Jer.	Jeremiah
BB.	Bava Batra	Josh.	Joshua
Ber.	Berakhot	JPS	The Jewish Publication Society
BK	Baba Kamma		
BM	Baba Metzia	JTS	Jewish Theological Seminary
Chron.	Chronicles		
Cor.	Corinthians	Jth.	Judith
Deut.	Deuteronomy	Judg.	Judges
Deut. R.	Deuteronomy Rabbah	Ker.	Keritot
EncJud	Encyclopaedia Judaica	Ket.	Ketubot
EH	Even Haezer	Kid.	Kiddushin
Er.	Eruvin	Lev.	Leviticus
Esd.	Esdras	Lev.R.	Leviticus Rabbah
Exod.	Exodus	LXX	Septuagint
Exod. R.	Exodus Rabbah	Meg.	Megillah
Gen.	Genesis	Men.	Menahot
Git.	Gittin	Mic.	Micah
Hag.	Hagigah	Mid.	Middoth
Hal.	Hallah	Mish.	Mishnah

Abbreviations

MK	Moed Katan	Sot.	Sotah
Naz.	Nazir	Suk.	Sukkah
Ned.	Nedarim	Tanh.	Tanḥuma
Neg.	Negaim	Tarq. Onk.	Targum Onkeles
Neh.	Nehemiah	TB	Talmud Bavli
Nid.	Niddah		(Babylonian Talmud)
Num.	Numbers	TJ	Yerushalmi
Num. R.	Numbers Rabbah		(Jerusalem Talmud)
OḤ	Orah Ḥayyim	Tos.	Tosafot
Pes.	Pesahim	Tosef.	Tosefta
Ps.	Psalms	Wars	Wars Against the Jews
RH	Rosh Hashanah	Yal. Shimoni	Yalkut Shimoni
Sam.	Samuel	Yev.	Yevamot
Sanh.	Sanhedrin	YD	Yoreh Deah
Shab.	Shabbat	Zech.	Zechariah
Shek.	Shekalim	Zev.	Zevahim
Shevu.	Shevuot		

PREFACE

DAUGHTERS OF THE KING [1]

The king's daughter is all glorious within,
Her clothing is of wrought gold
She shall be brought unto the king in raiment of needlework
The virgins her companions that follow her
Shall be brought unto thee.
With gladness and rejoicing shall they be brought
They shall enter into the king's palace.

Psalm 45 : 14ff.

In the past two decades, women have made tremendous advances in obtaining access to the sources of power in the Jewish community: traditional scholarship, positions of communal leadership, input into religious decision making and—the ultimate bastion of traditional male authority—the rabbinate. These advances, obtained at times through painful personal struggles, have been difficult to achieve. This has especially been the case when opponents of broadening women's roles argue that such advances fly in the face of "tradition," albeit a tradition very loosely defined.

As religious feminists who seriously seek to integrate Jewish practice with our contemporary sense of self-worth, we must grapple with troubling questions about how to relate to a patriarchal tradition with which we often find ourselves at odds. The first step in answering these questions lies in a critical study of traditional sources. Such a study is a necessary prerequisite when trying, in a thoughtful and educated way, to delineate lore from law and to harmonize religion with Western beliefs of equality, democracy, and pluralism.

Once the building blocks of the traditional sources are mastered, we can proceed to the next step: those very sources that have been used to limit women's participation in study and ritual can also be used to provide support for women's active involvement. There are several ways of accomplishing this. One is to interpret Jewish law so as to encompass new realities. Another is to develop creative exegesis in the form of *Midrash*. Technically, *Midrash* refers to collections of rabbinic interpretations, both legal (*Midrash Halakhah*) and narrative (*Midrash Aggadah*), of biblical texts. Today, that process of interpretation continues as a method of grappling with the meaning and significance of our holy texts. *Midrash* becomes a bridge between the static text and the contemporary reader, ensuring that classical Jewish sources remain eternally relevant and compelling.

Let us now apply this methodology to one scriptural verse, the mere citation of which has come to be used as a code to signify that a particular activity is off limits for women because it falls outside their traditionally prescribed role:

> *Kol kevudah bat melekh penimah,*
> *Mi-mishbetzot zahav levushah.*
>
> The king's daughter is all glorious within,
> Her clothing is of wrought gold.
> Psalm 45:14

This verse has been cited as proof that, according to tradition, women have divinely ordained roles that preclude any public activity. Rabbis throughout the ages, including our own, have cited this beautiful image to justify excluding women from public life, restricting their dress, and stressing that women's sole legitimate sphere of activity is *within* the home. The use of this phrase has become so widespread that it surfaces in most discussions about broadening women's role in Jewish ritual and communal life. It is often cited by Orthodox, Conservative, and other scholars who seek to exclude women from elected office in Israel,[2] from praying together in public places,[3] and from the rabbinate.[4]

Psalm 45 is a beautiful hymn written in praise of an earthly king. It describes the "kings' daughters" of other nations who have come to wait upon the Israelite king (Ps. 45 : 10). They are advised to forget their own people and devote themselves to the king.

By the rabbinic period, this verse was already taken out of its original biblical context, and endowed with completely different meanings.

An anecdote that appears several times in the Jerusalem Talmud and in *midrashic* literature praises a woman named Kimḥit for her unusual modesty.[5] The version, as it appears in the Jerusalem Talmud (Yoma 1 : 1, 5a), follows:

> Kimḥit had seven sons, and every one served as High Priest. The sages sent and asked her; "What good deeds have you done [to merit this honor]?" She told them, "[Terrible things] should happen to me if the walls of my home ever saw the hair on my head, and the borders of my frock." It was said: All flour is regular flour, but the flour (*kemah*) of Kimḥit is fine flour. And it was said of her, "The king's daughter is all glorious within, Her clothing is of wrought gold."

The classical eighteenth-century commentator on the Jerusalem Talmud, Korban ha-Edah, David ben Naftali Hirsch Fraenkel, explains the Talmud's use of the verse to mean that a woman who dresses modestly deserves to have a son who wears golden garments, that is, who serves as the High Priest.

This oft-repeated anecdote is meant to encourage modesty by stressing its rewards. Kimḥit's reward is vicarious. Paradoxically, the more private Kimḥit is, the more public will be her son's position.

The value of modesty is beyond the scope of this essay. While modesty may be a virtue, in practice it has often been translated into a restriction of women's activities. Both elements—modesty in dress and restriction of activity—are merged in the following *midrash*.

In *Tanḥuma*,[6] we find the following explanation for the rape of Dinah, the daughter of Leah and Jacob. It asserts that a woman's appearance in a public place is a temptation to men.

> A woman should not go out to a public place on the Sabbath wearing her jewelry . . . And our rabbis say that even on weekdays she should not go out to a public place, where people will gaze at her, because God provided jewelry to woman

only so that she could adorn herself within her home . . . [I]t is written: "The king's daughter is all glorious within, Her clothing is of wrought gold" . . . And it has already been said of this matter, hinted at in the Torah, that a woman shall not walk much in the marketplace . . . However, if she habitually would go to the marketplace, in the end she would come to ruin, to promiscuity. And this is what you find about Dinah, the daughter of Jacob. As long as she sat in her home she was not ruined by sin, but as soon as she went out to the marketplace, she caused herself to come to ruin.[7]

This *midrash* responds to the biblical phrase, "Dinah went out . . ." (Gen. 34:1) by implying that the rape was a result of her going out, a form of "loose" behavior. Had she remained in her home, as our verse from Psalms, "The king's daughter is all glorious within. . . ," advises, she would have remained safe. The *midrash*, in effect, blames the victim for the crime.

By the twelfth century, what had been offered in Talmudic and midrashic literature as advice became codified into law by the great Talmudist and philosopher, Maimonides, in his *Mishneh Torah*. In *Hilkhot Ishut* (The Laws of Marriage), 13:11, in a discussion of a husband's obligation to provide his wife with appropriate apparel, he says:

In a place where it is the custom for a woman to go out to the market not only with the cap (*kippah*) on her head [but also with] a veil that covers her entire body, like a *tallit*, he [her husband] gives her, included in her dress [allotment], the simplest type of veil. And if he is wealthy, he gives her according to his wealth, in order that she may go out in it to her father's house, or to the house of mourning, or to the house of feasting [e.g., for a wedding]. Because every woman may go and come to her father's house to visit him, and to the house of mourning, and to the house of feasting in order to do kindness to her friends or to her relatives, so that they will similarly visit her. For she is not in prison that she cannot go out and come in. However, it is shameful (*genai*) for a woman to always be going out, one time outdoors, another time on the streets. And a husband should stop his wife from this and should not allow her to go outside except perhaps once a month or perhaps a few times a month, according to the need. Because it is not becoming to a woman. Rather she should sit within her home (lit., in a corner of her home), for so it is written: "The king's daughter is all glorious within."

Thus, Maimonides acknowledges that a woman may appear in public but exhorts her husband to control and limit her movements. Interestingly, in his list of permitted reasons for a woman to leave her home, he does not include going to synagogue. Maimonides, and indeed all the sources cited here, contributes to establishing clearly delineated male and female roles in Judaism: The proper place for women is in the home and not in the public eye. For women, these two areas of activity are mutually exclusive.

To be fair, the very fact that this verse was used to restrict women to the home sometimes had positive practical benefits. The Talmud (Git. 12a) states that a husband is obligated to support his wife, even if she had to flee to a city of refuge. Citing "The king's daughter is all glorious within," the rabbis decide that a woman in a strange city cannot be expected to support herself and to seek employment, because she should remain within her home.[8]

Elsewhere, the Talmud (Yev. 72a) accepts as converts Ammonite and Moabite women but not Ammonite and Moabite men. The most famous of such female converts is Ruth, from whom King David was descended. The Bible bans the men because they did not provide bread and water to the Israelites when they were wandering in the desert (Deut. 23:4ff.). According to the Talmud, however, the women were not expected to do so, because "The king's daughter is all glorious within," and women are therefore not responsible to provide hospitality, which is a public act.

Even though these sources were clearly intended to help women, their assumption that women belong in the home implies a limitation on women's arena of activity. The liabilities inherent in such an assumption persist today, often in the form of apologetic literature justifying the exclusion of women from involvement in the public affairs of the community.

As women have become more active in seeking greater participation, the apologetic literature has become more vociferous. For example, Moshe Meiselman, in his widely read book, maintains that there are divinely ordained roles for women and men, and that women's role is private in nature, citing "the king's daughter is all glorious within."[9] He opposes all attempts by women to find fulfillment by expanding their religious observance into nontraditional areas that, even if not technically prohibited by Jewish law, are contrary to the "Divine imperative" to a female.

Determining "Divine imperative" has never been a simple matter. We do not claim to speak for the Divine. We maintain that Judaism, both in the past and the present, encompasses legitimate differences in belief and practice.

In all the above sources, men delineated the proper role for Jewish women. Today, women are defining their own roles. As we discussed previously, part of this process includes reinterpreting traditional sources through *midrash*, as a way of bridging tradition and contemporary concerns so that Judaism remains eternally relevant and compelling.

Tanḥuma, Num. 3, preserves the following explanation of why God wanted the Israelites to build a Tabernacle in the desert:

"And God spoke to Moses in the wilderness of Sinai, in the Tabernacle. . . ." Until the Tabernacle was erected, He spoke with him from the [burning] bush . . . afterward He spoke with him in Midian . . . and then He spoke with him in Egypt . . . and then spoke with him in Sinai. . . . Once the Tabernacle was erected He said, modesty is becoming . . . and He began speaking with him in the Tabernacle, and so David said "The King's daughter is all glorious within." The King's daughter is Moses . . . therefore, "The King's daughter is all glorious within. . . ."

This *midrash* understands "within" to mean within the Tabernacle, the special place from which God chose to communicate with humanity. The rabbis interpreted the word "daughter" figuratively to refer to Moses, the beloved of the King, who speaks to the King from within the Tabernacle.

We suggest a new *midrash* on the verse, "*Kol kevudah bat melekh penimah* . . . ," "The king's daughter is all glorious within." The King represents the sovereignty of God. Jewish women are God's daughters. "Within" refers to within the synagogue. Every synagogue, regardless of its location or physical structure, is considered to be a *mikdash meᶜat*, a small sanctuary, a place where God and humanity can meet.

God is waiting for the daughters of Israel to be brought into the inner courts of the palace—of the synagogue—asking them to leave the periphery where they have remained for too long. Their entrance should be accompanied by joy and celebration, as it says in Ps. 45:16, quoted at the beginning of this preface:

> With gladness and rejoicing shall they be brought
> They shall enter into the king's palace.

This idea, that women should more fully participate in all aspects of synagogue life and ritual, was the impetus that moved us to compile this volume.

Notes

1. We are well aware that our title reflects the use of masculine imagery when referring to God. We have avoided gender-linked God language wherever possible when using our own voice, in line with Maimonides, who explained that anthropomorphic language cannot truly describe God, as God has no body (Maimonides' commentary on Mish. Sanh. 10:1, Yesod 3). However, we have retained such language when it is found in primary sources and when used by our contributors.

2. See "Leah Shakdiel v. Minister of Religion, Supreme Court Justice Menachem Elon, Israel Supreme Court," 1987, no. 153, p. 32. Elon, who voted in favor of women on religious councils, cites Rabbi Kook, Israel's first Chief Rabbi, who used our verse to argue that women may not vote nor hold public office (p. 35).

3. For example, cf. Hershel Schachter, "Regarding Matters of the Synagogue and its Sanctity" (in Hebrew). *Or ha-Mizrah* 34:1–2 (Fall 1985): 66, and Rabbi Menashe Klein in "State of Israel's Brief against the International Committee of Women at the Kotel," BAGATZ 89:142, 1988.

4. Rabbis Simon Greenberg and Joel Roth both seem bound to respond to the traditional usage of this verse in their refutations of opposition to women's ordination. *See* Greenberg, "On the Question of the Ordination of Women as Rabbis by the Jewish Theological Seminary of America," in *The Ordination of Women as Rabbis: Studies and Responsa*, ed. S. Greenberg (New York: JTS, 1988), 82ff. (in English), 199ff. (in Hebrew); and Roth, "A Brief Position Paper on the Ordination of Women," ibid., 152–53.

5. Jerusalem Talmud (hereafter TJ) Yoma 1:1; TJ Meg. 1:10; TJ Hor. 3:2; Lev. R. 20:11; Num. R. 1:3 to end of *parashah*; Tan. Aḥrei Mot 33.

6. Tanḥuma, a collection of *midrashim* (*see* glossary), was probably edited sometime after 800 C.E., although it contains earlier materials. Cf. EncJud, s.v. "*Tanḥuma Yelammedenu.*"

7. Shlomo Buber, *Midrash Tanḥuma*, v.I. (Lemberg 1883), *Vayishlah* 85, 169–71 (in Hebrew).

8. When a person kills another by accident, the murderer flees to a city of refuge (*'ir miklat*), where he or she must remain until the death of the High Priest. The city of refuge provides sanctuary for the murderer from the vengeance of the relatives of the deceased. Ordinarily, a husband must support his wife. In this case, since his wife is not residing with him, one might assume that the husband no longer has the duty to support his wife so long as she remains in the city of refuge. The Talmud here teaches this is not so.

9. Moshe Meiselman, *Jewish Woman in Jewish Law* (New York: Ktav, 1978). Note especially pp. 14–15, 49, 79. He qualifies his remarks by acknowledging that men, too, have private roles, especially in prayer. However, ". . . the private sphere should be the dominant area of a woman's life," (p. 15).

DAUGHTERS
OF THE
KING

WOMEN
AND THE
SYNAGOGUE

Susan Grossman
Rivka Haut

INTRODUCTION: WOMEN AND THE SYNAGOGUE

Synagogue. The word first brings to mind the Jewish house of worship. Actually, the word *synagogue* comes from the Greek *synagogos,* a house of assembly.[1] Indeed, the most common word used for synagogue in Hebrew is not *beit tefillah,* house of prayer, but *beit knesset* (also originally from the Greek), house of assembly.[2] Throughout the ages, the synagogue has been more than the location for communal prayer; it has served as a focal point for Jewish community, for a sense of identity and belonging.[3]

Much has been written about the history and function of the synagogue and its role as a precursor to the church and mosque.[4] It is not our purpose to review or duplicate these fine studies here. In reading them, however, we have found that, with a few notable exceptions,[5] they largely ignore the role of women in synagogue life, aside from a discussion of the women's galleries. Nevertheless, there is material on this subject available in primary and even secondary literature, although it is scattered and often difficult to find. Compiling and analyzing such material has been one goal of this book.

The impact of the feminist movement on Judaism has brought to the fore the issue of women's role in the synagogue—both today and throughout history. The role of women in the synagogue is currently a major subject for debate among all branches of Judaism. The Orthodox community is in an uproar over the innovation of women's prayer groups. The Conservative Movement is facing a critical challenge regarding its recent decision to ordain women as rabbis and to invest women as cantors. The Reform Movement is struggling with the attempt to include a feminine element in traditional male-oriented liturgy. Innovative practices are now being introduced in all segments of the Jewish community. The fact that people are so concerned with these issues attests to the vitality of the synagogue and of Judaism in general.

What was the role of women in the synagogue? There is no simple answer. As with any question of history, circumstances varied with time and place. Moreover, gathering information about women's history is difficult because women's lives were largely ignored by the men whose writing remains for us today the primary record of Jewish life.[6]

A common theme running through many of the articles in this volume is that women considered the synagogue important to them. Women turned to the synagogue as the center of community and as an avenue for seeking communal justice. Women—as well as men—sometimes even interrupted the Torah reading to voice their grievances and seek redress (*see* Reguer, pp. 53–54).[7]

Many women expressed their affinity for the synagogue through regular attendance at Sabbath and holiday services. Others, more isolated examples to be sure, expressed their piety by daily attendance.[8] Baile Edels, wife of Rabbi Joshua ben Alexander Ha-Kohen (Falk) (mid-sixteenth to seventeenth centuries) had the key to the women's section because she was often the first to appear in synagogue each morning and the last to leave at night.[9]

Although women attended synagogue, their actual participation in services was extremely limited. Women were not counted in the quorum necessary for communal prayer, nor did they receive synagogue honors.[10] Women were also generally excluded from serving the congregation in any official capacity. They could not be rabbis, cantors, or synagogue presidents, nor, save for a few isolated exceptions, could they serve in any elected position.[11]

Despite the lack of an official role, some women served as leaders for other women. From the thirteenth century until modern times, women in Germany, Eastern Europe, and Italy served as prayer leaders (*firzogerin*) for women. Other women composed liturgical hymns for women (*see* Taitz, pp. 64–68).

Because their role in public worship was largely circumscribed, women expressed their relationship to the synagogue differently than did men. Men could show their affiliation by attending services daily, by receiving various honors during the service, and by serving as prayer leaders and communal officials. Contributing money to the synagogue was one way women had to make their presence known. A rich tradition of contributions by women can be traced back to the desert Tabernacle (*see* Grossman, p. 33, n. 50). From the ancient period, we find tombstones and synagogue inscriptions attesting to women's generous donations.[12] In medieval Cairo, women were so generous with their donations that their husbands sometimes complained to the rabbinical authorities (*see* Reguer, p. 55). Today, too, sisterhood groups are often in the forefront of fundraising efforts on behalf of their synagogues and national synagogue organizations.

It is important to keep such donations in perspective. For men, contributing money often bought power and influence in the community; for women, it seldom did.[13] Nevertheless, the act of giving served to make the contributors feel that they were part of the synagogue.

In addition to monetary contributions, women donated their handicrafts. This tradition also dates back to the Bible, which tells us that women wove curtains and donated them to the Tabernacle, the paradigm for the synagogue (Exod. 35:25). The Israel Museum in Jerusalem and the Jewish Museum in New York feature beautiful Torah mantles and curtains for the Holy Ark embroidered by women from different cultures and time periods. Many women embroidered Torah binders, called "wimpels," from the linen used during their sons' circumcisions. A woman who spent a great deal of time creating an intricate accessory for the Torah scroll probably did so out of deep religious feeling. Although she did not have physical contact with the Torah scroll during services, she could feel satisfaction in knowing that the work of her hands was embracing the most holy object of Judaism.

Women also contributed candles to the synagogue. A Talmudic tradition states that the Prophet Deborah supplied the Tabernacle with torches.[14] This custom of women providing light for holy places appears in such diverse Jewish communities as Eastern Europe and rural Iran (*see* Berger, pp. 75–76; Khoubian, pp. 221–22).

Women sometimes considered their voluntary offerings of physical labor to be signs of devotion and involvement. The idea of menial work as an act of worship is not unique to women nor to Judaism and is a common theme of Ḥasidism.[15] The seventeenth-century Anglican clergyman George Herbert, in his poem "The Elixir," wrote:

> Teach me, my God and King,
> In all things thee to see
> And what I do in any thing,
> To do it as for thee: . . .
>
> A servant with this clause
> Makes drudgerie divine;
> Who sweeps a room, as for thy laws,
> Makes that and th' action fine . . . [16]

Jewish women in certain cultures would clean the synagogue and dust the ark (*see* Regeur, p. 54; Khoubian, pp. 221, 223). In many synagogues today, it is the primary responsibility of the women to provide and set up the *kiddush*. These types of synagogue activities are, in effect, extensions of women's traditional homemaking responsibilities.[17]

Through acts of physical labor such as these, women have manifested a desire to attain greater connection to the community's center of sacredness. Women have expressed their piety in these ways because they were not prohibited from doing so (whereas they *were* prohibited from expressing it in other, more vocal and public ways). Such activities center around the synagogue without actually placing women in the public eye; they remain within the realm of what is considered traditionally feminine.

Ironically, women in certain times and places expressed their piety by not attending synagogue when they were menstruating, as they considered themselves capable of contaminating the sacred space with their ritual impurity (*see* Cohen, pp. 109ff.).

The synagogue was not necessarily the locus of women's piety: they had a rich spiritual life both within and outside the home. They excelled in acts of kindness and charity, caring for the sick, helping the poor, and dowering orphan brides. Women prayed privately in their homes. The kitchen, as the scene of preparations to honor the Sabbath and holidays, was a center for pious activity (*see* Sered, pp. 206, 207). The *mikveh* (ritual bath) was also a focus for religious activity, a place where women recited personal prayers and petitions.[18] Sephardic women still gather in groups at the *mikveh* to celebrate the first visit of a bride.

Women also gathered in groups to pray in cemeteries.[19] In some cultures, they gathered in homes to recite Psalms (*see* Khoubian, p. 223). In other cultures, women, uneducated in traditional prayers, gathered to recite women's oral traditions (*see* Sered, p. 209). These expressions of women's spirituality were largely ignored by the rabbis, who were not ordinarily interested in the activities of women that did not impact upon the male world.[20] Even modern scholars have tended to view such activities as expressions of folk piety (which often connotes a primitivism or an innocence), having assimilated the rabbinic standards for serious, legitimate religiosity. Women's piety did not generally involve the two traditional pillars of male hegemony: Talmudic study and synagogue ritual; but feminist scholarship has taught us to evaluate women's expressions on their own terms and not in comparison with male standards.

The architects of Judaism were, by and large, male. Consequently, Jewish law and tradition reflect male experience and were developed—in general—to meet male needs. By excluding women from serving as religious or political officials of the community, men retained the sources of power and influence.

Admittedly, rabbinic leaders always did their best to ensure that women received adequate protection from male insensitivity and that their physical needs were met. For example, the marriage laws in the Talmud are striking in their efforts to aid divorced and widowed women.[21] However, these efforts were paternalistic attempts to protect the rights of the weak, not to enfranchise them.

As far as we can ascertain, given the lack of available evidence for Jewish women's internal lives, most women accepted the existing social structures and found fulfillment on the margins of the synagogue and house of study. This began to change in the twentieth century, with the influence of broader educational opportunities for women and, later, through the impact of feminism on women's aspirations for social equality.

Until the early twentieth century, most Jewish women received a nominal Jewish education. They were often taught at home, receiving the minimum education necessary to keep a Jewish home and to pray. In early twentieth-century Europe, Jewish girls began to receive better secular educations and to question traditional values.[22] The renowned scholar Rabbi Israel Meir ha-Kohen, better known as the Ḥafetz Ḥayyim (d. 1933), ruled that girls should be taught Bible because their religious education should be on a par with their secular studies.[23] In 1918, with his support, Sara Schnirer founded Bais Yaakov, the first network of *yeshivot* for girls.

Once a precedent for women's education was established, more girls and women availed themselves of increasing opportunities. More than half a century later, Rabbi J. B. Soloveitchik, the acknowledged leader of modern Orthodoxy, taught one session in a Talmud class in Stern College (the women's college of Yeshiva University in New York) to indicate his approval of Talmud studies for women. Consequently, some *yeshivah* high schools now offer Talmud classes to girls as part of their regular curriculum. There are also a number of Orthodox institutions of higher Judaic studies for women, both in Israel and the United States.

In the Conservative Movement, in 1903, Henrietta Szold was a pioneer in gaining the acceptance of women as students in the Jewish Theological Seminary. However, she was allowed to study with the male rabbinical students only on condition that she would not seek ordination.

With the advent of the feminist movement in the 1960s and 1970s (*see* Monson, pp. 227ff.), women educated in Jewish studies began to realize that an advanced Jewish education was the key that could open many doors. Previously, without direct access to the primary sources that serve as the basis for all Jewish life, women had been dependent on the male rabbinate to serve as intermediaries between them and Jewish law and tradition.

Through feminism, religiously educated women learned to apply their knowledge to improve the status of women in Judaism. Religous feminists realized that women reading rabbinic texts are more likely to be sensitive to the concerns of women, and that they may arrive at different, equally legitimate, interpretations of those texts.[24] Religious feminists pointed out that the process of evaluating traditional texts to determine Jewish observance has necessarily been a subjective one, given the vast corpus of material reflecting varied and sometimes contradictory opinions.

It has only been in the last few decades that women themselves have been able to approach the sources, study them, and learn what options are really possible under Jewish law. Women in the Reform and Conservative Movements have demanded equal rights in the synagogue and equal employment rights as Jewish professionals, attaining acceptance into rabbinical and cantorial schools. Orthodox women are demanding remedies for the thousands of *agunot,* women who are unable to obtain Jewish divorces, and they are also seeking ways to participate more fully in religious rituals such as *Bat Mitzvot* and prayer groups. Many of these efforts for increased involvement focus around the synagogue, which remains the locus of Jewish identity and influence.

The contributors to this volume discuss the role of women in the synagogue from ancient times to the present. In the context of this volume, "synagogue" is loosely defined as a place where people regularly gather for prayer. It may be a rooftop or a living room, as well as a building specifically designed for that purpose.

The three main sections of this book address the following questions:

1. HISTORY: What role did women play in the premodern synagogue and in the ancient sacrificial services that preceded it?

2. HALAKHAH: What are the parameters under Jewish law regarding the participation of women in the synagogue?

3. CONTEMPORARY REALITIES: What new expressions of spiritual involvement are women developing today in all branches of Judaism?

After reading the varied articles and vignettes, readers may ask how the inclusion of female sensitivities and concerns will change the nature of Judaism. How are Jewish women's lives enriched by these changes, and what, if anything, is being lost? Are the gains worth the losses? Are women merely gaining access to what were previously men's roles, or will the roles themselves evolve with the inclusion of women? Are such changes bringing to light aspects of Judaism that were already present though ignored, are they creating a new Judaism, or are they a combination of both? What does equality really mean? Will women's and men's roles ever be truly equal? Should they be identical? Finally, what paths are we, today, blazing for the Jews of the twenty-first century? The volume concludes with a summation of what we can learn from the past as we look to the future.

Our contributors, both male and female, were carefully chosen to reflect not only different academic disciplines but also different personal backgrounds and movement affiliations. This reflects a growing tendency among religious feminists and the men who share their concerns to work together and support each other even when those concerns differ.[25]

No one book can exhaustively cover such a large and diverse subject as women and the synagogue. We have had to omit certain topics. Some of them, such as "new age" Judaism[26] or arguments against increasing women's involvement in the synagogue,[27] have been covered elsewhere. There are other topics that time and space did not allow us to touch upon. We can only hope that this volume will serve as the impetus for further serious study.

Notes

1. On the distinction between synagogue and proseuche (house of worship), *see* Lee Levine, "The Second Temple Synagogue: The Formative Years," in *The Synagogue in Late Antiquity*, ed. Levine (Philadelphia: American Schools of Oriental Research, 1987), 20–23.
2. *See* Ismar Elbogen, *Ha-Tefillah be-Yisraʾel be-Hitpaʾḥutah ha-Historit* (Tel Aviv: Dvir, 1972), 331–32. *See* the rest of that chapter for other names for the synagogue, pp. 331–57.
3. Other pillars of the community are the home and Jewish communal organizations.
4. Lee Levine, "Ancient Synagogues—A Historical Introduction," in *Ancient Synagogues Revealed*, ed. Levine (Jerusalem: Israel Exploration Society, 1981), 1. Other recent works on the synagogue include Levine, ed., *The Synagogue in Late Antiquity* (Philadelphia: American Schools of Oriental Research, 1987; both Levine volumes include bibliographies); Jack Wertheimer, ed., *The American Synagogue: A Sanctuary Transformed* (New York: Cambridge University Press, 1987); Samuel Heilman, *Synagogue Life: A Study in Symbolic Interaction* (Chicago: University of Chicago Press, 1973). A popular survey is Geoffrey Wigoder, *The Story of the Synagogue: A Diaspora Museum Book* (New York: Harper and Row, 1986).
5. For example, Bernadette Brooten, *Women Leaders in the Ancient Synagogue* (Chico, Calif.: Scholars Press, 1982), 206–30, 363–94. Wertheimer, *The American Synagogue*, includes articles on sisterhoods as well as on the *mehitzah*.
6. *See, for example*, a discussion on this issue by Paula Hyman, "Gender and Jewish History," *Tikkun* 3:1 (Jan./Feb. 1988): 35–38.
7. *See also* Paula Hyman, "Immigrant Women and Consumer Protest: The New York City Kosher Meat Boycott of 1902," *American Jewish History* 70:1 (Sept. 1980): 94, 100.
8. *See, for example, The Memoirs of Gluckel of Hamlen*, trans. Marvin Lowenthal (New York: Schocken, 1977), notably p. 130, and the last chapter.
9. Tur, YD, vol. 2, Introduction, by her son Rabbi Joseph Kohen ha-Tzadik, which includes a detailed description of his mother, Baile Edels. Today, we follow her interpretation that festival candles should be lit after saying the blessing, a reversal of the order followed during Sabbath candle lighting.
10. There are some theoretical cases whereby women could receive *aliyot* to the Torah (*see* Taitz, p. 64).
11. For example, *see* Maimonides, *Mishneh Torah*, Melakhim 1:5. However, there are isolated examples of women serving as religious leaders. For example, in the nineteenth century, Hannah Rachel Werbermacher, known as the Maid of Ludomir, served as the rebbe to a group of Ḥasidim in that Ukrainian town. S. Horodezky, *Ḥasidut ve-ha-Ḥasidim*, vol. 4, (in Hebrew) (Tel Aviv: Dvir, 1927), 69–71; Harry Rabinowicz, *World of Hasidism* (London: Vallentine, Mitchell, 1970), 205–7. *Also see* Horodezky, *Ḥasidut ve-ha-Ḥasidim*, for other examples of prominent women in Ḥasidism.

The issue of women serving in public capacities is still being debated, particularly in Israel. In the late 1980s, the Israeli rabbinate strongly objected to the election of Leah Shakdiel, the first woman on a municipal religious council.

12. *See* Brooten, *Women Leaders*, app., pp. 157–65.

13. One of the few exceptions to this rule is Doña Gracia, during the 16th-century Ottoman Empire, who financed the building of a number of synagogues and remained very involved in the operation of the synagogue she established in Constantinople. Cecil Roth, *Doña Gracia of the House of Nasi* (Philadelphia: JPS, 1977), 124–25, 128–30.

14. TB Meg. 14a.

15. For example, *see* Martin Buber, *Tales of the Hasidim: The Early Masters* (New York: Schocken, 1961), 3, 4.

16. Dudley Fitts, ed., *Herbert* (New York: Dell, 1966), 172.

17. *See* Jenna Weissman Joselit, "The Special Sphere of the Middle-Class American Jewish Woman: The Synagogue Sisterhood, 1890–1940," in *The American Synagogue: A Sanctuary Transformed*, ed. Wertheimer (New York, Cambridge University Press, 1987), 223.

18. *See, for example,* Chava Weissler, "The Traditional Piety of Ashkenazic Women," in *Jewish Spirituality*, vol. 2, ed. Arthur Green (New York: Crossroads, 1987) 245–75.

19. *See, for example,* Jack Kugelmas and Jonathan Boyarin, *From a Ruined Garden: The Memorial Books of Polish Jewry* (New York: Schocken, 1983), 77. *See also* Susan Starr Sered, "Rachel's Tomb and the Milk Grotto of the Virgin Mary," *Journal of Feminist Studies in Religion* 2 : 2 (Fall 1986): 7–22, and "Rachel's Tomb: Societal Liminality and the Revitalization of a Shrine," *Religion* 19 (1989), 27–40.

20. *See* Jacob Neusner, *Method and Meaning in Ancient Judaism* (Missoula, Mont.: Scholars Press, 1979), 85. Rachel Biale suggests that *halakhot* concerning women only reflect what men knew about women's daily lives. For example, in discussing why there is little rabbinic discussion of lesbians, Biale posits that perhaps lesbians existed in significant numbers but remained unknown to the male rabbinical authorities. Biale, *Women and Jewish Law* (New York: Schocken, 1984), 196.

21. Today these very same laws often are used to the detriment of women. *See* Irwin H. Haut, *Divorce in Jewish Law and Life* (New York: Sepher Hermon, 1983) for a full discussion of rabbinic sensitivity in the past and current rabbinic intransigence.

22. Deborah Weissman, "*Bais Yaakov:* A Historical Model for Jewish Feminists," in *The Jewish Woman*, ed. Elizabeth Koltun (New York: Schocken, 1976), 140–41.

23. Ḥafetz Ḥayyim, *Likutei Halakhot*, quoted by Elyakim Ellinson, *The Woman and the Mitzvot*, vol. 1 (in Hebrew) (Jerusalem: World Zionist Organization, 1979), 158. This set has recently become available in English translation.

24. This is an issue in wider feminist and literary studies, cf. James Atlas, "On Campus: The Battle of the Books," *New York Times Magazine*, Sunday 5 June 1988, 75.

25. One example of such cooperation was the 1986 Jerusalem Conference on *Halakhah* and the Jewish Woman, which brought together probably the largest gathering of women scholars ever in Jewish history, representing all the different Jewish movements. *See* Pnina Peli, ed., *Halachah and the Jewish Woman* (Washington, D.C.: B'nai B'rith; forthcoming). Another example is the International Committee for Women at the Kotel, which includes women from every stream of Judaism.

26. For example, Penina V. Adelman, *Miriam's Well: Rituals for Jewish Women Around the Year* (New York: Biblio Press, 1986).

27. For example, Moshe Meiselman, *Jewish Woman in Jewish Law* (New York: Ktav, 1978) and Baruch Litvin, ed., *Sanctity of the Synagogue* (New York: Ktav, 1987).

One

HISTORY

Remember the days of old,
Consider the years of ages past . . .
Deuteronomy 32:7

To know oneself is to know the history of one's people. For the Jewish people, especially, this has meant turning back to history and tradition to establish present and future practice. Each of the articles in this section focuses on a significant period in the development of the synagogue.

In the centuries following its destruction, the Jerusalem Temple became a paradigm for synagogue architecture and worship services. Susan Grossman suggests that, in forming their model of women's role in the synagogue, later generations focused on the segregation of women during one particular Temple ceremony. In a detailed survey of women's role in Temple ritual she shows that women shared with laymen almost equal access to and involvement in the Temple.

Even while the Temple still existed as the official religious center for the nation, the synagogue had begun to emerge as a local center of communal worship and activity. Hannah Safrai explores the prominent presence of women in the early synagogue from its beginnings through the seventh century c.e. She dis-

cusses the lack of evidence for the separation of the sexes and shows that some women seem to have served in leadership roles.

Safrai ends her study with the ancient synagogues of the Christian Byzantine period, at which point Sara Reguer directs our attention to the Cairene synagogues of the Islamic Middle Ages. Here, too, women were a prominent presence in the synagogue. They served as synagogue caretakers, were major contributors, and sometimes came to the synagogue as plaintiffs seeking social justice; all this despite the fact that the Jewish community was greatly influenced by Islamic culture, which at that time excluded women from the mosque.

Emily Taitz shows that women half a world away in Christian Europe created alternative forms of religious expression through the leadership of fellow women. She suggests that certain aspects of women's legal status in Judaism reflected the feudalism of the dominant Christian culture. Despite halakhic limitations on women's activities in the medieval and early modern periods, individual women managed to excel as religious singers and prayer leaders for women. In a companion article, Shulamith Berger discusses the development and significance of teḥines, petitionary prayers, many of which were written by and for women. Some collections of Yiddish teḥines are still available and in use today. To provide the English reader with the flavor of this genre, Berger translates two teḥines recited by women in the synagogue.

Readers coming from disparate perspectives may draw different inferences from these articles. Some may ask whether the spiritual lives of women in the past were richer than those of women today. Others may find that restrictions on women's roles were determined by time and culture. They may ask, to what extent should the past be a model for the future? The majority will find that collecting material about women, often from scattered sources, provides an invaluable resource for a fuller understanding of the development of Jewish history, literature, and practice, and our relationship to it.

Susan Grossman

WOMEN AND THE JERUSALEM TEMPLE[1]

Until its destruction by the Romans in 70 C.E., the Herodian Temple in Jerusalem stood as the official center of Jewish ritual and worship. Yet, ironically, its influence over popular Jewish practice and imagination may have been strongest only after its destruction.[2]

The idea that the Temple and its laws could exert influence over Jewish practice outside its physical, or temporal, boundaries began generations before its destruction, in the democratizing efforts of the Pharisees. The Pharisees applied the biblical commandment "You shall be a kingdom of priests . . ." (Exod. 19:6) to (lay) Israelite Jews, i.e., not only those of priestly lineage. The laws of ritual purity were applied to the home as well as the Temple. The table of God in the Temple became equated with the dinner table; the rituals followed by the priests before partaking of sanctified foods in Temple precincts were to be followed by lay Jews when eating unsanctified foods in their homes.[3] (Vestiges of these practices exist today, for example, in the Jewish ritual of washing one's hands before eating bread at the beginning of a meal.) Ironically, while their efforts, in effect, de-emphasized the importance of the Temple, the Pharisees—by applying Temple law beyond Temple boundaries—laid the foundation for their spiritual heirs, the rabbis of the Talmud, to establish the Temple as a paradigm for Jewish aspiration and observance after its destruction. Amoraic and post-Talmudic sources glorify the Temple, considering it to be, in the abstract, a sign of God's manifest favor and Israel's national independence.[4] The messianic desire for the rebuilding of the Temple, as the first stage in Israel's redemption, found expression over the next centuries in the central prayers of the liturgy.[5]

Perhaps most important for our purposes, the Talmudic rabbis established the Temple as the model for Divine worship. Throughout the following centuries, synagogue ritual practice and the physical design of the synagogue were often based on what was known about the Temple (*see* Cohen, pp. 106–08).[6]

Consequently, Temple practice had an impact that long outlived its actual existence. This has certainly been true regarding the role of women in Jewish public worship. In perhaps the most pointed example, traditionally oriented authors today cite what they consider to have been Temple practice, in seeking to justify the separation of the sexes by a partition (*meḥitzah*) in the synagogue.[7] However, upon examining early rabbinic material we can deduce that women were not generally segregated from men when they visited the Temple and that they also brought sacrifices.

Much has been written about the First and Second Temples.[8] While many works touch upon women's role in the Temple, the most complete studies are either not easily accessible to the English reader[9] or were written almost a century ago and therefore lack the benefit of modern scholarship.[10] Indeed, a comprehensive discussion on women's role in later Israelite religion, utilizing modern research methods, is worthy of a book in its own right.

Literary evidence regarding the role of women in the Temple can be gleaned from a number of different sources: the works of Josephus and non-Jewish writers, the Apocrypha and Pseudepigrapha, the New Testament, and the Dead Sea Scrolls. Yet, the richest source of information— and the one on which we will concentrate—is tannaitic material, early rabbinic literature of the Mishnaic period, dating until 200 C.E. Nevertheless, using such material in an effort to establish historical veracity is difficult. Compiled years after the destruction of the Temple, even tannaitic sources do not necessarily reflect the actual details and procedures of the predestruction Herodian Temple but rather the rabbinic conception of it.[11]

Given these caveats, this essay highlights the major ways in which women participated in the Herodian Temple and examines the integration and segregation of the sexes there, according to the rabbinic conceptions that have come down to us from the generations closest to the Temple's existence.

Our discussion must first be placed in context by making a brief survey of the biblical material on women's involvement in the rites of the central shrines that preceded the Herodian Temple: the Tabernacle [12] and the First and pre-Herodian Second Temples. While much of this material is collected elsewhere, it is presented here also for the reader's convenience. Such an overview highlights rabbinic views and the transformations the rabbinic imagination may have made of earlier materials on the role and status of Jewish women in various cultic activities.

Women in the Tabernacle at Shiloh

From the earliest biblical periods, we find women involved in a wide variety of cultic activities, from participation at communal festivals, to bringing sacrifices, to serving an official or semi-official function in the ritual surrounding the cult.

Women's active participation in the festivals is attested to in the books of Judges, Samuel, and Kings. Elkanah shares the sacrificial meal with his wives and daughters at Shiloh (1 Sam. 1:4–9). The family seems to have worshipped together there as well (1 Sam. 1:19).

In the Book of Exodus, only males are commanded to appear before the Lord [13] three times a year for the annual pilgrim festivals (Exod. 23:17, 34:24; Deut. 16:16; cf. Deut. 12:11–12, 18). However, according to the Book of Samuel, it seems unusual for the wife to remain behind. Hannah must explain why she will not accompany her husband Elkanah on his annual pilgrimage to Shiloh until her son Samuel is weaned (1 Sam. 1:21–23). [14]

Women, like men, also brought voluntary sacrifices as signs of thanksgiving. When Hannah weans Samuel and brings him to Shiloh to devote him to service in the Tabernacle, she brings along bulls, flour, and wine for an offering (1 Sam. 1:24–25). Another reference to Hannah may also be our earliest example of a woman's involvement in bringing the festival offerings (1 Sam. 2:19). [15]

Women participated in special national celebrations and sacrifices. They were included in the covenantal readings by Joshua (Josh. 8:34–35), which implies inclusion within the covenant.[16] Women also joined the celebration of David bringing the ark to Jerusalem and the eating of the sacrifice associated with it (2 Sam. 6:12–19).[17]

Women sang and danced at festivals. It was well known that young women danced at the annual "feast of the Lord" at Shiloh (Judg. 21:19–23). However, it is not clear whether the dances were part of the official cultic ceremony or just part of a general popular celebration of those who attended.[18] Women did dance and sing as part of victory celebrations, which—in the context of the times—were religious celebrations (e.g., 1 Sam. 18:6–7). In addition, the Bible records that there were female leaders of such celebrations, although not at Shiloh. Deborah (Judg. 5:1–31) and Jephtah's daughter (Judg. 11:34) lead, on separate occasions, songs and dances of thanksgiving after victories.[19]

There has been much debate as to the role of the women who gathered at the Tent of Meeting (1 Sam. 2:22; cf. Exod. 38:8). Some suggest that these women were used as cultic prostitutes by Eli's sons, even if their function was not normally such.[20] However, the term *tzvo'ot* is not used elsewhere when mention is made of prostitution.[21] Most scholars suggest that these women served some cultic role—either praying,[22] fasting,[23] offering sacrifices,[24] or serving as an honor guard at the Tabernacle.[25] While their role cannot really be determined without further evidence, the "Women who Gathered" provide, at the very least, evidence of an active female presence at Shiloh in the form of an identifiable group—as women.

References to the daughters of Shiloh who danced (Judg. 21:21, mentioned above) and the "Women who Gathered" seem to indicate that women congregated separately as women, both at ritual events to dance and at the Tabernacle to serve there in some way. Nevertheless, biblical material gives few other indications of the segregation of men and women during Divine worship,[26] covenantal Torah readings, or the bringing of sacrifices. All in all, women seemed to have had easy access to the Tabernacle. For example, Hannah is not chastised by Eli for being at the Temple of the Lord (*heikhal*), but only for appearing drunk there (1 Sam. 1:9–12). While not serving as priests at Shiloh,[27] women seem to have been an integral part of the people expressing their religious life in and around one of the central institutions of ancient Israel.

Women in the First and Early Second Temples

Biblical sources on women's roles in the First and early Second (pre-Herodian) Temples present a sketchy picture at best. As in the Tabernacle, no mention is made of the segregation of the sexes at the Temple site. There is no reference to a Women's Court in the First or pre-Herodian Second Temples,[28] as there is regarding the Herodian Temple (*see* below).

Women participated in Ezra's reading of the Torah (Neh. 8:2–3, 10:1–30)[29] and Nehemiah's sacrifice and celebration in honor of the re-dedication of Jerusalem's wall (Neh. 12:43). However, the Chronicler describes the inclusion of women at these events differently than did the earlier biblical author when mentioning the inclusion of women in the Torah reading by Joshua. In Neh. 8:2, we find Ezra bringing the Torah from the men to (ʿad, lit., until) the women. Neh. 12:43 can be read as an emphatic, that when Nehemiah offered the sacrifice, even the women and children (v-gam, lit., and also) were included. Such distinctions may imply that the men and women stood in separate areas during these ceremonies.

Male and female singers are mentioned in Ezra and Nehemiah as part of the community returning from exile (Ezra 2:65; Neh. 7:67). In both books, it is difficult to determine whether these women singers were part of the Temple retinue or just entertainers. Only male singers are mentioned when ceremonies or services are described (Neh. 10:29, 12:28–29, 42; cf. Neh. 12:46–47, 13:10). The Chronicler mentions Heiman's three daughters, in addition to his fourteen sons, in the context of his teaching his children the songs and instrumentation of the Temple service (1 Chron. 25:5–6). However, only the brothers are named and only they are assigned to the watches for service (1 Chron. 25:13–31). The daughters may have been involved in playing instruments, though, which could be supported by Ps. 68:26, citing maidens playing timbrels among the musicians as part of the procession bringing the ark to its place, probably in Solomon's Temple.[30] The women singers mentioned in 2 Chron. 35:25 lamenting Josiah's death are most probably mourning women, an ancient female profession,[31] rather than singers involved in Temple services.

In the earlier biblical period, the prophet Deborah stands out as a female religious leader and authority. In the First Temple period, Ḥuldah similarly serves as a prophet. The Bible records little about her except that King Josiah turns to her, instead of to her contemporary, the prophet

Jeremiah, to determine the status of a scroll found in the Temple Court. Huldah warns the King to obey what is written in the book, also referred to as a book of the Law (Torah) and a book of the Covenant (2 Kings 22:8–20; 2 Chron. 34:14–33).[32] Scholars are not sure what this scroll was; many suggest it may have been Deuteronomy.[33] Most important here, this scroll is seen as central to what has come to be known as the Josianic Reform, the destruction of local altars and the centralization of the sacrificial system in the Jerusalem Temple. Perhaps Huldah, too, should be credited with this reform that served as a watershed in Israel's early history.[34]

Women in the Herodian Temple

In the eighteenth year of his reign (c. 20 B.C.E.),[35] King Herod began his massive project to rebuild the Jerusalem Temple. He had the slopes and valley surrounding the Temple built up, doubling the area of the Temple Mount.[36] Construction continued after Herod's death for almost fifty years; changes and additions continued until shortly before the Temple's destruction.[37]

Women were in regular attendance at the rebuilt Temple. As in earlier periods, women joined their husbands and families for the festival pilgrimages.[38] Tannaitic material records that women often brought sacrifices to the Temple, for example, one dove as an offering for each bodily flux or miscarriage they had experienced since their last visit.[39] A woman, therefore, might have had to bring a number of doves as sacrifices. Demand was so high that the price of a dove reached a golden dinar. In a move that predicted modern market strategies by almost 2000 years, Rabban Shimeon ben Gamliel ruled that a woman could bring one dove to cover all her bodily emissions. Consequently, the price of doves fell to one-quarter their previous price (Mish. Ker. 1:7).[40]

Women who brought animal sacrifices were, at least sometimes, allowed to participate in the ritual surrounding the offering of the sacrifice. An eyewitness is reported to have seen women laying their hands on their animals to perform *semikhah* (TB Hag. 16b, *see* below).

Women also brought sacrifices after the completion of a period of naziriteship. Like men, women could devote themselves to God through a nazirite vow.[41] The reasons for taking the vow varied.[42] The Adiabene convert, Queen Helena, became a nazirite in the hope that her son would return safely from war (Mish. Naz. 3 : 6).[43]

Nazirites could not partake of strong drink nor cut their hair. At the end of the nazirite period, nazirites brought sacrifices, had their hair cut publicly in the Temple, and participated in the waving of their offering.[44] Women participated fully in the ceremony ending their nazirite period: They brought their own sacrifices (Mish. Naz. 4 : 4),[45] had their hair cut (Mish. Naz. 4 : 5), and had their sacrifices placed into their hands for waving by the priest, although women were not generally allowed to wave their offerings (Mish. Kid. 1 : 8).[46] Only one other category of women could wave the offering: the *sotah* (the woman suspected of adultery) (Mish. Kid. 1 : 8, *see* below).[47]

To prove the opinion of the Sages (that an interrupted nazirite sacrifice is valid and is continued from where it had been left off), the Mishnah brings an anecdote about one nazirite woman in the midst of bringing her sacrifice. Miriam of Palmyra (a central Syrian community, many of whose Jews came to Israel during the first centuries C.E.)[48] had completed her nazirite period. As the blood from one of her sacrifices was being thrown on the altar, she learned that her daughter was gravely ill. Miriam left to attend her but found she had already died. Ritually impure from contact with the dead, Miriam had to wait until she was purified before she could bring the rest of her nazirite sacrifices (Mish. Naz. 6 : 11; Tosef. Nezirut 4 : 10).[49]

In addition to sacrifices, women brought other types of offerings to the Temple in the form of handiwork and other contributions.[50] Women wove the curtains for the inner Temple (Mish. Shek. 8 : 5).[51] Queen Helena is perhaps the most famous of the female contributors, having donated a golden candelabra for the door (*petaḥ*) to the Sanctuary (*heikhal*), and a gold plaque on which was written the paragraph to be recited during the ritual trial by ordeal of a woman suspected of adultery (Mish. Yoma 3 : 10, Tosef. Yom Kippurim 2 : 3).[52] This trial was held in the Temple (*see* below). It is noteworthy that Helena contributed something that would be clearly identified with women: By providing the words of the oath on a plaque, Queen Helena shortened the woman's humiliating ordeal, because the priest would not have to find the words of the oath in a Torah scroll.

While one must be wary of drawing conclusions about historical realities from rabbinic materials, the above sources appear to indicate that, at least according to the rabbinic imagination, women continued to be active in the Herodian Temple much as they had in the previous Temples and Tabernacle, attending the festivals and bringing sacrifices.

However, with the Herodian Temple, we see the first mention of an area of the Temple specifically referred to as the Women's Court, the *Ezrat Nashim*.[53] The historical existence of the Women's Court seems certain; both the Mishnah (Middot 2 : 5 − 6) and Josephus (Wars V.v.2) mention it.[54]

The idea that the Women's Court served to segregate female from male worshippers is a popular misconception, probably furthered by the association of the term *ezrat nashim* with the women's section of the (Orthodox) synagogue. Sources indicate otherwise.

The Women's Court stood to the east of the inner Court. Though in total area smaller than the inner Court (135 by 135 cubits for the Women's Court compared to 135 by 187 cubits for the entire inner Court), the Women's Court provided a larger gathering area because the inner Court was divided into the Israelite Court, the Priestly Court, and the Sanctuary, which contained the Holy of Holies (Mish. Middot 2 : 5 − 6).[55] The Women's Court, and the chambers it contained, was a bustling area of activity: Male and female nazirites who had completed the period of their vows gathered there, as did cured lepers; priests who suffered a blemish (and therefore could not officiate over the sacrifices) prepared the wood for the altar there (Mish. Middot 2 : 5).[56] On Passover, priests (*kat shlishit*) would sit in the Women's Court after they completed their work with the paschal sacrifice.[57]

Yet there was one time during the year when the sexes were segregated: during the Water-Drawing Festival held annually on the second night of Sukkot.

Referred to as *Simhat Beit ha-Sho'evah* in tannaitic Hebrew,[58] the festivity has no biblical antecedent.[59] The Mishnah describes the festivities as beginning at nightfall after the first day of Sukkot, with the lighting of the golden menorahs in the Women's Court. Their light was so bright, all of Jerusalem was lit up. Pious men would dance in the Women's Court, tossing burning torches while singing. The entire Temple's musical retinue was there: Levites playing on harps, lyres, and cymbals; flute players; and *shofar* blasters. The event was seen to be so joyous that the Mishnah records the saying that, "Anyone who did not see the rejoicing of the Water-Drawing Festival had never seen rejoicing in his days." The water drawing itself continued at daybreak, with a procession to the Siloam, the drawing of water from it, and the pouring out of a water libation, as well as a wine libation, on the altar (Mish. Suk. 4:9, 10; 5:1−4).[60]

The Mishnah does not explicitly mention the separation of the sexes during these festivities. Mish. Suk. 5:2 states only that a great enactment, a *tikkun gadol,* was enacted in the Women's Court that evening, which both Talmuds understand to be the building of a balcony in the Women's Court to segregate the sexes during the festivities (TB Suk. 51b−52a, TJ Suk. 55b). Although not mentioned in the Mishnah, the building of a balcony to segregate the women is attested to in the tannaitic *Tosefta:*

At first, when they would watch *Simḥat Beit ha-Sho'evah,* the men would watch from the inside and the women from the outside. Because the Court (*Beit Din*) saw that they came to licentious behavior (lit., light headedness, *kalut rosh*), they made three balconies in the Court [of the Women] against three walls (*ruḥot*) that were there. Women watched the *Simḥat Beit ha-Sho'evah,* and when they would watch the *Simḥat Beit ha-Sho'evah,* there was no mixing [of the men and the women] (Tosefta Suk. 4:1).[61]

However, it is unlikely that the balcony was rebuilt every year at the festival. The Mishnah (Middot 2:5) describes the Women's Court with a balcony in it as a physical fait accompli. It is also hard to imagine that constructing a balcony to hold such weight would have been realistic at the time of nightfall after the first day, with so many people thronging around, especially since construction would not have been permitted on the festival itself.[62] It is also unlikely that women were restricted to the balcony all year round, as women also brought sacrifices (*see* above) and could even, according to at least one tannaitic tradition, perform a form of *semikhah* on the animal (TB Hag. 16b; cf. Sifra Lev. 4:10) (*see* below, p. 25).

If that is the case, what was the great enactment?[63] Tosafot (a standard collection of comments on the Talmudic text by medieval scholars of the French and German schools) notes that the Hebrew word *gadol* (great) sometimes indicates that there is a great need for an enactment.[64] What great need could exist to instigate the separation of men and women on the night after the first day of Sukkot, when separation of the sexes was not a concern only a few hours earlier during the festival itself?

An answer may lie in the nature of the *Simḥat Beit ha-Sho'evah* celebration, which, as mentioned above, has no biblical antecedent. Many scholars agree that the water libation itself was an appeal for rain, which finds many parallels in the Canaanite and Hellenistic cultures with which Judaism was in contact during the later Second Temple period.[65] The festive aspects of *Simḥat Beit ha-Shoʾevah* (the lighting of torches, torch-throwing, and dancing by distinguished men, which showed off their physical prowess)[66] are reminiscent of pagan festivals.[67]

Although men and women were not usually separated during Temple rituals, one could suggest that a special and concerted effort was made to separate them during *Simḥat Beit ha-Shoʾevah* to ensure that the celebration, similar to pagan festivals in so many ways, did not degenerate into what was seen as one of the most loathsome of pagan practices—sexual liaisons during, and as part of, ritual activities. This could have been considered a great enough need in the rabbinic imagination (following the reasoning above, based on *Tosafot*) to justify changing standard Temple procedure and segregating the women in a balcony during the Water-Drawing's evening festivities.[68]

It has been commonly accepted that the term "Women's Court" signified the closest women could come to the inner Court of the Temple, as indicated in several places by Josephus (Ant. XV.xi.5; Wars V.v.2,6; *Against Apion* II, 8). Tannaitic material, however, is not so clear. This issue also touches upon how involved women were in the bringing of their own sacrifices.

Mish. Kelim 1:8, in delineating who may enter each of the Temple's Courts, which increased in holiness as one proceeded into the interior of the Temple, mentions no restrictions on the access of women beyond the Women's Court. It implies that non-priests were permitted to enter the Priestly Court for the requirements of laying hands on the sacrifice (*semikhah*), slaughtering the sacrifice, and waving (or, perhaps more accurately, raising) it.[69] Theoretically, at least, women should have also been allowed to enter the Priestly Court for those purposes.[70] However, the tannaitic sources are contradictory; some imply that women did go further into the Temple than the Women's Court, while others imply the opposite.

For example, Mish. Men. 5:6 states that women's sacrifices require waving (raising). However, a *baraita* attached to the Mishnah in the Talmud clearly states that women do not perform their own waving (raising) (TB Men. 61b).[71] Similarly, while sacrifices slaughtered by women were valid, the Mishnah seems to imply that women did not generally slaughter their animals, nor were they encouraged to do so (Mish. Zev. 3:1).[72]

On the other hand, while Mish. Men. 9:8 excludes women from performing *semikhah* on their animal sacrifices,[73] one tannaitic sage, Abba Elazar, is reported to have witnessed women being brought their sacrifices in the Women's Court and performing *semikhah* on them there (TB Hag. 16b).[74] Since women were not obligated to perform *semikhah*, they would not have been allowed into the Priestly Court to do so according to the parameters set out by Mish. Kelim 1:8 (*see* above).

The female nazirite and the suspected adulteress (the *sotah*) were the exceptions to the prohibition on women waving their sacrifices; they had to perform their own waving, as mentioned above. However, it seems that the *sotah*, at least, did not pass beyond the Women's Court, according to the Mishnah; she waved her offering at the Eastern (Nicanor) Gate between the Women's and Men's Courts (Mish. Sot. 1:5).[75] While no location is given for the female nazirite's waving of her sacrifice, it is hard to imagine that numbers of women (and we have seen that a number of women were nazirites) would have been allowed into the Priestly Court, according to the rabbinic imagination, in view of the restrictions on other women.

At least according to the cumulative tannaitic record, women appear to have been present in the Temple and to have actively participated by bringing, and sometimes handling, their sacrifices. Nevertheless, women seem to have been excluded from the central areas of sanctity in the Temple, according to the rabbinic imagination. A male Israelite could enter further into the Temple than either a female Israelite or the daughter of a priest (*bat kohen*). (The *bat kohen* seems to have had no special sacrificial functions and could not serve as a priest,[76] although she was allowed to partake of some of the consecrated foods, as were all members of a priestly household.)[77]

There are two basic approaches to the question of why women could not enter further into the Temple. The most popular is the idea that such a limit on women's access prevented the mixing of the sexes.[78] However, as we have seen above, men and women freely mixed in the Women's Court (except one evening a year).

A more anthropological approach might consider that women, who experience regular discharges of blood during their menses, would somehow be considered to have an inherently stronger potential for defilement than would Israelite men, who would also have experienced regularly occurring periods of defilement through ejaculation. The discharge of blood was a powerful life-leak, a symbol of death, the ultimate contaminant of the sacred. For example, the only dead bodies Priests could come in contact with were those of close relatives; High Priests were not to come in contact with any dead, except for an abandoned body. Women, as a class, may have been excluded from the most sacred areas of the sancta as potential bringers, not only of life, but of the "little death" (in the loss of potential life through menses).[79] Centuries later in Yemen, women were prohibited from entering the synagogue because they were considered potentially defiling, due to the flow of blood they experienced during menstruation and childbirth (*see* Sered, p. 215, n.5). However, there seems to be no overt support for such a view in the Mishnah, and certainly not as regards delineating a court as *the* Women's Court, even though the tannaitic rabbis were not hesitant to rank levels of holiness (as we saw above in Mish. Kelim 1:8) nor to rank women in relationship to men (e.g., Mish. Hor. 3:7).

One could posit an alternative theory. Women may have been excluded from the most sacred areas of the Temple because, in the patriarchal society of the time, women's role in sacred areas was defined in such a way as to support the male-defined, largely familial role of women in the greater society; concomitantly, women occupied a lesser status than men in religions in which men comprised the leadership.

Limiting access to the holy center of temples was not singular to Judaism. Many Greco-Roman religions limited access to their temples to initiates or placed limits on how far nonpriests could enter temples. Married women, for example, could not enter the Temple of Artemis.[80] Religious leadership roles in the state cults were generally reserved for men.[81] The cults in which women played a leadership role, as priestesses or cultic functionaries, were strictly organized by the state to correspond to the social roles assigned to women, as wife and mother, and to the behavior expected of them, for example as a *univirai*, a woman who remained married to her first husband.[82]

The rabbis were very much part of the Greco-Roman world.[83] On one hand, Jewish ritual forms and architecture of the Mishnaic period show much in common with the surrounding Greco-Roman culture.[84] While such commonalities are often referred to as transference, they might be more appropriately described as part of the unconscious process whereby groups that share certain values and a similar heritage respond in analogous ways. However, as much as Judaism of the Greco-Roman period exhibited commonalities with the dominant culture, it did, nevertheless, enjoy its own heritage and values. Consequently, it stands to reason that the tannaitic rabbis made conscious efforts to distinguish Jewish practice from pagan practice.[85]

One example of this dichotomy may be the attitude the tannaitic sages had toward the involvement of women in the Temple.[86]

Although the rabbis inherited a long tradition of women's involvement (albeit limited) in the sacrificial system and attendance at Judaism's central shrine (in Shiloh and later in Jerusalem), they were part of a culture that seemed, in some ways, to place even greater restrictions on women's access to the sacred centers of its religions.[87] In such a context, it seems understandable that the rabbis could not conceive of women having the same access as laymen to the Temple's sacred areas. This may be one reason why a Women's Court is clearly defined for the first time in the Herodian Temple, rather than in previous Temples, since its structure, more than the structures of the previous two Temples, was influenced most by Greco-Roman culture and architecture. The Women's Court, then, may symbolize not the separation of the sexes but the relegation of women to lesser status in the Greco-Roman patriarchal world, a status that allowed for the integral involvement of women only in those cults that forwarded societal expectations of women, something the communal, public Temple rituals were not generally designed to do.

Nevertheless, if we follow the model suggested above, the rabbis would have sought to distinguish Temple practice from Greco-Roman practice. Their decision to build a balcony for the women during the Water-Drawing Festival on the second night of Sukkot may be an example of just such concern. A number of Greco-Roman cults had sexual aspects or overtones to their rituals.[88] The rabbis may have instituted the segregation of the sexes on the one evening of the year that most resembled pagan celebrations to avoid the possibility of sexual liaisons that resulted during similar (pagan) festivals, while still allowing women to attend.

Conclusion

The nature of ancient sources makes it difficult to establish the historicity of the role women played in Judaism's central shrines. The problem is compounded by the fact that the scanty material available covers such broad periods of history, each with its differing cultural contexts. As discussed above, some evidence exists that women gathered together separately from the men at Shiloh and later during the rededication of the Second Temple. Further, even biblical Israel never seemed to have allowed women to serve as priestesses at its central shrines. Nevertheless, until the period of the Herodian Temple, women seemed to have had as easy access to Judaism's central shrines as laymen.[89] The ambiguity of the cumulative tannaitic record, however, suggests that women did not have the same involvement in the physical offering of their sacrifices as did lay males.

Yet, even in the Herodian Temple, women were largely part of the general worshipping community. Men and women gathered in the Women's Court together. As in earlier periods, women attended festivals and brought various kinds of sacrifices. Even when women were relegated to a balcony one evening each year, during *Simḥat Beit ha-Sho'evah*, they would still have had an unobstructed view of the celebrations.[90]

Until this point, we have restricted our discussion of rabbinic material to that of the tannaitic period. While the seeds for restricting women's access to the central sacred areas of the religion may have been sown in the tannaitic period, they were raised to paradigmatic heights only much later in Jewish history. The rabbis of the later stammaic period (fifth to sixth century C.E., marking the editing and close of the Babylonian Talmud),[91] may have served as the unknowing springboard for the later severe restrictions on women's access to the main areas of Judaism's later sacred sanctuary, the synagogue.

The stammaic rabbis structured the Talmudic discussion of the building of the balconies for the *Simḥat Beit ha-Sho'evah* (and the consequent need to justify a change in Temple architecture) in a way that ascribed the separation of men and women during the Water-Drawing Festival to an effort to avoid the Evil Inclination. Citing the first-century Babylonian *amorah*, Rav, the Talmud (TB Suk. 51b–52a) states:

Rav said: They found a Scriptural verse and expounded [*drosh*]: "And the land will mourn, every family apart, and the family of the house of David apart, and their women apart" [Zec. 12:12]. . . . if in the future to come, when they will be engaged in mourning and the Evil Inclination has no power over them, the Torah says men apart and women apart, now that they are engaged in rejoicing [in the Temple] and the Evil Inclination has power over them, all the more so [should men and women be separated].

Unlike the parallel *sugyah* (component of Talmudic discussion) in the Jerusalem Talmud, the Babylonian rabbinic editors structured their *sugyah* to incorporate a large body of material on the Evil Inclination, which, at best, is tangentially related to the building of the balconies for the *Simḥat Beit ha-Shoʾevah* (cf. TJ Suk. 5:2, 55b). The concern with the Evil Inclination seems overriding. It sets a cultural context in which the stammaic rabbis would have assumed that separation of the sexes, being a desirable method for overcoming the Evil Inclination, would have existed in the Temple.

This view served to underlie all later decisions to segregate men and women, especially during prayer and other ritual events, but also in any situation that might lead to lightheadedness or frivolity, which was very widely defined.[92] The image of women segregated in the balcony during the Water-Drawing Ceremony came to dominate later evaluations of women's role in the Temple to the point of eclipsing their much more active role that is reviewed here.

A study of how the tannaitic materials were handled in the amoraic and stammaic periods is worthy of detailed examination. It is hoped that closer reading of the tannaitic texts, modestly begun here, will stimulate further discussion on the role of women in the Temple and the long and clearly not monolithic transition to their general exclusion from the central rituals of the synagogue.

Notes

1. I want to express my appreciation to Professors Tikva Frymer-Kensky, Shaye Cohen, Sarah Pomeroy, and the late Baruch Bokser z"l, for their comments. All errors are, of course, my own. I also want to acknowledge the support of the Jewish Foundation for the Education of Women while I researched this paper.

2. It is difficult to determine the degree to which the Jewish populace attended events at the Jerusalem Temple or to what extent the Jerusalem Temple served as the main or sole focus of Divine worship in different periods of Jewish history. According to Shmuel Safrai, while the people evinced great attachment to the Second Temple, the biblical injunction that all males appear before the Lord three times a year (Exod. 23:17, 34:23; Deut. 16:16) was interpreted in the Second Temple period as a non-obligatory act that was encouraged but not demanded. Safrai, "The Temple," in *Compendia Rerum Iudaicarum ad Novum Testamentum, Section One: The Jewish People in the First Century*, vol. 2, ed. S. Safrai and M. Stern (Philadelphia: Fortress, 1976), 865, 899–900. Cf. James Strange, "Archaeology and the Religion of Judaism in Palestine," in *Aufsteig und Niedergang der Romischen Welt* II (19.1) (New York: Walter de Gruyter, 1979), 646–85, esp. pp. 654–55; Menachem Haran, *Temples and Temple*

Service in Ancient Israel (Oxford, England: Clarendon Press, 1978), 294; and Lee Levine, "The Second Temple Synagogue," in *The Synagogue in Late Antiquity,* ed. L. Levine (Philadelphia: American Schools of Oriental Research, 1987), 9.

3. E. Urbach, *The Sages,* 2d ed., vol. 1 (Jerusalem: Magnes, 1979), 582–84.

4. For example, ibid., 55. Cf. Baruch Bokser, "Rabbinic Responses to Catastrophe: From Continuity to Discontinuity," *Proceedings of the American Academy for Jewish Studies* (1983): 37–61, esp. pp. 58–59.

5. The most notable examples are the recitations of the sacrificial service in the holiday and Sabbath *Amidot* and the traditional meditation following all *Amidah* prayers, calling for the rebuilding of the Temple.

6. Various aspects of worship (fasting, reading the sacrificial order, prayer) serve as substitutes for the ideal form of worship—sacrifices. *See* Urbach, The Sages, 2d ed., vol. I, 434, vol. 2, 879 n.51, though cf. vol. 1, 611. Cf. also Bokser, "Rabbinic Responses," esp. pp. 47–57. This trend continued in geonic and medieval times. Cf. Lawrence Hoffman, *The Canonization of the Synagogue Service* (Notre Dame, Ind.: Notre Dame Press, 1979), 54, 74, 92–93, 98. On later synagogue architecture, cf. Helen Rosenau, *Vision of the Temple: The Image of the Temple of Jerusalem in Judaism and Christianity* (London: Oresko Books, 1979).

7. E.g., Baruch Litvin, *The Sanctity of the Synagogue,* 3d ed. (New York: Ktav, 1987), citing R. Joseph Soloveitchik, p. 115, and R. Moshe Feinstein, p. 126ff.; H. E. Yedidiah Ghatan, *The Invaluable Pearl: The Unique Status of Women in Judaism* (New York: Bloch, 1986), 148–50. Cf. also R. Haut, p. 154 n.19 and Joseph, pp. 118, 122ff.

8. Although traditionally referred to as the First and Second Temples, the Second Temple period is perhaps more accurately divided into two distinct periods: the pre-Herodian and the Herodian Temples. Michael Avi-Yonah, "The Second Temple," (in Hebrew) in *The Book of Jerusalem,* ed. M. Avi-Yonah (Jerusalem: Dvir, 1956), 392. Cf. W. F. Stinespring, "Temple, Jerusalem," in *Interpreter's Dictionary of the Bible,* vol. 4 (New York: Abingdon Press, 1962), 550.

9. Most notable are Shmuel Safrai's works on the Second Temple. *See, for example, Pilgrimage at the Time of the Second Temple* (in Hebrew) (Tel Aviv: Am HaSefer, 1965), 88–91; "Was There a Woman's Gallery in the Synagogue of Antiquity?" (in Hebrew) *Tarbiz* 32 : 4 (1963): 331–33. A brief discussion can be found in English in his article "The Temple," 877–78 (*see* n.2 *supra*).

10. Ismar Peritz, "Women in the Ancient Hebrew Cult," *Journal of Biblical Literature,* vol. 17, pt. 2 (1898): 111–48; Solomon Schechter, *Studies in Judaism* (Philadelphia: JPS, 1896), 313–25. Though not specifically focusing on this subject or time period, Carol Meyers provides a lucid introduction to some modern scholarly concerns in her *Discovering Eve* (Oxford, England: Oxford, 1988), 157ff.

11. Many scholars have debated the relative reliability of the accounts of Josephus and the Mishnah, especially where they disagree in their descriptions of the Temple and its rites. French Catholic scholar R. P. Vincent is among the large body of scholars who favor Josephus, considering the Mishnah's depiction an idealized view of the Temple influenced by the vision of Ezekiel (Ezek. 40–48). *See, for example,* R. P. Vincent, "Le Temple Hérodien d'après la Misnah," *Revue Biblique* 6: 1 (Jan. 1954): 5–35. Israeli archaeologist M. Avi-Yonah is among those who prefer to rely on early Mishnaic authorities who, having witnessed the Temple in its last stages, would have been meticulous in gathering accurate details to serve as the basis for its restoration. Cf. Avi-Yonah, "Reply to the Article by Joshua Brand," (in Hebrew with English summary) *Tarbiz* 29: 2 (Jan. 1960): 218–21.

12. Discussion here will generally be limited to the normative cult at Shiloh. There is much scholarly debate as to the historicity of the desert Tabernacle. Cf. Haran, *Temples and*

Temple Service, 149, 189, 202–3 and Nahum Sarna, *Exploring Exodus* (New York: Schocken, 1987), 196–200, 240 n.27. Consequently, we will focus on biblical materials on the Shiloh Tabernacle, whose existence even Haran acknowledges, p. 201, cf. pp. 198–204. A discussion on women and the Tabernacle, as presented by the Priestly Code, can be found in Mayer Gruber's "Women in the Cult According to the Priestly Code," in *Judaic Perspectives on Ancient Israel,* ed. Jacob Neusner, Baruch Levine, and Ernest Frerichs (Philadelphia: Fortress Press, 1987), 35–48. He rejects the popular view that the Priestly Code (P) virtually excluded women from the cult. Rather, Gruber argues that P exhibits a tendency to include women in cultic activity, for example, by specifically mentioning women serving as nazirites, describing the women who gathered at the Tent of Meeting (*see infra*), and using the inclusive "non-sexist" expressions of *nefesh* or *adam* in referring to cultic acts to be performed by men or women.

13. Regarding the term "before the Lord," refer to N. Raban, "Lifnei HaShem," (in Hebrew) *Tarbiz* 23:1 (1951–1952): 1–8.

14. 2 Kings 4:23 (about the Shunamite woman) also seems to imply that women regularly attended festival and New Moon celebrations, although there it seems to refer to Elijah's headquarters as the cultic site.

15. According to Peritz, "Women in the Ancient Hebrew Cult," (p. 126 n.21), Hannah, as the subject of the verse, offers the yearly sacrifice. Cf. David Silber, "Kingship, Samuel and the Story of Hannah," *Tradition* 23:2 (Winter 1988): p. 66ff., who suggests that Hannah's prayer (1 Sam. 2:1–10) signifies her break with the sacrificial tradition surrounding the corrupt Eli.

In Judg. 13:23, Manoaḥ's wife, while not slaughtering the sacrifice herself, seems to fill the role of interpreter of the Lord's actions—that all will be well since the sacrifice has been accepted. It is also possible that Deborah, as a judge and prophet (Judg. 4:4), might have officiated at the victory sacrifice following Sisera's defeat, such celebrations being common (e.g., Josh. 8:30, Judg. 11:30–31, 1 Sam. 11:15). Pseudo-Philo 32:18 (first century c.e.) adds such a sacrifice and celebration, although it does not ascribe the officiation of the sacrifice to Deborah. As the prophet, it would have been her role, rather than Barak's, to offer the sacrifice. Saul, for example, loses Divine favor for usurping Samuel's right to sacrifice (1 Sam. 13:8–14). Cf. Peritz, "Women in the Ancient Cult," 143–44. Cf. Haran, *Temples and Temple Service,* who considers Deborah's seat of justice a site of cultic activity and sacredness, even though not a location of a temple, p. 53. Cf. n.14 above.

16. Josh. 8:34 specifies that Joshua read the blessing and the curse, indicating that this reading—and the hearing of the reading by the people—reaffirmed the covenant first contracted by the people through Moses. Cf. Deut. 27:11–30:20. Deut. includes women in the reading by Moses (Deut. 29:9–10) and in the reading of the Torah every seven years (Deut. 31:10–12). The Chronicler includes women in the reading of the Torah to the people by Ezra (Neh. 8:2–3, 10:1–30).

17. Mikhal's absence from the celebration emphasizes not only her disapproval of what she perceives of as David's unkingly behavior during spirited dancing (2 Sam. 6:16, 20) but her change in status, from the daughter and wife of kings to a consort no longer preferred by her husband and no longer important for his claims to the throne. Cf. Robert Alter, *The Art of Biblical Narrative* (New York: Basic Books, 1981), 123–25.

18. Haran, *Temples and Temple Service,* 299–300.

19. Cf. Miriam at the Reed Sea (Exod. 15:20–21) and Judith (Jth. 15:12–16:17). On Deborah, *see* n.15 above, *infra.* On the religious nature of such celebrations, *see* George Buchanan Gray, *Sacrifice in the Old Testament* (New York: Ktav, 1971), 189.

20. Phillip Siegel, "Elements of Male Chauvinism," *Judaism* 24:21 (Spring 1975): 235.

21. E.g., Deut. 23:18−19; Hos. 4:14.

22. Cf. Targ. Onk. Exod. 38:8.

23. LXX Exod. 38:26.

24. Cf. Gruber, "Women According to the Priestly Code," 36−37; Peritz, "Women in the Ancient Cult," 145−46.

25. Schechter, *Studies in Judaism,* 313−14.

26. With the exception of Miriam singing separately to the women, Exod. 15:20−21.

27. It is generally accepted that there is no biblical evidence that women ever served as priests in ancient Israelite religion. *See* Gray, *Sacrifice in the Old Testament,* (pp. 184−93, esp. pp. 191−92) who compares the linguistical evidence on the role of priestesses in Hebrew and ancient Near Eastern languages. However, the important work of Bernadette Brooten on women in the ancient synagogue raises questions about the assumptions we make in evaluating the available evidence. While we may not be able to prove women served as priests, we may need to wait for further study before categorically assuming that they could not have assumed such roles at any point in Israelite history or for any segment of the population (e.g., for women only). Bernadette Brooten, *Women Leaders in the Ancient Synagogue* (Chico, Calif.: Scholars Press, 1982), 73−99.

28. On the Solomonic Temple, *see* Yigael Yadin, "First Temple: Structure," under "Temple" in EncJud, vol. 15, 946−52. On the pre-Herodian Second Temple, *see* Shmuel Safrai and Michael Avi-Yonah, "The Second Temple: Structure," under "Temple," in Enc-Jud, vol. 15, 960−69. However, Safrai, author of one of the articles there, suggests that the Court, if not the appellation, existed earlier, based on a reading of Ezekiel's vision. *See also* Safrai, *Pilgrimage,* 88.

29. Cf. 1 Esd. 9:37−41.

30. Though, cf. Gray, *Sacrifice in the Old Testament,* 188−89, who argues that the procession was of secular character since it included the secular tribes of Benjamin, Judah, etc. On the attribution to Solomon's Temple, cf. Amos Hakham, *Book of Psalms* (in Hebrew), vol. 1 (Jerusalem: Mosad ha-Rav Kook, 1984) 401.

31. E.g., Jer. 9:16−17. Cf. *Pirkei de-R. Eliezer,* chap. 17, 41b (in English) trans. Gerald Friedlander (New York: Sepher Hermon Press, 1981), 121−22.

32. The Mishnah mentions two gates of Ḥuldah leading into the Herodian Temple from the South (Middot 1:3). These were the main entrances to the Temple for pilgrims. M. Avi-Yonah, "Excavations in Jerusalem: Review and Evaluation," in *Jerusalem Revealed,* ed. Yigael Yadin (Jerusalem: Israel Exploration Society, 1976), 22. Cf., in the same volume, N. Avigad, "The Architecture of Jerusalem in the Second Temple Period," p. 16; and B. Mazar, "The Archaeological Excavations Near the Temple Mount," pp. 25−27, 30. According to the Targum and Rashi on 2 Kings 22:14, these gates led to Ḥuldah's schoolhouse (*beit ulfuna*). For more information on Ḥuldah, *see* the index of Louis Ginzberg, *Legends of the Jews,* trans. Henrietta Szold (Philadelphia: JPS, 1911).

33. Cf. Yeḥezkel Kaufman, *The Religion of Israel* (New York: Schocken, 1972), 172−75; John Bright, *A History of Israel,* 3d ed. (Philadelphia: Westminster Press, 1981), 319.

34. On the Josianic Reform and its impact, *see* Bright, *A History of Israel,* 317−24.

35. Stinespring, "Temple Jerusalem," 550; cf. Josephus Ant. XV.xi.1.

36. Safrai and Avi-Yonah, "The Second Temple," 962; Mazar, "The Archaeological Excavations," 25; cf. Josephus, Ant. XV.xi.3.

37. Safrai and Avi-Yonah, The Second Temple," 962; cf. Josephus, Ant. XX.ix.7; John 2:20.

38. In determining in which situations a wife eats of the paschal sacrifice slaughtered for her by her husband, the Mishnah makes the assumption that women were present

(Mish. Pes. 8:1; cf. TB Pes. 87a) and that women and slaves cannot join together to make up the required fellowship for the eating of the paschal lamb (Mish. Pes. 8:7). On women's participation in *Pesah Sheni,* the one-day festival a month after Passover for those who missed the first Passover sacrifice, *see* Mish. Ḥal. 4:11 (cf. Tosef. Pes. 8:10; TJ Kid. 1:7; TB Pes. 91a–b). On women attending the *Hakhel* ceremony on Sukkot, *see* TJ Ḥag. 1:1, 75d; and Safrai, *Pilgrimage,* 90.

While not obligated to appear in Jerusalem for the festivals (Mish. Ḥag. 1:1), women were obligated to rejoice on the festivals according to tannaitic tradition. *See also* TB Ḥag. 2b–3a; Safrai "The Temple," 877 n.6. Cf. Tosef. Pes. 10:4; Saul Lieberman, *Tosefta ki-Feshuto,* vol. 4 (New York: JTS, 1966), 196; and Deut. 16:11–16. On the contradictory traditions about the wife of Jonah going up to Jerusalem for the festivals, cf. *Mekhilta de-R. Ishmael,* Bo: 17, 1:162–63; (Philadelphia: JPS, 1976) ed. Lauterbach, vol. 1, 154; TJ Ber. 2, 4c; TJ Er. 10, 26a; TJ Suk. 5, 55a; TB Er. 96a. Cf. Safrai, *Pilgrimage,* 91, 102, nn.44, 45. Large numbers of men and women appeared in Jerusalem for the annual festivals, though they still represented only a portion of the total population. Safrai, *Pilgrimage,* 24–26. Cf. n.2 above, *infra.*

39. While women did not enter Temple precincts during their menses (Josephus, Ant., V.v.6), they could enter the Temple after completion of their menses and their subsequent ritual immersion. Sacrifices were not necessary. On the sacrifices required after childbirth, *see* the statement by Simeon bar Yoḥai, TB Nid. 31b.

40. Cf. TB Pes. 3a.

41. There was one difference between a male and female nazirite: the female nazirite's vow could be annulled by her father (if she was an unmarried minor) or by her husband (if she was married), as could any other vow by a woman. *See* the fourth chapter of Mish. Naz. Cf. Num. 30:4–16. On the nature of the naziriteship, *see* Peritz, "Women in the Ancient Cult," 128.

42. *See* Mish. Naz. 2:7–10, in which a man vows to become a nazir if a son is born to him. Mish. Naz. 4:6 states a woman cannot place her son under a nazirite vow, even though in 1 Sam. 1:11, Hannah places her yet-to-be-born son, Samuel, under the nazirite vow. The Mishnah may be trying to preclude similar practices by contemporary women.

43. Cf. TB Naz. 19a–20a, on Helena's lengthy naziriteship, which implies that menses is not a cause for impurity in reference to interrupting the nazirite period.

44. Cf. Num. 6:18–20.

45. Cf. TB Naz. 24a–b.

46. Cf. TB Kid. 36a–b, TB Men. 61b.

47. Cf. Mish. Men. 5:6; TB Kid. 36a–b, Num. 5:18, 25. On the translation, "wave offering," *see* n.69 *infra.*

48. EncJud, s.v. "tadmor."

49. In addition to Mishnaic evidence on the female nazirites Queen Helena and Miriam of Palmyra, Josephus records what may have been another female nazirite, Bernice, the sister of King Agrippa (Wars II.xv.1).

50. The tradition of women's contributions is an ancient one, especially prominent in the Exodus traditions. Women, along with men, made free-will offerings of their gold jewelry for the building of the Tabernacle (Exod. 35:21–22). The wise (or skilled) women brought their spinning of linen and goat's hair (Exod. 35:25–26). The copper laver of the Tabernacle was made of the copper mirrors donated by the "Women who Gathered" (Exod. 38:8).

51. *See* Gedaliah Alon, *Studies in Jewish History in the Times of the Second Temple, the Mishnah and the Talmud* (in Hebrew) (Tel Aviv: Kibbutz Hameuhad, 1957), 297–98 n.3.

On hellenistic parallels, cf. Saul Lieberman, *Hellenism in Jewish Palestine* (New York: JTS, 1950), 168−69.

52. On the oath recited by the priest over the *sotah, see* Num. 5 : 19−22. Cf. TB Yoma 37b−38a, on whether the entire paragraph or just abbreviations of the verses were included on the tablet. According to the *Tosefta,* it seems the plaque was situated so that the first rays of the morning sun reflected from it for all to know the time of sunrise (and therefore the time for the recitation of the morning *Shema,* according to the *baraita* on TB Yoma 37b).

53. Cf. n.28 above.

54. Wars V.v.2 seems to imply that the Women's Court was built as an addition for the women. Adolf Buchler's suggestion that the Women's Court was built in 44 C.E. in response to increased attendance of women due to the standard of involvement set by Queen Helena seems·to be based on the assumption that Temple officials would not have allowed women to mingle with men in large numbers; therefore, women could not have been attending the Temple in large numbers earlier. Buchler, "The Fore-Court of Women and the Brass Gate in the Temple of Jerusalem," *Jewish Quarterly Review* vol. X (original series) (1898): p. 678−718. However, such an assumption does not seem to conform with earlier sources suggesting women's presence in the Tabernacle, First Temple, and pre-Herodian Second Temple, as discussed above, *infra.*

55. Cf. Safrai, "Temple," 866−67.

56. Josephus also mentions that men entered the Women's Court (Ant. Xv.xi.5, Against Apion II.8). On lepers, *see* Mish. Neg. 14 : 8. On the possibility of the Torah reading ceremonies being held in the Women's Court, *see* TB Yoma 69b, TB Sot. 41b, containing a tradition attributed to the third-generation Babylonian amorah R. Ḥisdah that the Torah readings by the High Priest on Yom Kippur and the King every seventh year on Sukkot were held in the Women's Court. Tannaitic tradition is less clear. Mish. Sot. 7 : 8 states that the *Hakhel* reading was held in the Court (*Azarah*), which usually refers to the inner Priestly Court, although cf. its usage in Tosef. Suk. 4 : 1. Mish. Yoma 7 : 1 is ambiguous, stating only "The High Priest came to read" (*ba lo Kohen Gadol likrot*). TB Yoma 69b records a tradition by the *tanna* R. Eliezer ben Jacob that the reading was held on the Temple Mount, which assumes the presence of the women, based on the precedent set by Ezra (Neh. 8 : 3).

57. Tosef. Pes. 3 : 12 (ed. Zuckermandel); 4 : 12 (ed. Lieberman).

58. For a discussion concerning the etymology and correct version of this title, *see* Raphael Patai, *Man and Temple* (New York: Ktav, 1967), 47 n.1; and Ḥanoch Albeck in his commentary to Mish. Suk. 5 : 1, p. 274.

59. Patai, *Man and Temple,* 24.

60. For a succinct presentation of the Water-Drawing ceremony, *see* Patai, ibid., 28−32. The Mishnaic material appears in the context of the rituals of Sukkot. Most of the material is presented anonymously, with some differing opinions by Rabbi Judah (second century, Usha). The general celebratory tone of the *Simḥat Beit ha-Shoʾevah* during the existence of the Temple is attested to in anecdotal material about the early Sages Hillel the Elder (Tosef. Suk. 4 : 3) and Yehoshua ben Ḥanina (Tosef. Suk. 4 : 5), both of whom lived during Temple days. Cf. also Tosef. Suk. 4 : 4 on Rabban Shimeon ben Gamliel.

61. Cf. the *baraita* cited on TB Suk. 51b; TB Kid. 81a, which assumes the same *baraita* as TB Suk. 51b; Rabbenu Ḥannanel on Suk. 51b; and especially Saul Lieberman, *Tosefta ki-Feshuto* on Tosef. Suk. 4 : 1. On differences between the *baraita* and the *Tosefta, see* B. De Vreis, "The Problem of the Relationship of the Two Talmuds to the *Tosefta,*" (in Hebrew with English summary) *Tarbiz* 28 : 2 (1959): 158−70.

62. *See* H. Albeck on Mish. Suk. 5 : 2, based on Mish. Middot 2 : 5, that it stood all year long but was only used for *Simḥat Beit ha-Shoʾevah; contra* Rashi, Suk. 51b, s.v. *Ve-hakifuhah*

gezuztra. Lieberman, while agreeing with Rashi, points out that Mish. Middot 2 : 5 seems to be referring to a balcony that stood all year, *Tosefta ki-Feshuto* on Suk. 4 : 1.

63. The term *tikkun gadol* appears nowhere else in tannaitic literature or in either of the two Talmuds. A term, *takkanah gedolah* (lit. a great enactment), does appear in several tannaitic sources (Tosef. Git. 7 : 13, [9 : 13, ed. Zuckermandel] and *baraitot* on TB Git. 36a, TB BK 103b, and TB Nid. 33a). The sense of *takkanah* (enactment) may be appropriate in our context, especially given the fact that the *Tosefta* speaks of the *beit din* (rabbinic court), which makes enactments, and the Babylonian Talmud's *baraita* uses *hitkinu*, as in to enact or promulgate a *takkanah.* Cf. Yosef Schechter, *Otzar ha-Talmud* (Jerusalem: Dvir, 1984), s.v. "takkanah."

64. Tos. Shevu. 45a, s.v.: *"gedolot me-khlal dikha ktanot,"* discussing *takkanah gedolah* (*see* n.63 supra), mentions only TB Git. 36a and BK 103b. This reasoning could also be applied to Nid. 33a, as an important safeguard. As for the attribution to R. Gamliel in TB Git. 36a: Tos Shevu. 45a, Tosef. Git. 7 : 13, and Rabbenu Ḥannanel TB Git. 36a have Rabban Shimeon ben Gamliel.

65. Patai, *Man and Temple*, 56–59. Cf. Theodor Gaster, *Festivals of the Jewish Year* (New York: William Morrow, 1953), 82–84.

66. Rabban Shimeon ben Gamliel, among other sages, is mentioned as participating, Tosef. Suk. 4 : 2–4, Mish. Suk. 5 : 4, TB Suk. 53a, TJ Suk. 5 : 4, 55b.

67. For pagan parallels to the torches and games, *see* Patai, *Man and Temple*, 34–36, 71–83; Gaster, *Festivals of the Jewish Year*, 82–83.

68. *See* Erwin Goodenough, *Jewish Symbolism in the Greco-Roman Period*, vol. 4 (New York: Pantheon, 1953–1968), 154–58. While the orgiastic Bacchanalia was severely curtailed by Senatorial decree in 186 B.C.E., other cults with orgiastic or erotic aspects maintained a wide appeal in the Greco-Roman Mediterranean for many centuries. The orgiastic cult of the Syrian goddess Ma, identified with Bellona, was widespread at the time of Marius (156–86 B.C.E.). The influence of the cult of the Egyptian goddess Isis, which contained clearly sexual elements, continued through the second century C.E. Cf. Robert Schilling, "Roman Religion: The Early Period," and Arnaldo Momigliano, "Roman Religion: The Imperial Period," in *The Encyclopedia of Religion*, ed. Mircea Eliade, vol. 12 (New York: MacMillan, 1987) 445–61, and 462–71, respectively; and Sarah Pomeroy, *Goddesses, Whores, Wives, and Slaves: Women in Classical Antiquity* (New York: Schocken, 1975), 217, 222–25. Philo, at least, seems aware of the orgiastic aspects of pagan festivals, which he severely criticizes. *See* Richard Baer, *Philo's Use of the Categories of Male and Female* (Leiden: Brill, 1970), 10–11. The cults of both Dionysus and Isis were practiced in Palestine and were well known to the Jews there. *See* D. Flusser, "Paganism in Palestine," in *Compendia Rerum Iudaicarum*, ed. S. Safrai and M. Stern, 1065–1100, esp. pp. 1067–69, 1083, 1085–86, 1099.

69. Cf. Josephus Ant. XIII.xiii.5, which discusses the separation of the Priestly Court from the Israelite Court. On defining *tenufah* as "raising," rather than "waving," *see* J. Milgrom, "Wave Offering" in *Interpreter's Dictionary of the Bible:* Supplementary Volume (Nashville: Abington, 1976), 944–45.

70. *See* Tosv. Kid. 52b, s.v. *"Ve-khi nashim ba-azara minayin."*

71. *See* Mish. Men. 5 : 5. On the relationship between the Mishnah and *baraitot*, *see* J. Epstein, *Introduction to Tannaitic Literature* (in Hebrew) (Tel Aviv: Dvir, 1957), 241ff.

72. Cf. TB Zev. 32a, and Gruber, "Women in the Cult," 46 n.37.

73. Unlike slaughtering, a priest or male Israelite cannot perform *semikhah* for women, as agency is not allowed for *semikhah* (Mish. Men. 9 : 9). Women's sacrifices are nevertheless valid without *semikhah* (Mish. Men. 9 : 8, cf. TB Pes. 89a, TB Ḥag. 16b). Peritz suggests that

women were obligated to perform *semikhah,* according to Leviticus, "Women in the Ancient Cult," 126–27.

74. *See* Sifra Lev. chap. 4, sec. 10 on the popularity of *semikhah;* cf. Urbach, *The Sages,* 2d ed., vol. 1, 591; vol. 2, 956–97 n.4.

75. *See* Josephus Ant. III.xi.6. On the biblical location of the *sotah*'s waving, *see* Raban, "Lifnei HaShem," 1–8. Nevertheless, Tos. TB Kid. 52b assumes both the *nazir* and *sotah* waved their sacrifices in the Priestly Court, in their discussion of Mish. Kid. 2:8 that a woman could be bethrothed through the holiest offerings that should not leave the priestly court. Cf. Saul Lieberman, *Tosefta ki-Feshuto, Seder Nashim,* vol. 8 (New York: JTS, 1955), 954. On the *baraita* on TB Kid. 52b, which seems to assume women cannot enter the Priestly Court, *see* Naz. 49b, which repeats the formulaic language with the particulars of the different relevant *mishnayot* substituted in the objections raised by cited *tannaim.* On the possibility of amoraic altering of *baraitot, see* De Vreis, discussing Epstein, "The Problem of the Relationship," 161–62.

76. *See* TB Kid. 36a and Lev. 2:2, 3:5, 6:7, 7:31. Cf. n.27 *supra.*

77. For a complete discussion on the *bat kohen,* cf. *Encyclopedia Talmudit* (in Hebrew), s.v. *"bat kohen."*

78. E.g. R. P. Vincent, "Le Temple Hérodien d'après la Misnah," 12.

79. Cf. Mary Douglas, *Purity and Danger: An Analysis of the Concepts of Pollution and Taboo* (Boston: Ark, 1984), 51, 121–28. This theory would seem to conform most closely with the levitical laws of the Priestly Code. However, according to Gruber in "Women in the Cult According to the Priestly Code," the Priestly Code (P) granted women a better position in the cult than is generally assumed (*see* n.12 above, *infra*). Douglas notwithstanding, it is important to note that blood taboos are culturally determined and by no means universally applicable.

80. Bickerman, "The Warning Inscriptions of Herod's Temple," *Jewish Quarterly Review,* vol. 38, no. 4 (April 1947), 389–90, 392, 404.

81. E.g., Livy (b. c. 59–64 B.C.E., Italy–d. 17 C.E), *History of Rome,* 34.7.8–10, on the lack of women priestesses in Republican Italy. Women did serve as priestesses and cultic functionaries in a number of Greco-Roman religions but:

> [T]he state religion of Rome traditionally excluded slaves, freemen, and of course women—with the exception of a few, including the six Vestals and two priestesses of Ceres—from its hierarchy, while those who did participate were carefully organized into separate categories [Pomeroy, *Goddesses, Whores, Wives,* 223].

Cf. Pomeroy, ibid., 77–78, 206–8, and Mary Lefkowitz and Maureen Fant, *Women's Life in Greece and Rome* (Baltimore: Johns Hopkins University Press, 1983), 113, 250–55.

82. Pomeroy, *Goddesses, Whores, Wives,* 206–7. On the different *Fortuna* religions, and the varying roles women played in them, *see* Jacqueline Champeaux, *Recherches sur le monde romain à Rome et dans le monde romain dès origines à la mort de César, vol. 1: Fortuna dans la Religion Archaïque* (Rome: Ecole Française de Rome, 1982). *See also,* Eva Cantarella, *Pandora's Daughters: The Role and Status of Women in Greek and Roman Antiquity,* trans. Maureen B. Fant (Baltimore: Johns Hopkins University Press, 1987), 151–52. However, for a critique of Cantarella, *see* Pomeroy's review of *Pandora's Daughters* in AHR vol. 93 (1988): 674. Women's involvement seems to have been somewhat less restricted in the Egyptian cults (*see* Pomeroy, *Women in Hellenistic Egypt from Alexander to Cleopatra* [New York: Schocken, 1984] 55–59), the very cults that remained widespread in Palestine during the rabbinic period. *See* Flusser, n.68 above, *infra.*

83. *See* Saul Lieberman's studies *Greek in Jewish Palestine* (New York: JTS, 1942) and *Hellenism in Jewish Palestine* (New York: JTS, 1950).

84. Urbach, *The Sages*, vol. 1, 581; vol. 2, 951 n.48. Cf. Lieberman, *Hellenism in Jewish Palestine*, 164–79.

85. Urbach, *The Sages*, vol. 1, 581.

86. Such a dichotomy seems to have influenced the Mishnah's version of the Passover *seder*. With its similarities and differences to the Greek symposia, the *seder*, as presented in the Mishnah, is an example of the balance—or tension—between cultural commonality and cultural distinction. *See* Baruch Bokser, *Origins of the Seder* (Berkeley: University of California Press, 1986), 57–66, and Mish. Pes. 10:7, 8, which Bokser presents as one of a number of examples of rabbinic efforts to distinguish the Passover rite from the ancient banquets and the symposia.

87. On the term "sacred center," *see* Michael Fishbane, "The Sacred Center: The Symbolic Structure of the Bible," in *Texts and Responses*, ed. M. A. Fishbane and Paul Flohr (Leiden: Brill, 1975), 6–27.

88. *See* n.68 above, *infra*. Cults with sexual components or overtones such as the Dionysus cult and the cult of Isis were present in Palestine. It seems that rabbinic leaders were aware in some detail of the rites of hellenistic cults and eastern cults such as that of Isis, which were absorbed into hellenistic culture. *See* Flusser, cited n.68 above, *infra*.

89. For a critique of the theory that women's status and participation in the Israelite cult suffered a steady decline, culminating in rabbinic literature, *see* Gruber (n.12 above, *infra*). A study of the visions of the Temple and views of the sacred in the Dead Sea Scrolls would probably contribute to delineating the transformation between biblical and rabbinic views of women's access to the sancta. However, such material awaits future study.

90. The Tosef. Suk. 4:1 stresses that the women would watch from the balcony.

91. On the stammaic period, *see* David Weiss Halivni, *Midrash, Mishnah, and Gemara* (Cambridge, Mass.: Harvard University Press, 1986), 76–92 and his multivolume commentary on the Talmud, *Mekorot u-Masorot* (Tel Aviv: Dvir, 1968 and New York: JTS, 1975–1982).

92. Cf. n.7 above, *infra*.

Hannah Safrai

WOMEN AND THE
ANCIENT SYNAGOGUE[1]

In ancient times the synagogue (*beit ha-knesset* or, as it is also called in the sources, *beit ha-ʿedah*) constituted a center for the Jewish community. Here the Jewish congregation assembled, not only for worship of God but also for a wide variety of public activities.[2] This congregation included men, women, and children.

In various contexts, the sources repeatedly mention that the women in the community functioned in the synagogue and found their place within it. According to the Book of Acts, even while the Temple stood, Paul, when he was still called Saul of Tarsus, expected to find women among the congregants when he anticipated visiting the synagogue in Damascus to uncover those who were sinning, erring, and believing in the forbidden new church.[3] Later, as a follower of Jesus, Paul visited a synagogue in Salonika (in modern day Greece) where he drew the attention of the women with his sermons.[4] Important women were among the multitude that heard him preach. In all cases, it is clear to the author of Acts that it was natural for women to be found in the synagogue. The presence of women did not arouse any amazement or surprise.

Philo of Alexander (20 B.C.E.–50 C.E.), in his *On the Contemplative Life*, describes the prayer assemblies of Therapeutae (a sect of Jewish ascetics, quite similar to the Dead Sea sect). He tells us that when the group gathered in public assembly, both men and women were found together, although they were seated separately. Together they sang songs of praise to the Creator of the World. Philo delights in the harmony of their singing; he is filled with enthusiasm for their devotion. He is not at all surprised that the women of the company are seated in the same meeting hall.[5] Elsewhere, in discussing the personal status and way of life of the Alexandrian Jewish community, Philo states that women must preserve their modesty and avoid appearing in public, except when they are on their way to the synagogue.[6] To Philo, as well as to the author of Acts, it is clear that women were found in gatherings of the community and in the location of these gatherings—the synagogue.

Often, in the course of rabbinic halakhic discussions, it is made clear that women's presence in the synagogue was common. In a city where all the inhabitants are priests (*kohanim*), everyone goes up to bless the congregation, "[A]nd who says 'Amen' after them? The women and children."[7] Women, as well as children, do not mount the platform to give a blessing, but there is no doubt that women are found within the synagogue when the priests are giving the blessing. This passage assumes there will never be a congregation lacking in women and children to answer amen. Tractate Sofrim assumes that both men and women attend the reading of the Torah, observing the holy scroll and the written words, and are obliged to say "*ve-zot ha-Torah . . .*" ("And this is the Torah . . .").[8]

In the same way, the synagogue is portrayed as a place that a woman can visit for a brief time in the course of her daily routine. "A woman puts her food pots upon the stove, leaving her non-Jewish servants alone at home, until she comes from the bathhouse or the synagogue, and is not concerned."[9] This means that a woman should not hesitate to leave her non-Jewish woman (servant) in her home for a brief time to go off to the public institutions where she normally would go. The rabbis chose the synagogue as one of the obvious examples of such an institution.

Likewise, there are halakhic discussions dealing directly with the attendance of women in the synagogue: Is a woman permitted to enter the synagogue during her menstrual period?[10] Is a jealous husband authorized to stop his wife from going to the synagogue because of his jealousy?[11] For our purposes here, the answers are not important; rather, what interests us is the reality that emerges from the questions themselves—women were accustomed to attend the synagogue.

Having established this fact, we may now inquire in more detail about women's place there. Where did women sit? Were women present in the synagogue building itself, or was there a separate location for their activities, an *ezrat nashim*? Did the women have defined roles in activities within the synagogue? What was their social or religious standing in the synagogue or in the organized community of the synagogue?

In an extensive and convincing article, Shmuel Safrai, my father and teacher, proved that there is no archaeological evidence from the ancient period, either in Israel or the Diaspora, to indicate that there was a special, separate place for women in the synagogue.[12] In addition, none of the literary and halakhic sources indicating the presence of women in the synagogue prove that women were separated from men. It is highly doubtful that a husband would be jealous of his wife if she would be sitting only among women. There is room for jealousy only if he envisioned her sitting among men and did not trust her.[13]

In the synagogue at Phocaea (a Greek settlement on the Aegean Coast of Asia Minor), a generous woman, known as Tation, was awarded a golden crown and the privilege of sitting in a seat of honor in the synagogue. From our archaeological finds we know that, in ancient synagogues, seats of honor were to be found in the front of the synagogue (*prohedria*). This esteemed woman could only have been sitting in a congregation where it was possible to honor women, as well as men, by seating them in a prominent location.[14] Paul, in his speech to the Corinthian congregation, warns the women not to speak up in the community, not even to ask any questions, but to inquire of their husbands at home.[15] His statement clearly indicates that women sat within the congregation, like their fellow men and husbands. This is the picture that emerges from both Jewish and early Christian sources: men and women sitting together during activities in the synagogue or community house.

As we examine the range of synagogue activities in which women participated, we must divide our discussion into two separate sections: (1) the erection of the building, its physical structure, and its administrative management; and (2) the worship of God that took place within its walls.

In her book *Women Leaders in the Ancient Synagogue,* Bernadette Brooten has gathered a wealth of material on the administrative role of women in ancient Jewish and early Christian congregations. From dedicatory inscriptions, as well as inscriptions found on tombstones throughout the Jewish Diaspora, we know of women who bore official titles related to the institution of the synagogue. We also learn about generous women who contributed to the building of synagogues. In addition to Tation of Phocaea mentioned above, archaeological excavations at the synagogue of Apamea (in what is north of Syria today), have uncovered nine inscriptions relating to generous women, five inscriptions on the generosity of women mentioned together with men, and two additional inscriptions describing donations made in honor of women.[16] A significant number of other inscriptions demonstrate the involvement of wealthy women in the building of synagogues thoughout the Jewish world.[17] There is, then, clear evidence that women felt themselves to be involved and responsible participants in this important Jewish institution.

From all these inscriptions, one can extract an impressive list of honorary titles connected to the synagogue that were awarded to women. Three women are titled "Head of the Synagogue,"[18] two inscriptions mention "leader" (fem. *manhigah*),[19] and six relate to "venerable women."[20] Two Greek inscriptions read "Mother of the Synagogue."[21] It had been widely assumed that these titles should not be interpreted as describing the actual participation of women in the synagogue but that they were only honorary titles. Brooten, however, quite justifiably claims that there is no proof that these titles, descriptive of positions filled by men, were only honorary when applied to women. We are not able to specify exactly what these distinguished women did, but the striking evidence before us is of women who were involved and active in these communities. The male holders of these titles were responsible for ongoing administration of the synagogue; it is reasonable to assume that women participated in these responsibilities as well.

The worship of God in the synagogue prayer service is focused around three areas: reading from the Torah (the most ancient of these practices), prayer, and the sermon and communal public study. It clearly emerges from our sources that women participated as part of the congregation and possibly even took part in every one of these areas.

Torah Reading

Tannaitic *halakhah* states: "Everyone is included in the *minyan* of seven [to go up to read the Torah on the Sabbath], even a woman, even a child."[22] In the early synagogue, it was customary for the same people who recited the blessings to read from the Torah. Essentially, women could have been among those reciting the blessings and reading the Torah.[23] However, in the *Tosefta* we find the reservation that prohibits women from reading the Torah for the congregation: "One does not call up a woman to read to the multitude."[24] Whatever the reasoning behind this reservation may be, it seems that, in fact, women did not read within the synagogue. The *Tosefta* continues, and clarifies: "[In] a synagogue that only has one person who reads, he stands and reads, then sits down, gets up and reads, then sits down . . . even seven times."[25] The one capable (male) reader will repeat the blessing and read (for each *aliyah*), but a woman will not be included among those who are called to read. In the Babylonian Talmud, we find a *baraita* that offers a kind of rationale for this practice: "But the Sages said, a woman shall not read, because of the honor of the congregation."[26] It becomes clear that at first women were permitted to be called up and recite the blessings during the Torah reading, but additional considerations served to distance them from this role in the synagogue.

The term "honor of the congregation" specifically refers to synagogue activities, yet its precise meaning is unclear. This phrase appears elsewhere: A *poḥeaḥ*—a person whose clothing is unkempt and immodest[27]—may not read from the Torah because of the honor of the congregation.[28] A prayer leader is not permitted to uncover the Torah scroll in public because of the honor of the congregation.[29] In the synagogue, it is prohibited to read from scrolls of individual books of the Torah rather than from a complete Torah scroll because of the honor of the congregation.[30] Regarding the women and the *poḥeaḥ*, it seems that we are dealing with matters of modesty. There is no doubt that the case of uncovering the Torah scroll is more related to burdening the public with additional time spent in the synagogue, and it seems that the prohibition of reading from individual books of the Torah is associated with the types of rituals suitable for the synagogue.

Perhaps an examination of the underlying rationale behind "honor of the congregation" in all of these prohibitions can aid our understanding of why it is considered improper behavior for women to serve as Torah readers in the synagogue. We cannot claim that the prohibition of women reading because of a concern for the "honor of the congregation" stems from a halakhic decision that women were not permitted to fulfill a public obligation.[31] A discussion elsewhere in the Babylonian Talmud rejects the suggestion that a decree of Rabban Yoḥanan ben Zakkai, prohibiting priests from wearing sandals when they bless the people, is based upon the concept of the "honor of the congregation." Rav Ashi there understands that Rabban Yoḥanan was concerned with the halakhic connotation of such an act disqualifying the priest from service rather than any concern for the "honor of the congregation."[32] The honor of the congregation, according to this and the above sources, seems to have been a social issue, whatever its exact meaning, and not an halakhically related item. Therefore, women were distanced from reading the Torah in the synagogue because, in the world of the ancient synagogue, having women readers seemed undesirable (*see* Hauptman, p. 163).

In none of our sources have we found that women were obligated in weekly or holiday Torah readings. In contrast, women were obligated in the *Megillah* reading,[33] and on this subject we learn: "All are obligated in the *Megillah* reading, all are fit [eligible] to read the *Megillah*. Including whom? Including women."[34] Women were obligated in the reading and, therefore, were able to fulfill this obligation for others, even men.[35] Indeed, here we do not find a dependence on the concept of the "honor of the congregation." Theoretically, women were able to recite the blessing or read. However, this was not acceptable in the social milieu of the ancient world. Since women were specifically obligated to read the *Megillah*, the prohibition of the "honor of the congregation" was not used to specifically forbid women from reading the *Megillah* in public.

What is the relation between obligation and the use of the rationale "honor of the congregation"? What should we infer from the different approaches reflected in our sources? Is the so-called social perspective more susceptible and changeable in the face of other issues? It is appropriate for us to ask: Did (or should) the nature of this social prohibition change in the different social realities of later periods? (*See* Hauptman, p. 169ff.)

Prayer

The Mishnah specifically states: "Women, slaves, and minors are exempt from reciting the *Shema* and from [wearing] *tefillin* and are obligated in prayer, in *mezuzah*, and [in reciting] the Grace after Meals."[36] It is doubtful that this *mishnah* obligates women in public prayer, as it contains only the basic obligation to pray and not specifically to join in prayer within a congregation. Nevertheless, we have already seen that women's presence in the early synagogue is beyond dispute. In Philippi (in contemporary Turkey), Paul walks from the town to the river, where the Jews are accustomed to meet in prayer. There he meets the women as well as the men.[37] It could be that the river was simply a meeting place and not a synagogue, but we may deduce that women did indeed participate in public prayer. So too, John Chrysostom (b. Antioch c. 347–407 c.e., Patriarch of Constantinople and Church Father) testifies that many women were accustomed to go to the synagogue on Rosh Hashanah for prayers and the blowing of the *shofar* as well as on other festival days.[38] Indeed, he urges husbands to forbid their wives from attending the synagogue or the theater.

Sermons

Women were present during sermons and Torah study in the synagogue, even though they were not considered to be under the same obligations as men to study.

Commenting on the verse, "You are all standing here today . . . your children, your *women* . . ." (italics added) (Deut. 29:10), the *midrash* states: "Even if they [the women] do not understand, they come to hear and to receive from everything. This teaches that everyone who enters the synagogue and hears the words of Torah, even though he may not understand, merits and receives four things as a reward. . . ."[39] According to the *midrash*, women are not erudite in Torah learning but they do come in order to listen and to merit the reward of one who frequents the synagogue and the house of study. The verse from Deuteronomy does not relate to the synagogue, but the author of this *midrash* views it as an example of synagogue activities. It is clear that everyone is present: men, women, and children. This reality seems to the expounder to be an outstanding mark of Jewish superiority. In addition, the expounder uses what seems to be a well-known homily,[40] which specifically indicates that women are not included in the obligation of learning Torah.

Similarly, we find elsewhere: "Because of this, young Israelite girls customarily came to the synagogues, so that those who bring them would merit reward, and so that they themselves would be rewarded."[41] This concept is also applied to the biblical verses relating to women's presence at the assembly for the reading of the Torah once every seven years (*Hakhel*)[42] and, to a certain extent, also at the giving of the Torah.[43]

According to these sources, women were incapable of study and were not obligated to study, but they were encouraged to be present in the house of study and the synagogue to listen. Perhaps they were not permitted to ask questions in public, but there seems to be no doubt that they were present during the time of the sermon. However, we seem to have no evidence of women preachers.

Preaching was not confined to the synagogue. As noted above, Paul went to the river outside the city of Philippi. There he encountered a woman named Lydia, who sold fine textiles. She listened to Paul speak and was convinced by his words.[44]

Sermons were often delivered in the study house, where women were also present. Targum Onkeles (second century c.e.) on the verse, "You will be praised among the women in the tent" (Judg. 5:24), states: "You will be blessed as one of the women who serve in the study house." The word "*ohel,*" tent, is interpreted as the study house, and there sit women who serve as students of the Sages; that is to say, women who sit and listen to their words. There is a well-known story about a woman who used to listen to the words of R. Meir every Sabbath eve, and ultimately aroused the ire of her husband.[45] This is a story of an independent woman who spent time in the house of study without her husband and learned from the scholars, contrary to her husband's wishes.

Summary

To summarize, the participation of women in the synagogue is well documented in our sources. Women occupied a distinguished position in the synagogue and certainly participated in its founding and administration. The involvement of women in the building of centers of worship is an ancient tradition, mentioned in the Torah. The responsibility that the daughters of Israel had toward the worship of God and the edifice designated as God's sanctuary goes back to the building of the Sanctuary in the desert. Exodus repeatedly makes this point: "Men and women, all whose hearts moved them . . ." (Exod. 35:22); "And all the skilled women spun with their own hands . . ." (ibid., 25); "And all the women who excelled in that skill . . . " (ibid. 26).

Although there is no evidence that women led prayers, it is clear that women were present in the synagogue for the worship of God conducted within its walls. The *midrash* for the section of the Bible about the giving of the Torah repeatedly emphasizes that the women stood alongside the men and took upon themselves the burden of the Torah and the obligation to observe the commandments.[46] Prayer is one of the commandments to which women are obligated. Moreover, as recorded in the Babylonian Talmud (Ber. 31a−b), the tradition of public prayer proudly reaffirms and emphasizes that the prayer of a woman, Hannah, is the model for the order of Jewish prayer. The nine blessings in the Rosh Hashana *Amidah* are ordered after the nine times Hannah mentioned the name of God in her prayer; Hannah originated the term "*Tzva'ot*" (Lord of Hosts) in her prayer; Hannah invented the silent prayer; Hannah stood to pray, from which the *Amidah* prayers derive ("*amidah*" means standing); and Hannah determined the structure of prayers within the *Amidah*, beginning with praise of God, followed by petitions, and ending with thanksgiving. Hannah's prayer is a classic example of Jewish worship.

The actual participation of women in the activities of the ancient synagogue and in its prayer service seems to have been interpreted by the social reality and the social attitudes acceptable at the time. Thus, we have no hard evidence for women serving as Torah readers, prayer leaders, or preachers. Nevertheless, it seems likely that women themselves made an effort to be included in the various events going on in the community, that they took part in the community's religious life, and that men assumed they were right to do so.

If applied to today, the role of women in the synagogue of the ancient world, as it appears in our literary and archaeological sources, would probably not be extensive enough to satisfy the modern woman's yearning for greater synagogue participation. Perhaps, though, the example of ancient women's involvement can serve as a starting point from which a new path for greater involvement can be forged, in a style appropriate to modern generations.

Notes

1. This chapter was translated from the original Hebrew.
2. *See* S. Safrai, *Be-shilḥei ha-Bayit ha-Sheni U-be-Tekufat ha-Mishnah* (in Hebrew) (Jerusalem: Misrad ha-Ḥinukh ve-ha-Tarbut; ha-Maḥlakah le-Tarbut Toranit, 1981), 143ff.

3. Acts 9:2.

4. Acts 17:1−4.

5. Philo, *On the Contemplative Life*, p. 32ff. He emphasizes here that women, just like men, also arrive regularly at these gatherings. It is possible that he meant to imply that there was something unique about this. It is also possible that nothing surprising is implied in this comment.

6. Philo, *On the Special Laws*, bk. 3, p. 171. He speaks about the sanctuary (*mikdash*), but we may assume that these words are only a use of Alexandrian terminology, and that he intends a reference to the house of worship in Alexandria, the synagogue.

7. TJ Ber., end of chap. 5.

8. Sofrim 14:14.

9. Av. Zar. 38a−b.

10. *See* S. Safrai, "Was There an *Ezrat Nashim* in the synagogue of the Ancient Period?" (in Hebrew) *Tarbiz* 32:4 (1963): 335.

11. TJ Sot. 1:2.

12. S. Safrai, "Was There an *Ezrat Nashim*," 331−33. Cf., more recently, a long and penetrating discussion by B. J. Brooten, *Women Leaders in the Ancient Synagogue* (Chico, Calif.: Scholars Press, 1982), 103−38.

13. *See* S. Safrai's discussion on this matter in "Was There an *Ezrat Nashim*," 336.

14. S. Reinach, "Une nouvelle synagogue grecque à Phocée," *Revue des Etudes Juifs* 12 (1986), 236−43.

15. 1 Cor. 14:34−35.

16. *See* n.12.

17. *See* Brooten, *Women Leaders*, 143, and the appendix listing inscriptions of women donors, pp. 157−65.

18. Ibid., 5ff.

19. Ibid., 35ff.

20. Ibid., 41ff.

21. Ibid., 57ff.

22. Tosef. Meg. 3:11.

23. *See* Safrai, "Was There an *Ezrat Nashim*," 335, and n.44.

24. Tosef. Meg. 3:11.

25. Tosef. Meg. 3:11−12.

26. TB Meg. 23a.

27. TJ MK 3:7.

28. TB Meg. 24b.

29. TB Sot. 39b.

30. TB Git. 60a.

31. However, *see* S. Lieberman, *Tosefta ki-Feshuta, Moed* (New York: JTS, 1962), 1176−78.

32. TB Sot. 40a. However, the Talmud continues, citing R. Ashi who disagrees with the reason, suggesting another.

33. TB Meg. 4a.

34. TB Ar. 3a.

35. *See* Rashi, ibid., s.v. "*le'atuyei mai?*"

36. Mish. Ber. 3:3.

37. Acts 16:13.

38. Adv. Jud. 2.4−6; 4.3.

39. *Midrash ha-Gadol* on Deuteronomy, ed. S. Fish (Jerusalem: Mosad Rav Kook, 1972), 639.

40. TB Hag. 3a; TJ Hag. 1:1; Num. R. 14:4, and others.

41. Sofrim 18:6.

42. *See* n.40.

43. Mekhilta de-R. Ishmael: Yitro, Masekhtah ba-ḥodesh, chap. 2 (ed. Horowitz), 207. Also, Exod. R. 28:2.

44. Acts 16:12–14.

45. TJ Sot. 1:4; Lev. R. 9:9; Num. R. 29:20; Deut. R. 5:15.

46. *See* n.43.

Sara Reguer

WOMEN AND THE SYNAGOGUE IN MEDIEVAL CAIRO

During the Middle Ages, more than half the world's Jewish population was under the rule of Islam. The centers of Jewish learning and culture were situated in Moslem countries and were greatly influenced by classical Islamic culture, which had rediscovered the Greek philosophers and introduced new styles of poetry and literature. During the classical period of Islam, from 900–1200 C.E., such luminaries as the philosopher and codifier Moses Maimonides and the poet-theologian Judah ha-Levi were so immersed in Islamic culture that they wrote some of their major works in the philosophical and literary styles then prevalent in the Moslem world. They even wrote in Arabic. Maimonides' *Guide to the Perplexed* and ha-Levi's *Kuzari* are just two significant examples of this body of medieval Jewish literature.

Islamic culture influenced all aspects of Jewish life. Synagogue architecture of this period is a conspicuous example of this cross-cultural influence. Many synagogues in the Islamic world reflected the architectural characteristics of mosques, with columned halls, ornamental lettering, and internal courtyards.[1] However, throughout Jewish history, Judaism has always maintained its own sense of tradition and religious uniqueness. Therefore, although synagogue architecture reflected many aspects of Islamic architectural detail, it did not reflect the architecture of the mosque in one very important detail.

In a society as segregated as that of Islam, women did not pray with men, nor did they enter a mosque during prayer. At the very beginning of Islam, women stood behind the men at Friday prayers. During the following decades, they prayed behind a screen. However, by the end of the Caliphate in 660 C.E., women no longer prayed in mosques. (Today, Moslem women usually do not participate in public prayer at all but pray privately.)[2]

This was never the case in the medieval synagogues of the Islamic world. Information from that period indicates that women not only attended synagogue reguarly, but were involved in synagogue life in several different ways.

Much of the information regarding medieval synagogue life under Islam came to light at the beginning of the twentieth century with the discovery of a treasure house of primary source material, the Cairo Geniza. Jews do not destroy anything with God's name written on it; such pieces of parchment or paper are usually buried. In medieval Cairo, this custom was extended to anything written in Hebrew. Instead of being buried, however, these items were placed in an attic of sorts in the Fostat Synagogue, in the older part of Cairo where most of the Jews lived; the arid conditions there preserved them.[3] After many years of study, scholars have pieced together a rather detailed picture of life in the Middle East during the Middle Ages. The most outstanding work on this topic is the multivolume opus of S. D. Goitein, *A Mediterranean Society.*

In Fostat, known as Old Cairo, each synagogue had a women's gallery, known as *bayt al-nisa,* "house of women." This gallery was reached via a staircase that led up from a separate entrance to the synagogue. Perhaps it was hoped that this type of construction would preclude the habit of talking and socializing that may have been a problem in the synagogue since its inception.[4] Men and women socialized both before and after prayer in the synagogue courtyard.[5] The courtyard was a central feature of the medieval synagogue, which, like the ancient synagogue before it, was generally part of a compound or complex of buildings built around a courtyard. This compound may have included an inn for travelers, an orphanage, a primitive hospital, and certainly, a *mikveh* (ritual bath) and a school.

Based on Geniza materials, Goitein divides the Jews of the Islamic world into different social classes: the upper classes, businessmen and professionals, urban craftsmen and laborers, and peasants.[6] The social class of a woman's father often determined the quality of the education she received. The level of their education would be important in respect to determining women's participation in the synagogue, in helping to decide whether they could pray on their own, and in ascertaining whether they could follow the services in the synagogue.

The Geniza contains a letter about hiring a private instructor to teach orphan girls to pray "so that they should not grow up like wild animals and not even know 'Hear Israel.'"[7] If such care was taken with orphans, we may safely assume that the higher social classes did at least as much for their own daughters. Girls were probably tutored at home, though we find evidence that there were classes composed entirely of girls and of teachers who were women.[8]

Women went to synagogue not only to pray and to socialize. The biblical concept "the people shall judge" (Num. 35:24) was very much alive in the Cairo community. The community or congregation in the synagogue was the highest juridical authority.[9] The communal structure was such that the Jews ran their lives autonomously, without any reference to Moslem institutions, and a powerful Jewish court system was one of the features of this autonomous structure.

Those who had not received satisfaction for their claims by regular legal procedure could interrupt public prayer and even stop the service until their complaint was heard by the whole community. This action was taken by women as well as by men. The interruption usually took place on the Sabbath, when the Torah scroll was taken out of the Ark. Women usually did not speak to the congregation themselves. Their complaints were read in the men's section by a representative. This did not preclude the possibility of a woman speaking out from the women's gallery. For example, two orphan girls appealed against two older married sisters, in a document that is probably a prototype for many others:

"By doing justice all the offspring of Israel will find glory with the Lord" [Isa. 45:25]. The orphans of Dosa (may God have mercy upon him). "In the name of the merciful and gracious God" [Exod. 34:6].

We appeal to God and to you, men of Israel! Do not forsake us! You used to pronounce a ban on the Mount of Olives on anyone who takes his heritage in a Moslem court. (But what can I do?) I am an orphan girl confined to the house and have a sister who is a mere babe. Yesterday, the two married sisters came and put their hands on the house and drove us out. We have two brothers, but they are absent. Thus, we, two orphan girls, confined to the house, have no one to assist us except the Lord of the Worlds and Israel, and their judges. The sin against us adheres to everyone who hears this appeal and does not secure for all of us a decision according to the law of inheritance of the Torah. Do not forsake us!

God can be trusted that He will not orphan any child of yours. Seize the opportunity for doing a good work by giving us satisfaction according to the law of the Torah. "And peace over all Israel!" [10]

In response to such an appeal, the heads of the congregation would promise that the case would be heard by the Jewish court and set a date for the hearing on the spot. Only when the complainant was satisfied could the synagogue service proceed.

Another item related to the court and synagogue involved the requirement of an oath, a neccessity decreed by the court in certain circumstances. Taking an oath was regarded with awe and trepidation in the medieval world. The oath ceremony was held in the synagogue. The Torah Scroll was removed from the ark and draped in black; a bier and a *shofar* were brought in as reminders of death and judgment. If a woman was to take an oath, she did so in the men's section, while holding the Torah scroll. [11]

Women served as synagogue caretakers. This came about as a result of the Jewish attitude that charity should be given in as honorable a way as possible. Widows, who would otherwise have been destitute, were appointed to the honorable position of synagogue or *mikveh* caretaker by the community. The two synagogues of Fostat, the Palestinian and the Iraqi, both had a *khadima*, the female equivalent of *khadim*, or beadle. [12] These women were paid in bread, clothing, and a little money. [13]

At the other end of the spectrum, wealthy women contributed to the upkeep of synagogues. These women were wealthy in their own right. Most Cairene Jewish women worked in various economic endeavors and were able to keep their profits, rather than turning over the profits to their husbands, once they had paid for those household duties for which they were responsible. These women bought honors for the men in their lives such as their fathers, brothers, husbands, and sons. The honors included reciting a section of the Torah or leading part of the liturgy. Women also donated Torah scrolls, oil for the lamps, and various kinds of books. Women even donated, for synagogue use, houses and apartments they had received as part of their marriage portion and which remained their property. By the Middle Ages, this was already an established custom, as verified by the mosaic inscriptions on ancient synagogue floors in Israel.

The Geniza contains letters written to rabbis by husbands who complained that their wives were overly generous and that the money donated should be returned to their families. The rabbis replied that this money belonged completely to the women, who could spend it as they wished. However, it should be noted that most of women's charitable actions were personal acts done as private individuals. Unlike men, women did not fill official communal leadership roles as a result of their donations to the community or their financial position in the community.

One interesting example of a woman donor is Karina, better known as al-Wuḥsha the Broker, daughter of ʾAmmar. She was an independently wealthy and notorious woman. Many extant documents tell of her affairs. Her will is of special interest because it lists her last dispositions, which included gifts to four synagogues "for oil so that people may study at night."

Her notoriety was based partly on a love affair she had after one of her divorces, from which she conceived a child. We know of this because her only son, born of this union, had to prove that his birth was the result of an irregular but not incestuous relationship, or he would not have been allowed to marry a Jewish woman. One result of the public flaunting of the affair and pregnancy was that when al-Wuḥsha went to pray on Yom Kippur, the Day of Atonement, at the Iraqi synagogue, she was expelled by the head of that institution. This was, in fact, against Jewish law, for even an excommunicant can join the prayers on that day. Obviously, the rabbi wanted to show that even a rich woman could not violate accepted rules of behavior. Al-Wuḥsha seems to have accepted this, for in her will she left money to that synagogue also.[14]

Despite the wealth and depth of information the Geniza contains on Jewish life in the Middle Ages, no evidence has yet been found of spiritual materials created by, or even for, women, comparable to those written in the European communities (*see* Berger, p. 74ff.). There is no "women's version" of the Torah readings in the vernacular, as appeared in Europe in the form of the *Tsenah-u-rʾenah*. Nor is there any evidence of the emergence of a woman's prayer leader—the *firzogerin* and *zogerke*, as in European communities (*see* Taitz, p. 64ff.).

This lack may indicate that women's knowledge of Hebrew in the Middle East was sufficient, so that there was no need for a genre of vernacular literature. Alternatively, women might have felt no need for specifically female-oriented liturgy because their interests lay in the pursuit of material gain, as was the case with most men of the Geniza communities. This materialism was tempered by service to God but not totally shaped by it. One might argue that the lack of spiritual matter by or for women indicates that they were effectively shut out of spiritual life and were merely second-class citizens of the synagogue, tolerated but not really wanted. However, the lack of specifically female prayer literature does not necessarily indicate women's secondary role in the synagogue, for the Ashkenazic women—who, one might argue, also had a secondary role in the synagogue—did develop a female prayer literature. Furthermore, while one might argue that women were seen as second-class citizens in regard to their participation in the actual synagogue services, we have shown that women were educated to pray and, moreover, looked to the synagogue as the house of God, where they could best appeal to the community's sense of justice and mercy.

The Cairo Geniza deals with a vibrant Jewish society within a vibrant Moslem world. The shattering of that world at the hands of the invading Mongols in the thirteenth century c.e., and then again a century later, marked the beginning of the major decline of Arab civilization. Except for the brief reprieve at the hands of the Ottoman Turks in the fifteenth and sixteenth centuries, the Middle East disintegrated as a center of culture and civilization. As the Moslem world moved, so did the smaller Jewish world within it. The Jews were shattered internally as well, by the dual tragedies of the Spanish Expulsion (1492) and the false messiah Shabbetai Zevi in the seventeenth century. Some scholars feel that the Middle Eastern Jews never recovered from the spiritual traumas of these two events.

Be that as it may, the world of women, inside the circumference of the Jewish world, declined spiritually to such an extent that many went to the synagogue only on Yom Kippur. It is only recently, within the new societies of North America, Western Europe, and the State of Israel, that women of Middle Eastern origin are again beginning to take their place in synagogue services and activities (*see* Sered, p. 21ff.). The key to this return lies in the revival of education for Jewish girls and women.

Notes

1. EncJud, s.v. "Synagogue."
2. Daniel Bates and Amal Rassam, *People and Cultures of the Middle East* (Englewood Cliffs, New Jersey: Prentice Hall, 1983), 46.

3. Raphael Levy, "First 'Dead Sea Scroll' Found in Egypt Fifty Years Before Qumran Discoveries," *BARev* 8:5 (Sept./Oct. 1982): 38–53.

4. According to Israel Abrahams in *Jewish Life in the Middle Ages* (New York: Atheneum, 1969), 24, "Gossip was inevitable in synagogue, for the latter was the chief meeting-place of Jews. The licensed conversation, however, occurred in the courtyard, not in the synagogue itself. . . . It became a fashion even with the most punctilious Jews, to reassemble after the service for the purpose of talking over the news of the hour, military and political." He cites Joel Muller, *Maseket Sofrim* (in Hebrew) Index (Leipzig: J. C. Hinrichs, 1878), 21 and Israel ben Pethahiah Isserlein, *Responsa Terumat ha-Deshen* (Venice: Daniel Bomberg, 1519), sec. 61.

5. Abrahams, *Jewish Life in the Middle Ages,* chaps. 1 and 2.

6. S. D. Goitein, *A Mediterranean Society,* vol. 1 (Los Angeles: University of California, 1967), 79. Goitein identifies five classes, dividing the businessmen and professionals into two layers.

7. Ibid., vol. 2, 184.

8. Ibid., vol. 2, 185.

9. This was practiced in Ashkenaz (Germany) also, but local social conditions determined whether this custom was accepted in a particular community. H. H. Ben-Sasson, ed., *A History of the Jewish People* (London: Weidenfeld, Nicolson, 1976), 506–7.

10. From the Elkan N. Adler Collection of Geniza Documents at the JTS, in New York, cited by Goitein, vol. 2 (Los Angeles: University of California, 1971), p. 324.

11. From the Tayler-Schechter Collection, University Library, Cambridge, England, cited by Goitein, vol. 2, p. 340.

12. Being a beadle, also known as a *shammash,* was a position of great honor. The beadle's duties comprised not only the maintenance of synagogue property—cleaning; care of books, ornaments, and textiles; and illumination—but also the service of the community. He served as messenger and assistant clerk of the court as well as attorney, trustee, and cashier. He had an intimate knowledge of all that occurred in the community (Goitein, *A Mediterranean Society,* vol. 2, 82–85). It is not known if women beadles fulfilled all these functions (*see* Interview with Iranian Women, pp. 223–24).

13. Tayler-Schechter Collection, (*see* n.11 *supra*) cited by Goitein,, ibid., vol. 1, 130.

14. Ibid., vol. 3, 346–52.

Emily Taitz

WOMEN'S VOICES, WOMEN'S PRAYERS: WOMEN IN THE EUROPEAN SYNAGOGUES OF THE MIDDLE AGES

"A Jew made a bet with his friend that his wife would obey him in all things. He went to her and said, 'Take off your veil.' She did it. He said to her, 'Call the cat and place it on your knees.' She did it. He said to her, 'Tie the cat with your veil.' And she did it. If he had ordered her to go and buy food for the house, that is reasonable, and if she did it, it would not have proved her love for him; but when he said senseless and bizarre things to her and she did them, in this way she proved her love for him.

"It is the same with us Israelites . . ." continues Joseph the Official, the writer of this thirteenth-century anecdote. Joseph then goes on to explain the purpose of God's "senseless" commandments.[1]

More than 600 years later, this analogy gives us important clues to some accepted ideas about women's place in the Middle Ages. As this writer and his contemporaries saw it, woman's relationship to man was directly parallel to man's relationship to God.

In the hierarchical society of the feudal era, equality was an unfamiliar concept. Every individual, man or woman, was the legal inferior of some-one else. The family functioned within this hierarchy and was a micro-cosm of it. The husband was lord of the household. His wife, children, and servants were all subservient to him. The wife might rule over her servants, young children, and female members of the household, but theoretically, the final decisions lay with the master—the head of the household.

It was always clear that women could not rule over men of the same social level. A noble woman could not marry a male serf since, in the natural order of things, she was his superior and thus could not properly be his wife. If such a marriage did occur, the woman would legally be assumed to have lost her noble status. If the situation was reversed, however, the marriage would be more acceptable.[2]

Although Jews did not fit exactly into the Christian class structure of feudalism, their social system contained a similar set of assumptions, reflected not only in *Sefer Joseph ha-Mekane* but also in much of Jewish literary and legal writings of the period. David ben Joseph Abudarham (a fourteenth-century scholar who lived under Christian rule in Spain) wrote, "The reason that women are exempt from positive time-bound *mitzvot* is because a woman is subservient to her husband to fulfill his needs."[3]

Jewish women lived under the lordship first of their fathers and then of their husbands. For this reason, the idea of women as leaders of men seemed incongruous. If it occurred, it was considered to be an exception or was explained away by scholars' interpretations. For example, when the rabbis of the Talmud discussed the permissibility of using women as witnesses, the Tosafists pointed out: Although Deborah was a judge, it was only because God spoke through her. She herself did not judge, but transmitted her ideas to the judges [males] who decided God's will by means of her interpretations.[4]

Beruriah, a scholar mentioned in the Talmud, was perhaps one of the few literary role models of a strong, intelligent, and assertive woman that existed in the early Middle Ages (except for biblical women). Nothing negative was said about her in the Talmud, but her character was denigrated by medieval scholars. According to the legend, Beruriah's husband, R. Meir, tested her virtue by arranging for her seduction by one of his students. When she failed the test, she committed suicide. Rashi, the earliest known sources for this information, was the first to have written about her immoral behavior and suicide. However, it is likely that he himself heard it from another source.[5] The lesson that was to be learned from Beruriah's sad fate was: Women who try to be like men come to a bad end.

In addition to the general medieval standard of female subservience, Jewish women who might have aspired to a more active role had to deal with two important precepts of Jewish law. These remain valid today among Orthodox Jews.

The first of the two precepts is that women are excused from observing positive commandments that must be performed at specific times (e.g., reciting the *Shema,* donning *tefillin*).[6] This concept implied that women's right to perform positive commandments was arbitrary, and since it was not *commanded,* was less important (*see* I. Haut, pp. 89ff. and Hauptman, pp. 162ff.).

The second problem facing women was a Talmudic statement attributed to Samuel that claimed: "The voice of woman is indecent" (*Kol b-ishah ervah*).[7] In TB Ber. 24a, this statement was applied to reciting the *Shema* prayer. The *Shema* was not to be recited by a man if he could hear a woman singing at the same time. The underlying reason was that her voice would divert him from his concentration on prayer.

Another example of this attitude can also be found in the Talmud. "If men sing and women respond [i.e., by singing after them, or joining them in the chorus], it is a breach of law, but if women sing and men respond, it is as if a fire was raging in a field of flax!"[8]

The acceptance of these ideas in the Middle Ages is clearly illustrated in works such as *Sefer Ḥasidim* from thirteenth-century Germany, where it is stated, "It is impossible for a bachelor to teach girls [Torah]." Part of the explanation for this is that "the voice of a woman is indecent. Rather, the father should teach his daughter and his wife."[9]

While this attitude toward women's voices was not as crucial in limiting women as was the precept excusing them from time-bound commandments, it nevertheless added another barrier. If women could not be heard, their ability to serve in communal situations was severely limited, except in an all-female environment.

In addition to these legal limitations, women were confronted with two other problems, which, although not directed specifically at females, served to discourage them from full participation. These were the general negative attitude of the Jews toward music following the destruction of the Temple[10] and the increasing discomfort occasioned by social interaction between the sexes, which was common in Christian and Jewish circles until very late in the Middle Ages. Among some Orthodox Jews it persists until today.

Early Christian sources continually warned that contact between the sexes led to sin. St. Jerome, in outlining his suggestions for educating a girl, warned that she must know nothing of boys and never hear "sensuous songs." Later in the Middle Ages, a popular writer, Walter Map, in his *Dissuasio Valerii* insisted that women cause evil by their very presence.[11]

Jewish sources echoed these feelings, but with a Jewish interpretation. The writings of R. Elazar of Worms (c. 1165–c. 1230) include a story of a man who taught his daughters to write so that they would not seek out other people (presumably men) to do it for them and get involved in sin or develop a bad reputation.[12] As late as the eighteenth century, a commentary to *Sefer Ḥasidim* by R. Ḥayyim Joseph David Azulai even stipulated that if men and women stood together in the same room during a *simḥah* (joyous occasion), you could not bless the celebration, "because there is no joy when there is an evil inclination."[13]

Yet, in spite of all these difficulties, women did participate in synagogue ritual. The extent and nature of that participation is not always clear. This is partly due to the scarcity of specific source material, especially in the earlier centuries. As we progress toward modern times, however, the evidence becomes more definitive.

We do know that, although women were excused from time-bound commandments such as reciting the *Shema* or sitting in the *sukkah*, they were obligated to pray. This is unequivocally stated in the Talmud and accepted by both Rashi (d. 1105) and his grandson R. Yaʿakov Tam (d. 1172).[14]

Did women ever sit together with men during prayer? Noted scholar Israel Abrahams insists that they might have, since separation of the sexes in the synagogue did not become a hard-and-fast ruling until the late twelfth or early thirteenth centuries. Unfortunately, there is no clear proof either way[15] (*see* Safrai, p. 41 and Baumel Joseph, p. 118).

The rabbis of the Middle Ages often spoke about women's participation in home or synagogue prayer. Their words suggest a reluctance to make a clear statement in favor of this. Occasionally, they allowed it with reservations or under specific circumstances, but the tone is rarely one of wholehearted approval.

In the Talmud (Ber. 45b) there is a discussion as to whether women should recite the Grace after Meals. Women were commanded to say the Grace, but because of the general belief that men singing together with women was improper, a problem arose. The women should not be counted among the three or the ten men required by Jewish law as the minimum number for reciting the communal prayer after meals. Could their obligation be fulfilled by the men?

In the commentary of the *Tosefot*, the example is given of a certain R. Abraham who encouraged his daughters to form their own group to say the introduction to grace.[16] However, the assumption is that these women are the exception. The Tosafists conclude that the ability of most women to read Hebrew and recite the prayers is deficient at best (*see* Hauptman, p. 162 and R. Haut, p. 156, n. 41).

In the fourteenth century, R. Nissim bar Reuben (Ran), in his commentary on the Talmud, discusses the legality of a woman who reads the *Megillah* on Purim. He is not opposed to it, explaining that when a woman reads, she fulfills the obligation on behalf of men, too, because in this instance, her own obligation is equal to his. In addition, if a woman is obligated to hear the *Megillah* (as stated in TB Meg. 4a), she should not be excluded from a quorum of ten (a *minyan*).[17]

In a separate book, *Ḥiddushei ha-Ran*, R. Nissim comments that minors are allowed to read and fulfill the commandment, but he is less explicit concerning women. Had he himself ever seen or heard about a woman chanting the *Megillah?* He does not say.[18]

Rabbi Jacob ben Moses (Maharil), who lived in the late fourteenth and early fifteenth centuries, deals with a related issue in one of his responsa. The question is not given. The answer begins with the words: "Again [alluding to the fact] that you were surprised that women are reciting the blessings of the Torah, and you disagreed. . . ." The general consensus among scholars today is that the "blessings of the Torah" refers not to individual women being called up to the Torah but to the morning prayers that include these blessings.[19] We do not know whether this referred to praying in the synagogue or at home. Whichever is the case, it is clear that women were reciting these prayers and that, for some men, the legality of their practice was open to question.

The Maharil's answer was an equivocation. Women who are educated and obey all the commandments may recite the prayers, but most, he concludes, do not fall into this category.

Some 200 years earlier, R. Tam had concluded that women were permitted to perform the commandments from which women were exempt. His reasoning was based on the Talmudic passage concerning Mikhal, the daughter of King Saul, who used to put on *tefillin*. The question arose: Did she say the blessings, or only put on the *tefillin?* The answer was that she said the blessings and even though she (as all women) was exempt, she nevertheless was allowed to do this. And so, R. Tam concluded, all women are allowed. And not merely "in order to please the women,"[20] but because it was legitimate to say the blessing ("Blessed art Thou . . . who has *commanded* . . .) on the acts they were performing despite the fact that they were not obligatory acts.[21]

R. Meir of Rothenberg (the Maharam, c. 1215–1293) gives one of the clearest statements in favor of women's active participation in the synagogue. However, it is stipulated only in a specific instance, one that is surely uncommon if not completely theoretical.

R. Meir says: "If a city contains only *kohanim* and there are no Israelites, after calling a *kohen* twice [to the Torah for an *aliyah*], they will then call a woman." The reason for this, he explains, is the Talmudic statement "all can satisfy the requirement of a quorum of seven, even a minor, even a woman." R. Meir recalls the *baraita* in the Talmud (TB Meg. 23a) that women are not called up to the Torah because of "the honor of the community" (*kavod ha-tsibbur*), but explains that this is not relevant when all are *kohanim*, since the honor of a *kohen* supersedes the honor of the community at large.[22]

Were there times and places where this ruling was actually followed? Again, there is no evidence either way. As early as the thirteenth century, however, there is clear evidence of women having their own leaders and their own auxiliary services in separate sections of the synagogue.

Worms, a major Jewish community in Rhineland Germany, had a woman's synagogue in a separate room adjoining the men's.[23] A woman named Urania (thirteenth century) is credited with being the cantor of the women there. Her tombstone calls her ". . . the eminent and excellent lady Urania, the daughter of R. Abraham, who was the chief of the synagogue singers." Not only is R. Abraham, her father, praised, but Urania, too, who ". . . with sweet tunefulness, officiated before the female worshipers to whom she sang the hymnal portions. . . ."[24]

Richenza was another women's prayer leader about whom we have some knowledge. She was from Nuremberg, and like Urania, lived in the thirteenth century.[25]

Dulcie of Worms, wife of the noted Rabbi Elazar (ha-Rokeaḥ), was said to have recited prayers in the synagogue, specifically the *Pitom ha-*

Ketoret and the Ten Commandments.[26] R. Elazar, author of a poem praising his wife after her untimely death, does not say whether she recited these prayers in the main synagogue or not. Nor does he specify where "she stands on every Yom Kippur to sing."[27] It is possible that she, too, like Urania, was a prayer leader in the women's synagogue at Worms.

As we progress through the later Middle Ages, evidence of women's galleries or rooms, women's prayers, and women prayer leaders, becomes more plentiful. These women were not always given titles or singled out. Probably the job fell to the most learned women in the community. Often they were the wives of rabbis, like Dulcie, or learned daughters, like Urania. These were the kinds of women most likely to possess the required knowledge.

It was helpful for women prayer leaders to know some Hebrew so that they could understand the liturgy. They may have taught prayers to other women or translated them into the vernacular for the women's congregation. As early as the eleventh century, Rashi, referring to four things a woman can do simultaneously, said that she can "teach a song to a woman for a fee," while she is at the same time watching the vegetables (on the fire), spinning flax, and warming silk worm eggs in her bosom.[28]

Although the songs referred to in Rashi's example might not have been for synagogue use, it is unlikely that, in the context of teaching, they were purely secular. The mind set of the medieval population tended to be religious, and although we know that there was no lack of love songs, cradle songs, and the like, Jewish law specifically frowned on all except religious music.[29]

We see in the poem written by R. Elazar of Worms that Dulcie ". . . says Psalms . . . sings hymns and prayers . . . recites petitions." In another verse, she is praised because "In all the towns she taught women (so that they can) chant songs."[30] Here again, although there is no proof either way, such a pious woman was not likely to be teaching secular songs.

Teaching songs and prayers seems to have frequently led to writing new prayers. Often, they were a loose translation of the Hebrew, with some additions, written out in the vernacular. Sometimes they were original creations.

Rebecca Tiktiner (d. 1550) of Prague is an example of a woman who wrote her own prayer-poems. She, too, was the daughter of a rabbi (R. Meir of Tiktiner) and thus belonged to the learned elite of the community. Among the liturgical poems that Rebecca wrote in Judeo-

German was a Simhat Torah song meant to be sung by women in the synagogue while they adorned the Torah in preparation for the holiday.[31] Rebecca also translated a popular treatise, *Duties of the Heart*.[32] In addition, she wrote a book called *Meneket Rivkah*, containing moral teachings and selections from the Talmud and Mishnah, all in Judeo-German. In Rebecca's introduction, she specifically addresses "all you dear, blessed, pious women." [33]

Rebecca Tiktiner was very likely a prayer leader in the women's congregation. She had the necessary requirements: learning and stature as the daughter of the rabbi. In the printer's introduction to her book, probably published after her death, she is referred to as a "rebbetzin-preacher." Other women writers of the Middle Ages probably filled that same role.

Deborah Ascarelli, an Italian Jew of Spanish descent, was known for her excellent translations of Hebrew hymns into Italian. She also translated two well-known works of her time written by the Italian Jewish scholar Moses da Rieti.[34] Since the norm was for men to be taught Hebrew, translations like those of Tiktiner or Ascarelli were assumed to be directed to an audience of women.

Toward the end of the Middle Ages, women's vernacular literature in the form of special prayers called *tehinot* (or *tehines* in Yiddish) multiplied. They were especially plentiful in Central and Eastern Europe, where most of the Jews had migrated after repeated expulsions from Western countries.[35]

The vernacular language for the Jews of Eastern Europe was Yiddish, and it is in this language that almost all of the women's *tehinot* from the late Middle Ages are written.

Although there are *tehinot* for a variety of occasions, a good many of them are meant to be recited in the synagogue. Prayers for the High Holy Days, *Rosh Hodesh* (the first day of the month, and considered to be a quasi-holiday for women), and Sabbath, all tend to indicate that women attended communal prayer during these times. Many of the *tehinot* have a direct connection with the synagogue liturgy.[36] Very often, they are addressed not only to God but to the Matriarchs, Sarah, Rebecca, Rachel, and Leah, as intermediaries. This custom seems to be a direct counterpart to the prayers that referred to the God of our Fathers, Abraham, Isaac, and Jacob (*see* Berger, p. 000).

In the movement of Jews from West to East, the old tradition of women prayer leaders was not lost either. We find evidence of it again and again in the Eastern European synagogue. Called a *firzogerin* (foresayer) in Yiddish, the prayer leader continued to lead the women and was an institution in synagogues throughout Russia and Poland until the early part of the twentieth century.

The *firzogerin*'s job was described by Mendele Mokher Seforim, a Yiddish writer and satirist of the late 1800s, as follows: ". . . It was she who showed the women how to pray: what hymns to say, when to rise, when to stand on tip-toe in the *Kedushah* prayer. . . . And in fact it was hardly possible to keep from fainting when Sarah read. She would read with great emotion, her melody melting the soul and pulling at the heart strings." [37]

Based on this description, her role seems to have changed very little from what it had been when Urania "sang the hymnal portions" in thirteenth-century Worms, or when Dulcie "taught women (so that they can) chant songs" and knew "the order of the morning and evening prayers." [38]

In a later period, Sarah bas Tovim was one of the more well-known of these women leaders, and one of the most important eighteenth-century writers of *tehinot*. Following a common pattern, she, too, was the daughter and granddaughter of rabbis, and thus among the small group of women who were well educated.

Many of her *tehinot* are intended for women to recite when they are observing their own special commandments (*hallah, niddah,* and candle lighting), [39] but Sarah also wrote prayers for the synagogue and often alludes to women's proper behavior there.

In *Shloysheh She'orim* (The Three Gates), a collection of her *tehinot,* Sarah urges, "I, Sarah, beg you young women not to sin by talking in the synagogue. . . ." And in the following paragraph, "Stand in the dear synagogue with fear and dread." [40]

Other *firzogerins* who composed prayers for women include Taube, wife of Jacob Pan of Prague (1609), Bella, wife of Josepho the Hazzan Horvitz (1705), [41] and Serel bat R. Jacob ha-Levi Segal of Dubnow, the wife of Rabbi Mordecai Katz Rapoport (mid-1800s). [42] There are many more prayer leaders whose names can be traced; probably thousands more have passed without a memory.

Women depended on these *firzogerins* to lead them through the intricacies of a service that few could understand unassisted. In addition, by relating their *tehinot* to the intimate details of women's daily lives, the literary creations of many of the *firzogerins* provided Jewish women with the personal spirituality that they needed and wanted.

The strong and continuing tradition of women prayer leaders through-out the Middle Ages and well into modern times points to the regular in-volvement of women in communal prayer. Although they may have been subservient to husbands, less well educated than their brothers, deprived (with few exceptions) of the privilege of study, and cut off from much of male spiritual activity, women nevertheless had an active spiritual and synagogue life. They created their own prayers and traditions, and fol-lowed their own leaders. They sometimes even lit their Sabbath candles in the synagogue and in general seem to have felt at home there.[43] Occasion-ally, individual women rose to high levels of learning or were known as experts in specific fields.

This spiritual and sometimes scholarly activity by women did not change the general attitude toward them in the nineteenth century any more than it had in the twelfth or thirteenth centuries. Despite the decline of feudalism, and the centuries of development in Jewish life and Jewish law, the story related by Joseph the Official in the work cited above, was still a recognizable paradigm some 500 years later.

Yet there is no evidence to indicate that women ever actively rebelled against what would today be considered second-class status. Like their Christian counterparts, both male and female, they accepted the feudal hierarchy of family life as ordained by God, and worked within it, creat-ing their own place and their own meanings.

Not until the end of the Middle Ages was there any change in how the Jewish community viewed women. Then the Enlightenment and the be-ginnings of reform took away the *firzogerin* together with the *meḥitzah* (the barrier dividing men and women in the synagogue). Female voices mixed with men's in reciting the traditional liturgy, but women lost a po-etry and a voice of their own.

Today, with women cantors and rabbis, women are coming into syn-agogue leadership in a new way—a way that Joseph the Official would hardly believe. At the same time, they are turning back to find the rem-nants of a woman's culture that was once a distinctive part of being a fe-male and a Jew.

Notes

1. This anecdote is part of an answer to the question "Why don't Jews eat pork?" which a priest asked a Jew. It is part of a thirteenth-century polemic work by a French Jew called Joseph the Official (*ha-Mekane*). The edition I used is J. Rosenthal, ed., *Sefer Joseph ha-*

Mekane, auctore R. Joseph b. R. Nathan the Official, (Jerusalem: Mekize Nirdamim, 1970), 47:60.

2. Theodore Evergates, *Feudal Society in the Baillage of Troyes Under the Counts of Champagne, 1152–1284* (Baltimore: Johns Hopkins University Press, 1975), 39. Evergates explains the difficulties arising when a noblewoman marries a peasant as being partly caused by the fact that she lives under a different set of laws than her peasant husband. In order to solve this problem, she must accept the (lower) status of her husband, and thus her children lose what would have been her lands. When the situation is reversed, the noble husband is permitted to "buy out" his peasant wife by paying the required tax to the overlord. The children then have the advantage of being able to inherit his land.

3. *Sefer Abudarham* (Jerusalem: Usha, 1962), 25. Abudarham explains that a husband might not understand if a wife neglects him to fulfill her religious duties. Therefore, God has excused her for the sake of domestic peace (*shalom im baʿalah*). Abudarham drew on Spanish, Provençal, French, and Ashkenazi materials.

4. Tosef. Nid. 50a.

5. References to Beruriah can be found in: Mish. BM 1:6; TB Er. 53b; TB Ber. 10a; TB Av. Zar. 18b. However, Rashi's commentary on TB Av. Zar. 18b, s.v. *"v-ika d-imir mishum maʿaseh d-Beruriah,"* is the earliest source mentioning anything negative about Beruriah. One theory about the legend's origin is based on the study of comparative folklore. M. Hershel Levine suggests that this legend is rooted in ancient prerabbinic motifs still circulating in Rashi's time. *See* his article "Three Talmudic Tales of Seduction," *Judaism* (Fall 1987): 466–70.

6. Mish. Kid. 1:7.

7. TB Ber. 24a.

8. TB Sot. 48a, cf. Rashi, s.v. *"k-esh b-neoret."*

9. *Sefer Ḥasidim,* Bologna ed., ed., R. Margulies (Jerusalem: Mosad HaRav Kook, 1970), 245, par. 313. This paragraph is translated by Rachel Biale in *Women and Jewish Law* (New York: Schocken, 1984), 35–36.

10. TB Sot. 48a.

11. For a discussion of these as well as other Christian sources on the separation of the sexes, see C. Erickson, "The Vision of Women," in *The Medieval Vision: Essays in History and Perception* (New York: Oxford University Press, 1976), 198.

12. This story is quoted by M. Gudeman in *Ha-Torah ve-ha-Ḥayyim,* vol. 1 (Warsaw: Ḥevnat Aḥiʾasaf, 1896; repr. ed., Tel Aviv: Madʿa ve-Sifrut le-ʿAm, 1968–1972), 168. The source he cites is a hand-written manuscript by R. Elazar of Worms," *"Ḥiddushim be-Otiot Ḥaserot."*

13. *See* Azulai's commentary to *Sefer Ḥasidim* in the Lemberg edition, ed. Margulies (Lemberg: B. L. Nechlis, 1863), 22, no. 168.

14. Rashi TB Ber. 20a, s.v. *"nashim;"* and Ber. 20b, s.v. *"b-tefillah p-shitah." See also* Jacob Tam, *Sefer ha-Yashar,* ed. S. P. Rosenthal (Berlin: Tz. N. Itskovski, 1898), 70:4 and n.3, p. 166; also ibid., 69:4; and *Tosafot* to Ber. 20b, s.v. *"Ve-ḥayavim be-tefillah."*

15. Israel Abrahams, *Jewish Life in the Middle Ages* (New York: Atheneum, 1975), 25.

16. For an elaboration on the question of joining in a *mezumman* for grace, *see* David M. Feldman, "Woman's Role in Jewish Law," *Conservative Judaism* 26:4 (Summer 1972): 38.

17. R. Nissim's commentary to TB. Meg., chap. 2, s.v. *"v-ha-kol."*

18. R. Nissim bar Reuben, *Ḥiddushei ha-Ran: Megillah, Moʿed Katan* (Israel: Makhon Harry Fischel le-Drishat ha-Talmud u-Mishpat ha-Torah, 1966), chap. 2, p. 34–35. *See also* Feldman, "Women's Roles and Jewish Law," 38.

19. The daily prayer includes a specific blessing praising God who commanded us to study Torah. Since the majority opinion held that this commandment did not include

women, the question of whether or not they might recite this particular blessing was perti-nent. This discussion is found in Jacob ben Moses ha-Levi Moellin, *Questions and Answers of the Maharil,* new edition (Jerusalem: Mifal Torat Ḥakhmei Ashkenaz Makhon Yerushalayim 1977), no. 45, p. 53.

20. TB Hag. 16b.

21. *See* Tosafot RH 33a, s.v. *"ha."* Although Maimonides disagreed and felt women should not be allowed to recite a blessing when performing *mitzvot* voluntarily, the Ash-kenazi communities have followed R. Tam (*see* I. Haut, pp. 93–97).

22. Calling a *kohen* to recite a blessing usually recited by an Israelite might suggest that the first *kohen* was not a "proper" *kohen (see* Safrai, pp. 43ff.).

23. Salo Baron, *The Jewish Community,* vol. 2 (Philadelphia: JPS, 1946), 140.

24. Quoted and translated by Abrahams, *Jewish Life,* 26.

25. Ibid.

26. Dulcie and her two daughters are described in an elegy, modeled after the *Eshet Ḥayyil* of Proverbs and written by her husband after their deaths at the hands of Crusaders. *See* A. M. Haberman, ed., *A History of Hebrew Liturgical and Secular Poetry,* Part 2 (Israel: Mas-sada Press, 1972), 197–99. Parts of this poem are reprinted in English in T. Carmi, *The Pen-guin Book of Hebrew Verse* (New York: Penguin Books, 1981), 387–88.

27. For a line by line analysis and translation of part of this poem see Ivan Marcus, "Mothers, Martyrs, and Moneymakers: Some Jewish Women in Medieval Europe" *Conser-vative Judaism* 38 (Spring 1986): 34–45. All my translations of this poem are taken from this article.

28. Rashi, TB Ket. 66a, s.v. *"Ve-shalosh ve-ʿarba be-vat eḥad.* Although "warming silk worm eggs" is probably purely theoretical, since the silk industry did not reach northern France in Rashi's time, there is no reason to assume that "teaching a song" was not a com-mon occurence among women.

29. Emily Taitz, "Kol Ishah—The Voice of Woman: Where Was it Heard in Medieval Europe?" *Conservative Judaism* 38:3 (Spring 1986): 50.

30. Ivan Marcus, "Mothers, Martyrs and Moneymakers," 42.

31. This poem, and a discussion about it, can be found in Khone Schmeruck, "The First Jewish Woman Writer in Poland," (in Hebrew) *Gal Ed* 4/5 (1978): 13.

32. *See* Sondra Henry and Emily Taitz, *Written Out of History: Our Jewish Foremothers* (New York: Bloch Publishing Co., 1979; reprint Fresh Meadows, N.Y.: Biblio Press, 3d print-ing 1985), 92, for a brief biography of Rebecca Tiktiner.

33. Rebecca bat Meir Tiktiner, *Meneket Rivka* (Cracow: 1618). This is a rare book, and the one extant edition I know of is in the Jewish Theological Seminary's Rare Book collec-tion in New York.

34. Henry and Taitz, *Written Out of History,* 127. Ascarelli's work was first published in 1601–1602 and then reprinted as late as 1925.

35. The Jewish community left England after the expulsion of 1290. By the early four-teenth century, the Jews of France had all but disappeared from within French borders, fol-lowing a series of expulsions. Then the major expulsions from Spain and Portugal in 1492 and 1497, respectively, effectively eliminated almost all Jewish communal life west of the Rhine River, with the exception of the Italian Jewish communities.

36. *See* Chava Weissler, "The Traditional Piety of Ashkenazic Women," in *Jewish Spiri-tuality,* vol. 2: *From the Sixteenth-Century Revival to the Present,* ed. Arthur Green (New York: Crossroads, 1987), 245–75, for an excellent discussion of these *teḥinot.*

37. Mendele Mokher Seforim, "Of Bygone Days," in *A Shtetl and Other Yiddish Novellas,* comp. and trans. Ruth Wisse (New York: Behrman House, 1973), 300–01.

38. Ivan Marcus, "Mothers, Martyrs and Moneymakers," 42.

39. These are three of the positive commandments that became identified as "women's commandments." They entailed: (1) separating a piece of dough when baking bread in memory of the tithe set aside for the High Priest during Temple times; (2) observing the laws of separation during menstruation, referred to as laws of family purity; and (3) lighting the candles on Sabbath and holy days.

40. *See* Henry and Taitz, *Written Out of History,* for a full translation of this part of *Shloysheh She'orim.* The original is available in a pamphlet from YIVO Institute for Jewish Research, New York, New York.

41. A. Z. Idelsohn, *Jewish Music in its Historical Development* (New York: Tudor Publishing Co., 1944), 440.

42. Henry and Taitz, *Written Out of History,* 193.

43. *See* Taitz, "Kol Ishah" 55, which cites Moellin's *Questions and Answers of the Maharil,* 45:53.

Shulamith Z. Berger

TEḤINES:
A BRIEF SURVEY OF
WOMEN'S PRAYERS

Teḥines are often referred to as supplicatory or devotional prayers. The concept of a prayer of this type is biblical in origin and hearkens back to Moses' prayer in Deut. 3:23: "I pleaded with the Lord at that time. . . ."[1] Moses used the word *va-etḥanan*, which is related to the word *teḥineh*, to characterize his request. The earliest use of the term *teḥineh* as a noun is found in the Prophets, where it is used in the sense of a prayer or request, and more particularly as a prayer of an individual. The word *teḥineh* is repeated throughout King Solomon's dedication of the First Temple in 1 Kings 8 and 2 Chron. 6. The most striking example of the term *teḥineh* occurs in 2 Chron. 6:29–30: "Any prayer or supplication (*teḥineh*) offered by any person among all Your people Israel—each of whom knows his affliction and his pain—when he spreads forth his hands toward this House, may You hear in Your heavenly abode, and pardon." This verse is virtually a repetition of 1 Kings 8:38, with some minor grammatical variations and the addition of the word *makh'ovo* (his pain). This verse links the *teḥineh* with the individual and the individual's situation or emotions, rather than with that of the nation as a whole.

The association of the *teḥineh* with personal prayers and requests was presumably the compelling reason that the genre lent itself so readily to the vernacular. It was in Yiddish, however, the vernacular of Ashkenazic Jewry, that the genre of the *tehineh* truly flourished and developed as a medium for women's expression and prayer.[2]

It is difficult to determine exactly when people started to recite Yiddish *tehines*. The Yiddish language originated in the tenth century c.e. and by the mid-thirteenth century was an independent language known to modern scholars as "Old Yiddish."[3] The first *tehineh* to appear in print was one for a woman to say before immersion in the *mikveh*. This *tehineh*, which was apparently translated from Hebrew, was included in *Seyder Mitsves Nashim* by Benjamin Aaron Selnik, published in Cracow in 1577. Although few *tehines* from this time period have survived, Yiddish *tehines* must have already been a well-known form. In the introduction to his book *Seyfer Shir ha-Shirim*, published in Cracow in 1579, Isaac Sulkash discussed the issue of *tehines* and the language of prayer. He suggested that women recite *tehines* in Yiddish rather than in Hebrew so that they would understand what they were saying. Sulkash could not have made his suggestion unless a substantial body of *tehines* was already extant in Yiddish.

The first known edition of *tehines* that was printed as an entity unto itself was a bilingual (Hebrew and Yiddish) edition published in Prague, probably in 1590.[4] Printed editions of Yiddish *tehines* became widespread in the seventeenth century. One such edition was published in 1666, apparently in Venice. By 1880 the bibliographer Benjacob noted that *tehines* for women were too numerous to count and list in a book.[5]

Benjacob's terse comment, however, fails to give a complete explanation of this statement. One popular format for printing *tehines* was as small, pocket-size books. Many *tehines* were printed individually on single sheets of paper or in pamphlets of just a few pages, with no mention of the publisher or place and date of publication, thus making it almost impossible for a bibliographer to record them. Moreover, the diminutive nature of these items caused them to be fragile and easily lost or destroyed. Although problematic for bibliographers, these items were convenient for users since they contained one or two *tehines* for specific occasions.[6] The proliferation of editions of *tehines* that Benjacob described attests to their popularity and indicates that *tehines* fulfilled certain needs.

Tehines were a popular and powerful medium of communication. They offered women a direct pipeline to God. The tone of *tehines* is conversational, addressing God respectfully but as a Yiddish-speaking friend or neighbor who will listen in time of need. The subject matter of *teḥines* is varied. There are *teḥines* to suit every occasion in personal and religious life, which were really one in the eyes of the *teḥineh*. *Teḥines* could also be said in various locations: the kitchen, the home, the ritual bath, the synagogue, and the cemetery.

Some *teḥines* include instructions advising that they be said along with certain prayers in the standard prayer service. There are also *teḥines* for the days of the week, the months of the year, the various holidays and fast days, and the High Holy Days in particular. Some of the types of *teḥines* mentioned above could be said in either the home or synagogue. Other *teḥines* were solely intended to be said in the synagogue, as indicated by the following kind of instructions that preceded the *teḥineh*: "One should say this *teḥineh* when the cantor says *anᶜim zemires*,"[7] or "Another *teḥineh* for a woman when she goes to synagogue after childbirth."[8] Many of those *teḥines* whose instructions can only be carried out in the synagogue center around the holidays, such as *teḥines* to be said when the *shofar* is blown, during *Yizkor,* or during the priestly blessing. This may indicate that there was a greater number of women in the synagogue during these special days.

A *teḥineh* that mentions women in the synagogue is "*Teḥineh Mah Tovu.*" *Mah Tovu* is the prayer that is recited upon entering the synagogue. The first sentence of the prayer is the following verse from Num. 24:5: "How fair are your tents, O Jacob, Your dwellings, O Israel!" The explanation of the verse given by the *teḥineh* is: "How good and dear are your tents, Jacob—these are the women's sections [*vaibershe shuln*] where Jewish daughters gather to praise God; your resting places, Israel—these are the holy synagogues and houses of study where men go to study and pray."[9]

A few *teḥines* bridge the gap between women's lives in the home and the synagogue. One of these is Sarah bas Tovim's *teḥineh* in *Shloyshah Sheᶜorim* (*The Three Gates*), which was recited on the eve of Yom Kippur when making memorial candles. Although the *teḥineh* was not recited in the synagogue, it posits a relationship between women and the synagogue and extends that relationship historically to the Temple in Jerusalem and possibly even to the *Mishkan,* the original mobile sanctuary in the desert, as is clear from the following passage from the *teḥineh*: "Let it be Your will that today, the eve of Yom Kippur, we will be remembered for good, since we bring the candles to the synagogue. Because of the commandment that we keep we should merit to give candles to the Holy Temple, as it was in the beginning, and the prayers that will be said near the candles should be with great piety and great awe. . . ." Perhaps one of the reasons this *tehineh* was so beloved was its assumption that women could participate in and contribute to the life of the synagogue and the prayer service. It also created a link between women's contemporary gifts to the synagogue, the gifts women had given to the Temple, and possibly even the women's contributions to the *Mishkan*—hence the reference to the present day candles as a "*mitzvah*" (commandment), which is not truly accurate in a technical or ritual sense.[10]

In contrast to this lofty realm, personal events and mundane concerns predominate in many *tehines*, such as *tehines* to be said when one's husband is on a journey, on the occasion of a son's circumcision, and in regard to making a living or baking *hallah*.

As befits a women's genre, *tehines* often focus on issues or events that are specific to women or traditionally associated with them. Many *tehines* revolve around pregnancy, childbirth, children, or childlessness. There are *tehines* for widows and *agunot*. *Tehines* for the Sabbath on which the new month is blessed—heralding the arrival of *Rosh Hodesh*, the semi-holiday that is particularly observed by women—were also popular. Numerous *tehines* were composed for the women's *mitzvot* known as the *Hanah mitzvot*, an acronym for *Hallah* (tithing dough), *Niddah* (laws of family purity), and *Hadlakat ha-ner* (lighting candles). The acronym is a reminder of the heroic Jewish women who bore the name Hannah (*Hanah* in Hebrew)—Hannah and her seven sons of Hanukkah fame and the biblical Hannah, who serves as a model of prayer and whose very name is onomatopoetically reminiscent of and linguistically related to the word *tehineh*. Furthermore, a self-evident conclusion is that if a woman observes the *Hanah mitzvot* scrupulously, as these great women of long ago did, she will be rewarded and blessed as they were.

Indeed, a significant characteristic of *tehines* is their frame of reference. In contrast to the standard prayer liturgy, which refers to the God of the Patriarchs, *tehines* invoke the merits of the Matriarchs or other biblical heroines as well as noted Jewish women to intercede on behalf of the petitioner.

This sensitivity to women's concerns indicates that *tehines* were truly women's province, written not only for women, but sometimes by women. The best known of these women was Sarah bas Tovim, whose pamphlet *Shloyshah She'orim,* mentioned above, first appeared in the eighteenth century. *Shloyshah She'orim* means *The Three Gates,* which are the *Ḥanah mitzvot,* the blessing for the New Moon and the High Holy Days, with particular emphasis on Yom Kippur. Sarah bas Tovim, however, was certainly not the only woman who composed *teḥines.* The women who wrote them were probably *firzogerins* (also called *zogerins* or *zogerkes*), women who guided the prayers in the women's section of the synagogue. The *firzogerin* attained her status because she was more knowledgeable than most of the women, and she might have used her expertise to compose new *teḥines* as the need or occasion arose (*see* Taitz, pp. 64ff.). There may have been an oral chain of transmission from one *firzogerin* to another, a *firzogerin* to her friends in the "congregation," or a mother to her daughter.[11]

Thus the genre of the *teḥineh* formed a folk liturgy, which served as an adjunct to the canonized Hebrew prayer service that was resistant to change and not readily accessible to the majority of women. The world of the *teḥineh* extended beyond the boundaries of the synagogue to encompass the home and daily life and to enrich them. *Teḥines* gave women a voice. They provided women with a vehicle by which to fulfill their spiritual needs and express their concerns in a concrete way. *Teḥines* enabled women to imbue their daily tasks with meaning and infuse their traditional roles with religious significance. Reciting *teḥines* let women know that they, too, were significant participants in the fabric of Jewish life.

Selections from *Teḥines*

The following two *teḥines* were both translated from *Shas Teḥineh Ḥadosheh: Mekor Dim'eh.* This collection of *teḥines* was edited by Ben-Zion Alfes. Alfes (b. Vilna 1850–d. Jerusalem 1940) was an Orthodox publicist who was particularly interested in bringing Jewish knowledge to the common people. He was a popular preacher in the synagogues and translated Hebrew ethical works into Yiddish. He was especially aware of the issue of women's education and often spoke to groups of women. Alfes expressed himself in the following manner: "And especially in this generation, when women play such an important role . . . we must make an effort to give their spirit good and healthy nourishment."[12] In 1900, he wrote *Mayseh Alfes* as a response to secular Yiddish works. *Mayseh Alfes* was an epistolary novel written from an Orthodox viewpoint. The letters are from a daughter on a journey to her father at home. *Mayseh Alfes* was so popular that the Vilna publishers asked Alfes to prepare commentaries by the same name on other works such as prayer books and Haggadot.[13] The first edition of *tehines* with the *Mayseh Alfes* commentary was published in Vilna in 1911 by the firm of Rozenkrants and Shriftzetser. In addition to the commentary, Alfes added some new *tehines* and reworked some of the older ones for his edition. Alfes's edition of *tehines* went through several printings and is still in print today.[14] The two *tehines* that follow were both translated from the 1925 edition.[15] The first *tehineh* was recited on the Sabbath when the month of *Iyar* was blessed. The second *tehineh* was recited on Rosh Hashanah. I incorporated the instructions from *Shas Tehineh Rav Peninim* (New York: Hebrew Publishing Co., 1916), where the same *tehineh* for Rosh Hashanah appears in an abridged form. I translated the parts of the *tehineh* pertaining to women, and included the headings of the other portions.

One should say this *tehineh* when one blesses the month of *Iyar*.[16]

> *Av ha-rahamim,* Merciful Father, who chose the people Israel, now we come to bless and sanctify the month of *Iyar*. In this month, we began to be Your beloved people, and You gave us the beloved, holy Sabbath. Remember the merits of our holy Sabbath, and because of the privilege that You gave us, women, the commandment of blessing the candles and the like, our fortune should be raised and You should save us from all ailments that could befall us in this month through nature that You created; the seasons change, winter goes away, and summer takes its place, and send us a cure as it says in the Torah—I am God your healer, Amen.
>
> Lord of the World, we are now going to bless the month of *Iyar*. In this month, at the time when You took the Jews out of Egypt, You caused the manna to rain from heaven, because of the merits of Moses our Teacher, may he rest in peace, and the well with water, which was created in the six days of creation on Friday before the Sabbath; and accompanied the Jews in the desert from the month of *Iyar* on, because of the merits of Miriam the Prophetess, may she rest in peace. Now, dear God, remember her merits. She said a song of praise with the women when the Jews came out of the sea as the verse states: And Miriam the Prophetess, the sister of Aaron, took the drum in her hand and all the women followed her with drums and musical instruments. And Miriam said to them: Sing to God because He did great miracles, He threw the horses of Egypt and their riders into the deep sea.[17] And so we should merit to say a song of praise with all the righteous men and righteous

women when the Messiah will come and redeem us from our troubles, speed-ily in our days, Amen.

Awake, awake, Miriam the Prophetess, arise from your slumber, and ap-pear before the King of Kings, God, blessed be He, and ask Him to have com-passion on us in this month of *Iyar*—that we should have enough food, that we should not, God forbid, become poor—the same way God gave the Jews the manna for the sake of your brother Moses' merits, and the well with water in honor of your merits. The crucial thing is that we should be cleansed from all of our sins, as the Jews in the desert were in this month, when they were about to receive the Torah. God, help Your people, and bless Your inheritance, and raise their fortune, and have mercy on them as a father does on his chil-dren, and bless the month of *Iyar* for us; to life, and health, and good fortune, and blessing, Amen.

A *teḥineh* for Rosh Hashanah, early in the morning. One says this *teḥineh* when one enters the synagogue on Rosh Hashanah. When Rosh Hashanah falls on the Sabbath, one does not say this *teḥineh*.

Remember the covenant of Abraham our father for our sake. . . .

Remember the merits of Sarah our mother for our sake.

Dear God, remember the virtues of our mother Sarah, who was redeemed on this day of Rosh Hashanah, and inscribe us in the Book of Life, and let us have children who are scholars. Lord of the World, You gave her an only son at the age of 90 years and promised her that her children will be as numerous and as important as the stars in the sky. Now, dear God, let her merits insure that her children, Your people, Israel, will not, God forbid, be wiped out, and inscribe us for a good life—myself, my husband, my children, and children's children, and all Israel, Amen.

Remember the binding of Isaac our father for our sake. . . .

Remember the merits of Rebecca our mother for our sake.

Remember, dear God, the merits of our mother Rebecca for our sake. She was raised by evil parents, Laban and Bethuel, and among bad people, and did not learn from their deeds. So, as she made certain that our father Jacob would receive the blessing from our father Isaac, so she will stand before Your throne today, Judgment Day, interceding on behalf of us, her children, to be inscribed for a good year, where our hearts will remain loyal to You, where we will not learn any foolishness from the wrong companions, and all the bless-ings of our father Isaac will be fulfilled speedily for us, Amen.

Remember the merits of Jacob our father for our sake. . . .

Remember the merits of Rachel our mother for our sake.

Dear God, remember the merits of our mother Rachel, who evaluated the situation of her sister Leah, that she must not be shamed when Jacob our fa-ther will speak to her and she will not know how to respond. In order to spare her sister, she withstood a great test and was torn from her happiness, from her beloved match, for which she had waited for seven years, and revealed to her sister the signs that Jacob our father had prearranged with her. Therefore, when Nevuzaradan led the Jews into exile past her tomb, and she cried and wailed and prayed to You for her children, You remembered her merits and promised her that You would return us to our land. Dear God, remember her merits for us today, Judgment Day, and give us a good year, and You should fulfill what You promised her without delay, and because we hear the *shofar* today, as You commanded in Your holy Torah, we should merit hearing the *shofar* of the Messiah soon and speedily, amen, let it be Your will.

Remember the merits of Leah our mother for our sake.

Remember, dear God, the merits of our mother Leah and heed our cry, as you accepted her cry that she should not fall in the lot of Esau, because You are merciful and hear the sound of weeping. Look down from heaven, and see how Your people all weep with bitter tears and tremble with fear of Your judgment, that we should not, God forbid, fall in the lot of Satan and the accusers who come to accuse us. It is better, Lord of the World, to turn to the voice of the good angels who stand before Your throne and pray for the good of Your people, Israel. Do not listen to the voice of Satan who says evil things about us. Shout so that he will not open his mouth; he will become confused and will not be able to say harmful things. And the sound of the *shofar*, together with our prayers, should rise before You in order to inscribe us for a good life in the Book of the Righteous, Amen.

Remember the merits of the tribes of Jacob for our sake. . . .

Remember the merits of Joseph the Righteous for our sake. . . .

Remember the merits of Moses our Teacher for our sake. . . .

Remember the merits of Aaron the Priest for our sake. . . .

Remember the merits of David our King for our sake. . . .

Remember the merits of righteous men and righteous women for our sake.

Remember, dear God, the merits of all the righteous men and righteous women who lived from the time of Adam, the first man, until today. Their merits should protect us, and our children should be Your loyal servants with happy hearts, and You should have mercy on us that the true redeemer should come soon. And the resurrection of the dead should occur and we should hear the *shofar* of the Messiah already, speedily in our days, Amen.

Notes

1. Translations of biblical passages are from *Tanakh: A New Translation of the Holy Scriptures According to the Traditional Hebrew Text* (Philadelphia: JPS, 1985). All other translations are my own.

2. It should be noted, however, that *teḥines* were not exclusively women's province. Men recited *teḥines* as well, but the form is primarily associated with women's prayer.

3. Max Weinreich, *History of the Yiddish Language*, trans. Shlomo Noble, with the assistance of Joshua A. Fishman (Chicago: University of Chicago Press, 1980), 727–33.

4. Khone Shmeruk, *Sifrut Yidish: Perakim le-Toldoteha* [*Yiddish Literature: Aspects of its History*] (in Hebrew) (Tel-Aviv: Porter Institute for Poetics & Semiotics, Tel-Aviv University, 1978), 51; and Shmeruk, *Sifrut Yidish be-Polin: Mehkarim ve-ʿIyunim Historiyim* [*Yiddish Literature in Poland: Historical Studies and Perspectives*] (in Hebrew) (Jerusalem: Magnes, 1981), 63–65, 70, 82–83.

5. Isaac Benjacob, *Otsar ha-Sefarim* (Vilna: Romm, 1880; repr. ed. New York: Hotsaʿat Yerushalayim, n.d.), 650.

6. The Venice?, 1666 edition and copies of *teḥines* published in small pamphlets are extant in the Joffe collection of rare Yiddish books in the rare book room of the Library of the JTS in New York.

7. *Teḥines u-Vakoshes* (Vilna: Romm, 1863), no. 11.

8. *Ḥaneh ve-Shiveh Baneha; A Naye Fil Fermehrte Shas Teḥineh* (Vilna: Romm, 1904), 214.

9. Ben-Zion Alfes, ed., *Shas Teḥineh Ḥadosheh: Mekor Dimʿeh, ʿim Mayseh Alfes ve-Rav Peninim* (Vilna: Rozenkrants and Shriftzetser, 1925), 48. For more information on Ben-Zion Alfes and his edition of *teḥines see infra*, pp. 77–78.

10. Sarah bas Tovim, *Shloyshah Sheʿorim* (Warsaw: Lebensohn, 1856), 6–7. For more information on Sarah bas Tovim and the custom of making candles on the eve of Yom Kippur, *see* Chava Weissler, "The Traditional Piety of Ashkenazic Women," in *Jewish Spirituality*, vol. 2, *From the Sixteenth-Century Revival to the Present*, ed. Arthur Green (New York: Crossroads, 1987), 253–56, 262–66. Further information on Sarah bas Tovim is available in: Israel Zinberg, *A History of Jewish Literature*, vol. 7, *Old Yiddish Literature from its Origins to the Haskalah Period*, trans. Bernard Martin (New York: Ktav; Cincinnati: Hebrew Union College Press, 1972–1978, 252–56); Sondra Henry and Emily Taitz, *Written Out of History: Our Jewish Foremothers*, 2d ed. rev. (Fresh Meadows, N.Y.: Biblio Press, 1983), 184–93; EncJud, s.v. "bas-Tovim, Sarah."

11. Chava Weissler, "The Religion of Traditional Ashkenazic Women: Some Methodological Issues," in *Association of Jewish Studies Review* 12:1 (Spring 1987): 85; Zinberg, *A History*, vol. 7, 23–24, 251; Henry and Taitz, *Written Out of History*, 187.

12. Ben-Zion Alfes, *Mayseh Alfes*, 2d ed. (Vilna: Rozenkrants and Shriftzetser, 1902), pt. 1, p. 6.

13. EncJud, s.v. "Alfes (Alfas), Benzion"; Zalman Rejzen, *Leksikon fun der Yidisher Literatur, Prese, un Filologye*, 3d ed. (Vilna: B. Kletskin, 1927–1929), v. 1, col. 107–11; *Leksikon fun der Nayer Yidisher Literatur* [Biographical Dictionary of Modern Yiddish Literature] (New York: Congress for Jewish Culture, 1956–1981), s.v. "Alfes, Ben-Zion," by Eliezer Raphael Malachi; Joshua Raidler-Feldman, *Mishpeḥot Sofrim: Partsufim* (Jerusalem: 1959 or 1960), 133.

14. The YIVO Institute for Jewish Studies catalogue lists a 1911, a 1922, and a 1927 edition of Alfes's edition of *teḥines*, all published in Vilna by the firm of Rozenkrants and Shriftzetser, but none of them could be located on the shelf. I used a 1925 edition, also published in Vilna by Rozenkrants and Shriftzetser. The 1925 edition is available in the Library of the JTS in New York. YIVO also has an undated reprint, published in New York by the Star Hebrew Book Co., apparently in the early part of the twentieth century. I purchased a reprint in a bookstore in Boro Park, Brooklyn, in April 1988 (Brooklyn: Mosheh Hoffmann: Bitahon Publishers, n.d.). This edition, which is probably a reprint of one of the Vilna editions, omits any mention of the editor, Ben-Zion Alfes.

Could Alfes, in his desire to bring appropriate Orthodox literature to the women of his day, also have been reacting to editions of *teḥines* put out by some of the *maskilim* ("enlightened" Jews)? (*See* Zinberg, *History,* vol. 7, 253; Weissler, "The Traditional Piety of Ashkenazic Women," 269 n.5 on the topic.) Although Alfes's edition first appeared in 1911(?), and *teḥines* by *maskilim* had been in circulation since the 1860s, Alfes might have been aware of the phenomenon. The *teḥines* of the *maskilim* may have been accepted by the women and become a part of the *teḥineh* liturgy by the time Alfes edited his work. Whether or not this conjecture is correct, there is no doubt that Alfes produced a charming work that addressed some of the religious and social issues of his day and that provides the contemporary reader with insights into the life of a particular segment of Jewish society in the early twentieth century.

15. Ben-Zion Alfes, *Shas Teḥineh Ḥadosheh: Mekor Dimʿeh* (Vilna: Rozenkrants and Shriftzetser, 1925), 135–37, 200–05.

16. *Teḥines* contain a great deal of biblical and midrashic material. Examples of uses of *midrash* in the *teḥines* presented here include the well created during the six days of creation (Miriam's well), Rachel's giving the signs to her sister Leah, and Leah's fear that she would be given in marriage to Esau. An English source for these *midrashim* is Louis Ginzberg, *Legends of the Jews,* trans. Henrietta Szold, from the German mss. (Philadelphia: JPS, 1909–1938).

17. A common practice in *teḥines* is to quote biblical verses in Hebrew and follow them with the Yiddish translation, as is the case here and throughout these *teḥines.*

Bibliography

Benjacob, Isaac. *Otsar ha-Sefarim.* Vilna: Romm, 1880; repr. ed. New York: Hotsaʾat Yerushalayim, n.d.

EncJud, 1972.

Ginzberg, Louis. *Legends of the Jews.* Trans. Henrietta Szold, from the German mss. Philadelphia: JPS, 1909–1938.

Henry, Sondra and Emily Taitz. *Written Out of History: Our Jewish Foremothers.* 2d ed., rev. Fresh Meadows, N.Y.: Biblio Press, 1983, 184–96.

Leksikon fun der Nayer Yidisher Literatur [Biographical Dictionary of Modern Yiddish Literature]. New York: Congress for Jewish Culture, 1956–1981.

Raidler-Feldman, Joshua. *Mishpeḥot Sofrim: Partsufim.* Jerusalem: [s.n.], 1959 or 1960.

Rejzen, Zalman. *Leksikon fun der Yidisher Literatur, Prese, un Filologye.* 3d ed. Vilna: B. Kletskin, 1927–1929.

Shmeruk, Khone. *Sifrut Yidish: Perakim le-Toldoteha* [Yiddish Literature: Aspects of Its History]. Tel-Aviv: Porter Institute for Poetics & Semiotics, Tel-Aviv University, 1978.

Shmeruk, Khone. *Sifrut Yidish be-Polin: Mehkarim ve-ʿIyunim Historiyim* [Yiddish Literature in Poland: Historical Studies and Perspectives]. Jerusalem: Magnes, 1981.

Tanakh: A New Translation of the Holy Scriptures According to the Traditional Hebrew Text. Philadelphia: JPS, 1985.

Teḥines. Various editions available in the Library of the JTS, and YIVO Institute for Jewish Research, both in New York City.

Weinreich, Max. *History of the Yiddish Language.* Trans. Shlomo Noble, with the assistance of Joshua A. Fishman. Chicago: University of Chicago Press, 1980.

Weissler, Chava. "The Religion of Traditional Ashkenazic Women: Some Methodological Issues," *Association for Jewish Studies Review* 12 : 1 (Spring 1987): 73–94.

Weissler, Chava. "The Traditional Piety of Ashkenazic Women," in *Jewish Spirituality*, vol. 2, *From the Sixteenth-Century Revival to the Present*, ed. Arthur Green. New York: Crossroads, 1987, 245–75.

Zinberg, Israel. *History of Jewish literature*. Trans. Bernard Martin, vol. 7, *Old Yiddish Literature from Its Origins to the Haskalah Period*. New York: Ktav, and Cincinnati: Hebrew Union College Press, 1975, 22–24, 248–59.

Two

HALAKHAH

Classical halakhah *(Jewish law) defined the aspirations and social roles of women and men, assigning separate roles to each. Today, all branches of Judaism are grappling with the tension between contemporary values and traditional observance, the acceptance of the ideals of equality and the tradition of role differentiation.*

The changing role of women in the synagogue has served as a catalyst for greater study of a number of relevant halakhic issues. A fundamental issue is that of ḥiyuv, *the obligation to observe religious commandments. The fact that* halakhah *has distinguished between women's and men's obligations has had a major impact on women's functioning in the community. A related issue is* kavod ha-tzibbur, *the honor of the community. This term has been used to limit women's active participation in synagogue services, with some people using the argument that women's participation insults and embarrasses men. The concept of* tumah, *ritual impurity, has also been used to limit women's religious lives, by seeming to imply that menstruation renders women impure and, therefore, unfit to enter a synagogue or touch a Torah scroll.*

A number of halakhic categories are concerned with ensuring that men are not sexually aroused during prayer by being made aware of the presence of women. Consequently, the sexes are traditionally separated during prayer by a meḥitzah, *a physical barrier. Women are also prohibited from having their voices heard by men (*kol ishah*) and having parts of their bodies such as hair and arms seen by men. The concept of modesty,* tzniut, *has also been an important factor in determining the height of the* meḥitzah *and in limiting women's public functioning.*

Irwin Haut and Shaye Cohen both examine the distinctions between law and custom regarding women, prayer, and the synagogue. I. Haut discusses the existential meaning of prayer and demonstrates that, according to classical Jewish law, women's obligation to pray is as important as men's. He criticizes attitudes that lead women, as well as men, to assume that the synagogue is rightfully the domain of men. Cohen traces the development of customs dictating that menstruants may not enter the synagogue nor touch the Torah scroll. He shows that these customs are not rooted in Jewish law. Rather, they may have been an outgrowth of women's efforts to express their piety by distancing themselves from the holy when they felt themselves to be ritually impure.

Another factor distancing women from the sacred center of Judaism has been the meḥitzah. *Today it distinguishes Orthodoxy from the other branches of Judaism. Norma Baumel Joseph discusses the laws surrounding the* meḥitzah, *concentrating on the views of the late leader of twentieth-century traditional Orthodoxy, Rabbi Moshe Feinstein.*

Rivka Haut, Judith Hauptman, and Annette Daum examine how the decision-making processes of each of their movements have handled attempts to expand the role of women in synagogue-related ritual. R. Haut describes the growing efforts of Orthodox women who, dissatisfied with the secondary role of women in the normative Orthodox synagogue, have created alternative prayer groups for women only. Despite severe criticism from the Orthodox rabbinate, these groups have continued to grow, producing a generation of Orthodox women learned in Jewish law and comfortable with leading prayers and reading the Torah.

Hauptman chronicles the struggles of the Conservative Movement to afford women greater ritual involvement in the synagogue, culminating in the decisions to ordain women as rabbis and invest them as cantors. She analyzes the social status of women in the time of the Talmud and how the social view of women determined their secondary role in the synagogue. She asserts that the changing status of women in contemporary society should be a consideration in the ongoing development of Jewish law.

Daum discusses one of the major feminist issues of the Reform Movement: the inclusion of feminine imagery in the prayer book. This takes two forms: includ-

87

Halakhah

ing female experience and role models and moving toward a gender-free representation of God. She surveys the current prayer books of the Conservative, Reform, and Reconstructionist Movements, showing the advantages and deficiencies of each in this regard.

These articles show that while women in all the major movements of Judaism are forging new paths, they still face disabilities. Readers may be led to ask whether limitations imposed upon women are an inherent aspect of Judaism or, rather, a reflection of social realities of particular times and places. Fundamental to this issue is whether one views halakhah *as a reflection of eternal, unchanging truths, as a constantly evolving system influenced by changing social realities, or, paradoxically, as both timeless and changing.*

Irwin H. Haut

ARE WOMEN OBLIGATED TO PRAY?

"Why are we told to recite the verse
    'O Lord, open my lips
    and let my mouth declare Your praise'
    before our most sacred prayer?
Like banks to a river
    lips form the outer edges of human speech.
We pray that God may release us from those limits,
    so that our mouths may declare
His endless praise."
             Shemuʿah Tovah 80 (Levi Yitzḥak of Berdichev) [1]

One Friday evening, a large number of men came to evening services at their neighborhood Orthodox synagogue. Some of them stood in the empty women's section. Then three women came to attend services. Since, according to Orthodox practice, men and women cannot sit together in a synagogue, the men had to leave the women's section. While the three women were comfortably seated in their section, behind the partition (*meḥitzah*), one of the men loudly complained that because of merely three women, the men had to be squashed into the men's section and could not use the women's section, as was customarily done when no women were present. When the women heard the man's complaint, they left the synagogue. With great joy the men took over the section so readily relinquished by the women.

This rather sad incident reflects an attitude that is quite pervasive among both Jewish men and women, namely, that the role of women in formal prayer is secondary at best, or, at worst, nonexistent. Such an attitude is completely wrong under *halakhah* (Jewish law), as this essay illustrates.[2]

Jewish law is perhaps unique among legal systems in that it applies to all aspects of life, from the purely personal such as the intimacies between a husband and wife, to matters of civil and criminal law, to matters of religious observance such as rules relating to the Sabbath and holidays. Jewish law deals with prayer as part of religious observance. Over the course of centuries, rabbinic leaders have established an elaborate system of formal prayers together with rules and obligations pertaining to them.

It is important to note, however, that there are no rules or regulations governing spontaneous prayer flowing from the inner recesses of the human spirit, by which men and women express their innermost needs and emotions. Such prayer neither needs nor is bounded by rules or regulations, whether motivated by human distress and need, awe, or thanksgiving. It is not that kind of prayer that either this article or Jewish law addresses. What is discussed is formal prayer, uttered either in the synagogue or elsewhere by both sexes.

Unlike spontaneous prayer, Jewish law does distinguish between men's and women's obligations in formal prayer. This differentiation is part of a larger distinction between men's and women's obligations to perform *mitzvot*.

Some introductory comments regarding Jewish law must be made here. Under *halakhah*, obligations, or commandments (*mitzvot*), are classified as being Toraitic (*de-oraita*), if the obligation to perform them derives directly from the Torah itself; or rabbinic (*de-rabbanan*), if the obligation to perform them flows from the inherent legislative power of the rabbis. The importance of this fundamental distinction becomes apparent below.

Women generally are relieved from the obligation to perform positive commandments ordained by the Torah or by the rabbis that are related to a particular time, with certain exceptions. Thus under Jewish law, for example, women are not obligated to put on *tefillin*, recite the *Shema*, or to dwell in booths on the Feast of Tabernacles, because these are positive commandments that must be performed at certain specific times, i.e., during daylight hours, or morning and evening, or during the holiday of Sukkot, respectively.

Women are, however, obligated to perform certain time-bound commandments such as eating of *matzah* (unleavened bread) during the Passover *seder*, hearing the *Megillah* on Purim, or drinking the four cups of wine during the Passover *seder*, either because they are specifically directed to do so in the Torah or for other reasons.

Moreover, women are generally equally obligated with men to observe positive commandments that are independent of time. For example, women are obligated to love their neighbors and honor their parents.

In addition, women are obligated to observe the negative commandments and, hence, must refrain from prohibited criminal activities, from violating the dietary laws, and from violating the Sabbath and holidays.[3]

Prayer is a positive commandment, not easily categorized as being either time-bound or independent of time. Women's obligation to pray has been defined differently by various rabbinic authorities. All rabbinic authorities agree that women are obligated to pray; they disagree as to exactly which prayers are obligatory. Some prayers, notably the *Shema*, are clearly time-bound, and therefore women are not obligated to recite them according to classical authorities. Other prayers are not so clearly defined as time-bound.

It is important to note that the Hebrew word for "prayer," *tefillah*, has two meanings. In its broadest sense it is used to connote "prayer," as that term is generally understood. In its narrow sense it is used to refer to the paradigmatic prayer called the *Shemoneh Esreh*, or eighteen benedictions.[4] The *Shemoneh Esreh* contains the essential elements of prayer under Jewish law, i.e., praise of God, petitionary prayers for one's daily needs, and thanksgiving to the Almighty for past beneficence.

We have thus far used the term "prayer" in its broader sense. Unless otherwise indicated, hereafter when we use "prayer," it is meant in the classical, narrower sense of the rabbinic literature, as referring to the *Shemoneh Esreh*.

The rabbis derived many rules regarding prayer from the description of the prayer of Hannah, mother of Samuel (1 Sam. 1 : 10–13). One *midrash*, in commenting upon the phrase ". . . [A]nd [Hannah] prayed . . . ," states as follows: ". . . From here we derive that women are obligated to pray, since Hannah recited the *Shemoneh Esreh.*" [5]

Other rules derived from the prayer of Hannah are that inner intention is a requisite of proper prayer; that private, personal, and silent prayer, with one's lips barely moving and with the words being inaudible to another is appropriate; and that, indeed, a loud or shouted prayer is inappropriate. [6]

The Mishnah, the first definitive statement of Jewish law by Rabbi Judah ha-Nasi, completed in approximately 220 c.e., sets forth the following rules:

Women . . . are not obligated to recite the *Shema,* or to put on *tefillin,* [but] are obligated to pray, to place a *mezuzah* on the doorpost, and to recite the Grace after Meals. [7]

The exclusion of women from the requirement to recite the *Shema* or to don *tefillin* derives from the rules discussed above, in that these represent time-bound positive commandments. The inclusion of women in the obligation to perform the commandments of *mezuzah* and Grace, set forth in the Mishnah, derives from the fact that such represent commandments that are not time-bound.

The inclusion of the obligation of women to pray has engendered much discussion. The Talmudic rabbis state that, according to the Mishnah: "[Women] are obligated to pray; for prayer is a matter of compassion [from God, the need for which also appertains to women]." [8]

In so doing, the Talmudic rabbis expressly reject the contention, which could possibly be argued, that women are relieved from the obligation to pray by virtue of its purported status as a time-bound positive commandment. [9]

Women's obligation to recite most prayers is dependent upon factors other than a relationship to time. A major factor in this issue is whether prayer is a Toraitic or rabbinic obligation.

Until Maimonides (1135–1204 c.e.), it had universally been accepted by all Jewish thinkers (with one exception) [10] that the obligation to pray was only rabbinic in origin, i.e., not mandated by God in the Torah. Maimonides, however, redeemed prayer from the level of a rabbinic obligation and transmuted it to the level of a Divine injunction or imperative, the force of which emanates from the Torah itself.[11]

This concept, the force of which proceeded from the genius of Maimonides, was actually deeply rooted in classical Jewish literature.

For example, an early tannaitic *midrash*, the *Sifrei* on Deuteronomy, edited around 300–400 C.E., comments on the biblical verse, "to love your God and serve Him (*l'avdo*) with all your hearts" (Deut. 11:13). It attempts to determine what the term *l'avdo* means: prayer or the sacrificial service.

The *Sifrei* concludes that the term refers to prayer and not to the sacrificial service because the verse includes the phrase "with all your hearts." The *Sifrei* reasons:

Is there then a [sacrificial] service of the heart? The term *l'avdo* must therefore be taken to mean prayer. . . . Just as the sacrifical service is termed *avodah* (service) so too must prayer be termed *avodah*.[12]

This portrayal of prayer as "the service of the heart," and its equation with the service of the Holy Temple, had profound influence on the legal literature of later generations, with deep and lasting psychological influences too, as will be seen.

Maimonides construed the *Sifrei* literally. He therefore ruled in his great code, the *Mishneh Torah:*

It is a positive commandment to pray every day, for it is stated, "you shall serve your God" [Exod. 23:25]. The oral tradition has taught us that service is prayer, for it is stated: "and serve Him with all your hearts." Our rabbis [accordingly] taught us: prayer constitutes the service of the heart.[13]

Maimonides, therefore, clearly construed the term "pray" as used in the Mishnah in its broader or more universalistic sense. In his great code he initially asserts that the obligation to pray is ordained by the Torah. He adds, however, that:

The Torah does not require a specific number of prayers, nor does it require a specific format or prayers at particular times.[14]

Maimonides took the position that women were, indeed, obligated to pray. According to him, this obligation is, as it is for men, Toraitic in nature and neither time-bound nor time related.[15] Maimonides may have had a variant reading of the Talmudic discussion, which perhaps influenced his views on this matter.[16]

In addition, Maimonides states:

Therefore, women . . . are obligated to pray since it is not a time-bound commandment. The [Toraitic] obligation to pray takes the following form: that a person shall entreat and pray to the Lord each day by declaring His praises, then petition for his [or her] needs, as necessary, and then he is to give thanks to Him for His beneficence.[17]

Under the view of Maimonides, therefore, the Toraitic obligation to pray, incumbent equally upon men and women, is fulfilled by the utterance of an informal prayer once a day, having the three aforementioned elements: praise, petition, and thanksgiving. It is the general consensus of opinion of codifiers and commentators that no particular form or wording is necessary or required,[18] although there is some substantial authority to the effect that such prayer must contain these three elements.[19]

Maimonides recognizes the existence of a rabbinic obligation to pray and discusses it at great length.[20] Unfortunately, he is silent as to the status of women with regard to the rabbinic obligation to pray daily and to recite the *Shemoneh Esreh* twice (or three times) each day. Although there exists some dispute in the matter, there is well-reasonsed authoritative opinion to the effect that under the view of Maimonides, women, equally with men, are obligated to recite the *Shemoneh Esreh* at least twice daily.[21]

Although it is perhaps open to question whether this is a correct interpretation of Maimonides' view, especially in light of his silence on the subject, it is nevertheless crystal clear that this would, indeed, be the view of Naḥmanides, his great adversary on this issue.

Naḥmanides (1194–1270 c.e.) follows and supports the prevailing view that prayer in general is mandated by the rabbis but not by the Torah (except in certain limited circumstances, which are discussed below).[22] Under his approach, all rabbinic statements that imply that the obligation to pray is Toraitic are to be interpreted figuratively.

Naḥmanides does, however, concede that in certain circumstances such as times of national distress ". . . there devolves a Toraitic obligation upon the community to cry out for help to the God of Israel."[23]

The rabbinic authorities, including Naḥmanides, who followed the view that the obligation of prayer was rabbinic in origin, construed the above quoted Mishnah and ensuing Talmudic discussion as relating to the rabbinic obligation of prayer.[24] They understood the Mishnah's statement that "[Women] are obligated to pray" in its narrow sense, as referring to the rabbinic obligation to recite the *Shemoneh Esreh*. Under this view, both women and men are obligated to recite the *Shemoneh Esreh* at least twice daily.[25]

From a modern perspective, and particularly from a psychological point of view, one could say that Maimonides has the better of the argument, since the need to pray appears to be universal in nature. Also, Nahmanides is forced to concede that in certain circumstances the obligation to pray is Toraitic.

Both Maimonides and Nahmanides viewed prayer as an emotion bursting forth from the innermost recesses and needs of the human spirit, as pointed out by Rabbi Soloveitchik, the recognized leader of modern Orthodoxy, in a lecture on the subject.[26] According to Rabbi Soloveitchik, both regarded prayer as meaningful only if derived from an awareness of the finite and limited nature of human existence and from a sense of inner pain and distress engendered thereby. They differed merely in their definition of the precise circumstances wherein such deep experience of prayer was prescribed by the Torah. To Nahmanides this was only when the entire community was faced with an external crisis, a public distress (*tzarah*). Maimonides, however, according to Rabbi Soloveitchik, viewed daily life itself as being:

Existentially in straits, inducing in the sensitive person feelings of despair, a brooding sense of life's meaninglessness, absurdity, lack of fulfillment. It is a persistent *tzarah* (distress) that exists daily.[27]

To Maimonides, according to Rabbi Soloveitchik, the need to pray arises out of the daily "depth crises" of life. This need is both sanctioned and, indeed, ordained by Divine fiat in the Torah.

Daily life crises afflict women and men equally. As regarding the rabbinic obligation to pray, surely under the prevailing view of Nahmanides, and possibly under the view of Maimonides, the obligation to pray daily is substantially similar for both sexes.

We have previously noted that the rabbis decreed the recitation of the paradigmatic prayer, *Shemoneh Esreh*, twice daily. According to Maimonides, the rabbis formulated the *Shemoneh Esreh* during the early Second Temple period.[28] They decreed that it be recited twice daily, to correspond to the morning and afternoon sacrifices. Indeed, on days when an additional sacrifice (the *Musaf* sacrifice) was brought such as Sabbaths and holidays, an additional recitation of the *Shemoneh Esreh* was mandated as well.[29]

The Rabbis also suggested the recitation of the *Shemoneh Esreh* in the evening to correspond to certain sacrificial activities that took place at night. This prayer was initially voluntary in nature, although its general acceptance by the public has rendered it obligatory.[30] However, it is generally assumed that only men took that obligation upon themselves. Consequently, it is accepted that women are under no obligation to recite the *Shemoneh Esreh* at night, even under the view of Naḥmanides; their sole obligation being to recite that prayer twice daily.[31]

That is not to say, however, that women are precluded from voluntarily reciting the *Shemoneh Esreh* at night. Indeed, one leading authority whose views we shall discuss more fully below, Rabbi Ovadiah Yosef, states:

And if women wish to pray [recite the *Shemoneh Esreh*] three times each day, they are worthy of blessing, and it is appropriate that they so do when time allows, and we are not concerned that in so doing they are making an unnecessary blessing [and hence, taking the Lord's name in vain] since the one who prays seeks compassion, and our Rabbis have taught us . . . would that people pray the entire day.[32]

This view, coming from the former Sephardic Chief Rabbi of Israel, is especially noteworthy since he adheres to the view of Maimonides in a related area of law. Maimonides, whose views are generally followed in Eastern or Sephardic communities, held the view that although women are not precluded from the actual performance of commandments to which they are not obligated, they should not recite the blessing in connection with the same.[33] The blessing says that God has sanctified and commanded us with regard to the commandment being performed. Reciting this blessing would constitute taking God's name in vain insofar as women are concerned, since they are not obligated to perform that very commandment.[34] Some Eastern, or Sephardic, authorities do follow Maimonides in this regard. Ovadiah Yosef reasons, however, that in matters of prayer, which invoke compassion needed by both sexes, more compassionate rules apply.

The rabbis of Western, or Ashkenazic, communities, on the other hand, follow the view of Rabbenu Tam, who held that women may perform all such commandments with any related blessings.[35]

We encounter a diversity of opinions (not an unusual phenomenon in legal systems) with respect to some formal details of prayers (other than the *Shemoneh Esreh*), regarding which some authorities distinguish between the obligations of men and women.

Some brief comments about these prayers are in order.

Prayers can generally be divided into three groups for our purposes:

a—Weekday prayers
b—Sabbath and holiday prayers
c—High Holy Day prayers

All three groups share a common element: The *Shemoneh Esreh* forms the central portion of each. Except for *Yom Kippur,* when an additional recitation is mandated, the *Shemoneh Esreh* is recited three times daily.

Other elements common to these groups are the *Kaddish* prayer, recited to honor the memory of the departed, and the *Hallel* prayer, which is a special prayer of praise containing psalms recited on holidays and semi-holidays but not on the High Holy Days.

The morning prayers are the most extensive. There are numerous additional prayers accompanying the *Shemoneh Esreh,* including introductory prayers of praise, the *Shema,* as well as the well-known *Aleinu* prayer, which is generally the concluding prayer at all prayer services.

The afternoon service is much briefer, consisting of the recitation of the *Shemoneh Esreh,* with brief introductory and concluding prayers.

The evening prayer is a bit longer, with the recitation of the *Shema* preceding the *Shemoneh Esreh.*

At the beginning of the Jewish month, the *Hallel* prayer is recited. On those occasions, known as *Rosh Ḥodesh* (New Moon), an additional recitation of the *Shemoneh Esreh* is mandated, called *Musaf.*

Sabbath and holiday prayers follow the same general format, including the additional *Musaf* prayer and, on festivals, *Hallel.*

On the High Holy Days, among the special prayers are the majestic *Kol Nidre* service, ushering in Yom Kippur, and the concluding service for that day, the beautiful and inspiring *Nᶜilah* prayer, which includes the fourth recitation that day of the *Shemoneh Esreh.*

Turning first to the weekday prayers, it is generally accepted by Ashkenazic authorities that women are obligated to recite those portions of the prayers that form an intrinsic or necessary part of the basic prayers such as the introductory prayers of praise in the morning daily services that precede or lead up to *Shaḥarit* (morning prayers).[36] Among Sephardic authorities the matter is in dispute. Some authorities, e.g., Rabbi Ovadiah Yosef, prohibit women from reciting the introductory prayers together with their accompanying blessing based on the theory that this constitutes the taking of God's name in vain. Other Sephardic authorities permit their recitation on a voluntary and nonobligatory basis.[37]

As noted previously, women are not obligated to recite the *Shema*.[38] Although not obligated to recite the *Aleinu* prayer, they are permitted and, indeed, encouraged to do so.[39]

The recitation of *Kaddish* by women has engendered much controversy. It had formerly been ruled that a daughter could not recite the *Kaddish* for a deceased parent, either in the synagogue or elsewhere, as for example, in the home of the deceased, although some authorities took the position that its recitation was permitted under the latter circumstances, when there were no surviving sons.[40]

There is, however, well-reasoned modern authority that permits its recitation by women when the requisite quorum (*minyan*) of ten adult males is present in a synagogue or elsewhere. In an article written in 1963 in a noted rabbinical journal, the much-respected Rabbi Yosef Eliyahu Henkin took the position that the recitation of *Kaddish* by women is proper, provided of course, that they recite it from their side of the partition (*meḥitza*) separating the sexes in Orthodox synagogues.[41] His opinion in this matter has recently been well-articulated and elaborated upon by his grandson, Rabbi Yehuda Henkin.[42]

Similar controversy surrounds the question of whether women are obligated, or indeed permitted, to recite the festive *Hallel* prayer. Since this prayer is recited only at certain specific times, it is contended by some authorities that women are not obligated to recite it, but that, as with any other time-bound commandment, they are permitted to do so based on the view of Rabbenu Tam.[43] This is the prevailing rule that is followed today in Ashkenazic communities.[44] Others, however, notably Rabbi Ovadiah Yosef, following the view of Maimonides, rule that women are prohibited from reciting that prayer, since the blessing preceding the recitation of *Hallel* states that its recitation is being performed pursuant to a Divine command, which is incorrect insofar as women are concerned.[45]

Similar views prevail with regard to the additional (*Musaf*) prayers recited on the Sabbath and holidays. Ashkenazic authorities generally hold, based on various theories, that women are obligated to recite such prayers. Sephardic authorities disagree as to whether women are enjoined from reciting such prayers or whether they are permitted, although not obligated, to do so.[46]

There appears to be unanimity among all authorities that women are obligated to recite the High Holy Day prayers since, again, they clearly invoke compassion, which is needed by all.[47]

The unifying element in such diversity of opinions is that if a particular prayer is viewed as invoking compassion, then its recitation is incumbent upon all. If, however, it lacks that element, the Ashkenazic authorities are, nevertheless, often ready to declare its recitation mandatory. Some Sephardic authorities, under the constraint of the view of Maimonides—i.e., that women are precluded from reciting a blessing in connection with a time-bound commandment—completely prohibit recitation of certain prayers while permitting recitation of others.

To sum up, it is quite clear that women's involvement with formal prayer under Jewish law has largely been underestimated, misunderstood, or ignored.

In the incident with which this article opened, when men showed their annoyance that women had attended Friday night services, the men were wrong in discouraging women's attendance, while the women were wrong in so easily being dissuaded from participating.

There should be no doubt of women's obligation under Jewish law to engage in formal prayer, despite the differences of opinion regarding some of the details. There should also be no doubt of the absolute right on the part of women to engage in and to participate in communal prayer, as desired, in an appropriate fashion.

In humanity's ongoing quest to attain new heights of spiritual experience, women of spirit seek to express their spiritual needs and their commitment to Judaism and its Torah. It is to the encouragement of that greatly desired goal that this paper is dedicated.

Notes

1. Quoted from *Your Word is Fire—The Hasidic Masters on Contemplative Prayer*, ed. and trans. A. Green and B. Holtz (New York: Paulist Press, 1977), 60.

2. On the attitude toward women and prayer, *see generally*, Blu Greenberg, *On Women and Judaism: A View From Tradition* (Philadelphia: JPS, 1981), 75–104; E. Ellinson, *Women*

and Mitzvot (in Hebrew) (Jerusalem: Jewish Agency, Alpha Press, 1979), chaps. 9–10; D. Auerbach, *Halihot Bayta* (in Hebrew) (Jerusalem: Machon Sharei Ziv, 1983), 35–59.

3. On women's obligations in *mitzvot, see* Ellinson, *Women and Mitzvot,* chap. 2; Saul J. Berman, "The Status of Women in Halakhic Judaism," *Tradition,* 14:2 (Fall 1973): 5.

4. Actually nineteen, if you count them. One was added after the other eighteen were already formulated, hence, the title "eighteen" remained. For further discussion, *see* EncJud, s.v. "*amidah.*"

5. Yal. Shimoni (Jerusalem, 1975), vol. 2, 715.

6. TB Ber. 31a–b.

7. Ber. 3:3.

8. TB Ber. 20b.

9. TB Ber. 20b. The Talmud seems to imply that if not for the fact that prayer was a matter of seeking compassion from God, a need applicable to both men and women, then women would be relieved of the obligation to pray by virtue of its status as a time-bound commandment. However, if it is assumed that the obligation to pray was only rabbinic in nature, then this would mean that the distinction between time-bound and non-time-bound obligations applies to rabbinic obligations as well. Indeed, from this text some authorities derive the rule that the distinction between time-bound and non-time-bound commandments applies generally (except for prayer, of course, for reasons stated in the text) to rabbinic commandments as well. *See Tosafot, ad. loc.,* 20b, s.v. "As to prayer."

10. *See* n.16 *infra.*

11. Rabbi Joseph B. Soloveitchik, *Ish ha-Halakhah-Galui ve-Nistar* (in Hebrew) (Jerusalem: Jewish Agency, Alpha Press, 1979), 240.

12. L. Finkelstein, ed. (New York: JTS, 1969), 87–88.

13. Rosenkrantz and Schriftsetzer, eds. (Vilna, 1900), *Laws of Prayer,* chap. 1, sec. 1.

14. Ibid.

15. Ibid., sec. 2.

16. It appears that Maimonides and his great predecessor, Alfasi (1013–1103 c.e.), had a textual variant of the Talmudic text under discussion. It was on this text that he based the obligation of women to pray, reasoning that such obligation was not a time-bound commandment. This is, of course, consistent with the view of Maimonides, discussed in the text. Under this textual variant the element of compassion, as a basis for such obligation, is unnecessary and, indeed, absent from the text of the Talmud quoted above at n.8. For further discussion *see* R. Rabinovitz, *Dikdukei Soferim,* Ber., 20a, n.2 (New York: M.P. Press, 1976) 19; Rabbi Ovadiah Yosef, *Yehaveh Da'at,* vol. 3. (in Hebrew) (Jerusalem: Hazon Ovadiah Seminary, 1980), 23–27. It would also appear that, at least in broad outline, Alfasi shared Maimonides' views on the subject; Maimonides supplied the rationale and details in his code. *See* the commentary of Menahem ben Solomon ha-Meiri (1249–1316 c.e.) on Ber. 20a–b, *Beit ha-Behira* (Jerusalem: *Mahon ha-Talmud ha-Yisra'eli ha-Shalem,* 1960), 69.

17. Maimonides, *Laws of Prayer,* chap. 1, sec. 2.

18. Ibid., sec. 3. For further discussion, *see* Israel M. ha-Cohen, *Mishnah Brura* (New York: Shulsinger Bros., 1952) chap. 106, sec. 1, subd. 4.

19. *See* Auerbach, *Halihot Bayta,* sec. 6, 35–36, for discussion of various views construing the view of Maimonides, including a minority view that women fulfill their Toraitic obligation to pray by uttering "any petition," even if it does not contain the three elements discussed in the text.

20. Maimonides, *Laws of Prayer,* chap. 1, secs. 4–9.

21. *See* Auerbach, *Halihot Bayta,* 35–37, and particularly, extensive discussion at pp. 36–37 (footnote). *See* however, Rabbi Ovadiah Yosef, p. 27, who holds that under the

view of Maimonides women are obligated to recite the *Shemoneh Esreh* only once daily, and accordingly, so rules. However, *see further* discussion on R. Ovadiah Yosef *infra*.

22. *See* comments of Naḥmanides to Positive Commandment no. 5 of *Sefer ha-Mitzvot of Maimonides*, ed. Lewin-Epstein (Jerusalem, 1947), 6–8.

23. Soloveitchik, *Ish ha-Halakhah-Galui ve-Nistar*, p. 241; *see also*, ibid., 7.

24. *Tosafot*, TB Ber. 20b, s.v. "As to prayer"; Naḥmanides, *see* n.22 *supra*.

25. Israel M. ha-Cohen, *Mishnah Brura*, chap. 106, sec. 1, subd. 4; Auerbach, *Halihot Bayta*, 37–39.

26. Rabbi Abraham R. Besdin, *Reflections of the Rav: Lessons in Jewish Thought—Adapted from the Lectures of Rabbi Joseph B. Soloveitchik* (Jerusalem: Jewish Agency, Alpha Press, 1979), 77–82.

27. Ibid., 80–81.

28. Maimonides, *Laws of Prayer*, chap. 1, sec. 4.

29. Ibid., sec. 5.

30. Ibid., sec. 6.

31. Israel M. ha-Cohen, *Mishnah Brura*, chap. 106, sec. 1, subd. 4; Auerbach, *Halihot Bayta*, 39.

32. Ovadiah Yosef, *Yeḥaveh Daʿat*, 27.

33. Maimonides, *Laws of Tzitzit*, chap. 3, sec. 9.

34. For full discussion, *see* Ellinson, *Women and Mitzvot*. Ellinson shows that there exists a substantial difference of opinion even among Eastern, or Sephardic, authorities as to whether the opinion of Maimonides is to be followed in this matter, at least regarding the *shofar* and *lulav*, even though these authorities generally adhere to and follow the rulings of Maimonides, their fellow-Sephardi. *See* particularly, pp. 56–58.

35. Ellinson, *Women and Mitzvot*, chap. 4, and particularly, p. 54. The view of Rabbenu Tam is presented at TB Kid. 31a, *Tosafot*, s.v. "I am not obligated."

36. Ellinson, *Women and Mitzvot*, 107.

37. Ibid.; Ovadiah Yosef, *Yeḥaveh Daʿat*, 10–13.

38. Rabbi Ovadiah Yosef would, with the utmost consistency, prohibit the recitation of the blessings accompanying the *Shema*. *See* Ellinson, *Women and Mitzvot*, 106–7.

39. Auerbach, *Halihot Bayta*, 53.

40. Ibid., 72–73; Ellinson, *Women and Mitzvot*, 70.

41. Yosef E. Henkin, "Recitation of *Kaddish* by a Daughter" (in Hebrew), *Ha-Pardes*, vol. 6 (1963): 5.

42. Yehuda Henkin, "Recitation of *Kaddish* by Women and Their Joinder to the Quorum From the Women's Section" (in Hebrew), *Ha-Darom*, vol. 54 (Sivan 1985): 34.

43. *See* n.35, *supra*.

44. Auerbach, *Halihot Bayta*, 54; Ellinson, *Women and Mitzvot*, 116–17.

45. *See* Ellinson, *Women and Mitzvot*, 116–17 and particularly n.12, discussing views of Rabbi Ovadiah Yosef in this matter. *See also*, ibid., 209, for Rabbi Yosef's comments that in this particular instance even Ashkenazic women should refrain from following the view of Rabbenu Tam. For further elaboration by Rabbi Yosef, *see Yeḥaveh Daʿat*, vol. 1, p. 223, and particularly the footnote at pp. 325–26.

46. Auerbach, *Halihot Bayta*, 41–42; Ellinson, *Women and Mitzvot*, 114–16.

47. Auerbach, *Halihot Bayta*, 43, 291; Ellinson, *Women and Mitzvot*, 116, 124.

Shaye J. D. Cohen

PURITY AND PIETY: THE SEPARATION OF MENSTRUANTS FROM THE SANCTA

Many Jews, both men and women, believe that menstruants are prohibited by Jewish law from touching a Torah scroll and participating in the synagogue prayer service. In this chapter, I briefly survey the tortuous history of this belief. For the sake of brevity, I present only the major evidence, reserving full discussion for another occasion.[1]

I begin with the relevant paragraphs of the *Shulḥan Arukh*, the classic code of rabbinic law, which permits menstruants to hold and read a Torah Scroll. The only individuals legally barred from touching the Torah Scroll were men who had seminal emissions (ejaculants), but the *Shulḥan Arukh* notes that this prohibition is universally ignored. Despite this clear statement of Jewish law, Ashkenazic Jewish women generally refrained from synagogue attendance during their menstruation. This practice was recorded and endorsed by Rabbi Moses Isserles in his gloss to the *Shulḥan Arukh*. In the central section of this chapter, I survey the evolution of the prohibition of access to the sacred by menstruants. This survey, which extends from biblical to medieval times, provides the background necessary for understanding the debate between R. Karo and R. Isserles. In the chapter's final sections, I survey post–*Shulḥan Arukh* developments and offer a few concluding reflections on the tenacity of this prohibition in Jewish piety.

The *Shulḥan Arukh*

In the *Shulḥan Arukh*, R. Joseph Karo (1488–1575) writes the following:[2]

All those who are impure may read the Torah, recite the *Shema,* and pray, except for the ejaculant, because Ezra removed him from the general category of the impure and prohibited him [to engage] either in the words of Torah or in the recitation of the *Shema,* or in prayer, until he immerses [in a *mikveh*] so that the Sages should not frequent their wives like roosters. Afterward, however, this enactment was abolished and the original law was re-established, that even an ejaculant is permitted [to engage] in the words of Torah, the recitation of the *Shema,* and prayer, without immersion and without washing in nine *kabim* of water. And this is the common practice.

R. Moses Isserles (c. 1525–1572) adds the following note:

Some have written that a menstruant, during the days of her discharge, may not enter a synagogue or pray or mention God's name or touch a Hebrew book, but some say that she is permitted [to do] all these, and this view is correct. However, the practice in these countries accords with the first opinion. However, in the white days[3] the custom is to permit [her to do all these]. And even in a place that follows the stringent practice, on the Days of Awe and other such occasions when many gather to enter the synagogue, they are permitted to enter the synagogue like other women, because it will be great sadness for them if everyone gathers [in synagogue] but they stand outside.

Elsewhere in the *Shulḥan Arukh,* R. Karo states that "All those who are impure, even menstruants, are permitted to hold a Torah scroll and read it, provided that their hands are neither soiled nor dirty."[4] Here R. Isserles has no comment.

The question addressed in these paragraphs is whether those who are impure (*teme'im*) may perform sacred acts, specifically read the Torah (a category that apparently includes also the study of Torah),[5] recite the *Shema,* and pray (that is, pray the eighteen benedictions, the *Amidah*). For R. Karo, a Sephardic authority, the matter is simple. He states that impurity does not bar any person—including menstruants, parturients, lepers, those who have come into contact with a corpse—from holding a Torah scroll or engaging in prayer and study. The only possible exception is the ejaculant, not because his impurity is greater than that of all the others, but because the rabbis sought to control male sexuality. If a pious son of Israel knows that after ejaculation he must immerse in a ritual bath (a *mikveh*) or wash himself thoroughly before he may read Torah or recite the prayers, the quintessential acts of rabbinic piety, he will restrain his amorous desires and not cohabit with his wife too frequently. However, even this possible exception is not really an exception because the requirement is everywhere ignored and the original law, which did not single out the ejaculant, is in effect. Thus R. Karo.

In his supplementary comment, R. Moses Isserles, an Ashkenazic authority relying on the work of various Ashkenazic predecessors, asks whether the status of a menstruant in relationship to the sancta should be distinguished from the status of other impure persons. Some authorities, R. Isserles states, prohibit the menstruant from the following four actions: (1) entering a synagogue, (2) praying, (3) mentioning God's name, and (4) touching a Hebrew book.

R. Isserles comments that this opinion is wrong because menstruants are not prohibited by law from these four actions. Nevertheless, "in these countries," that is, in Poland and other Ashkenazic areas, the custom (*minhag*) is to observe the prohibitions. Since there is no legal prohibition, R. Isserles remarks that two leniencies are followed: first, the prohibitions are followed only during the days of menstrual discharge and not during the seven "white" days; second, on the Days of Awe and other such occasions, menstruants are permitted to attend the synagogue (and, presumably, to pray),[6] even in those localities which otherwise follow the stringent practice.

To understand how this widespread custom developed, we need to look to the biblical and rabbinic sources for the origins of the concept that a ritually impure person should refrain from contact with sacred objects and places.

From the Torah to the *Shulḥan Arukh*

The focal point of the purity system in the Torah is the central sanctuary. After outlining the details of the impurity caused by sexual discharge from both men and women, God instructs Moses and Aaron to "keep the people of Israel separate from their impurity, lest they die in their impurity by defiling My Tabernacle that is in their midst" (Lev. 15:31). Impurity of any kind, whether that of the leper, the ejaculant, the menstruant, or a corpse, must be kept distant from the sacred space and the sacred objects of the Tabernacle. As long as the Temple stood in Jerusalem the realm of the sacred was clearly marked off from the realm of the profane. In the Temple and in proximity to persons and objects bound for the Temple, purity was an essential requirement; elsewhere the purity laws could be ignored. During the latter part of the second Temple period (mid-second century B.C.E. to 70 C.E.) various sects and pietistic groups extended the limits of the sacred to include daily life outside the Temple, especially all matters connected with food. This perspective, however, had only a minimal impact on the Jews at large, who continued to regard the Temple as the single locus of sanctity and the sole place that demanded ritual purity of its entrants.

With the destruction of the Temple in 70 C.E., the purity system lost its focal point and ultimately ceased to exist. In the absence of the sacrificial cult, the Jews elaborated and ritualized a system of worship through prayer and Torah study. In the absence of the Temple, the synagogue and the school emerged as the new central institutions of Judaism. Prayer, Torah study, and synagogues were part of Jewish piety long before the destruction of the Temple in 70 C.E., but the destruction endowed them with new prominence and meaning. They became the permanent replacements for an institution and a ritual that would return only in the messianic age.

Were these replacements fully equivalent to the lost originals? Obviously not, because the Torah contains prescriptions for the Tabernacle (which was understood to be the model for the Temple) and the sacrificial cult, but not a word about synagogues or ritualized prayer and study. However, in spite of this ideological weakness—or perhaps because of it—the Jews tried to assimilate the synagogue to the Temple and prayer to the sacrificial cult. The synagogue became home to rituals that originally were performed in the Temple (for example, blowing the *shofar* on Rosh Hashanah), was decorated with representations of the Temple and the Temple utensils (notably the *menorah*), and was outfitted with an ark and a perpetual light. The prayers were explicitly likened to the sacrifices and were said to replace them. This process lasted several centuries, and one of its results was the idea that prayer, Torah study, and entrance into a synagogue demand ritual purity.

At the earliest stages of this process, ritual purity requirements were not transferred. The Mishnah, the first document of rabbinic Judaism, states that an ejaculant may not recite aloud the benedictions of the liturgy or of the Grace after Meals.[7] The Mishnah does not give a reason for the prohibition but implies that the problem is not impurity in general but semen in particular. The Mishnah nowhere records a parallel prohibition for a leper, a man with an abnormal sexual discharge (*zab*), someone affected by corpse impurity, a menstruant, or any other impure person. Only the ejaculant and those who come in contact with semen must be purified before performing the liturgy. The *Tosefta,* a collection of material closely related to the Mishnah, correctly concludes:[8]

Men who have an abnormal sexual discharge (*zabim*), women who have an abnormal sexual discharge (*zabot*), menstruants, and parturients are permitted to read the Torah, and to study Mishnah, Midrash, laws, and homilies. But the ejaculant is prohibited from all these.

Why of all sources of impurity was ejaculation alone singled out? Both the Jerusalem and Babylonian Talmudim suggest that the reason was to restrain male sexuality ("so that Sages should not behave like roosters"). The law is primarily interested in men, not women, and in male actions and intentions, not purity and impurity.[9] Neither the Mishnah nor the Talmuds raise any obstacle before a menstruant who wants to attend synagogue, pray, recite the *Shema,* or study scripture.

Thus, the separation of the ejaculant from the sancta is far older and more authoritative than the analogous separation of the menstruant. In the thousand years or so between the completion of the Talmud and the publication of the *Shulḥan Arukh,* the case of the ejaculant was debated intensely by jurists. Some said that he was prohibited by law from praying unless he immersed in a *mikveh* or washed in a specific amount of water; others said that the custom had lapsed completely. But regarding Torah study, there was near unanimous agreement that an ejaculant was not required to do any special bathing or washing, because "the words of Torah cannot contract impurity." Following Maimonides (1138–1204 c.e.), R. Joseph Karo adopted a lenient position, permitting the ejaculant both to pray and to study Torah.[10]

Although there is no legal basis in the Talmuds for separating menstruants from the sancta, in the post-Talmudic period, in some circles, they began to be excluded (or to exclude themselves). This practice is the result of two developments. First, as archaeology demonstrates, the arrogation of Temple ideology by the synagogue continued apace. In inscriptions of the Byzantine period the synagogue is called "holy place," "house of God," and other such epithets that originally and properly belonged to the Temple in Jerusalem. The rules elaborated in the Talmud governing respect for the Temple were transferred to the synagogue. And since menstruants and other impure persons could not enter the Temple, logic dictated that they could not enter synagogues, the surrogates of the Temple. This conclusion should have affected ejaculants, lepers, and all other impure persons as much as it affected menstruants, but it did not. Menstruants were distanced from the synagogue, but impure men could still attend (even if many authorities stated that ejaculants could not pray).

Of all impure persons, menstruants alone were excluded from the synagogue, because only menstruants were dangerous as well as impure. In the conception of the Mishnah and the Talmuds the menstruant is impure and transmits impurity to persons and objects, but she is not a source of danger. She is ritually impure not dangerously polluted.[11] But a text known as *Baraita de Niddah,* probably written in the Land of Israel in the sixth or seventh century, documents a significant shift in attitude. A menstruant must not cut her fingernails, lest her husband or child accidentally step on or touch the clippings and, as a result, develop boils and die; a priest whose mother, wife, or any other female member of the household is menstruating, may not bless the people, lest his blessing become a curse; a Sage who partakes of food prepared by a menstruant will forget his learning; a menstruant's spit, breath, and speech cause impurity in others.[12] Earlier rabbinic texts did not contain any regulations like these. The identity of the group or school that produced the *Baraita de Niddah* is unknown, but the text had enormous impact on later Jewish piety.

Since *Baraita de Niddah* considers the menstruant dangerously polluted, it is surely no coincidence that it is the earliest Jewish text (post-70 C.E.) to prohibit menstruants from coming into contact with the sacred. A menstruant is prohibited from lighting the Shabbat candles. Men are prohibited from greeting a menstruant or reciting a benediction in her presence, lest she respond in kind or recite "Amen" and thereby desecrate the name of God. No impure person is permitted to enter a "house of prayer, because he thereby is rendering God's sanctuary impure," but this general prohibition is directed specifically at menstruants; in fact, they should not even enter a room filled with Hebrew books. Like menstruants, parturients too may not enter either synagogues or schools. These prohibitions apply not only to menstruants but also to those who come into contact with them. Men who have had contact with a menstruant's spittle are prohibited from entering a synagogue until they have been purified; a midwife who has delivered a child has the impurity of a menstruant and may not enter a synagogue or "stand before the Sages" without being purified.[13]

Thus, the impurity of the menstruant is not like that of other persons, because her impurity is dangerous to those around her. She must be distanced not only from her husband but also from the sacred. In the *Baraita de Niddah* the menstruant is explicitly prohibited from entering a synagogue or coming into contact with sacred books and is implicitly prohibited from praying and reciting God's name. These are precisely the four prohibitions mentioned by R. Isserles.

In the thousand years between the *Baraita de Niddah* and R. Isserles, these prohibitions, and the fundamental perception of the menstruant on which they were based, underwent vigorous debate, analogous to the debate concerning the impurity of the ejaculant. At first the rabbis of medieval Babylonia (the *geonim*) were opposed to the separation of the menstruant from the sancta. "Even if she is forbidden to her husband, she certainly is not exempted from the commandments" (of prayer, benedictions, etc.). However, by the tenth century the restrictive view began to triumph; a menstruant was in some quarters still permitted to pray, but the prohibition of entering a synagogue, certainly during the initial days of her period, became widespread.[14] In the emerging communities of the High Middle Ages, a curious pattern developed. Sephardic communities did not accept these prohibitions at all; Maimonides and R. Joseph Karo, the two great codifiers of rabbinic law, both of them Sephardim, omit them entirely. Both of them state explicitly that menstruants are not prohibited from holding a Torah scroll. Ashkenazic communities, however, accepted the prohibitions, if not as law then as custom.[15]

In Ashkenaz, menstruants observed these prohibitions not because men commanded them to but because they wanted to observe them. Here is the report of a work that derives from the school of R. Solomon ben Isaac of Troyes (known as Rashi, 1040–1105 c.e.):[16]

Some women refrain from entering a synagogue and from touching a Hebrew book during their menstrual periods. This is only supererogation (*ḥumrah be'alma*) and they are not obligated to act in this manner. For what is the reason for them to act this way? If it is because they think that the synagogue is like the Temple, then even after their immersion why do they enter it? . . . Thus, you see that (the synagogue) is not like the Temple, and they may enter it [even during their periods]. Nevertheless it is a place of purity, and they act properly, and may they be blessed.

From the point of view of law, there is no reason for menstruants to refrain from entering the synagogue; the purity system has lapsed; all Jews, both men and women, are impure, since they cannot bring an atonement sacrifice to the Temple; and, in any case, the synagogue does not have the legal status of the Temple. Nevertheless, oblivious to law and logic, the women of medieval France refrain from entering the synagogue during their periods because they internalized the fear of menstruation first attested by the *Baraita de Niddah*. Even without a legal basis, the custom is endorsed by the rabbi who reports it, and the women are praised for their piety. Similarly, a somewhat later authority, R. Eliezer ben Yoel ha-Levi (known as the Ravyah, c. 1160–c. 1240 c.e.) writes that menstruants correctly refrain not only from entering the synagogue but also from praying "in front of" other women.[17] In fourteenth-century Provence, a "border district" between Ashkenaz and Sepharad, parturients did not attend synagogue forty days after the birth of a son and eighty days after the birth of a daughter. In this case, our informant disapproves of the practice,[18] but here is further evidence that Jewish women voluntarily absented themselves from the synagogue during their menstrual periods.

Even in Ashkenaz, however, the prohibitions were not observed everywhere and were not approved by all legal authorities. R. Jacob Molin (known as the Maharil, d. 1427) seems not to have known the prohibition at all. When outlining the wedding ceremony, which was to take place inside the synagogue, he makes provisions for the fact that the bride might be a menstruant. This possibility requires special discussion, not because her impurity would exclude her from the sanctuary, but because her impurity would prevent the groom from touching her, even while placing the ring on her finger.[19] His younger contemporary, R. Israel Isserlein (c. 1390–1460) endorses the custom that menstruants refrain from attending synagogue but proposes that the custom should not prevent them either from attending on the Days of Awe and other such occasions or from reciting benedictions.[20] Perhaps the clearest evidence of the unevenness of the observance of the prohibitions by the women of Europe is a brief paragraph by R. Jacob Landau in his *Sefer ha-Agur* (published by the author in 1490). After quoting some of the Ashkenazic authorities who say that a menstruant should not enter a synagogue, pray, or recite a benediction, he comments.[21]

But I, the author, have seen in my country that women are accustomed to enter the synagogue, and they pray [there] and respond [amen to] all the sacred [benedictions, *ve'onot kol davar she-bi-Kedushah*). They take care only not to look at the Torah scroll when the sexton displays it to the congregation.

In R. Landau's "country," which probably means Germany (where he was born and educated) but might mean Italy (where he was living when he published the *Sefer ha-Agur*), women (that is, menstruating women) pay no attention to the customary prohibitions. They attend synagogue, pray, and recite amen to all benedictions; however—and here is yet another way of distancing menstruants from the sancta—they do not look at the Torah scroll when it is held aloft.

This welter of conflicting custom and practice in Ashkenaz explains the comments of R. Moses Isserles cited at the beginning of this essay. His gloss on the *Shulḥan Arukh* is not the result of either a reasoned legal opinion or a clearly conceived theory governing the separation of menstruants from the sacred. R. Isserles knows from his research and his observation that Ashkenazic women are accustomed while menstruating to separate themselves from the sancta. In some communities they refrain from attending the synagogue, in others they do not pray or mention the name of God, in others they do not touch a Hebrew book. R. Isserles does not explain why the separation of menstruants from the sacred is more severe than the separation of ejaculants, or why, of all impure persons, only menstruants suffer disability in the synagogue, because he has no need for an explanation. He is describing custom, not prescribing law. When R. Karo permits menstruants to hold a Torah scroll and read it, R. Isserles did not demur, because how often could a woman, menstruating or not, touch or hold a Torah scroll? In the synagogue women prayed in separate rooms or galleries and could never touch the Torah. No custom arose to prohibit that which was in any case impossible or extremely unlikely, and R. Isserles had no need to make a comment in the code of law.[22]

From the *Shulḥan Arukh* to Contemporary Times

The customs mentioned by R. Isserles persisted in Ashkenaz for another 200 years, although they occasionally provoked denunciation by legal authorities because the women carried them too far.[23] By the nineteenth century, however, in most of Ashkenaz these customs had all but died out; menstruants attended synagogue and recited benedictions without hesitation.[24] However, while the customs were dying out in most of Ashkenaz, in a peculiar and uninvestigated process they were becoming part of Sephardic women's piety. R. Joseph Karo writes that "nowadays our (menstruating) women do not have a custom to refrain from entering a synagogue,"[25] but in the following centuries the women of many Sephardic communities did have such a custom. In contemporary Israel, many women from "Oriental" countries do not attend synagogue or pray while menstruating, even though the Sephardic chief rabbi has told them that the custom has no basis in law (*see* Sered, p. 212 and Interview with Iranian Women, pp. 219–20).[26]

Concluding Reflections

Many Jews, both men and women, believe that menstruants are prohibited by Jewish law from touching a Torah scroll and from participating in the synagogue prayer service. Some Conservative Jews use this belief to support their opposition to the egalitarian impulse in Conservative Judaism and specifically to the ordination of women as rabbis.[27] Some Orthodox Jews use this belief to justify the separation of men and women in the synagogue.[28] I have tried to show that this belief is wrong, because the prohibition is based not on law but on custom, and the custom was never universally observed and was always subject to diverse opinions. The parallel prohibition for ejaculants is much older and much more securely rooted in the rabbinic sources than the prohibition for menstruants, and yet that prohibition is completely ignored.

The tenacity of the prohibition for menstruants cannot be ascribed only to male fear of women in general and menstruation in particular, because women too have long observed the prohibition, sometimes against rabbinic (male) opposition. The prohibition for menstruants is so tenacious because it is an expression of folk piety, and folk piety does not quickly relinquish practices that confirm some of its deeply held convictions. The separation of a menstruant from the sacred confirms not only her impurity—and all Jews, even those who do not observe any of the rules of "family purity," *know* that she is impure—but also the marginality of all women, menstruating or not, in the organized, public expressions of Jewish piety. In Judaism (at least until recently) public sacred space is male space, and the exclusion of menstruants from that space confirms that women, because they are women, are not its natural occupants.

As more and more women, even in Orthodox circles, assume prominent roles in synagogues and prayer groups, the power of these prohibitions will wane, because women are making themselves less marginal. Not coincidentally, women are making themselves less "impure" as well. Among many writers, both feminist and nonfeminist (or antifeminist), the language of impurity is being replaced by other terminology to explain and justify Judaism's elaborate system of menstrual taboos.[29] No longer "polluted" and no longer marginal, women, including menstruants, are less afraid to touch a Torah and to engage in sacred activities. "They act properly, and may they be blessed."

Notes

1. *See* my "Women and the Sacred: Menstrual Pollution in Judaism and Christianity," *Women's History and Ancient History*, ed. S. Pomeroy (University of North Carolina Press, 1991), 273–99. The fullest collections of material on this topic are Yedidyah Dinari, "The Violation of the Sacred by the Niddah and the Enactment of Ezra," (in Hebrew) *Te*ʿ*uda* 3 (1983): 17–37 (*Te*ʿ*uda* is the journal of the Chaim Rosenberg School of Jewish Studies of Tel Aviv University) and R. Ovadyah Yosef, *Yeḥaweh Da*ʿ*at* (in Hebrew) III (Jerusalem: n.p. 1980), 27–33. I am much indebted to each of them, especially Dinari. For a rabbinic discussion in English, *see* R. Avraham Weiss, "Women and Sifrei Torah," *Tradition* (Summer 1982): 106–18.

2. *Shulḥan Arukh*, Oraḥ Ḥayyim 88.

3. According to Lev. 15, menstrual impurity lasts only seven days, but in the Talmudic period women began to add seven "white" days after the cessation of the menstrual discharge (TB Nid. 66a). According to rabbinic law a woman has the status of a menstruant both during her discharge and during the seven "white" days, but in the matter of separation from the sancta, R. Isserles says that the seven "white" days are to be treated more leniently than the initial days.

4. YD 282:9. R. Karo is following Maimonides and R. Jacob b. Asher. *See Mishneh Torah*, Laws of *Tefillin, Mezuzah,* and *Sefer Torah* 10:8, and *Tur*, YD 282.

5. Note that R. Karo first uses the phrase *qorin ba-Torah* and then shifts to *divrei Torah*.

6. *See* R. Abraham Gumbiner (1637–c. 1683), *Magen Avraham*, n."c" on Oraḥ Ḥayyim 88.

7. Mish. Ber. 3:4–6.

8. Tosefta Ber. 2:12, p. 8, ed. Lieberman. The version in TJ Ber. 3:4, 6c is substantially identical with that of the *Tosefta*, while the version in TB Ber. 22a has been changed to reflect the later view that menstruants are prohibited from reading the Torah. TB omits *zabot* and parturients and substitutes "men who have intercourse with menstruants" for "menstruants." Thus, the version in the TB, unlike that of the *Tosefta* and TJ, does not explicitly permit menstruants to perform sacred acts. *See* Lieberman's commentary.

9. *See* TB Ber. 21b–22b and TJ Ber. 3:4, 6b–c.

10. Cf. Maimonides, *Mishneh Torah, Laws of Prayer*, 4:4–6, and R. Jacob b. Asher (c. 1270–1343), Tur, Orah Hayyim 88.

11. The only exception known to me is TB Pes. 111a; cf. too Shab. 110a.

12. *Baraita de Niddah*, pp. 3, 10, 12–13, 16, 18, 25, 36, 37, ed. Horovitz in *Tosefata Atikata*, pt. 5 (Frankfurt: Horowitz, 1889).

13. *Baraita de Niddah*, pp. 3, 6, 17, 26, 27, 31–33, 36, 37.

14. *See* especially B. M. Lewin, ed., *Otzar ha-Geonim* Berakhot, Teshubot, pars. 116–21, pp. 48–49. The quote is from par. 116, ascribed to R. Natronai. At the same time, the custom arose that a menstruant pronounces the benediction upon her purification only after emerging from the waters of immersion, not before (which had been the normal practice); *see Otzar ha-Geonim* Pesahim, Teshubot, pars. 25–26, pp. 8–9, and Dinari, "The Violation of the Sacred," 21–22.

15. R. Karo is familiar with the prohibitions but only from Ashkenazic sources. *See* the *Bet Yosef* on Tur, Orah Hayyim 88, end. On this distinction between Ashkenazim and Sephardim, *see* H. J. Zimmels, *Ashkenazim and Sephardim* (London: Oxford University Press, 1958; repr. London: Marla, 1976), 197–99 and 228–29.

16. *Sefer ha-Pardes*, ed. Ehrenreich, p. 3; cf. *Mahzor Vitry*, ed. Horowitz, p. 606 and *Sefer ha'Orah*, ed. Buber, pt. 2, pp. 167–68.

17. *Sefer Ravyah*, ed. Aptowitzer, vol. 1, p. 45. This passage is quoted by various Ashkenazic authors of the thirteenth and fourteenth centuries; *see* Aptowitzer's notes. Dinari suggests that the Ravyah is prohibiting not menstruants from praying in front of other (nonmenstruating) women but (nonmenstruating) women from praying in front of menstruants. The syntax of the Ravyah's Hebrew is difficult, but I am not convinced by Dinari's rendering; *see* his "The Violation of the Sacred," 27–28.

18. R. Yeroham, *Sefer Toledot Adam ve-Havah* (written c. 1340), Part II (*Havah*), chap. 26, p. 223d (ed. Venice, 1553). R. Yeroham is writing under the influence of Maimonides, *Mishneh Torah*, Laws of Forbidden Intercourse 11:15. The practice of the Provençal women may have come to them from either the women of Ashkenaz or the Karaites of Spain.

19. *Sefer Maharil*, ed. S. Spitzer (Jerusalem: Machon Yerushalayim, 1989), pp. 466–67.

20. R. Israel Isserlein, *Terumat ha-Deshen*, Part II, *Pesakim u-Ketavim* #132; *see also* R. Joseph b. Moshe, *Leket Yosher*, Orah Hayyim, p. 131, ed. Freimann.

21. *Sefer ha-Agur* ed. M. Hershler (Jerusalem: 1960), sec. 1388, p. 230.

22. Contrast the explanation of Weiss, "Women and Sifrei Torah," p. 111.

23. R. Abraham Gumbiner (1637–c. 1683), *Magen Avraham*, n."b" on Orah Hayyim 88, echoed by R. Abraham Danzig (1748–1820), *Hayye Adam* 3:38; *see also* R. Joseph Hahn (d. 1637), *Yoseph Ometz* (Frankfurt: Hermon 1928; repr. Jerusalem: 1965), pp. 342–43, and R. Joseph Kashman, *Noheg Katzon Yoseph* (published by the author in 1718; repr. Tel Aviv, 1969), pp. 116–17 (cf. p. 95 where he endorses the prohibition for parturients). That these prohibitions were part of women's piety is demonstrated by their frequent appearance in Yiddish *minhag* books.

24. *See* R. Israel Meir ha-Kohen Kagan (known as the Ḥafetz Ḥayyim, 1838–1933), *Mishnah Berurah*, n."z" on Oraḥ Ḥayyim 88 (first published in 1894). R. Kagan is describing the customs of Russia and Poland; in Hungary the prohibition seems to have persisted. *See* the *Ḥatam Sofer* (by R. Moses Sofer, 1763–1839) on Oraḥ Ḥayyim 88, and R. Solomon Ganzfried (1804–1886), *Kitzur Shulḥan Arukh*, pt. 4, 153:16.

25. *Bet Yosef* on Tur, Oraḥ Ḥayyim 88, end.

26. *See* the responsum of R. Ovadyah Yosef cited in n.1.

27. In his responsum permitting *aliyot* for women, R. Aaron Blumenthal felt obliged to address the question of whether a menstruant could receive an *aliyah* and touch a Torah scroll. (The answer is yes.) *See Conservative Judaism and Jewish Law*, ed. Seymour Siegel (New York: Rabbinical Assembly, 1977), pp. 277–78.

28. R. Eliezer Silver, *Conservative Judaism* 11 (Fall 1956): 52, and R. Yeḥiel Weinberg, *Seridei Esh* II (Jerusalem 1961): no. 12, p. 28a.

29. *See, for example,* Rachel Adler, "Tum'ah and Toharah, Ends and Beginnings," *The (First) Jewish Catalogue*, ed. Richard Siegel, M. Strassfeld, and S. Strassfeld (Philadelphia: JPS, 1973), 167–71, repr. in *Response* 18 (1973) = *The Jewish Woman: An Anthology*, ed. Liz Koltun (New York: Schocken, 1976), 117–27; and Aryeh Kaplan, *Waters of Eden* (New York: National Conference of Synagogue Youth, 1976). Both Adler and Kaplan defend, at least to some extent, the traditional system of menstrual taboos. For a more radical approach, *see, for example,* Penina Adelman, *Miriam's Well: Rituals for Jewish Women* (New York: Biblio Press, 1986).

Norma Baumel Joseph

MEHITZAH: HALAKHIC DECISIONS AND POLITICAL CONSEQUENCES

The separation of men and women in public places has a long and complicated history.[1] Biblical stories of women as singers, dancers, and mourners attest to their presence at communal events.[2] Other sources also indicate that women were participants at Temple public celebrations[3] (*see* Grossman, pp. 19ff.). The subject of this chapter is not the question of their presence but rather of their place in the synagogue, the place that has been the focus of public ceremonies since before the destruction of the Temple.

At present, a variety of seating arrangments exists, ranging from mixed pews to balconies and separate rooms. Many presume the separate seating model to be a replica of ancient patterns. However, as Professor Shmuel Safrai indicates, much more research must be done before anyone can conclusively date the use of a structural barrier between the sexes for the purpose of prayer.[4]

Of course, the absence of a *mehitzah* (barrier) does not automatically imply the existence of mixed seating. It could mean that men and women sat separately without a barrier or that no evidence of one remains. Others conclude that women did not attend synagogue.[5] However, since the evidence available does indicate that women frequently did attend services,[6] no absolute statement on seating arrangements is plausible. Whether its origin was in biblical, late antique, or medieval times, the *mehitzah* has become a symbol of denominational allegiances and policies in the twentieth century.[7] This chapter focuses on the debates in this century and on the use of ancient sources and texts to claim authority and legitimacy.

There was an *ezrat nashim* (Women's Court) in the Second Temple, according to rabbinic tradition. Men and women did congregate there. Talmudic references indicate that it became necessary to separate men and women for one specific celebration during Sukkot, namely, *Simhat Beit ha-Sho'evah* (the Water-Drawing Festival). The reasons given for this restriction or restructuring is the presence of *kalut rosh* (light headedness). The Sages understood this as frivolous or lewd behavior, the prevention of which becomes the key factor in later halakhic pronouncements and developments (*see* Grossman, pp. 22–37).

As clouded as the archaeological and historical records are, the halakhic issues are equally ambiguous. Questions remain about the requirement that the sexes be separated for prayer (with or without the *mehitzah*) as well as for all public occasions.[8] The wording of the Talmudic texts is unclear, and the codes nowhere explicitly require a *mehitzah*.[9] There is neither a direct prohibition nor a direct requirement; there are merely a few references to the *ezrat nashim*, indicating that there was such a thing.[10] Maimonides refers to the women's section in his compilation of laws dealing with the Temple and not in the section dealing with prayer and synagogue.[11] Other medieval texts specifically mention using a partition for public occasions such as the rabbi's lecture. The *Mordekhai*, a thirteenth-century German rabbinic authority, states specifically (Shab. 311) that a screen could be set up for such a purpose even on Shabbat. (One might question whether this permission to erect something on the Sabbath, an ordinarily forbidden act, might not indicate the absence of a permanent *mehitzah* in the synagogue.) It was not until the modern period, when the Reform Movement first removed the *mehitzah* and later instituted family pews, that responsa explicitly requiring a *mehitzah* for prayer services were written. Orthodox decisors today all agree that one can only pray in a synagogue with separate seating and a *mehitzah*. No matter what the historical record, the Temple pattern of that one day has thus been extended to the synagogue permanently.

The halakhic process surrounding this one issue involves many levels of interpretation, differential weighting of sources, a variety of reasons, and a serious difference of opinion concerning women's "disturbing" presence during prayer. In the last 150 years, the issue of a separation has taken on political overtones that impinge on the legal ones.

The legal questions raised are fascinating and begin with the ambiguous sources relied upon. The primary text is the Talmudic discussion of Mish. Suk. 5:2, which states that on *Simḥat Beit ha-Shoʾevah* they went into the *ezrat nashim* and made a great improvement (repair) or a major enactment (*u-matkinim sham tikkun gadol*).[12] There are other Mishnaic references such as Middot 2:5, and Sanh. 1:5, which add to the picture, but the Talmudic discussion in Suk. 51a,b–52a is the most elaborate (*see* Grossman, pp. 22–24).

What exactly was the "new enactment"? The legal decision to separate the men and women is clear in the Talmudic discussion in Suk. 51a–52a, but the questions as to how, why, and when remain. Was this reform, according to the Talmud, only for that one holiday, when levity reached a level that moral laxity was feared? Or does the Talmudic use of the text of Zech. 12:12–14,[13] which relates that men and women were separated for mourning, indicate a known policy on the separation of men and women? What is the legal relationship of that text to other biblical texts in which men and women mingle at public celebrations?[14] Furthermore, if men and women were separated for mourning, how is it that women still performed officially as wailers?[15] Is that text, then, extendable to all moments of holiness such as prayer? How did the Sages institute something new for the Temple? Even with the agreement of a special court of seventy-one,[16] how could any changes be made when 1 Chronicles contains the injunction *ha-kol be-khtav* (all this in writing),[17] which prohibits any change to the Temple structure? Given even that a physical structure is necessary, will only a balcony suffice? And finally, what does *kalut rosh* mean, what causes it, and are we to avoid it only during a prayer service?[18]

Consideration of all the above questions, plus other factors such as the equation of synagogue with Temple and the authority of biblical law versus rabbinic law, play a major role in the decision-making process of today's rabbinic authorities. Primary attention is given here to the responsa—*teshuvot*—of Rabbi Moses Feinstein, in an attempt to elucidate the halakhic process surrounding this one issue. As one of the major Orthodox rabbinic authorities of the twentieth century, his views and decisions on this issue are significant.

For Feinstein, separation of the sexes is mandatory and is *mi-de-oraita*—having biblical authority. He deals directly with *meḥitzah* in fourteen separate *teshuvot*. Many responsa in the collection *Igrot Moshe* (IM), the seven volumes of questions and answers authored by Feinstein, deal with the ways and means of separating men and women. For Feinstein, gender separation is essential in order to preserve biblically mandated morality. He strives to maintain this pattern in many different aspects of daily Jewish life, not just in the synagogue. For example, a large number of his decisions require separate schools for boys and girls, even at the primary level. Having taken such a consistently strong position on male-female separation, it is understandable that he will legislate a strict position on *meḥitzah*. It is interesting to focus on how he maintains the position, what sources he uses, what conditions he requires, and what leniencies he allows. Although he has a definite subjective position, he still must develop it through the traditional legal process, so that his use of sources, and the interpretations and emphases he uses to justify his position, become key signposts for us in understanding the role of the *meḥitzah* in American Orthodoxy. The need to stay within the legal parameters, to find halakhic precedents and decisions, and to respond to the social conditions of the community, create in his work a very interesting balance.

I hope this analysis is able to shed light on the halakhic process in the Orthodox world in general and, specifically, on how this particular issue has become the hallmark of the divisions that exist among American Jewry.

Orthodoxy's Biblical Basis for *Meḥitzah*

Underlying the argument is the Orthodox concern with change, with the ways and means of remaining traditional in a changing and disruptive world.[19] The perspective accepted is that the laws of God are immutable and therefore, Orthodoxy brooks "no change." This is the foundation of its argument with the Conservative and Reform Movements. It is precisely in this arena of synagogue structure that the argument has found its symbolic image. Orthodox synagogues maintain separate seating, whereas Conservative and Reform congregations allow men and women to sit together. Since the *meḥitzah* has become the physical symbol of the difference between Orthodox and non-Orthodox Judaism, the arguments for and against it have taken on quite serious implications.

In Feinstein's *meḥitzah* responsa, the argument has special significance, as it embraces three critical and fundamental themes: (1) the problem of change within Jewish legal categories, (2) the need to separate men and women, and (3) the relationship of his Jewish community to the world of Conservative and Reform Judaism. Given the underlying implications for Feinstein and for Orthodoxy, the arguments, and not just the decisions, are worthy of detailed analysis.

In brief, Feinstein's decision is not only that men and women must sit separately in the synagogue but also that there must be a wall, a *meḥitzah*, separating them—a wall that may not be less than, and is preferably higher than, sixty inches. A balcony is even better, as it provides the best defense against mingling and frivolous behavior. Finally, all this must be seen as emanating from the immutable law of Sinai, as derived from biblical texts.

Each piece of the above summation is repeated in several different responsa, but none is argued more uniquely than that the law is *mi-de-oraita*—of Torah authority.[20] The case for a biblical foundation is complicated and indirect. It is best seen in IM, Oraḥ Ḥayyim (OḤ) 1 : 39 and in the two articles (Hebrew and English) that appear in *The Sanctity of the Synagogue* by Baruch Litvin.[21] Feinstein uses the Talmudic source in Suk. 51a,b (which clearly states that the Sages instituted a great innovation) to prove that there was no change, that the separation of the sexes with a *meḥitzah* did not constitute a change from Temple practice. Even the balcony that was built on the second night of Sukkot is considered *mi-de-oraita;* though indirect or implied, for Feinstein, it is nonetheless immutable Torah law.

IM OḤ 1 : 39 is a remarkable text. In it, Feinstein struggles with two purposes: to issue a decision concerning *meḥitzah* and to clarify a complicated *gemara* text in such a manner that all the texts are harmonized so that there is no possibility of a dissenting opinion. He chooses the biblical statement from 1 Chronicles, "all this in writing"[22] to be the focal point of interpretation and the primary text to be developed. That text means that nothing in Temple practice, procedure, or structure can be changed, and that this principle rests on the absolute sanctity and authority of Scripture as understood by tradition. All possible relevant sources are then viewed as explicating and implementing that statement. In arguing for the conceptual unity of the Talmud and for the biblical basis of *mehitzah*, Feinstein indicates through both form and content the seriousness of this issue for him.

Given the clear biblical text forbidding changes to the physical structure of the Temple, and the absence of any special instructions to those in charge of the building, Feinstein reasons that there must have been a known requirement for a physical separation (IM OH 1 : 39). No rabbinic law or amendment could have overridden the injunction of 1 Chronicles (as is clarified in Hul. 83). He sees the *mehitzah* as "implicit in the verse as a pre-existing . . . Scriptural law." [23] In other words, it is *mi-de-oraita* by default. Only a Scriptural command could override the prohibition of change. Since the change was made, there must have been a known law. [24]

It becomes clear, then, that a balcony was necessary by original Biblical law, so that the women would be above and the men below, and then they would in no sense mingle or communicate. As the Mishnah states: [The wall of the women's court] was smooth at first, and then a balcony traversed its length, so that the women would see [the festivities] from above, and the men from below, and they would not be intermingled (Mid. 2 : 5). This proves that originally, though they were separated by an adequate *mechitzah*, they were considered as if commingling; such a situation violated Biblical law, which implicitly demanded, then, a balcony. [25]

The biblical source of the *mehitzah* is of such importance to Feinstein that he writes a separate letter to Litvin clarifying that the biblical law does not just prohibit mixed pews but prohibits prayer without a proper *mehitzah*. [26]

Why is Feinstein so insistent on the biblical base of the law when his Orthodox rabbinic colleagues do not make the same claims? It is possible to see the source of his claim in the ambiguous texts themselves. It is also possible to understand his perspective in twentieth-century America. His sense of the Jewish world is one of a world in chaos, losing its hold on tradition. He frequently makes disparaging comments about America, such as "in this country, because of our many sins. . . ." In that context, when a group of Jews appear—known as Conservatives—who change some of the rules, claiming their intent is to save Judaism and Jews, Feinstein needs to delegitimize their claims at every turn, especially in the realm of public synagogue practice. Therefore, it is important for him to show that they are violating Torah, i.e., biblical law, and not just rabbinic law. He also wishes to indicate to those who follow these leaders just how greatly they err. In the introduction to the Litvin essay, he assumes that many pray without a *meḥitzah* out of ignorance. He thus tries to impress upon them how serious is their straying and how obvious and sacred is the source forbidding this.

Having shown the biblical requirement of having a *meḥitzah* in the Temple, Feinstein argues that the extension of the *meḥitzah* to the synagogue is not just rabbinic, but has Torah authority also.[27] "Frivolity during prayer would then be proscribed by Scripture."[28] Feinstein's equation of Temple with synagogue is not new, as many rabbinic authorities (using the text of Meg. 29a) have so ruled.[29] What is new is his insistence on the biblical foundation of *meḥitzah* in synagogues. One questioner went so far as to imply that people enter synagogues for the purpose of *mitzvah* and therefore do not need separation. His response (IM OḤ 1:41) is that people entered the Temple in awe and for the purpose of *mitzvah,* and still, physical separation was required. Both synagogue and Temple are equatable in function and, therefore, in structure.

He then must clarify what kind of structure. The Temple had a balcony, and that is therefore preferable (IM OḤ 2:43). Interestingly, he does not make any case for the transferability from balcony to partition. Somehow he assumes that it is permissible to use a partition, and he writes many *teshuvot* on their required height, though not on their permissibility. The minimum height required, as indicated in Shab. 92a (*see* Rashi and *Tosafot, ad. loc.*) is three *amot* or eighteen *tefaḥim* (handbreadths).[30] Feinstein rules that five and one-half feet, or sixty-five inches, is a satisfactory translation of those ancient measurements (IM OḤ 3:23, 4:31). However, because we live in difficult times, Feinstein allows himself the leniency to use the solitary opinion of Rashbam (BB 100b) that requires only seventeen *tefaḥim.* Thus, he permits sixty inches (IM OḤ 3:23, 4:29–31) and in one place even allows fifty-eight inches because women are shorter(!) today (IM OḤ 3:24).[31]

For Feinstein, the whole discussion of height is intelligible only in the context of the reasons given for separation. If we know why we must sep-

arate—what it is the separation must prevent—then the decisor can respond accordingly. The most intricate part of this whole approach lies in
his understanding of why: why the Bible requires a *meḥitzah*.

Kalut rosh, translated as frivolity, is the forbidden state. Feinstein
claims that frivolity occurs when people are able to talk, to communicate
in any fashion (IM OḤ 1:39). The partition must therefore be high
enough to prevent the communication and mingling that bring with them
frivolity (IM OḤ 1:41). Both verbal and physical contact are classified as
mingling and are, therefore, forbidden (IM OḤ 3:23).

Feinstein further explains that these acts are matters of public behavior, recognizable (*nikar*), and thus of a different genre from other experiences that require separation (IM OḤ 1:40). In fact, he is very careful to
distinguish the laws of *meḥitzah* from other laws that appear similar but
are due to reasons of personal moral laxity such as those that fall into the
category of *ervah* (nakedness, *see* below) or *yiḥud* (the prohibition that
man and woman, other than husband and wife, not have the opportunity
for intimacy). *Meḥitzah*, he insists, is not required to prevent men from
seeing women.[32] "The obligation of the *meḥitzah* is due to frivolity and not
gazing" (IM OḤ 1:40). Therefore, a glass partition fulfills the legal requirements of a *meḥitzah*—though perhaps not of *ervah* (IM OḤ 1:43,
3:23). A balcony, which inherently prevents mingling, does not require a
partition such as a curtain to block the view of the men (IM OḤ 1:41).
His reasoning is quite consistent and rests on the Talmudic discussion of
the seating arrangements in the Temple. At first the men were outside and
the women were inside. Then the men were inside and, according to
Feinstein, unable to see the women, but there was still a problem with
levity that required the balcony.

And so, if women are on an upper level, even without a screen or curtain, or if
they are below, but behind a veritable, high *mechitzah*, so that there be no fear of
levity, it is of no consequence if the women are visible.[33]

In a series of responsa, Feinstein examines the prohibition involved in
looking at women. The laws of *ervah* prohibit a man from looking at a
woman if his intent is to receive pleasure; but intent is not the only determining characteristic. Equally important is the nature of the exposed
area. If it is a part of the body that is usually covered, then it is prohibited
for a man to look and he cannot pray under such circumstances. On the
other hand, if women usually appear with this area uncovered, then it is

not *ervah*, and prayer is not prevented. The Talmud warns that the hair of a woman contains an erotic element that requires covering.[34] The same is true for a woman's shoulders and arms. For Feinstein, as well as for a significant segment of Orthodox Jewry, these warnings have been translated into a specific dress code. A married woman must cover arms and hair. Problems arise, however, in pinning down the legal consequences of these warnings. Even though he wants married women to cover their hair at all times, especially in the synagogue (IM OḤ 4:32), he rules that it is permissible to pray, to say the *Shema*, and hear the Torah read even if men can see the uncovered hair of married women (IM OḤ 1:42). Since it is not the custom of women today to cover their hair, it cannot be considered *ervah* or nakedness. Hence, the *meḥitzah* can be shoulder height, covering the arm and shoulder areas that are still *ervah*, but allowing for the visibility of hair.

The legal decision in this case is determined to a degree by public custom. Looking at women, deriving pleasure from that act, involves a personal code of modesty and license and affects men and women differently. *Meḥitzah* applies to public behavior and to men and women equally (IM OḤ 1:43). Though he prefers that men never look at women, he rules that female visibility does not enter into the category of *kalut rosh* and that *erva* is not the reason for *meḥitzah* (IM OḤ 1:40). Despite his preferences, Feinstein will not allow anyone to confuse the issues or to argue for *meḥitzah* on the wrong grounds.

Though halakhic flexibility and leniency emerge from careful definitions and separation of issues, Feinstein is not satisfied with the minimum standard. His ideal design forbids all forms of contact between the sexes, either visual or verbal. Thus, after stating that visibility does not prevent prayer, he is quick to add that it is best to be strict and have a high *meḥitzah* that will prevent all visibility (IM OḤ 1:40). He is especially careful to warn all those who are capable of higher standards, the "God fearers," to look away and never gaze at women (IM OḤ 1:40, 42; 4:29). To reinforce his division between minimal practices and the preferred ideal, he always prefaces statements of acceptance of lowered standards with such expressions as: "because of our many sins," "in extremis," "in this country," "in our day." He is not an idealist, although he presents an ideal standard. He does not like the exigencies of daily living, but he understands and writes with practical concerns.

In one case dealing with separate seating without a *meḥitzah*, his decision indicates his constant practical approach combined with his view that there are layers of possible, preferred, and prescribed patterns. Thus, he rules that mixed seating is a graver sin than prayer without a partition but with separate seating (IM OḤ 1:44).[35] He reasons that if people transgress a minor law, they should not be encouraged or allowed to transgress in a more serious arena. In fact, he claims that the proper procedure is to convince a mixed seating congregation to at least sit separately. This is the first and only indication that, for Feinstein, separate seating is a more serious matter than *meḥitzah*.

Separation Between Orthodox and Conservative or Reform Judaism

In this matter, as in many others, Feinstein's approach is that if the ideal is not possible, we must do what we can. In one related area, however, he insists on a consistent standard. One must not pray or attend any service in a non-Orthodox congregation.[36] A synagogue that is Conservative is considered a community of *kofrim* (deniers), even if they do not know any better. He extends this category to Reform congregations and rabbis in other responsa. It is therefore forbidden to pray in their building (IM OḤ 4:91, sec. 6). Even if they establish a special room with an acceptable *meḥitzah* for those who wish it, it is still forbidden to pray there (IM OḤ 2:40). Feinstein argues that one must not do anything that will bring suspicion (*ḥashad*) upon one's self, nor do anything whose appearance might be misinterpreted, thereby leading others astray (*marit ʿayin*). Entering the building of such a synagogue falls into these categories. If someone is seen entering a Conservative synagogue, he or she will be suspected of being Conservative or will lead others astray by example. In his terms, the non-Orthodox synagogue benefits both financially and morally, as it can claim that it satisfies all needs. For both halakhic and social reasons, then, Feinstein prohibits praying in such a room, even if it has a proper *meḥitzah*. However, if the same arrangment exists but the synagogue in question considers itself Orthodox, he permits praying in a separate room with a *meḥitzah* (IM OḤ 4:91, sec. 6). If the Orthodox congregation uses a microphone or does not have a proper partition (and there are some), the members are not considered *kofrim*. They have accepted the *mitzvot* and are just disrespectful in this one area. Avoidance is therefore not required.

Intent and motive play a significant role in his halakhic scenario in general, but especially so in *meḥitzah* cases. The *meḥitzah* must separate men from women and Orthodox from non-Orthodox Jews.[37] Anyone who tampers with this division comes under suspicious scrutiny. His or her motives might stem from a desire to cross these sacred boundaries. Even if the act might be halakhically permissible, it becomes forbidden in this context of interdenominational polemics.

Women, even those who keep the commandments, fall under suspicion when they ask for any change in this arena. Thus, when a group of women requested a change from a balcony to a kosher *meḥitzah* on the main floor, Feinstein prohibited it. He explains in his responsum that we know (*nikar*) that the women really want mixed seating, and this is only the first part of their campaign. The claim of the women that they find climbing the stairs difficult is quickly discounted as an untruth. He states that the women would willingly climb the stairs for physical pleasure. If they were acting "for the sake of heaven," there would be no difficulty.[38] He insists that the women only wish to change the traditions of the people, and that is forbidden (IM OḤ 2:43). Since the attributed motive is unacceptable, the act becomes illegal.

There is no evidence as to why Feinstein discredits the women's request. He neither provides halakhic evidence for this decision nor explains why he assumes the women have "wrong" motives. The responsum is very brief, a statement of opinion rather than a legal brief with precedents. In fact, he mentions that for legitimate reasons the change can of course be made. More space for the women might be such a legitimate reason. The rabbi's job security is another acceptable justification. If he might lose his job, then Feinstein allows the change that is, after all, well within halakhic requirements. Earning a living does not excuse all, but it is a powerful alibi. In a different case, Feinstein permits a man who is a cantor in a Conservative synagogue to write a *get* (Jewish bill of divorce). He has transgressed, he has prayed in a place of mixed seating with a microphone, but only in order to earn a living. The category of *kofer* can only be applied to one who knowingly and willfully denies God. Feinstein does not give him permission to remain in his post, but he does declare him a kosher scribe (IM Even ha-Ezer 2:20).

In those cases where he assumes that the intention of the individual or group is to transgress the law, in open defiance of God and Torah, Feinstein is very harsh in his condemnation and his decision is on the strict side. However, when he assumes the practice in question is the result of ignorance or economic need, and not rebellion, then he writes a careful and detailed responsum whose purpose is to educate and set the record straight. In such cases there is room for leniency. Some changes are permitted, some motives are acceptable; those that appear to breach sacred borders are quickly denied.

Feinstein's purpose is to promote and preserve Jewish separateness. Separation of the sexes is part of his strategy. Part of it also involves separating the elite "God fearers," those capable of extra effort, from ordinary Jews.[39] For Feinstein, the most significant battle is waged to separate not Jew from non-Jew, but Orthodox Jews from Conservative and Reform Jews. The *mehitzah* is the symbol of this separation and the focus of this battle. Feinstein's commitment to the *mehitzah*—and in this he is typical of all Orthodoxy—is also part of his campaign against all things Conservative or Reform.[40] Truly, the *mehitzah* is the "great divide," separating male from female, elite from ordinary, and Orthodox from Conservative and Reform.

For the past 150 years, all Orthodox responsa have consistently maintained the *mehitzah* requirement.[41] In Europe, when the Reform Movement removed the *mehitzah* while still retaining separate seating, the response of Orthodox rabbis was swift and condemning.[42] However, when the Reform Movement instituted mixed pews in America, the Orthodox Movement for the most part ignored the action and kept to itself.[43] On the other hand, when the Conservative Movement moved to change seating patterns a generation later, the Orthodox entered the debate. Between the two World Wars, some Conservative congregations began to be built without separations. Though one of the two synagogues at the Conservative Movement's Jewish Theological Seminary continues to have separate seating, it is not the policy of most member congregations. By 1955, Marshal Sklare could write that mixed seating was the practice in the majority of Conservative congregations.[44]

It was not until the 1950s that the debate became a central focus of the denominational divisions, and stands that were taken became frozen principles of faith.[45] For Conservative Jews, the mixed pews were accepted as the way of the people that did not require formal responsa. According to the Conservative Movement's position, the absence of a codified requirement for *mehitzah* allowed for re-evaluation. Therefore, "No official responsum has ever been issued to justify this move."[46] Robert Gordis, a professor at the Jewish Theological Seminary, explained that this was a real case of custom overcoming tradition:

No halakhist has thus far been able to validate the family pew from traditional sources, nor has it ever been adopted as a *tagganah* by a recognized rabbincal body. The tacit surrender of the segregation of the sexes in synagogues of all tendencies is another example of *minhag* triumphing over accepted law. In this instance, it is *minhag America.*[47]

Certainly, the Orthodox polemic against the Conservative community points to this absence of responsa permitting mixed seating. In Orthodox terms, the Conservative stance remains illegitimate and unjustified. On the other hand, from the Conservative point of view, there are no recorded laws specifying the *meḥitzah* in ancient times; "if a prohibition is not specifically mentioned and promulgated as such by the Talmud or Codes, the restriction is, at best, a *minhag* or local ordinance of regional validity."[48]

The halakhic issue aside, the debate became one of denominational polemic that reached its peak in the 1950s in America.[49] At that time, there were Orthodox congregations that had mixed seating. The Orthodox Movement's Yeshiva University even allowed rabbinical students to accept posts in mixed seating congregations, with the hope that they would influence their congregants to change. Both those practices are no longer permitted.[50]

Legal battles were fought in the 1950s in America, as Jews used the civil courts to force one or the other practice.[51] One of the most famous cases was the Mt. Clemens case, in which one man, Baruch Litvin, sued his congregation for depriving him of his rights by changing the seating to mixed pews. The court ruled in his favor and the *meḥitzah* remained. This case was an important element in the hardening of the Orthodox position.[52] Litvin collected various rabbinic sources, statements, and responsa in the book, previously cited, *The Sanctity of the Synagogue*. Though Orthodox responsa forbidding mixed pews had been written before, after the publication of Litvin's volume, all Orthodoxy became defined by this one practice. Today, an Orthodox congregation is largely defined by the presence of a partition.

The *Meḥitzah* as a Symbol of Communal Allegiance

The *meḥitzah* is now the symbol of one's communal allegiance. Therefore, the debate today over women's place and position in synagogue practice is seen as threatening the denominational borders that were drawn by the *mehitzah* debate. In this context, Feinstein's suspicion of the women's motives regarding the balcony becomes understandable, if not acceptable. "Ultimately, observance of the law becomes secondary to correct ideology and political loyalty." [53] The debate is, of course, voiced in legal rhetoric, but the conflict is political. Feinstein and most of his Orthodox collegues wish to suppress pluralism within the Jewish world. The question remains; why is the *mehitzah*—which restrains women and even removes them visibly—the issue chosen through which to supress pluralism? [54] There are, of course, other areas of conflict and dispute. Thus, in one responsum (IM OH 1 : 104), Feinstein forbids a *Bat Mitzvah* because the idea comes from the Conservative Movement. Thus, the opposition to things non-Orthodox is the determinant, but in the process, women are effectively suppressed.

Furthermore, problems arise with the reasoning process underlying the debate, and also with the attitudes the *mehitzah* appears to engender. Does *mehitzah* indicate that women are irrelevant to the service? The men's section is called the *beit knesset,* the synagogue, by Feinstein. This usage also occurs consistently in Litvin's book. [55] Is the *ezrat nashim* not in the *beit knesset?* Are women too distracting to the men? What about men being distracting to the women? Feinstein and his colleagues would be quick to deny any attributions of secondary status to women. In fact, Feinstein insists that seeing and distraction are not the primary problems; however, he does prefer that men should not look at women. And even though he claims *mehitzah* applies equally to men and women, he is only concerned about men looking at women. So the problem remains that the *mehitzah*, though not necessarily established to limit women [56] nor to treat them as irrelevant or secondary, nonetheless sometimes leads to these ends.

As a great divide, *mehitzah* would appear to be the restricting factor in women's participation in synagogue life. This is not necessarily so. It is possible to construct a synagogue such as the Hebrew Institute of Riverdale, New York, wherein the partition splits the room exactly in half. The women have theoretical access to both the *bimah* and the ark. This structure would appear to fit Feinstein's perspective of *mehitzah* being a communal obligation equal for men and women. Under such circumstances, it is possible to speak of women sitting separately as Jews before God—on their own, not as adjuncts to the men in their lives—protected from the distractions of any male presence. The laws and customs that limit women do not result from the requirement of a *meḥitzah*. Restrictions on women's ability to be called to the Torah or to serve as prayer leaders are derived from other laws and customs (*see* Haut, p. 137). However, *meḥitzah* has become the symbol of women's limited participation.

As the separation of men and women became linked with political ideology and practice, the limits on women's participation appear to have increased. The great divide stands as Feinstein envisioned it: Separating men and women, elite from ordinary, and Orthodox Jews from Conservative and Reform Jews.

Notes

1. Louis Epstein, *Sex Laws and Customs in Judaism* (New York: KTAV, 1967 [1948]), chap. 3, 67–103.

2. Miriam led the women in song and dance, Exod. 15:20, 21; Deborah sang her song of victory to the assembled armies, Judg. 5; Hannah prayed in the Sanctuary, 1 Sam. 1; women were professional public mourners, Jer. 9:16; women participated in the choral services of the Temple, Ezra 2:65.

3. Women were included in the public reading of the Bible, known as *Hakhel*, Kid. 34a; they were present at *Simḥat Beit ha-Shoʾevah, see infra;* they were permitted to participate in the laying on of hands (*sʾmikhah*), part of the sacrificial ritual, Ḥag. 16b; and women were obligated to participate in the Passover sacrificial meal, Pes. 91b. *See* S. Berman, "The Status of Women in Halakhic Judaism," *Tradition* 14 (Fall 1973) 5–28, for interesting examples of women's obligations.

4. S. Safrai, "Was there an *Ezrat Nashim* in the Ancient Synagogue?" (in Hebrew), *Tarbiz,* 32 (1963): 329–38. The Talmud records the use of different types of temporary partitions—jugs and reeds—that were used when men and women gathered (Kid. 81a: Abaye made a partition of jugs; Raba made a partition of canes; trans. H. Freedman, London: Soncino Press, 1966). *The Sanctity of the Synagogue,* ed. B. Litvin (New York: Litvin, 1962), 231; the editor cites sources claiming that these barriers were used to separate men and women other than in the synagogue, implying that there was always a permanent *meḥitzah* for prayers. The Talmud, however, is unclear as to when these barriers were used and nowhere specifies the use of a partition for prayer. Even Litvin (ibid., 230) must include the reference from *The Jewish Encyclopedia* (1916) that there is no mention in "the old sources" of the separation of the sexes in the synagogue and that the archaeological record is obscure on this point. Epstein, *Sex Laws,* 81, argues that the temporary barriers were in use only when the synagogue was used for a general public assembly, at which times women came in large numbers. He claims that they were not used for regular worship, as women did not frequently attend. However, there are many sources that indicate women did attend services and were active in synagogue life; for example, *see* B. Brooten, *Women Leaders in the Ancient Synagogue* (California: Scholars Press, 1982). *See also* n.6 *infra.* Cf. Grossman, pp. 22–29.

5. Litvin, *The Sanctity,* 225.

6. TB Ber. 17a; TB Sot. 22a; Lev. R. 9:9; Sofrim 18:6. Solomon Schechter, "Women in

Temple and Synagogue," in *Studies in Judaism*, vol. 1 (Philadelphia: JPS, 1911), 313–25. Cf. Safrai, pp. 39–49.

7. Jonathan Sarna, "The Debate Over Mixed Seating in the American Synagogue," in *The American Synagogue; A Sanctuary Transformed*, ed. J. Wertheimer (New York: Cambridge University Press, 1987), 363–94.

8. Litvin, *The Sanctity*, 139–40. Some of the rabbis treat the requirement for separate seating differently than the requirement for a *meḥitzah*. Rabbi J. B. Soloveitchik claims that separate seating is a "Pentateuchal injunction" (*issur de-oraita*), having Divine provenance, while a *meḥitzah* is only a rabbinic ordinance. This article by Rabbi Soloveitchik is a reprint of a letter to Rabbi Lapidus, originally published in *Conservative Judaism*, vol. 11 (Fall, 1956): 50–51. As we shall see later, Rabbi Feinstein does not accept such a bifurcation of the law.

9. Litvin, *The Sanctity*, 145, 167.

10. Medieval European synagogues definitely had a separate women's section, frequently called the *Weibershul*. This area, sometimes a room or annex, was so separate that some women, called *firzogerin*, would lead the others in prayer. The communities in Worms and Frankfurt built separate buildings for the women. EncJud, s.v. "*meḥitzah*" and ibid., 192, 226.

11. Cited in Litvin, *The Sanctity*, 98, 209.

12. The word *tikkun* might simply refer to a physical alteration, a repair. It might also imply a major halakhic enactment.

13. "And the land shall mourn, every family apart: The family of the house of David apart, and their wives apart; . . . All the families that remain, every family apart, and their wives apart" (Zech. 12:12–14).

14. 2 Sam. 6:22; Exod. 15:20; Judg. 16:27, 21:21; Jer. 31:12.

15. Jer. 9:16. Women as official wailers raises interesting questions about the prohibition of *kol ishah*, the voice of a woman. 2 Chron. 35:25 also lists women as official singers at funerals.

16. Sanh. 1:5. According to legislative procedure, no additions could be made to the city or the courts of the Temple without a *Beit Din* (court) of seventy-one Sages. It is unclear whether a balcony would require such a rabbinic process or whether it was part of the original plan.

17. 1 Chron. 28:19. "All this in writing, as the Lord hath made me wise by His hand upon me even all the works of this pattern."

18. The literal meaning is light headedness, but different decisors vary on the conditions that bring it about, from gazing to physical mingling.

19. Many studies confirm this concern, such as: D. Ellenson, "Jewish Legal Interpretation: Literary, Social and Ethical Perspective," *Semeia* 34 (1985), 93–114; J. Gurock, "Resistors and Accomodators: Varieties of Orthodox Rabbis in America, 1886–1983," *American Jewish Archives* 35, (Oct. 1983), 100–130; Norma Joseph, "The Traditional Denial of Change: Women's Place in the World of Rabbi Moses Feinstein," *Journal of Religion and Culture* 2 (1987), 190–201; I. Robinson, "Because of Our Many Sins," *Judaism* 35 (1986), 35–46. In Litvin, *The Sanctity*, 43, Saul Bernstein claims that the Oral Torah is "unchanging and unchangeable. . . ."

20. *Mi-de-oraita* is best translated as having the authority of Torah. Many scholars use the words biblical, Scriptural, or Pentateuchal as acceptable translations. However, there is a definite difference between the concept *mi-de-oraita* and the genre of the written Torah, *Torah she-be-khtav*. They are not necessarily equatable. Rabbi Feinstein uses the word *mi-de-oraita*. Although the English translators in Litvin's book, *The Sanctity*, use the word bibli-

cal, I think it is not justified. The words do not necessarily have to be written in Scripture in order to have the authority of Torah as long as they are derived from the Bible. For Feinstein, separate seating with a *meḥitzah* is derived from the Bible, though it does not explicitly say so. Rather, he presents a long argument to prove that *meḥitzah* is implied in the Torah and, therefore, can qualify as *mi-de-oraita*. In the process, Feinstein adds a new mode of *mi-de-oraita* by allowing the later part of the Bible and not just the Pentateuch to provide the source for this category. I am indebted to Jack Lightstone for this clarification.

21. *See* n.4.

22. *See* n.17.

23. Feinstein, in Litvin, *The Sanctity*, 120.

24. Alan Yuter also describes Feinstein's reasoning and originality on this issue. "Mehitsa, Midrash and Modernity: A Study in Religious Rhetoric," *Judaism*, 28 (1979): 152.

25. Feinstein, in Litvin, *The Sanctity*, 122.

26. Feinstein, ibid. 125.

27. Feinstein, ibid. 124; cf. R. Nessim in his novellae to Meg. fol 26; TB Meg. 29a.

28. Feinstein, in Litvin, *The Sanctity*, 124.

29. Ibid., 98, 169−73.

30. An *amah* (pl. *amot*) is an ancient measurement. Translated as a cubit or an ell, it measures between 446−521 mm. (EncJud, s.v. "Weights and Measures.") Feinstein takes it to be approximately 22 inches.

31. This statement is not based on any empirical evidence but rather derives from his acceptance of a twofold meaning for the word *gadol*—great, large. The ancients were *gedolim,* greater than we are today. We are less in stature, both spiritually and physically. It is unusual for a play on words to have halakhic consequences, although distinctions based on physical differences between "now" and "then" is a consistent Orthodox strategy.

32. There are others who claim that viewing women is part of the problem, e.g., Rabbi Aaron Kotler in Litvin, *The Sanctity*, 125−39.

33. Feinstein, in Litvin, ibid., 123.

34. TB Ber. 24a; EH 21 : 2; OḤ 75 : 2.

35. In this he comes closer to the ruling of Rabbi Soloveitchik (*see* n.8 *supra*) who differentiates between separate seating, without a partition, and segregated seating, with a *meḥitzah.* For both of them, separate seating is a grave matter that cannot be overturned under any conditions.

36. Rabbi Soloveitchik also takes an uncompromising position on prayer in a Conservative or Reform synagogue. He rules that it is preferable to pray alone, even on Yom Kippur, than to enter a synagogue where there is no separation (Litvin, *The Sanctity,* 110).

37. Feinstein restricts contact with Conservative or Reform institutions in a number of responsa. He even forbids answering "amen" to a Conservative rabbi's blessing. IM OḤ 2 : 50, 51; OḤ 3 : 21, 22. *See* Robinson, "Because of Our Many Sins," pp. 40−41.

38. This is consistent with other rulings concerning women's increased ritual participation. If they were righteous women, their motives would be for the sake of heaven, and therefore, the acts that are nowhere forbidden, would be permitted. OḤ 4 : 49, and a responsum written with his approval by his grandson, 4 Sivan 5743; unpublished. (*See* Haut, p. 146, n.1b.)

39. Robinson, "Because of Our Many Sins," 38.

40. Ibid., 40−41, 44. Yuter, "Mehizah, Midrash and Modernity," 153−54.

41. Litvin, *The Sanctity,* chap. 2, 147, includes letters from many representative groups within Orthodoxy as well as the statements of Chief Rabbi Isaac Halevi Herzog, Rabbi

Abraham Isaac Kook, Rabbi Joseph B. Soloveitchik, Rabbi Moshe Feinstein, and Rabbi Aaron Kotler. "One could go on, page after page, enumerating all the similar responsa, without a single dissenting orthodox legal opinion, which appeared over the last 150 years" (Litvin, 147).

42. Litvin, *The Sanctity,* chap. 3, pp. 142–220, especially pp. 193, 198. The sharpest condemnations of the Reform Movement in the nineteenth century came from Maharam Schick, Ḥatam Sofer, and Rabbi Eliyahu Guttmacher.

43. David and Tamar De Sola Pool, *Old Faith in a New World* (New York: Columbia University Press, 1955), 100. Toward the end of the nineteenth century there was an unsuccessful movement in Shearith Israel, the leading Sephardic synagogue in New York, to remove the balcony and institute family pews. Many women protested against such radical innovations.

44. Cited in Sarna, "The Debate Over Mixed Seating," 380.

45. Ibid., 378. Sarna commented: "In time, 'separate seating' and 'mixed seating' became shorthand statements, visible expressions of differences on a host of more fundamental issues that lay beneath the surface." His article offers an excellent analysis of the history of mixed seating in the American synagogue.

46. Lawrence Kaplan, "The Dilemma of Conservative Judaism," *Commentary* (Nov. 1976): 145.

47. R. Gordis, "Seating in the Synagogue: Minhag America," *Judaism,* 36 (1987): 53.

48. Yuter, "Mehizah, Midrash and Modernity," 151. The Conservative position is presented in a special edition of the journal, *Conservative Judaism* 11 (1956).

49. The debate continues to split congregations to this day.

50. Litvin, *The Sanctity,* 340–41; Rabbi Soloveitchik states that even though some members of the Rabbinical Council of America occupy pulpits in congregations with "improper seating arrangements," it is still against *halakhah.* Ibid., 141. *See also* N. Lamm's article in ibid., 311–38.

51. Sarna, "The Debate Over Mixed Seating," 381–86, has shown that in the Reform and Conservative Movements the issue of *meḥitzah* was presented on the basis of family togetherness, women's equality, and the modernity of Judaism. In the Orthodox world, the debate focused on a dissociation from all things Reform and Conservative, which were seen as ultimately being imitations of church patterns.

52. Lawrence Schiffman, "When Women and Men Sit Together in American Orthodox Synagogues," *Moment,* 14:7 (Dec. 1989); 48–49.

53. Yuter, "Mehizah, Midrash and Modernity," 158.

54. Sarna notes that only American Orthodoxy defines itself by the *meḥitzah.* British Orthodoxy separates itself from the non-Orthodox world through its position on mixed choirs, German Orthodoxy on the use of an organ, and Hungarian Orthodoxy on the position of the pulpit. Ibid., Wertheimer, *The American Synagogue,* p. 394, n.109.

55. *See* n.4 *supra.*

56. The pattern of separation of the sexes might be embedded in social etiquette and would not necessarily indicate a desire to limit women for fear of their sexuality. *See* Epstein, *Sex Laws and Customs,* chap. 3, pp. 69–83.

Rivka Haut

WOMEN'S PRAYER GROUPS AND THE ORTHODOX SYNAGOGUE

Women's *tefillah* (prayer) groups, developed and organized by Orthodox women, have set the "Torah world" in turmoil. They have been discussed, and denounced, in virtually every major rabbinic journal and periodical,[1] banned in sermons from the pulpits of major Orthodox synagogues, and proclaimed by rabbinic responsa to be against Jewish law. Yet they grow, proliferate, and are thriving. Although only about fifteen years old, the women's *tefillah* movement is becoming a permanent part of Jewish life.

Women's *tefillah* groups are communities of women who meet regularly, usually once or twice a month, to pray together. Sometimes they meet for Shabbat *minḥah* (afternoon prayers, during which a Torah portion is read); sometimes for *Rosh Ḥodesh* (the New Moon); and, most often, on Shabbat mornings. They conduct a full service, with the exception of prayers for which a *minyan* of men is necessary, which are therefore omitted. The prayer groups conduct a complete Torah and *haftarah* reading. Men are not present. In the absence of men, women are halakhically permitted to lead prayers, to receive Torah honors, and to read from a Torah scroll.

To comprehend the significance of women's *tefillah* groups, it is necessary to understand the role of women in the Orthodox synagogue.

Women and the Orthodox Synagogue

An Orthodox synagogue is immediately recognizable as such. This is true not only of a small *"shteibel"* located in a private house and filled with praying Ḥasidim, but also of a large "centrist" (modern Orthodox) synagogue with its own building, hundreds of congregants, a rabbi, a cantor, and perhaps even a choir. What immediately marks these synagogues as Orthodox is the fact that women and men are separated by a physical barrier, a *meḥitzah*. The *meḥitzah* may be a partition that is ten feet high, or it may be camouflaged as a decoration, for example, as flower pots or plants. Often it is a balcony, or even a separate room. Whatever type of separation, it is clear that the men's area is the center of activity, and the women are on the periphery.[2]

Sometimes the *meḥitzah* cuts the women off from any possible connection with the services by severely limiting their ability to see, or even to hear, what is taking place. This fact has been recognized by the renowned authority Ḥafetz Ḥayyim (d. 1933). In speaking of the obligation of women to hear the *Megillah* read on Purim, he states: ". . . [I]n some places it is customary that they [women] go to the synagogue to the women's gallery to hear the reading, and this requires study as to how the women there can fulfill their obligation because it is impossible to hear there as is required?"[3]

Even in those synagogues where women are able to hear and have visual access to the *bimah,* their presence is not recognized in any meaningful way. None will receive any synagogue honors, none will be called to the Torah, none will be a rabbi, cantor, or choir member. The presence of a *Bat Mitzvah* girl, or a bride, or a mother of a *Bar Mitzvah* boy, will not be reflected or acknowledged in the religious ritual.[4] It makes no practical difference if hundreds of women are present, or if none are there, for they have no active role in any part of the service.

Today the exclusion of women from all public participation in the prayer service is not because women are considered inferior to men, nor because they are believed to have lesser spiritual needs. The passive role of women in the normative Orthodox synagogue has been defined by *halakhah,* classical Jewish law, as reflecting the assignment of different religious obligations to women and men.

Women are obligated to pray daily (*see* I. Haut, p. 92 and Hauptman,

p. 162), but their prayer obligation is private in nature. The Bible is replete with examples of women who prayed and who even composed prayers. Deborah the judge, for example, wrote a song of praise.[5] The Talmud contains the statement that many laws regarding prayer are illustrated by the story of Hannah and the manner in which she prayed.[6] Orthodox women have always been devout; they take their prayer obligations seriously (*see, for example,* Gelernter-Liebowitz, p. 240). However, they tend to leave the public aspects of prayer such as synagogue attendance to men.

According to classical Jewish law, a *minyan,* which is the minimum requirement for public prayer and public Torah reading, is made up of ten adult male Jews. The rabbis derived this number from a close examination and comparison of biblical texts,[7] which they interpreted to mean that women, as well as minors and slaves,[8] could not be counted in a *minyan.* The rabbis never definitively stated exactly why they excluded women from the obligation of public prayer, and many reasons have been offered. According to some, the rabbis did not want to burden women, who were subservient to their husbands' wishes, to have to attend to their Creator at regular and specific times, because that might interfere with their husbands' needs.[9] According to others, women's sphere of activity should be limited to the home as much as possible.[10] Whatever the reason behind the *halakhah,* the *halakhah* is definitive. Women may not be counted in a *minyan.*[11]

As women are not obligated in public prayer, they cannot lead public prayer; one who is not obligated cannot perform the obligation for those who are.[12] For example, since a woman is not obligated to say the *Kedushah* prayer, she cannot lead men in saying that prayer, for if ten men are present, they are obligated, while she is not. (A prayer leader may discharge the prayer obligations of those who hear him and pray together with him, particularly if they do not know how to pray, and merely answer amen.) Furthermore, women are not permitted to lead prayers for men because of the prohibition of *kol ishah,* which means that a man may not listen to a woman's voice, for this might lead to his sexual arousal (*see* Taitz, p. 61).[13] Therefore, according to classical Jewish law, women are not permitted to serve as cantors nor as prayer leaders. Neither may they sing in a synagogue choir.

One element of public prayer services is the reading of a Torah portion. The Torah is read on Sabbath mornings and afternoons, on Mondays and Thursdays, on New Moons, and on holidays and fast days.[14] This public Torah reading (and *haftarah* reading as well) was ordained by Ezra the Scribe, so that Jews should not go for more than three days without hearing words of Torah. It is a public obligation, incumbent upon the community. Because of its public nature, women are not obligated to hear the readings[15] and may not read for men, who are obligated. Therefore, women do not read from the Torah (nor do they chant *haftarah*) in Orthodox synagogues.

Women in Orthodox synagogues do not receive *aliyot*. In the distant past, one who received an *aliyah* was expected to actually read the Torah portion.[16] Although being called to the Torah no longer means that one is expected to read from it, and the Talmud says that women are included in the seven *aliyot* for Shabbat, yet women are not called because of "*kavod ha-tzibbur*," the honor of the congregation.[17] If women were called, the congregation might be embarrassed because this would imply that not enough men know how to read. (The fact that today almost every synagogue has a special Torah reader, the "*baʿal koreh*," has not affected the custom of not honoring women with *aliyot*.) Therefore, in Orthodox synagogues today, women are never called up to the Torah.

Women are not accepted as students in any Orthodox rabbinical seminary, and they are not ordained as rabbis. Since they cannot serve as rabbis, it is extremely rare for a woman to deliver a speech during services, as this is generally the prerogative of the rabbi.[18]

In short, women in Orthodox synagogues cannot be heard, either as individuals, or as a group. They cannot perform any ritual act in that setting—they do not even open the ark, an act that requires neither speaking nor being called by name. They are able to pray along with the congregation and to hear the Torah reading, but they remain private participants, like playgoers who, although absorbed in the action and perhaps even singing along with the music, allow the actors to direct the activity.

The marginal status of women in the Orthodox synagogue has often been explained by referring to the place of women in the ancient Temple. Rabbi Herschel Schachter, an Orthodox scholar, has expressed the view held by many rabbis and scholars that the women's sections of synagogues correspond to the "*Ezrat Nashim*" of the Temple and, as such, their ". . . degree of holiness is lesser than that of the *main* part of the synagogue . . ." (italics added).[19] It is clear that, for him, the synagogue is rightfully the domain of men, the women's section being of secondary significance (*see* Grossman, p. 16).

Need for Women's Prayer Groups

Over the centuries, Jewish women seem, for the most part, to have accepted their role in the synagogue. There is no record of any group of Orthodox women demanding *aliyot;* there does not seem to have ever been a rebellion about this matter. Women found other outlets, outside of the synagogue, by which to express their spirituality. Sometimes they adopted the custom of going to cemeteries to pray near tombs.[20] In certain times and places they had their own prayers and prayerbooks (*see* Berger, pp. 73ff.). Almost all of these avenues are lost today, especially in the Western world. Modern Orthodox women desire to pray, in a synagogue setting, the prayers that make up the normative liturgy, in Hebrew and not in Yiddish. This restricts them to the standard *siddur,* which contains prayers that have very few allusions to women, prayers that never refer to the Matriarchs, and prayers that are written in masculine specific language— prayers written by men, for men, to a "masculine" God. Modern women have lost the richness of the past. Without replacing it, emptiness reigns.[21]

This situation is especially dire because of the achievements and equality that women have attained in most other areas of life. Women may be lawyers, doctors, teachers, soldiers, firefighters, or politicians. The modern Orthodox woman may even enter the law or medical schools of Yeshiva University.[22] She is encouraged to develop herself as a professional. It is only in the synagogue that she is forced to take a passive role. Only in the synagogue has she made so little progress.

While many, perhaps even most, religious women are satisfied with the private role assigned to them in the traditional Orthodox synagogue, an increasing number are finding this situation intolerable. This is especially true as women acquire a better Jewish education. The words of the author of Ecclesiastes (1:18), "For as wisdom grows, vexation grows," are particularly descriptive of the modern Orthodox woman and her position in the synagogue.

Despite the difficulties created by halakhic limitations on the participation of women in public religious ritual, women who desire more active participation in the synagogue and yet who are committed to classical Jewish law have chosen to remain within the Orthodox Movement, retaining a life-style that offers the individual an intense and enriched spiritual life, membership in a warm and vibrant community, and the benefits of an excellent *yeshivah* educational system.

While maintaining their commitment to Orthodoxy, these dedicated women have created a halakhically viable option for Orthodox women who want to draw nearer, to come closer, to experience communal prayer from the center, and not the sidelines. Today, in many Jewish communities, women are forming their own *tefillah* groups, congregations of women who pray together in the absence of men. These women adhere strictly to classical Jewish law, and yet are able to conduct services, lead prayers, receive Torah honors, read from the Torah, and give *divrei Torah*.

Not a *Minyan*

Women's prayer groups are not *minyanim*.[23] This means that they omit all prayers, including *Kaddish*, *Kedushah*, and *Barekhu*, for which a *minyan* is necessary. They do not have the halakhic status of a *"tzibbur,"* a public prayer group. Only those prayers that are recited when an individual, whether male or female, prays privately, are said.

The decision not to be a *minyan* was, and is, a painful one. To a certain extent, the issue is still unresolved.[24] Not being a *minyan* means having to omit beautiful prayers. It also means not being able to accommodate those who are saying the Mourner's *Kaddish*.[25] More importantly, it involves the recognition, and a measure of acceptance, that any number of adult women cannot constitute a *"tzibbur,"* in the technical halakhic sense, while ten males, even ten adolescents, can. Polemics aside, this belies the apologetics of "equality" in Jewish law between women and men. Acceptance of this severe limitation by the Orthodox women involved in prayer groups is only possible because of their deep commitment to classical Jewish law and their unwillingness to step beyond the boundaries of *halakhah*.

Nor is the issue of women not being permitted to make up a *minyan* universally accepted, even in the Orthodox world. When he was Chief Rabbi of Israel, Rabbi Shlomo Goren responded in the affirmative to an inquiry from Baltimore, Maryland, as to whether women can say *devarim she-be-Kedushah,* those prayers said only in the presence of a *minyan.* In a five-page responsum, he first presented all the reasons why they should not. Then he cited the opinion of Rabbenu Tam, a twelfth-century Tosafist who ruled that women are permitted to recite blessings for commandments that they observe optionally. These blessings are not considered to be taking God's name in vain.[26] This principle has been accepted by Ashkenazic Jewry. It is the reason, for example, that Ashkenazi women recite the blessing over *lulav* and *etrog* on Sukkot, and recite a blessing upon hearing the *shofar* on Rosh Hashanah. Rabbi Goren applied this ruling to women's prayer groups and decided that, in the absence of men, women may say all prayers. He added, on the first page of the responsum, that it was private, and not for publication. As of this writing, it has not been published, but it has been widely circulated.

There has been much controversy surrounding this responsum. Its very existence has been denied, and it has been said to apply only to the Baltimore group for whom it was written. The responsum definitely exists, and there can surely be no reason that only women in Baltimore are permitted to form a *minyan.* Recently, another Orthodox rabbi, Eliezer Berkovits, also expressed a positive view about women's prayer groups constituting themselves as *minyanim.* Nevertheless, neither Rabbi Goren's ruling nor Rabbi Berkovits's opinion has been followed by most women's prayer groups.[27] Instead, the stricter opinion of the revered Rabbi Moshe Feinstein, to be discussed below, has been accepted.

Reading the Torah

Despite the fact that women's prayer groups are not *minyanim,* they do have complete Torah and *haftarah* readings. The readings are not for the purpose of fulfilling the halakhic "public" Torah readings, as in normative synagogues, for, as noted above, women have no such obligation. These Torah readings are, technically, for educational purposes. As such, they are permitted under Jewish law, as any individual Jew, male or female, may read from a *Sefer Torah* for learning purposes.[28]

Women may approach a Torah scroll at any time, whether or not they are menstruating (*see* Cohen, p. 104). Interestingly, this halakhic factor, while never mentioned by rabbis who oppose women's prayer groups, is almost always brought up by women. Many women do not yet know that women may read from a *Sefer Torah* at any time.[29] This erroneous notion carries with it psychologically unhealthy assumptions regarding women's bodies that serve to strengthen the idea of women's inferiority.

Women's prayer groups encourage young girls to take prayer seriously and to develop a love for Torah. The Torah is carried around so that all present may reach out and kiss it. (This is in sharp contrast to the situation in most Orthodox synagogues, where women have no access to the Torah.) Young girls are often given the honor of singing the concluding part of the service. Although they may once have been upset to watch their brothers receive this honor in the synagogue while they were excluded (*see* Alter, p. 279), now they too may participate in this way.

Development of Prayers, Rituals, and Study Groups

Women's *tefillah* groups offer Orthodox women an opportunity to thank God publicly for the good things in their lives, to celebrate life's significant events in a religious way. *Bat Mitzvot* are often celebrated. The young girl may read from the Torah, chant the *haftarah*, deliver a talk, and receive the honor of being called up to the Torah for the first time.[30] Engagements and marriages are also celebrated.[31] Baby namings are frequent occurrences.[32]

The *siddurim* used in the Orthodox Movement do not contain prayers specifically celebrating the important events in women's lives such as *Bat Mitzvah*, or marriage. Women's prayer groups are slowly beginning to incorporate new prayers for special events. Some groups encourage women to compose special *"mi she-berakh"* prayers for individual brides, for women who are going on *aliyah* to Israel, or even for students who are embarking upon a year's study in Israel. One prayer that is becoming widely accepted in many prayer groups is concerned with *agunot* (women unable to obtain a religious divorce) and expresses the hope that God will infuse rabbis with the wisdom to free these women from their "dead" marriages. One approach for creating new prayers is to look at the *tehines* literature for models of women's prayers, translating them from Yiddish into Hebrew (which is the language used in women's prayer groups) and adapting them for use today.

Women in prayer groups are trying to add feminine experience to their prayers wherever permissible under *halakhah*. Women are called to the Torah by the names of their mother, as well as of their father. Some women add the names of the Matriarchs, as well as the Patriarchs, to the *Amidah*.

New rituals are cautiously being developed. Brides are often called up for an *aliyah* accompanied by singing and dancing. Some groups choose a bride to have the honor of being called for the first *aliyah* on Simhat Torah, which begins the new cycle of Torah readings.[33]

Some of the arguments marshalled against women's *tefillah* groups assert that they destroy family life.[34] The fact that so many events celebratory of family life take place in women's *tefillah* groups points out the absurdity of this argument.

Women's prayer groups are encouraging the creation and development of women's Torah interpretations. Many prayer groups sponsor classes for women. Some meet occasionally such as on Shavuot night or to read the *Megillah* on Purim.[35] One group has a regular Shabbat afternoon Talmud study class. Women giving *divrei Torah*, a form of women's *midrash*, during services are encouraged to write them down and send them to the Women's *Tefillah* Network so that the best of these may eventually be made available for use in study groups.

Development of Community

A hallmark of women's *tefillah* groups is the sense of community that exists among the members. In the normative Orthodox synagogue, women new to the congregation frequently enter and leave the synagogue unnoticed, whereas a man, new to the congregation, will usually be invited to receive an *aliyah* and will be welcomed as an addition to the *minyan*. A new woman will often be lost in the crowd. In some synagogues, women are not even members in their own right; they are regarded as included in their husbands' membership.[36]

Most prayer groups resemble *havurot*, in that both groups aim to create an intimate circle. Newcomers are generally invited to stand up, at the close of the service, and introduce themselves. Efforts are made to invite them to someone's home for lunch following services. Many groups have hospitality committees, who organize the hosting of new people.

Another way in which prayer groups resemble *havurot* is the absence of paid professionals. All synagogue functions are carried out by volunteers. Roles are filled by different people each time. Everyone has a chance to lead prayers, to deliver talks, to serve as *gabbai* (the person responsible for giving out synagogue honors).

Clearly, women's *tefillah* groups are a means of bringing women closer to Judaism through prayer and study. Their entire purpose and reason for existence is to enhance and enrich the spiritual lives of their participants.

Historical and Halakhic Precedents

The modern "tradition" of women's prayer groups is really not a radical innovation in Judaism. The first women's prayer group was initiated by Miriam the prophet, Moses' sister. When the Jews were delivered from Egypt, the women, on the banks of the Reed Sea, formed their own "prayer group," separate from the men, in order to thank God for the miraculous delivery[37] (Exod. 15:20, 21).

Throughout Jewish history, women have gathered together to pray. S. Baron writes of twelfth-century Worms, where the women prayed in a separate building. The names of their precentors have been preserved.[38] There is evidence that in Italy, in the late sixteenth century, women also prayed separately from the men.[39] In Eastern Europe, from the Middle Ages until quite recently, the *firzogerin* carried on a tradition of women leading other women in prayer (*see* Taitz, p. 67 and Berger, p. 77). They stood in the synagogue in the women's gallery and prayed aloud so that those who did not know how to pray could follow them. Today, in most Orthodox girls' *yeshivot,* girls and their women teachers gather together for morning prayers, with a *ḥazzanit* singing aloud to lead them.

A scene of women praying together is found in the *Zohar,* the classical Jewish mystical text. An angel, privy to heaven's secrets, describes to R. Simeon ben Yoḥai a number of heavenly chambers for righteous women. In one of them, Jochebed, mother of the prophet Miriam, leads the women in Paradise in praising God three times a day. In another, Deborah the prophet does the same.[40] This kabbalistic vision of Paradise is now reflected by earthly reality. Today women again join together in prayer, echoing Miriam's song of praise.

In addition to historical parallels, there are also halakhic models for women's prayer groups. Women have always participated in certain forms of group prayer. Three women (or three men) who have eaten together should collectively praise God. After an individual eats a meal, he or she says the Grace after Meals. When a group of three or more individuals, of the same sex, eats a meal together, they begin the prayer with an Invitation to Say Grace. The words of the blessing change if three people of the same sex have eaten together.[41]

The *Gomel* prayer is a prayer that is to be recited by an individual after surviving a dangerous experience. Childbirth is considered to be such an experience, and so the *Gomel* prayer is generally said after a woman gives birth. There is a rabbinic view that a woman may recite the *Gomel* prayer in the presence of nine women and one man.[42] These two cases (chanting the Invitation to say Grace and reciting the *Gomel* prayer) represent instances of women functioning as a group, in halakhically acceptable ways, for the purposes of prayer.

Rabbinic Response

In the Orthodox world, change in the status quo is generally approached with hesitation and greeted with resistance. New movements generally have to go through a period of proving themselves and their staying power before being accepted. For example, the Ḥasidic Movement was bitterly opposed at its inception by rabbis of the non-Ḥasidic world, yet today Ḥasidism is generally accepted as a legitimate option for religious Jews.[43] Women's *tefillah* groups have similarly been targets for sustained and vigorous opposition from individual rabbis and rabbinical organizations.

In the past, rabbis generally reacted to women's customs and rituals favorably, or they ignored them, viewing them as harmless activities. Women did not question or challenge men's superiority in religious matters; men were not upset by the small pieties in which women indulged. Men did not covet cleaning the synagogue (*see* Khoubian, p. 220). Women's prayers were recited in an inferior language, not in Hebrew. Women accepted their marginal status and did not rebel.

In the Orthodox community today, observant women organize concerts and theatrical presentations that are restricted to female participants and female audiences.[44] Rabbis sanction these activities, particularly as the events often raise money for charity. Orthodox women are encouraged to entertain themselves, to attend women-only teas, shows, even health clubs. Women's classes led by learned women are often looked upon with favor. However, the development of women-only prayer groups has provoked condemnation in many Orthodox circles.

The rabbinic response to women's *tefillah* groups has been, with the exception of very few rabbis, extremely negative. From their inception, the groups have been attacked.

In 1984, the late Rabbi Moshe Feinstein, who was almost universally accepted as the leading *posek* (rabbinic decisor) of our times, was asked about the halakhic permissibility of the groups. In a responsum written by his grandson, in his name, Rabbi Feinstein said that, in theory, they are permissible, but only when they are clearly not *minyanim*, and not *"tzibbur,"* and only when the women comprising the groups are "righteous women" (*tzidkaniot*), and are praying in this manner only "for the sake of heaven." This responsum is important to women's prayer groups for it represents an endorsement, of a sort, by the *"Gadol Hador,"* the great rabbi of the generation. It created such a furor that Rabbi Feinstein later issued a short "clarification," in which he emphasized that what he had said applied only to groups of women that were "righteous" and that, in reality, it is almost impossible to find such groups. He added that it is also impossible to find such groups of men. However, he did not suggest that men, if they are not "righteous," may not pray together.

The most severe reaction has been that of the so called "centrist" Orthodox world, the sector of Orthodoxy that many of the women involved in prayer groups look to for rabbinic leadership.[45] In 1984, a group of rabbis from Yeshiva University issued a *teshuvah* (responsum, halakhic statement) in response to a question from Rabbi Louis Bernstein, then president of the Rabbinical Council of America, as to the halakhic permissibility of women's *tefillah* groups. That one page responsum, signed by five rabbis, who became known as the "Riets Five" (Rabbi Isaac Elhanan Theological Seminary), created an atmosphere of tension and of public and private rancor between the supporters of women's *tefillah* groups and those who oppose them.

The Riets Five responsum declared that women's *hakafot* (carrying the Torah around the synagogue while singing and dancing) on Simḥat Torah, women's *"minyanim,"* and women's *Megillah* readings are categorically prohibited. It offered three reasons for the prohibitions. The first is *"ziyuf ha-Torah,"* falsification of Torah. Women cannot constitute a *minyan*, and the women involved in prayer groups are falsely creating the impression that they are a *minyan*. This is a false statement. Every woman who prays in an Orthodox prayer group is well aware that the group is not a *minyan* because prayers such as *Kaddish* are omitted. The non-*minyan* status of prayer groups is readily acknowledged by all involved.

The second objection raised is that women's prayer groups are against tradition, and traditions regarding the synagogue are particularly to be adhered to. This statement, too, is misleading. There are precedents well within Jewish tradition for prayer groups, some of which we have discussed above. Moreover, even in the Orthodox Movement, "traditions" are constantly changing. The very existence of Yeshiva University, whose motto is "Torah and Science," itself represents a "new" tradition.

The third halakhic objection raised in the responsum is that women's prayer groups are influenced by non-Jews and are a direct result of the feminist movement, whose goal is "promiscuity." The rabbis who signed the responsum are apparently not aware that many Jewish women were among the founders of the feminist movement, and that its goal is the equality of women before the law and in all areas of life.

The signators of the responsum asked their fellow rabbis to strongly oppose these "breaches" of *halakhah*, for "who knows what will be the end result of them."

Subsequent to the publication of the Riets Five *teshuvah*, one of its signators, Rabbi Herschel Schachter, wrote two articles explaining his views.[46] In addition to his halakhic opinions, these articles contain personal attacks on the women involved in prayer groups and on the rabbis who support them. He questions their motivations and even their "normality." He implies that the women are heretics, and are part of "Korah and his group" (*see* Num. 16).

A major point in Rabbi Schachter's articles is that it is immodest for women to act "publicly." He stresses that the *Shekhinah*[47] is not present where there is immodesty. Rabbi Schachter insists that women may not separate themselves from the *tzibbur* (community). Although he stresses that women are not counted as part of the *tzibbur* (they are not part of a *minyan*), he feels that they may not form their own *tzibbur*. As a group, their prayers are acceptable only when men are present on the other side of a *mehitzah*.

The lack of respect for religious women exhibited by Rabbi Schachter, who is considered by many to be one of the great scholars of our time, is symptomatic of the paralysis afflicting many in the Orthodox world regarding the role of women. The fact that a scholar of his stature would devote so much of his time and energy toward attacking women's prayer groups is an indication of the uneasiness gripping the modern Orthodox world in the face of the new class of Orthodox women that they have helped to create, women who are learned in both secular and Jewish knowledge, active in all spheres of life, and dissatisfied with the limitations of the role they have been assigned—women who are demanding and precipitating change.

Not all Orthodox rabbis have responded negatively to women's prayer groups. Some have been quietly encouraging; a few have been actively supportive. Rabbi Avi Weiss, rabbi of the Hebrew Institute of Riverdale, New York, has been a strong ally from the inception of the movement. The prayer group formed by the women of his congregation meets in the *beit midrash* of his synagogue. An increasing number of rabbis are now following suit. Some of the largest synagogues in the New York area now encourage women's prayer groups and provide suitable space for them. Meeting in synagogues is preferable to meeting outside them for a number of reasons. This not only indicates the support of the synagogue, but allows families to join together after services for a joint *kiddush*. It keeps the community together.

The opposition of the organized rabbinate has actually had a positive effect, for it has galvanized women into action and has been directly responsible for the formation of the Women's *Tefillah* Network.

Women's *Tefillah* Network

The Riets Five responsum, discussed above, received a great deal of publicity when it was first issued.[48] It was circulated widely, referred to by many pulpit rabbis, and used by a number of rabbis as justification for barring women's prayer groups from meeting in their synagogues.[49]

The women involved in prayer groups were angered by the Riets Five *teshuvah*, especially because of the lack of research on the part of the rabbis who signed it, none of whom were apparently familiar with the actual practices of the prayer groups, as evidenced by the continual reference to "women's *minyanim*."

The publicity surrounding the Riets Five *teshuvah* made clear to the women involved in prayer groups that they were in an untenable situation. Whereas the rabbis who opposed their practices had many forums in which to voice their opinions (their rabbinical journals, their classrooms, their pulpits), the women had no means by which to bring the issue to the larger Jewish community. In an effort to decide how to handle the attack on prayer groups, a meeting was held, and women from all prayer groups in the New York metropolitan area were invited. The need for support and exchange of ideas among prayer group members was recognized, as was the necessity for a united voice. It was unanimously decided to form the Women's *Tefillah* Network.

The Women's *Tefillah* Network is the umbrella organization of halakhic women's prayer groups. It has accomplished much since its inception. The Network publishes a quarterly newsletter, which is mailed to hundreds of members. It has sponsored two conferences, bringing together women from various prayer groups, thus facilitating the sharing of ideas and information. Its speakers' bureau has sent women to many communities across the United States to provide information about women's *tefillah*. The Network has made available tapes of women's voices chanting prayers, as well as Torah and *haftarah* cantillation. It sponsors a lecture series and has organized essay contests for school girls on topics relevant to women and Judaism.

One of the first acts of the Network was to write to the Rabbinical Council of America, protesting the Riets Five responsum. The Rabbinical Council responded by saying that ". . . The Rabbinical Council of America has not taken any official position on the question of *tefillot*." [50] This response, by the official rabbinical organization of centrist Orthodoxy, indicating refusal to explore a question of *halakhah*, highlights the fact that women's prayer groups have become, for many rabbis, a political, and not an halakhic, issue.

Although the women have not yet succeeded in establishing a dialogue with the organized Orthodox rabbinate, and perhaps thereby obtaining official sanction and encouragement, the prayer group movement is nevertheless flourishing.

Achievements

The women's prayer group movement continues to grow. New groups are forming, and existing groups are gaining members. Groups are appearing on college campuses.[51] An increasing number of girls have celebrated their *Bat Mitzvot* in women's prayer groups. Most Orthodox women and men are aware of the existence of the groups. They have already become a "tradition" in Jewish life.

In 1988, the women's prayer group movement received world-wide attention when a halakhic women's prayer service was held at the *Kotel*, the Western Wall, in Jerusalem (*see* R. Haut, p. 274).[52] Since then, despite fierce and often violent opposition, women have continued to pray there together, thus asserting their right to worship together not only privately but also in public sacred space. The "Women of the Wall" have received tremendous grass-roots support from Jewish women and men all over the world.

The women involved in women's prayer groups are not encouraging other women to pray exclusively in women-only groups. On the contrary, most groups meet only once monthly because their purpose is not to take women away from the synagogue but to provide an additional prayer experience in which women can participate fully and directly. A major goal is for every Orthodox Jewish community to support a women's prayer group as an alternative form of prayer for those women who choose that option.

The survival of women's prayer groups is especially remarkable in that religious women, a group that traditionally has sought rabbinic advice on every issue, have found the strength to question and counter rabbinic edicts, even those coming from the strongest and most influential authorities. Learned women are now sharing halakhic information with other women.[53] Women are turning to the Network with questions pertaining to prayer and other matters affecting religious women.

The inception of the women's prayer group movement has motivated experimentation with alternative prayer experiences that offer equal religious expression to women in the Orthodox world. For example, there is an Orthodox *ḥavurah* in New York City that has egalitarianism as its goal. That group prays together on Friday nights, for *Kabbalat Shabbat*. Sometimes two women lead prayers,[54] and sometimes a man is *shaliaḥ tzibbur*. The women's prayer movement, by focusing attention on the problems caused by denying women the ability to publicly participate in prayer services, has served as a catalyst for creating alternative forms of prayer while still remaining firmly rooted within the halakhic system.

Progress toward more sensitivity to women within a traditional Orthodox framework has also been made. In an increasing number of synagogues the *meḥitzah* now is positioned so that women do not feel excluded from the services, and the Torah scroll is brought to the women's section as well as the men's when it is carried around the synagogue. *Bat Mitzvot* are acknowledged in some way, such as presenting the girl with a gift, a practice unheard of in Orthodox synagogues ten years ago. More synagogue Talmud classes are open to women than ever before. The Orthodox community is becoming sensitized to the spiritual and intellectual needs of women.

A model for rabbinic encouragement of women's yearning for more active participation in religious ritual is found in the Talmud (TB Hag. 16b). An eyewitness account of an incident in the Temple relates that a group of women wanted to perform *semikhah* on their sacrificial animal. This consisted of placing their hands on the animal's head and pushing down. It symbolized a direct action on the part of the donor of a sacrifice, connecting the donor with the sacrificial act itself.[55] The Talmud stresses that men were required to perform *semikhah*, whereas women were exempt. However, the group of women who wished to participate in that optional (for them) act, were permitted to do so, in order to give them *"naḥat ruaḥ,"* spiritual pleasure.

The women involved in today's prayer groups consider themselves spiritual heirs of those women of the Second Temple who were not content with observing only those *mitzvot* that they were obligated to do but who desired greater expression of their spirituality. Those women of antiquity and women of today share the awareness that more active personal participation in ritual helps one to attain a greater feeling of closeness to and communion with God. Judaism can only benefit by the infusion of women's energies in communal worship.

Notes

1. The following is a partial listing of articles denouncing women's prayer groups, followed by a listing of publications in favor of them:

PUBLICATIONS AGAINST WOMEN'S PRAYER GROUPS

a. Responsum written in response to an inquiry by Rabbi Louis Bernstein, then President of the Rabbinical Council of America, and signed by Rabbis Nissan Alpert, Abba Bronspiegel, Mordechai Willig, Yehuda Parnes, and Hershel Schachter. It was written and circulated in 1984 and was published in *HaDarom*, vol. 54 (1985): 49–50.

b. Rabbi Hershel Schachter, "Go Out in the Footsteps of the Sheep," (in Hebrew), *Beit Yitzḥak*, vol. 17 (1984–1985): 118–34.

c. Rabbi Hershel Schachter, "Some Matters Concerning the Synagogue and its Sanctity," (in Hebrew), *Ohr HaMizrach*, vol. 34 (Tishrei 1985): 54–67.

d. Rabbi Abba Bronspiegel, "Separate *Minyanim* for Women," *HaDarom*, vol. 54 (Sivan 1985): 51–53.

e. Israel Shepanksy, "The Tumult About Women's *Minyanim*," editorial, *Ohr HaMizrach*, vol. 34 (Tishrei 1985): 1–3.

f. Yaacov Amitai, "Sanctity and Self Expression," *The Jewish Observer*, 18:3 (Feb. 1985): 23–25. In the May issue, in a letter to the editor, it was admitted that Yaacov Amitai is a pen name, and that the author refuses to reveal his identity.

g. Rabbi Kenneth Auman, "Orthodoxy Requires Sage Discussion," *Sh'ma* (18 Oct. 1985): 145–46. This article represents a reversal of his previously expressed views on the issue. *See* n.49 *infra*.

h. J. David Bleich, "Religious Experience? *tefillah be-tzibbur?*" *Sh'ma* (18 October 1985): 146–49.

i. Rabbi Menashe Klein, "*Mishneh Halakhot*" (in Hebrew), *Makon Mishneh Halakhot Gedolot* pt. 4, siman 78 (1977): 120–21.

PUBLICATIONS IN FAVOR OF WOMEN'S PRAYER GROUPS

a. Rabbi Avi Weiss, *Women at Prayer: A Halakhic Analysis of Women's Prayer Groups* (Hoboken, N.J.: Ktav, 1990).

b. Responsum of Rabbi Moshe Feinstein—unpublished to date. It is available through the Women's *Tefillah* Network, P.O. Box 236, Brooklyn, NY 11230.

c. Responsum of Rabbi Shlomo Goren—unpublished. It is available through the Women's *Tefillah* Network (*see supra*).

d. Rabbi Michael Chernick, "In Support of Women's Prayer Groups" *Sh'ma* (7 May 1985): 105–8.

e. Rabbi David Singer, "A Failure of Halachic 'Objectivity'," *Sh'ma* (7 May 1985): 108–10.

f. Rivka Haut, "From Women: Piety Not Rebellion," *Sh'ma* (7 May 1985): 110–12.

g. Rivka Haut, "Women and Prayer Groups" (tentative title) in *Halakhah and the Jewish Woman*, ed. Pnina Peli (Washington, D.C.: B'nai B'rith, forthcoming).

There have also been many newspaper articles, too numerous to list, discussing women's prayer groups and the controversy surrounding them. Examples include Larry Kohler's articles in the *Long Island Jewish World*, "Women's Prayer Group Gets a Torah," 13; 27 (13–19 July 1984); "Orthodox Rabbis' Responsa Condemns Women's Prayer Groups," 14; 37 (15–21 Feb. 1985). Many more have been written dealing with the Women of the Wall and the attempt to conduct women's prayer at the Kotel; see n.52.

2. There are a few Orthodox synagogues in which the women's section is exactly equal, both in size and appearance, to the men's section. In the Hebrew Institute of Riverdale, New York, the only way to differentiate between the women's and men's sections is by reading the signs on the entrance doors leading to the separate sections. In this synagogue, both sections have equal access to the *bimah*, which is in the center of the sanctuary, and to the ark, which is at the front, both of which are centered exactly mid-point between the sections. Most striking is the fact that there are entrances, from both the women's section and the men's, to the *bimah*. There are also ramps for the handicapped, leading up to the ark, in both sections. This synagogue's rabbi, Rabbi Avi Weiss, insisted upon equal access to the *bimah* and the ark from both sections, so that the architecture would not reflect exclusion of women from the centers of activity, thereby making the women feel physically distant.

3. Israel Meir ha-Kohen, *Mishneh Berurah* (Shulsinger ed.), vol. 6, p. 305.

4. On the other hand, a *Bar Mitzvah* boy will receive his first *aliyah*, a groom will receive a special *aliyah* (*aufruf*), and the father of a *Bar Mitzvah* boy will receive an *aliyah* and recite a special prayer.

5. Judg. 5.

6. TB Ber. 31a.

7. *See* Mish. Meg. 3 : 2 and the Talmudic discussion of this *mishnah* at TB Meg. 33b. For the halakhic decision, *see Shulḥan Arukh*, Oraḥ Ḥayyim, siman 55, par. 1: ". . . [A]nd we do not recite [*Kaddish*] with less than ten physically mature, adult, free males, and this is also the case with *Kedushah* and *Barekhu*. . . ."

8. Caananite slaves were considered to be "almost Jews." They were circumcised and were obligated to keep all *mitzvot* obligatory upon women. Upon being freed, they were officially converted.

9. *Sefer Abudarham* (Jerusalem: Usha, 1962), 25.

10. *See* Moshe Meiselman, *Jewish Woman in Jewish Law* (New York: KTAV, 1978), 15: Public and private are necessary aspects of the lives of both men and women. Neither sex is restricted to either area, but tradition did say that the private sphere should be the dominant area of a woman's life.

For a different interpretation, *see* Saul J. Berman, "The Status of Women in Halakhic Judaism," *Tradition* (Fall 1973): 5–28, where he argues that while the rabbis did not mandate a specific role for women, they did leave open the possibility of choice for those women who preferred a private role by not requiring women to take part in public religious functions.

11. There are exceptions. *See* Weiss, *Women at Prayer*, 50–56, who enumerates them. For example, women are counted in a *minyan* for *Kiddush HaShem* (martyrdom). But these instances are not normative. No Orthodox synagogue will count women in its *minyan*.

12. Mish. RH 3 : 8 ". . . This is the general rule: One who is not obligated in a particular *mitzvah* may not discharge that obligation for the majority [who are obligated]."

13. TB Ber. 24a: ". . . A voice in a woman is licentiousness." In some Orthodox synagogues, this prohibition is taken so seriously that women never sing aloud along with the prayer leader. They intone the words in a whisper. In synagogues where women do sing, they are permitted to do so because their voices are not the only ones heard; the men sing louder and so drown out individual women's voices. I have been told of more than one instance when individual women were asked, by the rabbi, to lower their voices.

14. TB BK 82a.

15. *See* E. Ellinson, *Women and Mitzvot*, vol. 1 (Jerusalem: Jewish Agency, Alpha Press, 1979), 70 n.15, for sources for this lack of obligation. However, there is one time during the year when, according to some authorities, women are obligated to hear the Torah read. That is *Shabbat Zakhor*, before Purim, when the Torah section dealing with *Amalek* is read. That is the one Shabbat when halakhic women's prayer groups do not meet.

See also ibid., 68–74, where he discusses some opinions that hold that women may discharge obligations for men, but only when women are similarly obligated. For example, reading of the *Megillah*.

16. TB Meg. 21b.

17. TB Meg. 23a. The statement that having a woman read would compromise the "honor of the congregation" presumes that "the congregation" means the men.

There is one instance where the halakhic literature specifies that women are to be called to the Torah. This is the case of a "city of *kohanim*." In such a congregation, calling a *kohen* for the third *aliyah* might imply that the first and second *kohanim* were not true *kohanim*, and thus the "honor of the congregation" would be impugned. Therefore, in order to avoid calling yet another *kohen* for the third *aliyah*, a woman is called. *See* R. Meir of Rothenberg (*Maharam*), cited in *Sefer Abudarham* (Jerusalem: Usha, 1962), 130.

18. There are very few exceptions. Sometimes a *Bat Mitzvah* girl speaks, but this generally takes place after services. In a few synagogues, here and in Israel, women are sometimes permitted to speak during services.

19. *See* Schachter, "Some Matters Concerning the Synagogue," 61.

20. Some women still do. *See* Susan Starr Sered, "Rachel's Tomb and the Milk Grotto of the Virgin Mary: Two Women's Shrines in Bethlehem," *Journal of Feminist Studies in Religion*, 2:2 (Fall 1986): 7–22; and "Rachel's Tomb: Societal Liminality and the Revitalization of a Shrine," *Religion* 19 (1989), 27–40. [*See* Sered, p. 208.]

21. For example, in the largely Orthodox neighborhoods of Boro Park and Flatbush, Brooklyn, a women's magazine called *ESRA* is widely distributed. In the Oct. 1985 issue (4:10), p. 6, the "editorial," called "Spotlight," which discussed the High Holidays, had this to say: "I'm also wondering about the *shul* seating plan. I never remember. Is it hotter upstairs or downstairs? I do know that whichever is cooler always has a longer davening. They say life is a trade-off. But the big puzzle is what to wear. . . ."

22. Yeshiva University, the educational institution of the modern Orthodox Movement, permits women to enroll as students in all of its schools, with the exception of its rabbinical and cantorial schools.

23. An exception to this was a Baltimore group, which followed Rabbi Goren's opinion, discussed *infra*, and functioned as a women's *minyan* for ten years.

24. To be or not to be a *minyan* was a major issue at the second Women's *Tefillah* Network conference, on Jan. 30–31, 1988. At that conference, noted Orthodox scholar and feminist Blu Greenberg suggested that it is time for women's prayer groups to become *minyanim*.

25. Women saying *Kaddish* have to find other options such as not praying with their women's prayer group for eleven months or, if they live in a community that has an early *minyan*, attending services there to say *Kaddish* before coming to their women's group.

Women reciting *Kaddish* are often those who seek greater participation in prayer. Women's recitation of *Kaddish* is supported by most women in davening groups.

In many Orthodox synagogues, it is still very difficult for a woman to say *Kaddish*. Many synagogues are not set up to accommodate women on weekdays. (Men take over the women's section or daven in a smaller room where there is no women's section.) Not all will answer to a woman saying *Kaddish*. One woman recently told me that, rather than go to her synagogue on weekdays to say *Kaddish*, where she will feel that she is making a spectacle of herself, she says *Kaddish* by herself, in her home, and imagines that the angels are answering her. Cf. Sara Regeur, "*Kaddish* from the 'Wrong Side' of the *Mehitzah*," in *On Being a Jewish Feminist*, ed. Susannah Heschel (New York: Schocken, 1983), 177–81.

26. *Tosafot* at TB RH 33a, s.v. "*ha-Rabbi Yehudah*."

27. Rabbi Goren's ruling is available through the Women's *Tefillah* Network; *see* n.1a *supra*, under publications in favor of women's prayer groups. Rabbi Berkovits's view is to be found in his book, *Jewish Women in Time and Torah* (Hoboken, New Jersey: KTAV, 1990), 83. Recently, as a response to the Women of the Wall, Rabbi Goren maintained, in a letter included in the State of Israel's brief against women's group prayer at the Kotel, that his responsum was meant only in a theoretical sense. He said this despite the fact that when he wrote the responsum he was informed that he was being asked a practical question on behalf of a functioning prayer group.

28. *See* Weiss, "Women's Prayer Groups," 81–82.

29. In women's prayer groups, it is very common for women who are attending for the

first time to refuse to touch or kiss the Torah or to accept an *aliyah,* because they believe that if they are menstruating, they can defile the Torah. *See* Cohen, p. 112 and Rabbi Avi Weiss, "Women and Sifrei Torah," *Tradition* (Summer 1982): 106–17, for further discussions of this topic.

30. *Bat Mitzvot* are now widely celebrated in the Orthodox community, usually by having parties. In some "modern" synagogues, the rabbi may offer a "*mazel tov*" to the *Bat Mitzvah* girl and her family, and the girl may be permitted to deliver a talk at a *kiddush* following services; however, she plays no active role in the services themselves.

31. A groom, the Shabbat before his wedding, has an "*aufruf,*" at which time he is called up to the Torah for an *aliyah.* The bride often does not attend, particularly if the *aufruf* takes place a week before the wedding, when it is traditional for the couple not to see each other. Even if she does attend, she plays no active role in the prayer service. "*Aufrufs*" for brides are now common in women's prayer groups.

32. A baby girl is named in the synagogue, on the first Sabbath, or first occasion for reading the Torah, after her birth. (Baby boys are named at their circumcisions.) The baby's father is called up to the Torah, at which time he announces the baby's name, and says a prayer for her (and for her mother). The mother is often not present. In *tefillah* groups, the new mother names her baby daughter herself.

33. The man chosen for this *aliyah* in the synagogue is called *Ḥatan Breishit* (the groom [for the reading of] Genesis). Therefore, choosing a bride for this honor is particularly appropriate.

34. Rabbi Menashe Klein, a *posek* (rabbinic decisor) of stature (see n.1, *supra*), responded to an interested rabbi who asked him about the halakhic permissibility of women's prayer groups. Rabbi Klein maintains that women's prayer groups destroy the family:

> But the women neglect their obligations and *mitzvot* that they are commanded to keep and leave the home to the husband and the children to some gentile housekeeper . . . and these modern women run to congregate and to make women's *minyanim,* which is not their obligation and not their *mitzvah.* They refuse to bear children and do all sorts of things to bar conception, and from this alone we see that their motivation is not for the sake of heaven . . . and since '*the glory of the King's daughter is within,*' it is apparent that to create their own congregations is the opposite of what they have been commanded, which is to remain within the home.

(Translated by this author, from a private correspondence to the above rabbi, which he sent to me. This responsum is included in the State of Israel's brief against women's group prayer at the Kotel. Bagatz 89, p. 142.)

35. This is particularly appropriate since women are equally obligated with men in hearing the *Megillah,* and since the holiday of Purim so obviously involves women.

36. Sometimes, women cannot vote. Often, a single woman, or a widow, are the only women permitted to become members in their own right and to vote.

37. In discussing Miriam and her "prayer group," Rabbi David Luria states that the biblical phrase ". . . went out" connotes ". . . that they went out *ḥutz la-maḥaneh* (out of the camp) in order to sing, so that their voices would not be heard by the men." Cf. David ben Judah Judel Luria (Radal) (1798–1855), gloss to Exod. R. 40:3, s.v. "If you will go with me to Ḥazor."

Another "women's prayer group" may also be mentioned in the Bible. The account of the "*tzov'ot,*" at Exod. 38:8, according to the biblical commentator Ibn Ezra, is referring to a group of women who ". . . would only come every day to the door of the Tent of Meeting, *to pray* and to hear about the *mitzvot.* . . ." *See* Ibn Ezra, *ad. loc.* For further information on this as a precedent for women's *tefillah* groups, *see also* my article "Women and Prayer Groups," cited in n.1, *supra (see* Grossman, p. 18).

38. S. W. Baron, *The Jewish Community,* vol. 2 (Philadelphia: JPS, 1942), 140.

39. In the records of the Jewish Community of Casale, Monferat, Italy (1589–1670), [original in the Casale archives] this entry is preserved for 1595:

The following matter was agreed upon: Since the lease of the house of Moroco Matoto, which was made into a women's synagogue [*beit ha-knesset*] for the time being, was about to expire, it was necessary to rent it anew and fix it, for some more years, as the lease of the men's synagogue [*beit ha-knesset*] still had seven years to go. . . .

It seems clear that the women's and men's synagogues were housed in different structures. The original of this manuscript is in Hebrew. The translation is that of Dr. Pinchas Doron, who brought the manuscript to my attention and showed me a photocopy of it.

40. *Zohar* 3, 167b. Here is the scene described:

In another chamber is Jochebed . . . and thousands and tens of thousands with her . . . three times a day she praises the Lord of the Universe, she and all the women who are with her. And they sing the Song of the Sea every day . . . and all the *tzadikim* in *Gan Eden* [Garden of Eden] listen to her sweet voice. And some holy angels praise the Holy Name with her.

In another chamber is Deborah the prophet, and here too, all the women who are with her thank [God] and sing the song that she sang in this world. . . .

41. *See Shulḥan Arukh*, 199, siman 6. Three women may (and, according to some views, are required to) say the same blessing that three men say when they have eaten together. Women and men may not join together to constitute the group of three. Each group must be made up of members of the same sex. If a group of women eats together with three men, the men lead the Grace. However, the women may, if they desire, break away from the men's group and form their own group to say Grace. But ten women are not permitted to say the blessing that ten men say when they have eaten together.

42. Mish. Berurah (New York: Shulsinger Bros., 1952), chap. 219, sec. 3. An Orthodox scholar, Rochel Millen, has explained to me that the single male represents, in a symbolic way, the *tzibbur*.

43. *See* EncJud, s.v. "Ḥasidim."

44. *See* Chana Shloush, "Making Music for Women Only," *Lilith*, (Spring 1988): 15–16.

45. The acknowledged leader of centrist Orthodoxy is Rabbi J. B. Soloveitcheik. He has never written or spoken out publicly on this issue. However, he has been quoted by a number of rabbis as having expressed the view that, while he would not encourage women's prayer groups, he does not believe that they are against *halakhah*. *See* Weiss, *"Women at Prayer,"* p. 112, n.39.

46. *See* n.1 b,c, under articles denouncing women's prayer groups, *supra*.

47. God's presence or immanence in the world. Interestingly, *Shekhinah* is a feminine form, used in kabbalistic literature to refer to the "feminine" aspects of the Divine.

48. *See* n.1, *supra*.

49. For example, Rabbi Kenneth Auman, rabbi of the Young Israel of Flatbush, Brooklyn, had originally been a supporter of women's prayer groups. The bulletin of his synagogue had said about him: "Rabbi Auman feels that Orthodoxy has to confront this matter [women's role in the synagogue] . . . with regard to the recent innovation of the 'women's prayer groups,' as long as the services are conducted in accordance with *halakhah* and women are not pressured to attend, this service should be one of the options that Orthodox congregations should consider." Upon publication of the Riets Five *teshuvah*, Rabbi Auman reversed his position, did not permit the Flatbush prayer group to meet in his synagogue, and wrote an article critical of women's prayer groups. *See* n.1 g, *supra*. For his former, positive position, *see* "Meet Our New Rabbi, Kenneth Auman," *The Turret*, Young Israel of Flatbush bulletin (Sept. 1985): 6.

50. Letter dated 26 Feb. 1985. Copies are available through the Women's *Tefillah* Network, *see* n.1a under articles in favor of women's prayer groups, *supra*.

51. For example, Columbia University now has a women's prayer group. Hadassah, a secular women's Zionist organization, has formed a *Rosh Hodesh* prayer group.

Each issue of the Network newsletter has a listing of member groups, and the number is steadily increasing.

52. There have been many news reports and articles written about this group, which calls itself *Shira Chadashah*, also known as the "Women of the Wall." Some examples are: *The New York Times*, 2 Dec. 1988, p. 10; Phyllis Chesler, "The Walls Came Tumbling Down," *On The Issues*, vol. II, (1989): 7–11 (repr. in *The Jewish Week*, 31 March 1989); Haim Shapiro, "Women's Service at Wall Causes Near Riot," *Jerusalem Post*, 2 Feb. 1989; Yossi Klein Halevi, "Women of the Wall," *The Long Island Jewish World*, 16 June 1989; M. C. Henry, "Women of Wall Somber in Garden Setting," *The Jewish Week*, 13 Oct. 1989.

53. See back issues of Women's *Tefillah* Network newsletter. Representatives of the Network are often asked to help new groups by explaining the *halakhot* involved in women's prayer and by helping women acquire synagogue skills.

54. Regarding the proscription of *kol ishah*, this group has accepted a halakhic opinion that two women's voices together, rather than the voice of a single woman, is halakhically acceptable.

55. According to one Orthodox scholar, the act of *semikhah* was a symbol of active participation on the part of a donor of a sacrifice before handing the animal over to the priest. The women desired to perform *semikhah* because they too wanted this participation. *See* Rabbi Mayer Herscovics, "The Dispute Regarding Semikhah: The First Dispute in Israel," *Ohr HaMizrach* (in Hebrew), 23:3–4 (April-July 1974): 96–101.

Judith Hauptman

WOMEN AND THE CONSERVATIVE SYNAGOGUE[1]

In the last two decades many women have begun to examine Jewish observances and texts from a fresh perspective. They note that Judaism,
though ethically valid and spiritually satisfying, seems deficient when
subjected to feminist criteria. Judaism appears to favor men. It imposes on
them myriad ritual obligations that, although demanding, make it possible for those who observe them regularly to sense God in the world and
delight in God's Torah. Women, upon whom the Jewish tradition does
not impose the same ritual obligations and who therefore may not participate fully and publicly in prayer and study, do not have available to them
the same opportunities for religious and intellectual expression.

Troubled by the realization that exemptions make life easy but shal-
low, Jewish women have begun asking a number of pointed questions:
For what reason were women assigned fewer ritual obligations than men?
Is differentiation between men's and women's roles and responsibilities an
essential, divinely ordained part of Judaism? If not, is there today any
halakhically defensible way to alter the status quo?

To find answers to these questions, it is necessary to study Judaism in
its formative period. Although grounded in Torah, the practice of Judaism
as we know it today can be traced to the period of the Talmud, approxi-

mately 2000 years ago. By examining rabbinic material on the development of Jewish prayer and study and the relationship of women to these activities we may begin to understand why the system evolved as it did and whether or not it can be changed.

Prayer in Ancient Judaism

Berakhot, the first tractate of the Mishnah, is a good source of information about prayer. It focuses on three major forms of prayer: *Shema*, a collection of biblical verses that acknowledge God's sovereignty and define the terms of God's covenant; *tefillah*, fixed daily supplications; and occasional blessings. Among other things, the Mishnah prescribes time parameters for the recitation of various prayers, notes the proper mental state for praying, and fixes the contents of many prayers.

A close reading of Berakhot shows that a significant feature of prayer was its communal or public nature. For instance, the Mishnah says that if a *shaliah tzibbur* (group representative) errs in reciting a blessing, it is a bad sign for the group that appointed him, and he must be replaced by someone else (Mish. Ber. 5 : 3,5). Statements like these indicate that it was standard practice for one individual to recite the prayers for others. Theologically speaking, these sources also suggest that how smoothly and correctly the leader prays affects God's response to the community's prayer.

Later in the tractate, in a discussion of *birkat ha-mazon* ("Grace after Meals"), the Mishnah implicitly provides a reason for group prayer by prescribing a simple call to Grace if only a few are joining in the prayer, a more elaborate call with reference to God if a group of ten is to recite these blessings together, and even more elaborate calls with increasingly rich praise of God if 100, 1000, or 10,000 are present,[2] the Mishnah (Ber. 7 : 3) suggests that the greater the number of Jews joining together in prayer, the greater the glory of God. A different, less theological, reason for advocating communal prayer is given at the end of Tosef. RH 2 : 18. When asked by Rabban Gamliel why an individual is appointed to lead the congregation in prayer, the Sages respond that while those who are able to recite the prayers for themselves must do so,[3] the illiterate and inarticulate may fulfill their obligations through the prayers of a *shaliah tzibbur*.

From other *mishnayot*, we infer that not only was group prayer the norm, it was even essential in certain instances. A quorum of ten men was necessary for reciting *Shema* responsively, passing before the ark to lead the group in prayer, reciting the priestly blessing, and reading Torah and *haftarah* (Meg. 4:3). Ten is the minimum number of persons required for these rituals because ten gives the sense of an *ʿedah,* of an assembly. Note that what all these rituals have in common is that they require a competent individual to perform them for the group or to lead the group in reciting the appropriate words.

After establishing the need for a leader, the Mishnah goes on to determine who is and is not eligible to serve as one. It states that a child may not lead *Shema* or the fixed prayer or the priestly blessing but may read from the Torah and translate; a person dressed in rags (*poheah*), whose limbs are exposed, may lead *Shema* (from his place, where he will not be seen) but may not read from the Torah or lead the fixed prayers or the priestly blessing (Meg. 4:6).

It is tempting to speculate (and many have done so) that a minor may not lead the group in prayer because he is not obligated to pray; however, that cannot be the basis of his ineligibility, for Ber. 3:3 obligates minors to recite the fixed prayers. A more likely reason for not allowing a minor or someone dressed in rags to serve as prayer leader is that he compromises the dignity of the congregation by his age or his immodest attire.[4] That is, social considerations seem to play a role in the performance of religious ritual.[5]

This brief survey of sources dealing with prayer indicates that praying communally, with one appointed to lead the group, benefits both God and humankind. It benefits God because Jews who join together in prayer honor God, like servants gathering to praise their king. Communal prayer benefits human beings because a group can appoint its most talented liturgist as *shaliah tzibbur,* thus increasing the likelihood that the prayer of all will be answered. Moreover, praying together enables those who are unable to pray by themselves, who do not know the words or who are not articulate, to discharge their responsibilities by someone who is qualified.

Women and Prayer

Having noted the essential public nature of prayer, we now turn to a discussion of women and prayer. The key source on this topic is Ber. 3:3, which states that women are exempt from reading *Shema* and donning *tefillin* but are obligated to recite the *Tefillah* (the set of eighteen fixed blessings recited daily), hang a *mezuzah*, and recite Grace. It is not surprising that women are exempt from *Shema* and *tefillin* because we learn elsewhere that women are exempt in general from positive time-specific *mitzvot* (Kid. 1:7). However, it is surprising that they are obligated to recite the *Tefillah*, also a positive time-specific *mitzvah*. The Gemara briefly comments that women are obligated to pray because prayer is synonymous with petitions (TB Ber. 20b). What this seems to mean is that each woman is best qualified to ask God for what she wants, whether it be for herself or for others.[6]

Given that women are obligated to pray and recite *birkat ha-mazon*, it would seem to follow logically that they may join and lead the quorum, for one who is obligated to perform a certain ritual act may do so on behalf of others (RH 3:8). Ber. 7:2 states, however, that one may not include women, slaves,[7] and minors in the *zimmun*, the invitation to join a quorum of three that will recite the Grace together. The previous *mishnah* also excludes others from the quorum of three for Grace: non-Jews, a servant (or any person) who has eaten less than an olive-sized amount of food, and someone who has eaten food from which the *kohen*'s and *levi*'s gifts were not separated. These people are clearly rejected on technical legal grounds: either they are not Jewish, have eaten too little to be obligated to recite Grace, or have eaten forbidden food. The exclusion of women, children,[8] and slaves, all of whom are obligated to recite Grace and may each form their own *zimmun* (TB Ber. 45b), must therefore be for a different reason altogether.

Women are similarly unable to join a men's quorum of ten for prayer or Grace. Strangely enough, the Gemara presents several opinions that a slave or minor may join the quorum in pressing circumstances (TB Ber. 47b–48a). If only nine men gather to say Grace, they may allow a slave or minor to complete the quorum of ten. This rule forces us to conclude that, at least according to some, slaves and minors are technically eligible to join the quorum but, even so, are undesirable, probably because of their lower social standing.[9] The silence of the text here concerning the possibility of women joing the quorum of ten for Grace or prayer suggests that even though they are ritually equivalent to slaves and therefore eligible (according to some), it is unthinkable to allow women to do so.

These sources together indicate that women were obligated to pray, but since Jewish prayer was communal, they could not become full-fledged members of the prayer community. It seems that their exclusion stems more from social realitites than from theological distinctions.

Even though the Talmud does not allow women to complete a prayer quorum, it examines the possibility of women assisting men in discharging various other ritual responsibilities. The third and fourth chapters of Mish. Meg. speak of the public Torah reading on Sabbaths and holidays. It is hard to know when this practice began—the Talmudic sources attribute it to Moses and Ezra[10]—but it was certainly in place by the time of the Mishnah. Deut. 31:12 requires a public reading of the entire Torah once every seven years at the end of the Sabbatical cycle (*mitzvat hakhel*) and explicitly requires that women and even children be in attendance. The Talmud makes no statement at all about women's obligation to hear the weekly portion read, but it does raise the possibility of women reading the Torah for the congregation.[11]

When discussing the number of people to be called to read from the Torah on various occasions, the Gemara cites a *baraita* (tannaitic source) that says a woman may be counted among the seven called to read on Sabbaths, but the Sages ruled that a woman should not read the Torah in public because of the dignity of the congregation (TB Meg. 23a). This statement needs to be understood in the context of several others that indicate that communities sometimes lacked a sufficient number of competent Torah readers.[12] Hence, the *Baraita* seems to say that a congregation, if unable to find a male reader, may turn to a female who, we are told, is clearly eligible to read from the Torah.[13] Yet, the Sages add, she should not read because by doing so she will compromise the dignity of the congregation. Although the Sages did not offer an explanation, it seems clear that they viewed women as members of a group generally considered socially or intellectually inferior. If women were of equal social status with men, a female reader would not affront the community's dignity.

In a similar vein, Mish. Suk. 3:10 says that if *Hallel* is recited for a man by a woman, he must repeat after her whatever she says—and he deserves to be cursed. He is required to repeat the verses because one who is not obligated to recite *Hallel*, e.g., a woman, may not discharge the responsibilities of one who is obligated (RH 3:8). However, why does he deserve to be cursed if she recites it and he repeats it? Possibly it is because he should have learned how to recite it himself and did not do so. However, the mishnah goes on to say that if an adult male reads *Hallel* for him, he answers *Halleluyah* after each phrase and need not repeat the words. In such a case, he is not cursed. It follows that the reason for the curse in the first case is that he is dependent for fulfilling his responsibilities on some-one of lower social status who is assumed to be less capable than he.[14] Were that not so, were he only deserving of a curse because he did not study and know enough to recite *Hallel* for himself, then he would de-serve to be cursed no matter who recited it for him, even an adult male.

A third reference to women leading men in prayer is found in TB Ber. 20b. In discussing the mishnah's rule that women are obligated to recite *birkat ha-mazon*, one rabbi asks if women's obligation is biblical, thus al-lowing them to say *birkat ha-mazon* for men, who are also biblically obli-gated, or whether women's obligation is only rabbinic, thus denying them the option of reciting *birkat ha-mazon* for men. In response to this ques-tion, the Gemara cites a *baraita* stating that a woman may recite *birkat ha-mazon* for her husband, but cursed be the man whose wife does recite Grace for him. This *baraita* is again suggesting that a learned woman shames an unlearned man, because women occupy a lower social stand-ing. The *baraita* also seems to indicate that women's obligation to recite *birkat ha-mazon* is biblical, because a woman is permitted to recite Grace for a man. However, since the Gemara later limits the scope of the *baraita* to a specific instance, it leaves the question about women reciting *birkat ha-mazon* for men unanswered.

In short, these sources tell us that women are obligated to pray the fixed daily prayers but may not join or lead the quorum or assist men in performing any of their other ritual obligations, even though women are technically eligible to do so.[15] A close reading of the text reveals that the rationale for these restrictions is women's social inferiority. This conclu-sion is distinctly different from the popular view that because women are not obligated to pray they may not join or lead the quorum.

Women and *Tefillin*

A ritual closely related to prayer is the donning of *tefillin*. Derived from the words of the *Shema* themselves, *tefillin* are worn while praying; in the Talmudic period they were also worn while studying Torah. They serve as a constant reminder of the covenant between God and the Jewish people, in which God promised health, prosperity, and security in exchange for worshiping God and performing God's *mitzvot*.

As noted above, the same Mishnah that obligated women to pray daily exempted them from reciting *Shema* and donning *tefillin*. Both of these are positive time-specific *mitzvot*, and it is consistent with the rules found in Kid. 1:7 that women are exempt. What needs to be clarified is whether or not women, although exempt, were permitted to wear *tefillin* if they so desired.

A *Baraita* in TB Er. 96a reports that Mikhal bat Kushi (also known as Mikhal, the daughter of King Saul) wore *tefillin* and the Sages did not protest. The Talmud, conducting an inquiry about the time limits of *tefillin*, asks if it necessarily follows from the account of Mikhal that *tefillin* is a non-time-specific *mitzvah* that a woman is obligated to perform, or if it is a time-specific *mitzvah* that, according to the Sages, a woman (although not obligated to do so) may choose to perform. The answer given is that the same *Baraita* that speaks of Mikhal bat Kushi also reports that the Sages did not stop the wife of Jonah from making the festival pilgrimage to Jerusalem;[16] since making the festival pilgrimage is certainly a time-specific *mitzvah*, so too is *tefillin*. The Talmud concludes that, according to the Sages, women may perform *mitzvot* from which they are exempt and may thus wear *tefillin*.

It is interesting to note that despite the Talmudic leniency, post-Talmudic decisors ruled stringently. *Tosafot* (s.v. *Mikhal bat Kushi*) comment that there are those who hold that women are not allowed to wear *tefillin* because *tefillin* need a clean body, and women are not careful about their personal cleanliness. In the sixteenth century, Joseph Karo merely states in the *Shulḥan Arukh* (Oraḥ Ḥayyim 38:3) that women are exempt from wearing *tefillin*, but Rabbi Moshe Isserles (Rema), Karo's contemporary, adds in his glosses that women must be stopped from putting them on.

Women and *Tzitzit*

Tzitzit (ritual fringes), like *tefillin*, serve to remind a Jew of the commandments (Num. 15:39). In the time of the Talmud, *tzitzit* were tied on the *tallit*, a four-cornered sheet-like cloak worn by most Jews over their clothes. A statement in the Talmud says that because God loves the Jewish people, God surrounds them with *mitzvot:* tefillin on their heads and arms, *tzitzit* on their garments, a *mezuzah* on their doors, and a sign of the covenant in their flesh (TB Men. 43b).

In the course of a lengthy discussion of the rules of *tzitzit*, we find a disagreement over whether or not women must wear them: the Sages, who regard *tzitzit* as a non-time-specific commandment, claim they are obligated; R. Simon, who views *tzitzit* as a time-specific *mitzvah* because it does not apply at night, asserts that women are exempt (TB Men.43a).[17] It is interesting to note that at least two later Talmudic rabbis tied *tzitzit* on the garments of their wives because, like the Sages, they held that *tzitzit* is a non-time-specific commandment that applies all the time and hence obligates women as well as men.[18]

In the post-Talmudic period, because of a change in the style of dress, men no longer wore four-cornered outer garments to which they could tie *tzitzit*. In order to fulfill this *mitzvah*, they began instead to wear a large fringed shawl for prayer and a small fringed garment (*tallit katan*) the rest of the day. It is possible that these changes led to the increasing stringency regarding women and *tzitzit*. Karo, ruling like R. Simon, exempts women from wearing them (Oraḥ Ḥayyim 17:2). Rema goes further, commenting that although women are permitted to wear *tzitzit*, it is arrogant for them to do so, for there is no absolute obligation to wear *tzitzit*, only the requirement that if one wears a four-cornered garment he must tie on *tzitzit*. This may be true, but a few sections later Karo writes that a Jew should make every effort to wear *tzitzit* all day long or, at the very least, when he prays (Oraḥ Ḥayyim 24:1). In any event, because post-Talmudic codists turned exemptions into near prohibitions, *tallit* and *tefillin*, the two garments that, through symbolic associations, help a Jew concentrate on his prayer, became off-limits to women.

Women and Testimony

The topic of women as witnesses does not relate directly to prayer but must be considered here because of its contemporary relevance to women serving as rabbis. Shevu. 4:1 states that the oath of adjuration (*shevuʿat ha-ʿedut*), which was administered to force witnesses to come forward and testify, applies to men but not to women—to those fit to be witnesses but not to those unfit to be witnesses. It follows from here that women were not eligible to testify in a court of law. The Gemara's commentary on the Mishnah provides a biblical prooftext for this restriction. By reading Deut.

19:17, "And the *two men* shall stand," in conjunction with Deut. 19:15, "All matters shall be established on the basis of the testimony of *two witnesses*" (both emphases added), the rabbis derive (by means of a textual analogy) that the two witnesses must be male.[19]

Nonetheless, other *mishnayot* indicate that the rule of women's exclusion from testimony was not consistently upheld. For instance, if a married man went abroad, and a woman came and reported that he died, her testimony was accepted, and his widow was given permission to remarry (Yev. 16:7). Or, if a man sent his wife a *get* (bill of divorce) from abroad, a female bearer of the *get* was allowed to testify that in her presence the *get* was written and signed, and the *get* was deemed valid (Git. 2:7). Similarly, if one woman testified that another woman was unfaithful to her husband, the testimony was accepted and the husband instructed to divorce his wife (Sot. 6:2). In general, in any instance in which the testimony of only one male witness was deemed sufficient, a woman's testimony was also accepted.

These exceptions to the rule indicate that women's testimony was probably not rejected on the grounds of unreliability. If that were so, marital matters, which have serious and far-reaching consequences, would not have been resolved on the basis of women's testimony. What seems more likely is that women in general were not allowed to testify because of their lower social standing. However, in those instances in which not accepting their testimony would have led to unnecessary and excessive social and economic hardship, creative exegesis of verses allowed exceptions to be made.[20]

The Rabbi's Role During the Talmudic Period

A rabbi's job in the time of the Talmud, not unlike today, was multifaceted. His most prominent role was that of legislator. As evidence of this, there are the thousands of rabbinic dicta found in the Talmud, which set standards of Jewish practice in all areas. Another one of his roles was to act as a judge. Numerous case histories indicated that rabbis settled disputes and decided practical matters. A third role, less evident in Talmudic sources, was as a preacher. Through public lectures delivered on Sabbaths and festivals, rabbis tried to inspire people to greater religious observance.

They also attempted to alleviate people's suffering at the hands of an oppressive foreign government by speaking to them of a glorious messianic future.[21]

Training to become a rabbi involved many years of studying with a mentor and serving as his apprentice, after which time a student who qualified could be ordained. The ongoing close association of teacher and disciples created fellowship circles of rabbis and their devoted students.

Not one of the hundreds of rabbis named in the Talmud was a woman. It does not seem that there were religious obstacles standing in the way of a woman becoming a rabbi, for there is no rule in the Talmud that precludes women from filling the teaching and preaching aspects of the rabbinate. What probably made it impossible for women to become rabbis was the fact that in the patriarchal, sex-segregated society of the Talmud women could not mingle freely with men.

Women in Ancient Society

A brief sketch of women's place in ancient Jewish society will help us view the laws mentioned above in their broad social context. A survey of Talmudic legislation affecting women reveals that in most areas of life women were controlled by men: a woman could not initiate or terminate marriage, manage even her own financial assets within marriage, keep any money she earned or found, inherit from her father or husband, fulfill her vows if her father or husband objected to them, or associate with someone of whom her husband disapproved (Ket. 4:4, 6:1, 8:1; Sot. 1:2).

To make sure that wives were not exploited by husbands, laws were passed that obligated the husband to feed and clothe his wife, satisfy her sexually, guarantee her alimony should he predecease or divorce her, ransom her if kidnapped, cure her if she fell ill, and bury her in proper style (Ket. 4:4, 8–12, 5:6). These rules may have placed significant limitations on the husband's behavior, but at the same time they clearly demonstrated that his wife was subordinate to him and economically dependent on him.

A married woman's role in Talmudic society was to satisfy her husband's needs, bear and rear the children, prepare the food, produce the clothing, and run the home (Ket. 5:5). Although clearly of higher status than a slave, wives were sometimes referred to as servants.[22] Outside of marriage, men and women were not to engage in any form of private social interchange for fear it would lead to sexual immorality; men could not chat with women, spend time alone with them, or look at any part of a woman's body (TB Ned. 20a, TB Shab. 64b).

This picture of women's subordination to men gives us a better understanding of some of the restrictions described above. A woman's general inability to function independently explains why she was exempt from fulfilling certain *mitzvot*. If a woman were obligated to perform ritual acts at specific times, it would lessen her husband's dominance over her because she would have to cease temporarily from serving him and instead serve God.[23] Rather than place her husband in competition with God, the rabbis did not require women to observe time-specific rituals. Although many have attributed these exemptions to a woman's responsibility to care for her children, there is no evidence that this was the case.

Women's social inferiority also explains why, despite their obligation to pray daily, they could not recite prayers for men. As noted above, a man was shamed if he found himself religiously dependent on those under his control, who presumably were less competent than he. Finally, women's subservience explains why many *mishnayot* group together women, slaves, and minors. What these three classes have in common is their subordinate status: wives are controlled by husbands, slaves by masters, and minors by parents.

The Modern Period: The Process of Change in the Conservative Movement

The inescapable conclusion of this survey of key institutions of Jewish religious expression is that the Talmudic laws that govern our lives today are inextricably bound up with the social realities of the past. As much as we try to view these rules as the outgrowth of God's perfect Torah, we must notice that they are also predicated on a set of assumptions about society and relationships between women and men within society. The question that arises is: Does this mean that the socially motivated and rabbinically mandated religious inferiority of women, which today we no longer find valid, is an integral, immutable part of Judaism? It seems not.

Ours is not the first generation to find it difficult to accept the underlying social assumptions of *halakhah*. Anyone who reads the Talmud with an open mind soon notices that the rabbis of the past frequently found themselves similarly troubled, but with great ingenuity they were able to solve the problem. When they sensed that the traditions transmitted to them were ethically deficient, they reinterpreted sacred texts in order to implement desired and necessary changes. For instance, displeased with the fact that the Torah does not allow a *kohen* to bury his wife—only parents, siblings, and children (Lev. 21:1–3)—the rabbis interpreted *"sh'ero"* (relative, flesh) in verse 2 as wife, thus stretching these norms to fit their emerging social outlook (TB Yev. 90b). Of course, they did not openly admit to altering the original intent of the biblical laws, but it is rather evident that that is exactly what they were doing.[24]

The trend to infuse Jewish law with one's own social thinking continued to develop in the post-Talmudic era as various eminent rabbis were called upon to set religious policies for their day. A good illustration is the lengthy comment written by Rabbenu Tam, a prominent twelfth-century Tosafist, on the question of allowing women to blow a *shofar* at home on Rosh Hashanah (RH 33a). He rules that women, even though they are exempt from hearing the blasts, may blow the *shofar* without breaking festival law. Moreover, he writes, women may in general perform a religious act from which they are exempt and recite the accompanying blessing without mentioning God's name in vain. To support his decision, Rabbenu Tam cites Talmudic precedents in which women's requests for expanded opportunities for religious expression were met by the Sages of their day. The most famous example is R. Yossi's report of Abba Elazar's decision to permit women to lay their hands on the head of the sacrificial animal on a festival—even though they were exempt from doing so—in order to give them *naḥat ruaḥ* (spiritual satisfaction, TB Hag. 16b).

Today, the Conservative Movement is home to those Jews who think like Rabbenu Tam, who accept *halakhah* as binding and yet recognize that as ethical and social thinking becomes more refined, it becomes necessary to modify religious practices. Upon reading his responsum, a Conservative Jew realizes that Rabbenu Tam could have chosen to deny women permission to blow the *shofar* by finding a set of precedents to support a stringency, but his desire to allow women greater opportunity for religious expression led him to develop a lenient line of argument. That is, a Conservative Jew understands that there is an element of subjectivity in rendering halakhic decisions, that there is more than one way to interpret a source, and that what predisposes a decisor to rule in a particular manner is his own set of ethical sensitivities and his perception of the socio-religious realitites of his day.[25] Unfortunately, this is a hard point of view to defend, because nowhere in his responsum does a decisor ever admit to subjective, ethically motivated interpretation. On the surface, there is only objectivity; however, by comparing conflicting responsa one begins to notice that the same corpus of traditions may be used by different writers to arrive at diametrically opposed conclusions.

In the last thirty years, the Conservative Movement has issued a number of responsa addressing specific requests by women for greater equality of opportunity in ritual areas. What characterizes these halakhic decisions is the attempt to reinterpret and explicate relevant traditional sources in order to propose a way to bring past legislation into alignment with present thinking. Although not all rabbis subscribe to all of the responsa,[26] it is consistently true that these responsa remain within the halakhic framework, using the same methods of reasoning as did the rabbis of the past to arrive at new conclusions.

Women Being Called to the Torah, 1955

The first request to increase women's opportunity for participation in the public service was made before the birth of feminism in the mid-1960s. In 1955, a number of papers were prepared by members of the Committee on Jewish Law and Standards, the official halakhic body of the Conservative Movement, on the topic of women being honored with an *aliyah* to the Torah. The most liberal opinion, advocating full equality for women, was written by Rabbi Aaron Blumenthal.[27] It is evident from his discussion of the issue that the motivation for this change was ethical—the need to give women equality of status in the synagogue. The main objection to granting women *aliyot* in the past was social, the idea that it was offensive to the community to honor women in this way. Today, he argues, this reason no longer applies because women are regarded as occupying equal social standing with men.

In his responsum, Blumenthal cites codists who discuss which *aliyot* of the seven a woman may have, whether more than one woman may be called on a given Sabbath, whether all of the readers may be women, whether women may have *aliyot* on festivals when fewer than seven are called, and whether a menstrual period prevents a woman from having an *aliyah*. These discussions, all of which assume that one may call women to read, provide ample basis for the view that it is halakhically defensible today to institute the practice of calling women to read from the Torah.

Women Counting in the *Minyan*, 1973

In 1973, one year after a Jewish women's group called *Ezrat Nashim* (see Monson, p. 227) publicized its feminist critique of Judaism and called for changes benefiting women in marital and ritual law, several members of the Committee on Jewish Law and Standards wrote position papers recommending that women be allowed to count in the *minyan*. Others wrote papers opposing it. Those who advocated the equality of women and men with respect to the prayer quorum based themselves on Talmudic analogies between women and minors or women and slaves. They claimed that since slaves and minors, in certain circumstances, could be counted as part of a quorum, women, who are ritually equivalent to slaves and minors, should also be counted. The Committee on Jewish Law and Standards did not adopt any one of the papers as its official position, but instead passed a *takkanah*, an independent enactment, allowing women to count in a *minyan* equally with men.[28]

Women Participating Fully in Synagogue Ritual, 1974

It is important to note that halakhic norms for Conservative Jews are not officially set by individual rabbis but by the Committee on Jewish Law and Standards, a group of twenty-five rabbis who study halakhic problems brought to their attention by members of the Conservative Movement's Rabbinical Assembly. Any resolution approved by at least three[29] of its members becomes an official position of the Committee and hence a legitimate option for Conservative rabbis to implement in their congregations.[30] In 1974, the Committee on Jewish Law and Standards adopted a series of proposals that equalized women and men in all areas of Jewish ritual.[31] For instance, as of that time, a Conservative rabbi could allow a woman to serve as *shaliah tzibbur* (prayer leader), count in the quorum for *birkat ha-mazon* (Grace after Meals), and function as a witness.

Women Serving as Rabbis, 1983

The issue that proved most difficult for the Conservative Movement to come to terms with was the ordination of women. Allowing a woman to fill the pivotal role of religious leader of the synagogue seemed a greater break with the past than allowing women to count in the *minyan,* which, halakhically speaking, was far more radical. For almost ten years this issue was debated. Fact-finding panels were established, testimony was collected in Conservative synagogues across the United States, and a report was written by the Commission for the Study of the Ordination of Women as Rabbis.[32] The majority of Commission members, like the majority of the Conservative laity, favored ordination of women. The minority opposed ordination because of its purported halakhic indefensibility.

Both sides agreed that most contemporary rabbinic functions, such as religious role model, teacher, and preacher, could be filled by women without making any halakhic adjustments. Although women did not engage in all of these activities in Talmudic society, there were no explicit laws preventing them from doing so. The only objections raised to ordaining women involved the ancillary rabbinic roles—leading prayer services and serving as a witness at weddings and divorces. The opponents of ordination noted that the Conservative rabbi of today is frequently called upon to serve as *shaliaḥ tzibbur,* often as the only competent prayer leader present in the *minyan.* It followed that if women were ordained, they too would find themselves pressed into service; however, the minority claimed, *halakhah* does not allow a woman to serve as a *shaliaḥ tzibbur;* Meg. 4:3 states that only men may count in the quorum of ten for prayer, and only men—who are themselves obligated to pray—may discharge the prayer responsibilities of others.

This objection to ordaining women overlooks the fact that the Talmud explicitly requires women to pray and in no way distinguishes their obligation from that of men (Ber. 3:3; TB Ber. 20b).[33] Admittedly, other sources in the Talmud make it clear that women, although technically eligible to be part of the *minyan,* for social reasons could not join men in prayer. However, as shown above, it should not be difficult to write a responsum arguing that today times have changed, that women occupy the same social standing as men, and therefore that women should be able to join a quorum on an equal basis with men and even lead it in prayer.

A responsum written by Rabbi Joel Roth on the ordination of women approaches the issue from a different perspective.[34] It discusses the possibility of women accepting upon themselves the obligation to pray daily at fixed times and hence becoming able to join men in a quorum and lead it in prayer. That is, although he does not say so explicitly, Roth, like some of the codists, holds that women are exempt from fixed daily prayer. He opens the discussion of self-imposed obligation by citing a statement of Magen Avraham (Rabbi Abraham b. Ḥayyim ha-Levi Gumbiner, seventeenth century) that although women are exempt from counting the *omer* (the fifty days between Passover and Shavuot) they have accepted this *mitzvah* upon themselves.[35] Roth finds precedents for this seemingly unprecedented legal decision. He cites, for example, the discussion by Ravyah (Rabbi Eliezer ben Yoel ha-Levi, end of the twelfth to beginning of the thirteenth centuries) about the widespread custom of adding *al ha-nisim*, the Ḥanukkah prayer, to *birkat ha-mazon*. In this instance, Roth argues, Ravia treats self-imposed obligation like externally imposed obligation: the codist decides that if one forgets to include *al ha-nisim* when saying *birkat ha-mazon* on Ḥanukkah, he must say Grace a second time, because adding *al ha-nisim* is no longer optional but obligatory.[36]

It follows, according to Roth, that once a woman has imposed upon herself the obligation to pray, she has equalized her prayer obligations to those of men, and she may count in the *minyan* and lead it in prayer.[37] He predicts that as a result of his responsum there will be different classes of Jewish women: those who will continue to regard their requirement to pray as voluntary and those who will regard their requirement to pray as obligatory.[38] Only women in the latter category could function as prayer leaders and count in the *minyan* and hence have no problem serving as rabbis.

As for women serving as witnesses, Roth argues that the rabbis of the Talmud derived a biblical prohibition against accepting women's testimony because they considered women unreliable. Since times have changed, he continues, and women's reliability is not in question, there is no longer any reason to exclude them. He therefore recommends invoking the ultimate halakhic act, active abrogation of a biblical proscription.[39]

Roth thus proposes a well-reasoned plan for changing certain aspects of Jewish law in order to allow for the ordination of women. What is strange, though, is his insistence that the issue of male-female equality plays no role in his thinking on the subject.[40]

Rabbi Mayer Rabinowitz also wrote a responsum approving ordination of women.[41] He solves the problem of women's ineligibility to serve as *shaliaḥ tzibbur* by asserting that the function of the *shaliaḥ tzibbur* today is different from what it was in the past. Originally, the *shaliaḥ tzibbur* led services in order to enable those who did not know the prayers to fulfill their obligations to pray; today, since we all have access to *siddurim* (prayer books) and can pray in either English or Hebrew, the *shaliaḥ tzibbur* may not discharge our obligations for us. The *shaliaḥ tzibbur*'s principal usefulness is to enhance the service, to ensure that the community prays together as a group. Thus, there is no reason to exclude a woman from acting as *shaliaḥ tzibbur*. As for women serving as witnesses, Rabinowitz challenges the notion that the prohibition is biblical, pointing to a number of commentators who seem to think it rabbinic, and hence easier to change. The prohibition can be relaxed today, according to Rabinowitz, because we no longer consider women unreliable but view them as independent, trustworthy adults.

Other Conservative responsa reached the conclusion that one cannot ordain women within the parameters of *halakhah*. One respondent focuses exclusively on the status of self-imposed obligation, deciding that a woman may impose new obligations on herself but may not discharge the responsibilities of others who are externally obligated.[42] He supports this conclusion with two early responsa that prohibit women from reading the *Megillah* for men, even though women themselves are obligated to hear it read. The codists who wrote these responsa, he informs us, relied on an alternate reading of the text of the Talmud to derive the stringency.[43] Another respondent, after stating that a woman's self-imposed obligation to pray daily does not allow her to function as *shaliaḥ tzibbur*, adds that a rapid decision to ordain women as rabbis will constitute "a break with the historical school of which the Conservative Movement is the heir, which looks to the past for guidance in its religious decision-making."[44] He recommends instead that women begin to increase their participation in Jewish life by serving as ritual slaughterers and circumcisors who are "religiously more important" than rabbis.

The issue of women's ordination, first approved by the Committee on Jewish Law and Standards in 1974, was also endorsed by members of the Jewish Theological Seminary faculty in October 1983. The various faculty papers on the ordination of women gave the basis for voting either in favor of or against the admission of women to the Rabbinical School. Even so, when the faculty voted to admit women, it did not predicate its decision on the acceptance of any particular paper. However, when implementing the faculty vote, it was decided to admit women as candidates for ordination only if they indicated that they had accepted upon themselves the same obligation to perform religious rituals as men.

According to Dr. Anne Lerner, author of one of the faculty papers,[45] the Roth responsum is followed mainly at the Seminary itself. In general it is impractical because it requires asking each woman if she may be counted in the *minyan*. Outside the Seminary, there are very few synagogues that implement the responsum. Most congregations ask no questions of women when counting them in the *minyan* because the general public posture is egalitarian.

Women Serving as Cantors, 1987

As unlikely as it may seem, four years passed after the decision was made to ordain women as rabbis before the Roth responsum was applied to the investiture of women as cantors. The same arguments given above for allowing a woman to act as *shaliah tzibbur* obviously apply to permitting women to act as cantors. It is interesting, though, that if we remind ourselves of the reasons for praying communally, with a *shaliah tzibbur* leading the group, we reach the decision to allow women to serve as cantors by an alternate route. Approaching the issue of women cantors from the broad perspective of the essence of Jewish prayer, we easily note that the two major goals of praying communally are achieved without any consideration of gender. If we pray in a group to enhance the glory of God, then the larger the gathering the better, the presence of women notwithstanding. And if we also pray in a group in order to exert greater influence on God to grant our wishes, then we must choose as prayer leaders those individuals who are most capable of praying effectively, regardless of gender.[46] Thus, it is possible to justify women as cantors on both a broad analytical basis and a technical halakhic basis.

Conclusion

Ultimately, we are all torn between the past and the present. Adhering to the past without introducing any changes in Jewish ritual gives a feeling of continuity and legitimacy, of doing things right. After all, it is not easy to base one's religious practice on a God-given Torah and then adopt extensive change. The forces to leave things in place are very great. Yet, it is hard for many of us to live with the past alone. It is impossible to maintain the status quo after our eyes have been opened to the feminist critique of Judaism. The arguments are so compelling and the system of law so clearly sexist that we have no choice about change. Luckily, what paves the way toward introducing changes is the fact that Jewish law itself underwent significant change over time in response to a social and ethical critique.

What I have attempted to show in this chapter is that Talmudic law in general, and the institutions of prayer in particular, derive not just from religious categories set forth in Torah (as many current writers believe) but have also assimilated some of the social mores of the past. Specifically, tradition imposed fewer ritual obligations on women because of their inability to function independently in a social context. The unfortunate outcome of this differentiation was to limit sharply women's opportunities for religious expression. Since the changes sought by women today do not involve basic restructuring of Jewish ritual but only neutralizing the pervasive bias toward men, it is possible to accommodate these requests within the confines of *halakhah*. In fact, careful study of Talmud and Codes shows that throughout halakhic history one of the main objectives of the decisor was subtly to infuse the socio-ethical dictates of his day into the transmitted corpus of *halakhah*.

The Conservative Movement continues today to seek that same goal by introducing a number of changes to expand women's role in synagogue services. Although women had been sitting side by side with men in mixed pews for many years, until recently women played no active role in the synagogue service. Since 1972, when Jewish women first began to seek greater opportunities for participation in communal worship, changes have occurred rapidly.[47] Today, many women receive *aliyot*, read from the Torah, celebrate becoming a *Bat Mitzvah*, wear a *tallit* and even *tefillin*, identify themselves with both patronym and matronym (as do many men), count in the *minyan*, and serve as rabbis and cantors.

Virtually every Conservative synagogue in the United States has found it necessary and appropriate to expand women's participation. Resistance can be felt in some congregations, but on the whole the changes are

warmly embraced. What marks this increase in opportunity in most synagogues is a sense of women coming of age religiously, of women finally
entering the mainstream of Jewish intellectual and spirtual life.

Notes

1. I wish to thank Professors Richard Kalmin, Anne Lerner, Mayer Rabinowitz, and Alvin Sandberg for making many suggestions to improve this chapter. I would also like to acknowledge the research funds provided by the Maxwell Abbell Research Fund.

2. For three the opening phrase is, "Let us bless"; for 10, "Let us bless our Lord"; for 100, "Let us bless God, our Lord"; for 1000, "Let us bless God our Lord, the Lord of Israel"; for 10,000, "Let us bless God, our Lord, the Lord of Israel, the Lord of Hosts who dwells among the cherubim, for the food that we have eaten."

3. This rule still applies today. The *shaliah tzibbur* may not discharge the responsibilities of those who are able to pray. *See* Orah Hayyim 124:1.

4. The reason a minor may not recite the priestly blessing, according to Rashi (Meg. 24a, s.v. *"v'eyno nosei et kapav"*), is that it offends the honor of the congregation to be dependent on a minor's blessing.

5. That the Torah may be read by a minor, although he may not serve as *shaliah tzibbur*, suggests that reading Scripture aloud for the group to hear is different from reciting prayers on its behalf. That a minor may read from the Torah but not a person dressed in rags (*poheah*) suggests that youth is regarded as less problematic than inappropriate garb.

6. *Tosafot* (s.v. *"bi-tefillah"*) explain the Gemara as saying that one might consider the Mishnah's ruling obvious. But that is not so, because it is possible to think that *Tefillah* is a time-specific commandment and therefore does not obligate women; however, since prayer is essentially petitions, even though time-specific, it is still incumbent upon women. Rashi, whose text of the Gemara here is different from that of *Tosafot*, argues that since *Tefillah* is rabbinically ordained, it may not be classified either as time-specific or not time-specific, for these categories only apply to commandments originating in the Torah. It follows that according to Rashi, women are obligated to pray just as men are (*see Arukh ha-Shulhan,* Hilkhot Tefillah, 106:5, 6, 7). The parallel section in the Jerusalem Talmud (Ber. 6b) says that women are obligated to recite the *Tefillah* "so that each person will himself petition God to have mercy on him." That is, the essence of fixed prayer is petitions.

Despite the Mishnah's clear-cut statement that women are obligated to recite the *Tefillah* as men are, post-Talmudic codifiers limited women's obligation, requiring them at the most to recite the morning and afternoon prayers each day but not the evening service (*Mishnah Berurah,* Orah Hayyim 106:4) and, at the least, merely to utter some petitions (*Magen Avraham,* Orah Hayyim 106:2) (*see* 1. Haut, pp. 94–95).

7. All references in Talmudic literature to slaves per se speak of a male or female non-Jewish slave purchased by a Jew, generally to serve as an attendant in the home. A male slave was to be circumcised within twelve months of purchase. A slave was required to live a Jewish life and even perform *mitzvot,* except for positive time-specific ones. Were his or her owner to emancipate him or her, upon immersion in a *mivkeh* (ritual bath) he or she would become a Jew in all respects (TB Yev. 47b–48b).

8. R. Nahman ruled that a (male) child who is old enough to know to whom he prays may join the quorum of three for Grace (TB Ber. 48a). However, Rema (R. Moses Isserles)

later decided that we may not count minors in either the quorum of three or ten for Grace (Oraḥ Ḥayyim 199:10).

9. R. Joshua b. Levi's dictum about slaves, as interpreted by the Gemara, also allows a slave to complete a quorum for prayer. Some Tosafists, most notably Rabbenu Tam (Ber. 48a, s.v. "*ve-leyt hilkheta*"), similarly allow a minor to complete a quorum of ten for prayer.

10. TJ Meg. 75a.

11. *Masekhet Soferim*, a post-Talmudic halakhic compilation, explicitly obligates women to hear the Torah reading (18:4); however, later codists do not agree and even note that the women of their day are accustomed to walk out during the reading (*Magen Avraham*, Oraḥ Ḥayyim 182:6).

12. *See* Tosef. Meg. 3:12, 13; TJ Meg. 75a.

13. According to Saul Lieberman, *Tosefta ki-Feshuta, Megillah* (New York: JTS, 1962), 1176–78, the *Tosefta's* statement (3:11) "All may be counted in the quorum of seven, even a woman, even a child; one does not bring a woman to read for the group," applies to a case where no man at all is able to read, for a woman may not read the entire section. If one man reads, however, then Moses' enactment of one male adult reader has been fulfilled, and women are allowed to read (*Or Zarua*, Meiri, and others). This explanation differs sharply with the one found in the Babylonian Talmud, which explains the rule in social rather than religious terms. Note that in the Jerusalem Talmud, R. Zeira, in the name of R. Jeremiah, says that a slave may count in the quorum of seven readers (Meg. 75a). No mention is made of women.

14. Rashi (Suk. 38a, s.v. "*ve-tavo lo me-ayrah*") says that a man shames his Maker by choosing such a representative. *Tosafot* (s.v. "*utehi lo me-ayrah*") softens the impact of Rashi's statement by saying that the shame derives from the fact that a woman is not obligated to say *Hallel*.

15. Women reading *Hallel* for men is an exception to this rule, because women are not obligated to recite *Hallel*, which is a time-specific commandment.

16. In the Jerusalem Talmud, Ber. 4c, the same *baraita* is cited. It is introduced as a challenge to the statement that women are exempt from Torah study and *tefillin*. Following the *baraita*, R. Hezekiah, in the name of R. Abahu, says that the Sages returned Jonah's wife and protested Mikhal bat Kushi's actions.

17. In the Jerusalem Talmud (Ber. 6b), *tzitzit* is listed in a *Baraita* as an example of a non-time-specific *mitzvah*; R. Simon disagrees, asserting that it is a time-specific *mitzvah* because nightclothes do not require *tzitzit*. A similar *Baraita* appears in the Babylonian Talmud (Kid. 33b) but lists *tzitzit* as a time-specific *mitzvah*.

18. TB Men. 43a reports that Rabbi Judah (the *amora*) did so (*see* Rashi, s.v. "*de-inshei beitei*"). TB Suk. 11a reports that Rabbi Amram also did so (*see* Rashi, s.v. "*le-pirzuma de-inshei beitei*").

19. Women were similarly not allowed to fill the role of judge. *Tosafot* (TB BK 15a, s.v. "*asher tasim lifneihem*" and TB Nid. 50a, s.v. "*kol ha-kasher ladun*") point out that one may not cite the biblical figure Deborah as proof that women may judge because she did not render her own decisions but was a conduit for the word of God. It is also possible, they say, that she did not judge cases but taught people law.

20. In post-Talmudic codes, there was a slight increase in the kinds of cases in which a woman could testify; *see Encyclopedia Talmudit*, s.v. *Ishah*.

21. Gedalyahu Allon, *Toldot ha-Yehudim be-Eretz Yisra'el be-Tekufat ha-Mishnah ve-ha-Talmud* (Merchavia, Israel: Hakibbutz Hameuchad, 1967) 294–306.

22. TB Ned. 38b, TB Sanh. 39a: In her clever response to an infidel who claimed the Jewish God was a thief because God stole a rib from Adam while he slept, the daughter of

Rabban Gamliel exclaimed: Was it not pleasing to Adam that God took a rib from him and replaced it with a handmaid to serve him?!

23. Rabbi David Abudarham, *Abudarham ha-Shalem* (in Hebrew) (Jerusalem: Usha, 1962), 25. He writes that a woman was subservient to her husband and instructed to take care of all his needs. Were women obligated to fulfill time-specific commandments, they might find themselves having to choose between pleasing God and pleasing a husband. Thus, to promote harmony in the home, God exempted women from time-specific commandments.

24. On occasion, the rabbis of the Talmud justify their right to devise new legislation. For instance, they cite "*lo tasur*" (do not deviate from what they [the judges] tell you, Deut. 17:11) as the Torah's mandate to the authorities of each generation to answer questions and develop laws according to the needs of the times (TB Shab. 23a).

25. For a lengthy discussion of this point of view, *see* Louis Jacobs, *A Tree of Life* (London: Oxford University Press, 1984), 9–17. For many fascinating examples of socially motivated change, *see* pp. 122–66. *See also* Menachem Elon's discussion in *Ha-Mishpat ha-Ivri* (in Hebrew) (Jerusalem: Hebrew University Press, 1973), 682–86, for socially motivated changes in inheritance law, and pp. 539–46 for socially motivated changes in marital law. *See also* Elon's survey of the family law enactments of the Israeli Chief Rabbinate from 1943 to 1950, pp. 669–75.

26. A group of Conservative rabbis and laymen who oppose these changes, notably the decision to ordain women as rabbis, formed an organization called the Union for Traditional Conservative Judaism, now called the *Union for Traditional Judaism*.

27. "An *Aliyah* for Women," *Conservative Judaism and Jewish Law*, ed. Seymour Siegel (New York: The Rabbinical Assembly, 1977), 266–80.

28. *See* the Rabbinical Assembly's unpublished booklet on Women and *Minyan*, 5 October 1973.

29. Recently the minimum number of votes required for issuing an official position was raised to six.

30. A Conservative rabbi is free either to exercise a new option, e.g., call women for an *aliyah*, or not to exercise the option, e.g., maintain the status quo of limiting public participation in synagogue ritual to men. A standard only becomes binding on Conservative rabbis if eighty percent of the Committee members approve it and a majority of the Rabbinical Assembly convention votes in favor of it.

31. For a full report on this series of decisions, *see* Aaron Blumenthal, "The Status of Women in Jewish Law," *Conservative Judaism*, 31:3 (Spring 1977), 24–40. For an updated survey of decisions by the Committee on Jewish Law and Standards relating to women in the synagogue, *see* Mayer Rabinowitz, "The Role of Women in Jewish Ritual," *Conservative Judaism* 34:1 (Fall 1986), 7–33.

32. This Commission was established in October 1977 by then Chancellor Gerson D. Cohen at the request of the Rabbinical Assembly. The final report of the Commission is published in full in *The Ordination of Women as Rabbis, Studies and Responsa*, ed. Simon Greenberg (New York: JTS, 1988), 5–30.

33. *See Arukh ha-Shulḥan*, Hilkhot Tefillah, 106:5, 6, 7 for a survey of interpretations of the Talmud's statement that women are obligated to pray. *See also* n.6, *supra*.

34. S. Greenberg, *The Ordination of Women as Rabbis*, pp. 127–87.

35. Ibid., 136.

36. Ibid., 139. Other examples cited by Roth are allowing women to obligate themselves to wear *tzitzit* even though they are exempt (Rabbi Shimshon bar Zadok, thirteenth

century), and requiring women to recite *musaf* even though they are exempt, because they have already accustomed themselves to praying it (Isaac di Molina, sixteenth century).

37. Ibid., 146.

38. Ibid., 148.

39. Ibid., 171.

40. Ibid., 170.

41. "An Advocate's Halakhic Responses on the Ordination of Women," *Judaism*, 33 (Winter 1984): 54–65. Also in S. Greenberg, *The Ordination of Women as Rabbis*, 107–23.

42. S. Greenberg, *The Ordination of Women as Rabbis*, 43, paper by Israel Francus.

43. For an excellent discussion of the issue of women reading the *Megillah* for others, *see* Joel Roth, *The Halakhic Process: A Systemic Analysis* (New York: JTS, 1986), 354–64.

44. David Halivni, "On Ordination of Women," (unpublished paper), 18.

45. S. Greenberg, *The Ordination of Women as Rabbis*, 93–106.

46. The issue of *kol be-ishah ervah* (the sexual distraction of a woman's voice) originates in the Talmud in reference to a man reciting *Shema* while hearing his wife's voice (TB Ber. 24a). The post-Talmudic commentators are divided on whether or not *kol ishah* applies to other contexts. As noted above, the Talmud (TB Meg. 23a) does not deny women the opportunity to read from the Torah in public for this reason but for other reasons relating to communal dignity. The Conservative Movement therefore does not see *kol ishah* as an obstacle to women serving as cantors. *See* Emily Taitz, "*Kol Ishah*—The Voice of Women: Where Was it Heard in Medieval Europe?" *Conservative Judaism* 38 : 3 (Spring 1986): 46–61.

47. Celebrating a girl's reaching *Bat Mitzvah* started in the 1920s, and *aliyot* for women began in the 1950s; however, neither of these practices became widespread until the 1970s.

Annette Daum

LANGUAGE
AND LITURGY

The *siddur* (prayer book) is traditionally regarded as the mirror of the Jewish soul, a metaphorical reflection of the spiritual and historical development of the Jewish people, expressing the religious and ethical ideals, the trials and tribulations, the joys and sorrows, the hopes and aspirations of the Jews over more than three millennia. As Dr. Joseph H. Hertz, the late chief rabbi of the British Empire, noted in *The Daily Prayer Book*, the *siddur* is both the gateway to communion with God and the bond that unites Jews with their "brethren" scattered throughout the world. Through the ages, the gate has been controlled, the opening filtered through the eyes of the men who developed, translated, interpreted, and taught that tradition.

Prayer, as the link between God and humanity, is a universal phenomenon, which takes many forms: from expressing the highest praise, thanksgiving, and adoration for God's protection from the terrors of life, to making humble petitions for help at times of great distress. The Hebrew word for prayer, *tefillah*, from the root, "to judge," is usually understood

Annette Daum passed away before publication of this book. We hope that this article will contribute to the work on liturgy to which she devoted her life.

as "self-examination." No matter what the form of expression, prayer inspires us to re-examine and renew our convenantal relationship with the One God Who loves us and Whom we, in turn, approach with all the devotion of our hearts, our minds, our souls, and our might.

There are many ways of reaching out to God. In ancient days, Jews communicated with God by offering sacrifices that were accompanied by rituals and ceremonies,[1] including the singing of Psalms and the chanting of prayers. Eventually, these ceremonies became so complicated that only special religious leaders (Temple priests and levites) could conduct them or lead the singing.

Prayer as a Substitute for Sacrifices

Religious practices began to change after the destruction of the First Temple in 586 B.C.E. Without a Temple, the priests could no longer offer sacrifices; therefore, a new form of worship was required. In exile, in Babylonia, the Jewish people began to gather on the Sabbath to study the Holy Book and to reach out to God directly with words and without priests, altars, or sacrifices.[2]

The custom of coming together to study and pray in a neighborhood synagogue continued even after the Jews returned to their land, even though the Temple at Jerusalem was rebuilt. It was the existence of the synagogue that enabled Judaism to survive. After the fall of the Second Temple in 70 C.E., Jews were able to continue to worship the One God, using prayer as a substitute for sacrifices, incorporating ancient practices such as the singing of Psalms and chanting of prayers as the heart of the service.

There are some indications that these practices were associated with the sanctuaries that predated the Temple in Jerusalem (1 Chron. 16:37–42). While sacrifices were accompanied by prayer, prayers were independent of sacrifice. The transition from sacrificial cult to synagogue worship was not accomplished without controversy about the restructuring of Jewish life and institutions. Even the obligation of every man to attend public services three times a day, corresponding to the times when sacrifices were offered, was not readily accepted.[3] Since the prayers were preserved and transmitted orally, and since there were already differences within and between Babylonian traditions, variations in the texts and even the principles of liturgy developed from place to place, even from congregation to congregation in the same area. Differences also arose regarding the desirability of fixed prayer texts.

The liturgy grew through the continuous improvisations of religious spirits in moments of inspiration. Men used to create prayers for their private devotion; and only after their compositions found favor in the eyes of the people, were they gradually incorporated into the public worship. It took more than 900 years of continuous growth for the liturgy to reach the state as presented in the first prayer-book compiled by Rav Amram (875).[4]

This first compilation, according to the Babylonian tradition, was followed shortly by the *siddur* of Saadya Gaon, which was based on Palestinian ritual. The Sephardic rite emerged out of the Babylonian tradition. The Ashkenazic rite that emerged out of the Palestinian tradition has a Western branch, the German *minhag* (custom) and an Eastern branch, the Polish *minhag*. The two major traditions today represent compilations and compromises with these various rituals.

Many of our most beloved prayers, which today are an integral part of traditional liturgy, are comparatively recent. For example, the ancient *Kaddish* prayer was first recited by mourners in the thirteenth century, during the persecutions of the Crusades. The *Kabbalat Shabbat* service welcoming the Sabbath was largely created by the sixteenth-century mystics of Safed. Reciting *Yizkor*, the memorial service of Yom Kippur and the Festivals, did not become standard practice until the seventeenth century.

The only controversy regarding the recitation of the *Kaddish* by mourners today centers on the sex of the mourner, as women were prohibited from reciting *Kaddish* (*see* I. Haut, p. 98).[5] For more than a century, only Reform Judaism offered women the privilege of reciting the *Kaddish*. Now, women in most non-Orthodox, as well as in some Orthodox, synagogues may recite *Kaddish*.

Since the prayer book has never been canonized, changes were introduced to meet the needs of people throughout the ages. After the destruction of the Temple, the *Avodah* prayer, traditionally recited by the priest after offering sacrifices, was changed to express the hope that the Temple would be rebuilt and sacrifices be restored. While the Orthodox *siddur* still retains this formulation, the Reform prayer book omitted such references and the Conservative Movement reinterpreted this prayer as a recollection of the sacrificial service.

Although Hebrew is *the* language of liturgy, linking Jews of various lands in a universal bond of worship, prayers were sometimes offered in the vernacular. The *Kaddish* has been traditionally recited in Aramaic—the language of the people in Palestine during the period of the Second Temple. Hellenist Jews, from approximately the third century B.C.E. to the beginning of the Common Era, used the Greek vernacular in worship, reading the Torah in translation. The prayer book was translated into several languages in later centuries, since many Jews, now living in the Diaspora, no longer understood Hebrew.

Since the covenant at Sinai was made with the Jewish people as a community as well as with each individual Jew, Jewish prayer is largely communal in nature, conducted mostly in the first person plural. Even the language of prayers originating in the Bible in the first person singular were changed to the plural form to accommodate this concept. For example: "Heal me, O Lord, and I shall be healed: save me, and I shall be saved; for Thou art my praise" (Jer. 17:14) was changed to "Heal us, O Lord, and we shall be healed; save us, and we shall be saved; for Thou art our praise." [6]

In his introduction to the new Conservative *Maḥzor* for the High Holy Days, Dr. Jules Harlow, the editor, illustrates how the framers of the prayer book deliberately mistranslated Scripture for a specific purpose. The example he provides, a biblical passage from Exodus 34, which occurs after Moses prays to God to forgive the Israelites for worshiping the golden calf, reads, "The Lord, the Lord God is gracious and compassionate, patient, abounding in kindness, and faithfulness, assuring love for a thousand generations, forgiving iniquity, transgression, and sin; *yet He does not completely pardon the guilty* . . . " (italics added). In the prayer book, the words "and granting pardon" (*ve-nakeh*) replace "yet He does not completely pardon the guilty. . . ," which significantly alters the text. The passage as changed stresses the concept of a compassionate God, emphasized on Yom Kippur, as a basic tenet of Judaism, overriding the concern for strict justice.

Liturgical creativity, which often took the form of the insertion of poetry from other than biblical sources, was initially met with opposition by such outstanding scholars as Maimonides, while it was supported by equally outstanding authorities such as Rashi. Centuries later, rabbinic authorities fought with vigor against the omission of such poetry.

During the Middle Ages, apostates (Jews who converted to Christianity) falsely denounced Hebrew liturgy to Church authorities, claiming that certain prayers were directed against Christianity. Church censors then forced elimination of "suspicious" passages. The *Aleinu* prayer was changed to eliminate the words "for they bow down to vanity and emptiness and pray to a god that cannot save," even though this portion of the prayer was based on the Book of Isaiah, which was written centuries before the birth of Christianity. Printers also arbitrarily changed the text of some prayers by either introducing or omitting material.

As the prayer book evolved, every addition, omission, and translation represented a re-formation, a re-interpretation. New prayer books could and did appear from time to time to reflect the needs and new understandings of the Jewish people. Dispersed throughout the Diaspora, different traditions formed around the central core of common prayers that remains recognizable from culture to culture, from country to country. The prayer book is meant to reflect the experience of the people, to be the property of the people, not only of rabbis and scholars.

Prayers from A Male Perspective

Until now, however, the prayer book has expressed the spiritual yearnings of half the Jewish People, the men who were the writers, editors, and translators of a liturgy that was designed for use by men. Still, many of the prayers reflect human experience such as prayers for health, wisdom, forgiveness, and justice as well as praise and thanksgiving. Feminine imagery appears, for example, in the *Hallel*, which speaks of barren women becoming mothers. It is difficult to determine whether the prayer reflects female yearnings or male priorities—the desire for progeny—which women internalize.

No matter how sensitive, these prayers, written from a male perspective, assume that women's only priority is to fulfill her biological function—to bear children. These prayers are highly selective, reflecting a biblical perspective (male) that features the Matriarchs as revered female role models. The editors of our prayer books traditionally excluded prayers by other biblical women, such as Miriam and Deborah, which offer alternative role models. Through the centuries, male editors of the prayer book stereotyped the role of women in the eyes of those at worship. The language of liturgy is also unrelievedly masculine, creating the overriding impression that worship is a male prerogative. Since services were traditionally conducted in Hebrew, which has no neuter gender, it was only natural that prayers, written and selected by men, would appear only in masculine form, further excluding women—whether or not intentionally. Translations in the vernacular such as English, which does have a neuter gender, were nevertheless couched in solely masculine terms, compounding the problem.

As Jews, who have suffered for centuries because of the stereotyped images that were used to exclude us from the mainstream of society, we are particularly sensitive to the way language is used to foster and perpetuate prejudice. Yet, when the question of masculine-biased language in liturgy is raised, the subject is often trivialized, the hostility hidden under the guise of humor. Women, themselves, sometimes object to suggested changes. They may be going through a process of denial, for the price of recognition may be too painful, or they may simply be unaware that change in language and liturgy is in good Jewish tradition.

In biblical days, even the names of revered Patriarchs and Matriarchs were changed when a radical change in character took place. Abram became Abraham when he received God's blessing (Gen. 17:5). Sarai became Sarah as she became the mother of the Jewish people (Gen. 17:15). Jacob's name was changed to Israel as a result of his transformation of character (Gen. 32:29). Religious equality for women signifies a similar change in status, necessitating inclusion in the language of liturgy and, thus, the elimination of sexist language.

The problem of masculine-biased language has been addressed on two levels. It has been relatively easy to reach a consensus on the need to change language referring to humanity. Resistance to the elimination of masculine imagery about God is much more pervasive, indicating the profound emotional impact of the language of prayer.

The Shift Toward Women's Equality

In 1972, the year that the first woman rabbi in the United States was ordained by Hebrew Union College (the Reform rabbinical seminary in New York), a Task Force on Equality of Women in Judaism was formed as an official committee within Reform Judaism. Since the elimination of sexist language in liturgy is a high priority item on their agenda, the Task Force developed a *Glossary of Substitute Terminology* for masculine-biased liturgical language.

The Glossary serves as a consciousness-raising device which compels us to think in new ways. It requires a re-orientation away from a male-dominated tradition, a change in men's attitudes towards women and, of greater significance, a change in women's attitudes towards themselves. The Task Force also addressed the importance of Biblical translation and commentary, recommending the elimination of unnecessary and inaccurate masculine references. Whether referring to humanity in general or to God, such language leads us in the wrong direction. For women as well as men are created in the image of God who, in Judaism, is beyond sexuality.[7]

The Reform Movement adopted the principle of religious equality for women as early as 1846. Yet, changes in language did not begin until 1975. Rabbi Sally Priesand (the first woman to be ordained as a rabbi) was consulted during the preparation of *Gates of Prayer* (New York: Central Conference of American Rabbis, 1975), the new weekday and Shabbat Reform prayer book. It was the first official Jewish prayer book to avoid masculine terminology when referring to humanity, as a matter of principle. The Conservative prayer book *Sim Shalom* (New York: Rabbinical Assembly, 1985), makes a number of changes, though not as inclusive as the Reform prayer book. We now examine some of the issues involving inclusive language and the changes that have been made in the various movements.

Prayers Offensive to Women

No prayer more accurately reflects the fact that worship services have been the province of a men's club than the traditional prayer still recited every morning by Orthodox males, "Blessed art Thou, Lord our God, King of the Universe, Who hast not made me a woman."

Both Phillip Birnbaum and Joseph Hertz, in their different editions of the daily prayer book, indicate that this prayer merely signifies men's gratitude for the "God-given" privilege of performing *all* the *mitzvot*, many of which are not incumbent upon women. Hertz explicitly states that "no derogation of women is implied."[8] Jewish feminist critics assert that greater privilege for men implies inferior status for women.

No matter how interpreted, a prayer thanking God for not making one a woman has negative implications for women if only because of its place in the prayer book—immediately following a group of prayers in which men thank God for not creating them heathens or slaves, clearly undesirable categories of lesser status. Despite protestations to the contrary, considered in context, it would appear that, in the eyes of the men responsible for the prayer book, Jewish religious life conferred lesser status on women.

The traditional companion prayer, to be recited by women, thanking God ". . . Who has made me according to Thy will," however interpreted, contains a not-so-subliminal message that women are expected to accept second-class religious status as ordained by God.

This prayer must have been troublesome to sensitive Jewish men from different traditions who sought solutions to this problem. Reform Judaism specifically rejected this prayer, dropping it completely shortly after the formation of the movement.

A century later, Conservative Judaism, confronted with this same dilemma, found a different solution, substituting a prayer thanking God "for making me an Israelite," to be recited by both men and women.

After searching through the sources, the late Professor Louis Ginsberg demonstrated that one of the true versions of that prayer (thanking God for not making me a women) did not contain such an expression (prior to the eighth century C.E.); it appears to have been added in medieval times by a scribe who made the addition without authority.[9]

The prayer thanking God for not making the worshiper a woman, recited today by Orthodox Jewish males, was rejected by the majority of Jews long before the feminist movement sensitized the community to the way language is used to perpetuate and foster prejudice.

There are other prayers that offend women such as *"modeh ani"* (an early morning prayer), in which the worshipper thanks God for the gift of the soul; for, written traditionally only in the Hebrew masculine form, the assumption is that the reader is a male and that women are not included in the congregation.

The Conservative prayer book *Siddur Sim Shalom*, published just as the first Conservative woman rabbi was ordained, reflects the dramatic improvement in the status of women in Conservative Judaism since the movement was challenged by *Ezrat Nashim* (*see* Monson, p. 227).

While prayer books of the Reform Movement take no special notice of women's participation, simply taking it for granted, the new Conservative *siddur* makes significant changes that affirm women as full participants in worship.

As the editor, Dr. Jules Harlow, indicates:

The language of the liturgical formulas reflects the reality that in many congregations both men and women participate in the service. They also include reference to both the patriarchs and the matriarchs. Passages designated for use on Simḥat Torah, when the conclusion and the renewal of the annual cycle of Torah readings are celebrated, include texts appropriate for those congregations which designate women as well as men as honorees. The prayer on behalf of the congregation recited after the Torah reading on Shabbat morning has been amended to reflect the fact that women as well as men are members of a congregation.[10]

The *siddur* also encourages individuals to add their own words of prayer that "are as authentic at certain times as those of an ancient or medieval sage."[11] As there are many routes to prayer, Dr. Harlow notes, "Each person must find his or her appropriate path."[12]

For the first time in any prayer book, the Hebrew has been changed in some instances to include the feminine gender so that women, as well as men, may pray in appropriate language. The weekday morning prayer expressing gratitude for the gift of our souls now adds "*modah ani*" (in the feminine) in parenthesis as a feminine alternative to "*modeh ani.*" Similarly, the feminine forms are added to other prayers, notably the prayer accepting the obligation of "fulfilling my Creator's *mitzvah* in the Torah" and the morning blessing that praises the God "who made me free." Even more important, the *gomel* prayer recited by those who have recovered from a serious illness appears in inclusive form, for males and females are called to the Torah, as does the *mi-she-berakh* prayer, which also adds the names of the Matriarchs in Hebrew as well as in English. (It should be noted that in the Orthodox *siddur* the *mi-she-berakh* for someone who is ill is written in both feminine and masculine forms, for sick men and sick women, although the prayer does not include mention of the Matriarchs.)

Of even greater significance than the change of language itself is the addition of the feminine form in the Hebrew prayers before putting on *tallit* and *tefillin,* clear indications that Conservative women may also engage freely in ritual practices traditionally regarded as reserved for men.

The inclusion of a prayer for a *Bat Mitzvah* on Shabbat morning signifies that Conservative Judaism is moving away from *Bat Mitzvah* ceremonies (for girls) that are conducted exclusively on Friday evenings when the Torah is not traditionally read and that have therefore been less significant than *Bar Mitzvah* ceremonies. The implication that the *Bat Mitzvah*, too, is called to the Torah on Shabbat morning, provides an opportunity for the *Bat Mitzvah* to assume an importance for girls as great as the *Bar Mitzvah* for boys.

Aliyot (going up to the Torah) on Simḥat Torah, which marks the conclusion of the cycle of Torah readings and the beginning of the next cycle, are provided in both male and female form in the Hebrew to indicate that Conservative women as well as men are called to rejoice in the Torah, to be part of the assembly that completes the reading and is ready to begin again, and to share both the reverence and the joy of participation in worship services.

Traditional liturgy generally omits references to women; for example, the first blessing of the *Amidah* mentions the Patriarchs but not the Matriarchs. In the new Reform prayer books, translations of the phrase *"ve-elohei avoteinu"* (God of our Fathers) reflect the innovative approach to the elimination of masculine-biased language about humanity. "God of our ancestors," "God of all ages," "God of all Israel," "God of all generations," "God of the past and the future" or, alternatively, "God of our Mothers" followed by the names of the Matriarchs and "God of our Fathers" followed by the names of the Patriarchs, are substitute phrases that appear in different sections of the prayer book. However, these changes and additions appear only in the English translation. No changes were made in the Hebrew.

The new Conservative *siddur* also includes the Matriarchs in English and provides an opportunity to substitute non-sexist language in an English alternative of the *Amidah* for Sabbath morning services. Another place in which mention of women is omitted in the traditional prayer book is the Song of the Sea, the *"mi kamokhah"* before the *Amidah*. Following the Song, the biblical story indicates that Miriam "took a timbrel in her hand; and all the women went out after her with timbrels and with dances, and Miriam sang for them . . ." (Exod. 15:20–1). Although this passage clearly shows Miriam in the role of a religious leader of women, in traditional liturgy, the biblical quotes used end before the verses mentioning Miriam.[13]

Only when prayers reflecting the important roles played by women in Jewish history are incorporated into a prayer book in which the language of liturgy has been changed to avoid masculine bias will women begin to feel truly included, as children of God, in the worship experience.

While progress is being made, women are not yet equal participants, their joy of participation diminished by the retention of masculine-biased language referring to God.

In Jewish tradition, language about God changed to reflect changes in Jewish experience that altered our understanding of the nature of God. At various stages of Jewish history, God is referred to as Shepherd, Redeemer, King, and Lord. That these reflect masculine imagery is not surprising.

The Reform Task Force's *Glossary of Substitute Terminology* eliminates references to God as "King" and "Lord," suggesting Ruler/Sovereign or God/Creator/Eternal as alternatives. In some instances, God is referred to as "You" rather than as "He," which enables people to perceive God as being both near and far, in good Jewish tradition. Since "*Adonai*," which means "My Lord," is actually a substitute word for the personal name of God (the Tetragrammaton), which, according to Jewish tradition, was only pronounced by the High Priest, the Task Force recommended it not be used in prayer.

The Task Force was not trying to develop a feminine theology but rather more inclusive ways of describing the indescribable. The substitute language offers people a wide latitude of choice regarding the way they conceptualize God, which serves to reinforce the thrust taken by the Central Conference of American Rabbis in providing a choice of ten Shabbat services for the *Gates of Prayer.* Today women merely seek to expand the possibilities, to reach out in more meaningful ways to the One Who is our Eternal God.

The Conservative prayer book, *Sim Shalom,* also exhibits sensitivity to the problem of portraying God as masculine. A portion of the Mishnah, Shab. 2:5, included as a source for study in Shabbat services, eliminates the usual sexist translations, substituting "One who . . ." for "He who . . ." and "Sovereign" for "Lord."[14]

Feminine Imagery

There is some attempt to go beyond nonsexist language and actually include feminine imagery when referring to God. In *Sim Shalom,* in supplementary readings for Sabbath evening services, God is described as a Mother who comforts Her children.

Such additions are not sufficient for everyone. Some traditionally oriented women, feeling alienated from such male oriented services, have formed women's *minyanim* (*Editor's Note: These groups are not to be confused with the Orthodox women's* tefillah *groups; see R. Haut, p. 135*) developing their own prayer books.

The Women's *Minyan* established at Brown University in Rhode Island developed a prayer book that emphasizes the feminine aspects of God and attempts to reflect women's experience. God is referred to as "She" exclusively and described as "Mother" and "Creator." However, referring to God in only feminine terms is no more acceptable than the use of only masculine language. Because of the lack of the neuter gender in Hebrew, these feminists are experimenting with references to God as "*Shekhinah*," sometimes alternating forms between the masculine and the feminine.

Rita Gross, a feminist author, offers a different approach based on the *Kabbalah*, which teaches that one of the causes of *galut* (exile) is the alienation of the masculine from the feminine in God, the alienation of God and the *Shekhinah*.

When the masculine and the feminine aspects of God have been reunited and the female half of humanity has been returned from exile, we will begin to have our *tikkun*. The world will be repaired.[15]

She proposes the use of both "*ha-kadosh barukh hu*" (The Holy One Blessed Be He) and "*ha-kadosha barukha hi*" (The Holy One Blessed Be She).

The initial impulse of most Jews who regularly attend synagogue services—whether Orthodox, Conservative, Reconstructionist, Reform, male or female—to deride this suggestion reflects the ingrained nature of masculine concepts of God that are accepted as "natural." It will not be easy to transform time-honored tradition, but this concept is advanced by women engaged in a struggle to add the feminine dimension of the Divine to the worship experience, to be taken seriously as full spiritual partners in the practice of Judaism.

While this may offer one solution to the problem of Hebrew formulation in worship, worshipers may be left with the masculine imagery of God solely portraying the image of a powerful ruler (e.g., *avinu malkeinu*—Our Father, Our King) and the feminine imagery of God solely portraying a nurturer (e.g., Mother). Such an approach perpetuates the stereotype of separate roles for men and women at precisely the moment that men are beginning to uncover their ability to nurture, and women are discovering that they may be powerful. As God is both powerful and compassionate, so each man and woman, created in the image of God, is a unique combination of these qualities. It becomes essential, then, to search for a satisfactory way of drawing on all these images while attempting to communicate with God.

The guiding principles for the new Reconstructionist prayer book suggest the addition of prayers reflecting a feminine aspect of God such as *Ha-Raḥaman* or the *Shekhinah*.

The *Shekhinah* is generally understood metaphorically as the numinous essence of God in the world but not traditionally regarded as part of the Godhead. The more personified concept of the *Shekhinah* as the feminine principle in the world of the Divine appears in the *Kabbalah*, a thoroughly masculine oriented doctrine, where she takes on sexual symbolism as the consort of God. Using the term *Shekhinah* in referring to God during Friday evening services carries with it overtones of goddess worship, especially since sexual union between husband and wife on Friday evening at midnight is considered a *mitzvah*—in imitation of the sexual union between God and *His* consort, the *Shekhinah*. This would appear to reinforce the concept of God as totally masculine, focusing solely on the sexuality of the female principle, a concept abhorrent to most Jewish feminists. Use of this term during Shabbat evening services relegates the feminine element to second-class status since Shabbat morning services, when the Torah is read, are regarded, by some, as more important than Shabbat evening services.

The personification of the Sabbath as a Bride and Queen dates back to Talmudic times.[16] In Jewish mystical tradition, the Sabbath is also viewed as the Divine Queen, the Consort of God. "*L'kha dodi,*" the sixteenth-century song now prominent in every prayer book in the Friday night liturgy, also presents the Sabbath Queen in sexual imagery. Some feminists are, therefore, troubled by the focus on either the *Shekhinah* or the Sabbath Queen. They are relegated to incomplete, inferior roles, as essentially male concepts that celebrate the sexuality of these feminine images.

Jewish feminists are searching for a way to describe God that includes both masculine and feminine aspects: as a total Parent, as both Mother and Father, King and Queen, powerful and nurturing. This avoids any implication that there are two gods or that Jewish feminists are promoting a return to goddess worship.

My own search to resolve the dilemma of sexist language led to an unexpected, overwhelming surge of emotion—a feeling of closeness, warmth, and joy when I began reaching out to God as "You" rather than "He." While, in Jewish tradition, God is both near and far, both immanent and transcendent, in an increasingly alienated world, emphasis on the near, on the more intimate "You" may have benefits beyond the elimination of sexist bias.

Translations

Every translation is an interpretation, subject to the particular biases of the translator. Some translations move beyond the words themselves, adding different meanings and new material to compensate for the bias of earlier times. There are also cases where the plain meaning of the Hebrew is ignored in favor of a different meaning in the English that is deemed more appropriate to modern society. Questions have been raised about whether the free translation of prayers culled from biblical and rabbinic sources may distort the intended message, doing a disservice to the readers. A similar problem, however, is inherent in the traditional custom of using verses in a way that may alter the original contextual meaning of the verses (as in Jer. 17 : 14 discussed above). Wherever changes are made in the translation of sacred texts for liturgical purposes, care should be exercised to maintain the intent of the Hebrew while adapting the language to meet the needs of modern worshipers.

Unlike the Hebrew, which, as mentioned earlier, has no neuter gender, the use of English translation provides us with the opportunity to develop a liturgy that is far more sensitive to women's needs. Some members of the all-male Central Conference of American Rabbis' Liturgy Committee [17] preparing *The Gates of Prayer* pressed for the elimination of all sexist language to reflect Reform Judaism's historic commitment to religious equality for women. Others, arguing that language changes advocated by the women's movement might not reflect a permanent need, urged a more cautious approach. The result was an uncomfortable compromise. Masculine terminology was eliminated when referring to humanity, but retained when referring to God. Subsequently, in the High Holy Day *Maḥzor, Gates of Repentance*, significant changes were made regarding God-language. In some passages, the traditional formula for blessings usually translated as "Praised be Thou, O Lord our God, King of the universe" is changed to "Blessed is the Eternal God" or "Praised be the One. . . . "

There are several ways of translating a verse to avoid masculine-biased language. The plural can be used, as in the free translation of the verse, "Then all shall sit under their vines and under their fig trees, and none shall make them afraid" (Mic. 4:4).

Translation of the Book of Genesis in the Torah presented a greater challenge. By examining two different translations of two verses (Gen. 1:26–7), it is possible to track the thoughtful process followed, which is faithful to the context as well as sensitive to the flow of language. The 1962 Jewish Publication Society translation of the Bible [18] translates these verses as follows:

And God said "Let us make man [*adam*] in our image, after our likeness; and let them have dominion over the fish of the sea. . . . And God created man in his own image, in the image of God created He them; male and female created He them.

Translating the Hebrew word "*adam*" (used in the Genesis verse cited above in the original Hebrew) as "man" obscures the real meaning. In this verse, "*adam*" is the generic term for "human being." "*Adam*" does not become the name of a specific male until the second story of creation found in a later chapter, when Eve is created out of Adam's rib to be his partner.

The Gates of Repentance (the High Holy Day prayer book for the Reform Movement) uses terms similar to those suggested by the Task Force on Equality of Women in Judaism:

And God said: Let us make a being in our image, after our likeness, and let it have dominion over the fish . . . thus God created us in the divine image, creating us in the image of God, creating us male and female. [19]

According to Dr. Harry Orlinsky, elimination of gender-biased language often enables interpreters to provide a more accurate translation as well as a better understanding of the text. He notes:

It is not generally realized, not even by Bible translators, that the way the Bible is translated is determined by the conditions—political, economic, social, cultural, religious, literary—that prevail at the time and in the country that the translation is being made. It is far from being a haphazard happening. [20]

Since many passages in the prayer book are biblical in origin, establishment of the principle that translations of Torah may be changed to eliminate masculine-biased language represents a crucial step in the progression toward an egalitarian service.

Other Torah portions were changed to focus on inclusive language. Lev. 19:17, familiar to most people as "Thou shalt not hate thy brother in your heart," now reads, "You shall not hate your brother or sister in your heart."

The Jewish Reconstructionist Foundation published a new prayer book in 1989. In the process, the Prayer Book Commission adopted a set of guidelines that reflect the principle of equality of men and women, similar to the pattern set by Reform Judaism, as well as the pattern adopted by the Conservative Movement to alter both the Hebrew and English in certain significant places. Adherence to these guidelines will move the Reconstructionist prayer book beyond the Reform and Conservative Movements, although their principle of authentic translation of sources may still allow for the retention of some sexist language.

Adding Women's Experiences

The desire of Jewish women, traditionally denied a meaningful role in public worship, to express their spirituality is not a new phenomenon. Generally not taught Hebrew, the language of liturgy, Jewish women in Eastern Europe were well versed in Yiddish, the language of the people. An entire culture of *tehinot*, poems and personal prayers, were produced in Yiddish mostly by women for women. Appeals were made to the God of the Matriarchs (Sarah, Rebecca, Leah, and Rachel) rather than to the God of the Patriarchs (Abraham, Isaac, and Jacob). These prayers reflected feminine concerns—prayers for the health and safety of husbands, children, widows, and orphans; special prayers after childbirth as well as prayers regarding the three *mitzvot* performed by women (*hallah, niddah,* and candle lighting) (*see* Taitz, p. 66 and Berger, p. 73). God was rarely addressed as "He," but rather referred to as "Your Holiness," "Creator," or "Your Will." Women's efforts to find more inclusive language about God predate the modern feminist movement.

Prayers and optional readings by prominent Jewish women such as Nobel Prize winner Nelly Sachs, Holocaust martyr Hannah Senesh, poet

Muriel Rukeyser, and educator Molly Cone are included in the Reform prayer book, *Gates of Prayer*. *Gates of Repentance* features an additional reading from the Talmud that refers to Beruriah, a noted second-century female scholar.[21]

The Reconstructionist liturgy commission's call for the development of a special meditation and *Rosh Ḥodesh* liturgy provides an opportunity for inclusion of women's experience not yet afforded in the other prayer books.

Summary and Conclusions

The *siddur* is, by nature, in a constant state of flux, re-examined, re-inter-preted, and re-formed by generation after generation as the Jewish com-munity developed new understandings and new spiritual needs in changing societies. The appearance of many new prayer books, published by different branches of Judaism in the last decade, reflects the ferment in modern society, particularly the re-evaluation of every aspect of Judaism fostered by Jewish feminists, who focus on the need to develop liturgy that eliminates masculine-biased metaphor. The single certainty is that changes regarded as radical today will undoubtedly be accepted as tomor-row's tradition, just as yesterday's controversies are firmly imbedded as to-day's "traditional" *tefillah*.

The Reform Movement's *Gates of Prayer* and *Gates of Repentance*, the Conservative Movement's *Siddur Sim Shalom*, and the Reconstructionist Movement's *Kol Haneshamah* provide choices in services and optional readings to meet the varying needs of their congregations that are autono-mous and thus free to use the official prayer book of their movement, de-velop their own *siddur*, or use any of the countless others on the market.

The gates to communion with God, while still controlled primarily by men, are being pried open under the persistent pressure of women edu-cated in Judaism, who are deeply involved in all branches of Judaism and who seek full participation in the life of the synagogue. Sensitive editors of prayer books in the Reform, Conservative, and Reconstructionist Movements are responding in different degrees to those new demands. Progress in the prayer book, still overwhelmingly the province of male rabbinic committees, is predictably slow and inconsistent. The process is, however, irreversible.

In this time of transition, Jewish feminists seeking a true egalitarian worship experience have few options. In some Reform and Reconstructionist synagogues, male and female rabbis consistently use only inclusive language. In the main, rabbis, both male and female, confine themselves to the language of the prayer book, content to provide an occasional "creative" nonsexist service.

A few synagogues, frustrated by the lack of a completely nonsexist *siddur*, are producing their own inclusive language prayer books. Temple Shaarai Tefilla in New York City, compiled *Tefillot Chaim*, a nonsexist *siddur*, specifically designed for children to use on the High Holy Days.[22]

Although there is steady improvement as each new prayer book appears, Reform Judaism, which has been in the forefront of the movement to change the language of liturgy, has not yet produced a single service that is totally devoid of sexist language. Since it is unlikely that new Shabbat or High Holy Day services will be published by the movement in the near future, the best recourse for it may be the publication of soft cover nonsexist supplements to the Sabbath and High Holy Day prayer books using the Task Force's suggestions as a model. In the process, since Reform synagogues are using more Hebrew in their services, the question of adding the feminine form in the Hebrew needs to be addressed. The Conservative Movement might consider publishing its own supplement, introducing inclusive language about humanity and God in the English translation.

If such supplements are not soon made available, feminists from all branches of Judaism will have to turn to the new Reconstructionist prayer book, *Kol Haneshamah*, perhaps the most satisfactory Jewish nonsexist prayer book to date. It contains, however, only the Friday night service.[23]

Elimination of masculine-biased language is, however, only the first step in the creation of prayer books that meet the spiritual needs of all Jews. Until now, the prayer book has reflected mostly the experiences and aspirations of Jewish men. Some feminists are exploring ways of including women's experiences and introducing feminine God imagery, addressing prayers to the *Shekhinah* in the Hebrew.

Other feminists find focusing on either the *Shekhinah* or the Sabbath Queen unacceptable because, as male concepts, they celebrate the sexuality of these feminine images in their secondary role as consort to God who is still "King" and "Lord." A totally feminine concept of God as "*Shekhinah*" is no more acceptable than the totally masculine "*Adonai*," and borders on goddess worship. Since God is beyond sexuality in Judaism, a more satisfactory solution for some is language that reflects an androgenous God concept, incorporating both masculine and feminine aspects of the Godhead.

One solution to this dilemma is simply to print the four Hebrew letters of the personal name of God (the Tetragrammaton). This usage first appeared in the revised edition of the Reform *New Union Haggadah* and was incorporated into its festival prayer book. In good Jewish tradition, this device allows participants the option of using whichever substitute term for the name of God is most meaningful to them.

Often, services that reflect nonsexist language in many ways still fail to do so consistently. For example, the Reform festival service is most consistent in the elimination of masculine-biased language. However, a memorial service appears as an intrusion, reverting once again to ancient and sexist translations.

Feminists are now struggling to move beyond the questions of pronouns, to develop new imagery, new prayers and blessings that add women's experiences and describe their search for spirituality. Such prayers might celebrate nurturing for both women and men. Prayers about the wonder of Creation might center not just on the majesty of mountain and sky, but the miracle of birth, of creating a new generation. Jewish women, like Deborah, Miriam, Ruth, Esther, Huldah, and Beruriah, have played many essential roles in Judaism as judges, religious leaders, prophets, and scholars, which need to be acknowledged.

Prayers for justice and peace should call not just for special care for the widow and the orphan but for the creation of a just society—both sacred and secular—where women would no longer be penalized or impoverished because of their sex—a world where Shalom includes *Shalom Bayit*—the creation of a whole, healthy, secure family relationship based on equal sharing of joys and responsibilities in the home, of a community that fosters the total well-being of women as well as men. Serious attention needs to be paid to the nature of spiritual practices, to heal the spiritual scars of women who anguish to be full participants in Jewish life.

As people of the Book, whose most revered prayer is the *Shema* (Hear O Israel), the command to hear and heed the words that have shaped the religious beliefs of over half the world's population, we cannot underestimate the power of words. We have a special responsibility to reverse the damaging effects, on both men and women, of centuries of language that misrepresents women and misleads us as to the very nature of God. We must respond positively to the needs of those who are still struggling to be treated justly, with dignity and respect, as human beings created by the God whom they wish to serve.

Notes

1. A. Z. Idelsohn, *Jewish Liturgy and Its Development* (New York: Holt, Rinehart, and Winston, 1967), 9.

2. While the origin of the synagogue is obscure, it is generally thought that houses of assembly and prayer developed during the Babylonian exile, after the destruction of the First Temple. There is evidence for the existence of synagogues in addition to the Temple in Jerusalem during the days of the Second Temple.

3. Idelsohn, *Jewish Liturgy*, 28. Idelsohn quotes Abba Benjamin, at TB Ber. 6a, as stating, "The prayer of man is accepted only in the synagogue." Cf. similar statements by *amoraim*, TB Ber. 6a, 7b.

4. Idelsohn, *Jewish Liturgy*, 29.

5. *See* Sara Reguer, "Kaddish from the 'Wrong' Side of the *Mehitzah*," in *On Being a Jewish Feminist*, ed. Susannah Heschel (New York: Schocken, 1983), 177–81.

6. Idelsohn, *Jewish Liturgy*, xi.

7. Annette Daum, "Responses in Reform Judaism to the Use of Sexist Language," American Psychological Association, Canada, 1980.

8. Joseph H. Hertz, *The Authorized Daily Prayer Book* (New York: Block, 1948), 21. Phillip Birnbaum, *Ha-Siddur Ha-Shalem* (New York: Hebrew Publishing Co., 1949), 17.

9. Benjamin Z. Kreitman, *Keeping Posted* (leader's ed.), 25:5 (New York: Union of American Hebrew Congregations), 15. Cf. *Tosef.* Ber. 6:18.

10. Jules Harlow, ed., *Siddur Sim Shalom* (New York: Rabbinical Assembly, 1985), 25.

11. Ibid.

12. Ibid., 29.

13. *See The Five Scrolls* (New York: Central Conference of American Rabbis, 1984), 83.

14. Harlow, ed., *Siddur Sim Shalom*, 271.

15. Rita Gross, "Female God Language in a Jewish Context," in *Womanspirit Rising*, ed. Carol P. Christ and Judith Plaskow (San Francisco: Harper and Row, 1979), 173.

16. TB Shab. 119a. Cf. Raphael Patai, *The Hebrew Goddess* (New York: Avon, 1978), 231–33.

17. The Reform Movement now includes women rabbis on their Liturgy Committee and has consulted prominent lay women in the preparation of their new prayer books.

18. *The Torah* (Philadelphia: JPS, 1962), 4.

19. *Gates of Repentance*, 197.

20. Harry Orlinsky, "The *Bereshit* Blunder," *Keeping Posted*.

21. *Gates of Repentance*, 238.

22. Esther-Ann Asch et al., eds., *Tefillot Chaim* (New York: 1981). Like many other prayer books, it retains "*Adonai*" when referring to God.

23. *Kol Haneshamah: Shabbat Eve* (Wyncote, Pa., 1989).

Three

CONTEMPORARY REALITIES

From the oriental Jewish communities of the East to the American Jewish communities of the West, women are experiencing the tension between the security of the traditions of the past and the uncharted possibilities of the new freedoms of modernity.

In the two articles by Susan Starr Sered and Rela Geffen Monson and the interview with the women of the Khoubian family, the impact of modernity on the role of women in the synagogue is explored. Sered and the Khoubians provide a glimpse into oriental Jewish culture. Significantly, both articles depict the richness of oriental women's spiritual experiences, a richness that, in many other cultures, has unfortunately been lost beyond recovery.

Sered documents that the women of Kurdistan, excluded from the synagogue, celebrated separate women's traditions, gathering on rooftops to sing religious songs. With the community's transition to modern Israeli society, where these women can attend synagogue, the women have lost many of their own ceremonies. It is especially valuable, therefore, to have an oral history of the Khoubian family, which allows three generations of women to speak in their own authentic voices, thereby preserving a record of the older traditions. The voices of the Khoubians provide a glimpse into an oriental society in which women felt very connected to the synagogue, a situation that contrasted with Kurdistani culture.

Again, as these women experienced the mobility of the modern world, first by moving from a small Iranian city to the large cosmopolitan city of Teheran, and then by emigrating to New York City, many of their customs were lost.

In contrast, Monson shows that modernity—specifically, the rise of the feminist movement—has spurred American women's greater involvement in the synagogue. She discusses the growth of Jewish feminism in each of the major branches of American Judaism, documenting women's demands for change and their efforts to attain leadership positions in the synagogue.

Monson's article serves to introduce a collection of personal vignettes. These first-person accounts record history in the making. The struggles and achievements of these women, often on the cutting edge of change in their communities, serve to provide a glimpse into the motivations and concerns that fuel their striving for growth and fulfillment.

An evaluation of the past leads to a projection of the possibilities for the future. In this volume's concluding article, Paula Hyman points out that Judaism was never monolithic in its treatment of women: women's involvement in the synagogue varied with time and place. Yet, it is only in the modern period that women en masse have begun to challenge their traditional roles. Hyman projects that the synagogue of the future will be enriched by the growth and acceptance of women's involvement, the beginnings of which we are witnessing today. She raises a number of questions as to the direction in which these changes will lead us.

Susan Starr Sered

THE SYNAGOGUE
AS A SACRED SPACE
FOR THE ELDERLY
ORIENTAL WOMEN
OF JERUSALEM

While the notion of setting aside certain space as "sacred" or "holy" may be universal,[1] there is considerable variation in the location, the content, and the nature of the activities carried out in such spaces. Furthermore, even within one particular cultural context, different categories of people may have access to or make different uses of the various spaces that are identified as sacred. This chapter focuses on the use of one particular type of sacred space—the synagogue, by one particular Jewish population— elderly oriental women living in Jerusalem.

In 1984 and 1985, I conducted fieldwork among a group of pious Oriental Jewish women, the majority of whom made *aliyah* (immigrated) to Israel from Kurdistan, Yemen, or Turkey approximately sixty years ago. All of these women regularly attend a senior citizen's day center in one of Jerusalem's ethnic neighborhoods. Using a mixture of participant-observation and interviewing techniques, I attempted to find answers to such questions as how these women define female religiosity (versus male religiosity), what they understand to be the essence of religion, in what circumstances women develop and perform their own religious rituals, and how a sub-group of women relate to the larger patriarchal Jewish tradition. In the course of this work, I observed the women as they visited and used a number of types of sacred space. These spaces, in an ascending order of holiness (according to the evaluation of the women themselves) are: the kitchen of one's own home (where the woman is responsible for *kashrut* and where the bulk of Sabbath and festival preparation takes place), the senior citizen's day center (in which lessons in Judaica are given three times a week), the synagogue, and cemeteries and holy tombs (including the Western Wall). To appreciate the role of the synagogue in the religious lives of these women, it must be seen in the context of the other important sacred spaces that they frequent.[2]

Of the four sacred spaces discussed here, only one (the kitchen) is domestic; the other three lie in the public sphere. The public spaces are perceived by the women as being holier than the domestic one. Prayers made at synagogue and at tombs are more effective than prayers made at home. The women of this study emphasize that it is only as old women, or more specifically as widows, that they are able to spend time at public holy places. When they were younger, they could rarely leave their houses to participate in public, religious events. The women explicitly state that one of the advantages of old age is the greater mobility and control of their time that allows them to conduct their religious lives in the public sphere. For these oriental women the synagogue is a relatively new holy space—during most of their lives they did not attend synagogue.

Other Sacred Spaces

Their repertoire of sacred spaces clearly reflects a female experience. The men who live with these women do not relate to the kitchen as a holy space, whereas the women see in food preparation an essentially sacred activity. At the most obvious level, for the husbands and brothers of these women, holiday celebrations are focused in the synagogue—it is the various special liturgies and synagogue rituals that define the holy days. For the women, holiday celebrations are focused in the kitchen. I asked the women questions such as: What does your ethnic group do on Rosh Hashanah? What is Shavuot? What is done by you on Ḥanukkah? Their answers consistently related to food and food preparation. "On Rosh Hashanah we eat the head of a fish so that you will be the head." "Shavuot is when we eat rice cooked in milk. I prepare a separate little bowl of this for each of the children." "On Ḥanukkah I make a kind of fried dough—my family loves it."³ I am not claiming that the women reduce the complex observances, meanings, and symbolism of each holiday to food. Yet, it does seem that for these elderly women, food is the central symbol of each holiday and food preparation is the most important ritual activity that they, as women, perform.

In addition, because of Jewish dietary laws, women in their role as preparers of food are in fact ritual experts. The women of this study do not consult rabbis in matters of *kashrut.* "We do not have any questions [about *kashrut*]." And finally, the women believe that they receive divine merit for feeding the hungry. On many occasions the women explained that the greatest *mitzvah* one can perform is giving cooked food to a hungry beggar. Providing meals not only gives physical nourishment, it also forges one of the most important links that the women's children and grandchildren have to traditional Judaism. The women are afraid that their descendants are not sufficiently observant in or knowledgeable about the old ways. Traditional Shabbat and holiday foods tie the children to Judaism at a time in which many other rituals and customs have been discarded. The kitchen itself absorbs some of the holiness of the activities that take place there. The son of one of the women described how on Friday night his mother blesses each of the children while touching the *mezuzah* on the kitchen doorway. "For my mother the kitchen *mezuzah* is the holy ark."

The second sacred space frequented by these women is the senior citizens' day center. The day center located in their neighborhood is operated by the municipality and formally open to all senior citizens regardless of gender. In fact, only women attend. (Elderly men are more likely to attend special classes held at the local synagogues.) The women have a certain amount of control over the activities of the day center, and they consistently choose religious activities. The day center schedule includes two lessons each week by a rabbi, one lesson by a *rabbanit* (a rabbi's wife), and, when possible, an organized trip to a holy tomb. As the classes at the day center are geared for the illiterate female members, the women can understand the lessons (unlike lessons held in the synagogue that are directed toward men who can read). The subjects of these lessons include the weekly Torah reading, holiday laws, Bible stories, and miracle tales. Since the women did not have a suitable framework for study when they were younger, they see old age as an opportunity for increasing their knowledge of Jewish ideas, rituals, and laws.

Cemeteries and holy tombs are visited mainly by female pilgrims. In many oriental Jewish societies, women are considered responsible for caring for the dead ancestors. It is women who tend the family tombs, light candles at the graves, collect blessings from rabbis on the anniversaries of deaths, and give money to charity in memory of their deceased relatives. As a result, women feel that they may request the righteous dead to intercede with God on behalf of living descendants. The women function as a link between the ancestors and the descendants—they care for the dead in order that the dead will assist the living. At several of the popular holy tombs (e.g., Rachel's Tomb and the Tomb of Rabbi Meir ba'al ha-Ness) women control the larger, more comfortable, and holier area. Women visit the tombs in order to pray at a place that is particularly meritorious (a saint is buried there), but pilgrimage is also an important social event. The women may spend several hours at the holy tomb, distributing sweets to other pilgrims and chatting with their friends. For these women, there are numerous differences between praying at a saint's tomb and praying in synagogue. First, in synagogue the men control the better space, whereas the women sit in a balcony far away from the ark and the Torah scrolls. At the tombs, women can stand right next to the grave, and touch and kiss the tombstone. Second, the prayers at the tombs are wholly personal and spontaneous—one does not have to be able to read the formal service to pray at the tombs. For the uneducated, illiterate women this is a critical difference. A last point is that the women believe it is more efficacious to pray at holy tombs than at synagogue—that at the tombs there is a kind of hot line to God. Thus, a woman who has a really serious problem (an infertile daughter, a grandchild who needs an operation) will make a vow to come to a tomb to pray.[4]

Women in the Synagogue in the Old Country

Because the women of this study are illiterate and their traditional culture was a highly sexually segregated one in which the synagogue was understood to be the territory of (literate) males, we must expect a certain amount of ambivalence in their relationship to the synagogue. In Kurdistan, women normally did not attend synagogue. Indeed, there was no women's section in the synagogue at all. In Yemen, women were actually barred from the synagogue; it was considered a sin for a woman to learn to read or to enter a synagogue, as women were considered potentially defiling because of menstrual and childbirth blood.[5] There are a few hints in the ethnographic literature that in Kurdistan very old women could sit in the men's section of the synagogue, while other women would, on important holidays such as Yom Kippur, sit on nearby roofs.[6] Holy tombs were far more central in the religious lives of Jewish women in Kurdistan, and women's pilgrimage ceremonies were elaborate and considered necessary for the well-being of the entire community.[7] Women's synagogue attendance in the Old Country had no community-wide significance.

On Shabbat, Kurdish Jewish men spent much of the day in synagogue. While the men were away, the women would do the necessary housework and then dress up in their Shabbat clothes and visit brides or mourners at home. Young women would meet to dance, or sit on roofs and sing.[8] Unfortunately, the content of the women's songs has already been, to a major extent, lost. Women's culture was passed down orally from mother to daughter—few women knew how to read or write.

One of the few women's oral traditions that has been preserved is "*Lel-Huza*," a women's lament that was traditionally recited on the Ninth of Av.[9] On the evening of this day of national mourning, women would gather on a roof and sit in a circle around one woman who knew the dirge well. The other women would participate by sighing and crying. "*Lel-Huza*" is the story of the destruction of the Temple and Exile personified into the stories of one young man and two young women. One woman escapes being raped by seven infidel men by drowning herself in the ritual bath. The other woman is killed by her father-in-law as a sacrifice imposed by divine edict in order to end a famine. The content of this one extant dirge is explicitly female, but I am hesitant to do more than hazard a guess that this type of feminizing of Jewish tradition was typical of the religious culture of the Jewish women of Kurdistan.

Women in the Old Country would gather together at numerous religious and quasi-religious occasions. A common feature of these gatherings was dance. Debbi Friedhaber, in her study of dance customs of Kurdish Jews, mentions several occasions at which the women in Kurdistan would get together and dance. These included the Shabbat before a wedding, Passover, childbirth and first pregnancy, Shavuot, and the first Shabbat in Adar. Women's autonomous dancing no longer exists in modern Israel. At weddings today all except the oldest women dance in a style that is identical to that of the men.[10]

We have a bit more information concerning Jewish women in Yemen. Nina Dubler Katz has demonstrated that Jewish men and Jewish women in Yemen had different musical traditions. Women, excluded from the synagogue, did not even hear men's religious rituals and music. Instead, the women created their own "second world" of fantasy, storytelling, and singing. Men's music was developmental, antiphonal, without instrumental accompaniment, without a definite rhythm, based on fixed texts, religious, and sung in Hebrew or Aramaic. Women's music was repetitious, never truly antiphonal, rhythmic, usually secular, and sung in Arabic with improvised texts.[11]

The picture that emerges of the traditional religious world of Jewish women in Kurdistan and Yemen is one that includes dance, song, storytelling, mourning, food preparation, and cemeteries. The synagogue was at most peripheral to the religious lives of the Jewish women of Asia. *Aliyah* to Israel has resulted in the near total destruction of traditional Jewish women's culture. Instead, women have become increasingly assimilated into the "mainstream" (male) religious institutions. However, *aliyah* has had far less impact upon the reasons and motivations that inspire the women to perform religious rituals. The desire to break up the monotony of their day-to-day lives, to get together with friends and relatives, to celebrate and commemorate their communal past—none of this has changed. In addition, the bulk of the women's rituals, both in the Old Country and in Israel, are directed toward protecting the health and happiness of their families. In the Old Country the women made great use of amulets and spells.[12] In Israel, such "normative" rituals as the recitation of Hebrew blessings and prayers have replaced the old amulets and spells. But the motivation is the same—women, and especially old women, are responsible for the well-being of their children. The women of this study, like their mothers and grandmothers, cook, clean, nurse, and launder for their families. Yet they know that wholesome food and expensive medicines will not help if God does not decree health. The women frequently exclaim that "Everything is in God's hands." These elderly oriental women have begun to attend synagogue in Israel. The synagogue has become a major part of their religious landscape. However, they have adapted the synagogue to their personal religious needs—the women interpret synagogue ritual in light of their traditional female role of family guardian.

Women's Synagogue Attendance in Israel

Most oriental synagogues in Israel do include women's sections. In most of the synagogues in the neighborhood of this study, the women's section is a balcony closed in by thick, opaque curtains. Although the majority of the women of this study attend synagogue regularly (especially the widows, many of whom go twice each day), they have a number of complaints about the way the synagogue is organized. Most of the women are hard of hearing, so they resent prayer leaders (*shliḥei tzibbur*) who chant and sing in soft voices. Also, a number of the women have attended literacy classes in recent years and so can follow parts of the service (especially the *Amidah*) if they are recited slowly. However, the men leading the service generally read too quickly and too softly for the women to be able to follow. Unlike in Eastern European synagogues, in oriental synagogues there is no special role for a woman who can read Hebrew and lead or assist the other women. All of the prayer leaders are men. On several occasions the women compared the synagogue to the day center. "It is better here [at the day center] where we all sit . . . in a circle." Other women pointed out that at synagogue one has to pay for a permanent seat, whereas at the day center each woman can sit wherever she wishes. In short, the formal and male-oriented nature of the synagogue bothers the women but does not prevent their frequent attendance.

The women are very aware of the fact that only old women go to synagogue regularly, with young women coming on such special occasions as Rosh Hashanah and Yom Kippur. In Shai's study of a Kurdish neighborhood in Israel, she found that the younger women never go to synagogue—they are embarrassed to go because it is an old women's activity.[13] The widowed women of my study stress that before their husbands died they were too busy at home to go to synagogue. For example, on Shabbat morning they had to set the table and prepare the salads. "Since my husband died 14 months ago I have begun covering my hair [a sign of female piety] and going to synagogue." The women are pleased when the women's section is full. "This week it was so crowded for *havdalah* that the women sat shoulder to shoulder squeezing in. It was very nice. Even many young women were there."[14]

In widowhood most of the women find new independence, free time, and a deepened piety. Widowhood also has the effect of forcing the women out of the domestic and into the public sphere for the performance of certain religious rituals. The women are usually reluctant to take on rituals that they understand to be male rituals. The widows will not perform *havdalah* or light the Ḥanukkah candles by themselves, even though their rabbi tells them that they are required to do so. Instead, they seek out public places in which the rituals are performed. For example, the widows go to synagogue to hear *kiddush*, a ritual that their husbands used to perform at home. Hearing *havdalah* and selling *hometz* before Passover are two other rituals for which they must now leave the house as a result of their widowhood. "Now [that I am a widow] I go to synagogue four times every Sabbath . . . to hear *kiddush*, to hear *havdalah*."

Several of the women mentioned menstruation as a reason for not attending synagogue when they were young. One woman explained that she would not go to synagogue when menstruating, nor would she bless the Sabbath candles (her husband would do it instead). Other women claimed that a menstruating woman may attend synagogue, but she must sit as far back as possible. In fact, the women spent most of the years between menarche and menopause pregnant or nursing, and so menstruation was an unusual rather than a monthly occurrence. I suspect that a more important reason for the increased synagogue attendance of older women concerns the changing nature of women's religiosity. As old women they have both the autonomy to move into the public domain and the responsibility to ensure (on a spiritual level) the well-being of their children and grandchildren. Thus, these old women who devote a great deal of time to praying on behalf of their descendants, prefer to petition God from a place in which the sacredness of the space itself maximizes the efficacy of their petitions.

Women's Synagogue Rituals

The women visit the synagogue for both social and religious reasons. Before and after the service they greet friends, relatives, and neighbors, although almost no active socializing goes on during the service itself. Women of several ethnic groups attend the day center and go on pilgrimages, but each ethnic group has its own synagogue. Thus, at synagogue, women are more likely to meet old friends and kin. As one woman said,

"All of my friends go to the same synagogue." The importance of the synagogue as a gathering place should not be underestimated. Most of the women of this study find it difficult to leave their immediate neighborhood—they have trouble negotiating buses and unfamiliar streets. They cannot or will not join organizations, go to movies, or attend public lectures. Thus, for many of the women, synagogue attendance ensures that they are involved in social interactions on a daily basis. Without the synagogue, many of these women would sit inside their homes, cut off from the life of the neighborhood.

The women are well aware that the synagogue is male sacred space. They realize that men control the larger and better furnished sections in the synagogue and that men are in charge of all of the public rituals. On the other hand, the women have a number of their own synagogue rituals of which the men are probably not even aware. On weekdays, for example, after the evening service one woman will pass around perfume to all of the other women. They will then smell and anoint themselves with the perfume, putting some on their wrists and foreheads and say the blessing over pleasant smells. Other women distribute grapes or small candies so that the women will have more opportunities to recite the appropriate blessings. Most of the women learned the Hebrew blessings recently and are very proud of their new ritual skills.

The women have special shawls, sweaters, and kerchiefs for the synagogue. Lower arms and foreheads, parts of the body that do not need to be covered at other times, must be covered in synagogue. This has little to do with the men being distracted by the women's sexuality—the men cannot even see into the women's section. Rather this is an important element in the relationship between the women and God. When the women were asked why they cover their foreheads and arms in synagogue, common answers included, "Because God can see everything we do."

A third series of women's rituals at synagogue involves hand gestures, kissing, and bowing. Since very few of the women can read, most are hard of hearing, and only some understand Hebrew, it is clear that they do not attend synagogue in order to recite the formal, written prayer service in the same way in which the men do. On the other hand, the women do not conduct their own autonomous service. Instead, they participate in the formal service through a series of gestures. The most important of these involves standing up, bowing slightly, reaching forward and then motioning with the hands back toward the body when the Torah is raised up. They will often pull back the curtain in front of the women's section at this time, so as to get a better view of the Torah. The women make a special effort to attend synagogue on Shabbat, Mondays, and Thursdays when the Torah or "*Sefer*" is read. When the Torah is raised up, the women make personal petitions, as this is a time when such petitions are most likely to be granted. Petitions made at this time are similar to those made at holy tombs—health, a speedy recovery, peace, for the soldiers to return unharmed, for a relative to rest in *Gan Eden* (heaven). During the recitation of certain parts of the prayer service (specifically the *Amidah* and *Kaddish*) the women eagerly say "amen" and roll their hands, kiss their fingers, and then touch their foreheads with their fingertips. Another common ritual is that of kissing the prayer book as they leave the synagogue. (Most do not actually use the prayer book during the service.)

The women believe that one receives merit from God for going to synagogue. Thus, in the words of one elderly woman, it does not bother her that she cannot hear the prayer service because "God knows if you have the desire to go to synagogue, so that even if you cannot hear you get the *zekhut* (merit)." The notion of *zekhut* is crucial to an understanding of the religious lives of the elderly oriental women. Most of their religious rituals have strong apotropaic elements, and it is a person's accumulated *zekhut* that makes those rituals effective. Furthermore, these women do not usually distinguish between *halakhah* (law) and *minhag* (custom). Anything that is traditionally Jewish is pleasing to God and is a potential source of *zekhut*. The fact that Jewish law does not require women to attend synagogue does not affect the *zekhut* that a woman receives for attending.

A last category of female synagogue rituals consists of cleaning the synagogue and cooking and serving ritual meals there. The women volunteer to clean the synagogues both because they take pride in their communities' public places of worship and also because tending a holy place gives one merit. A woman does not need to be able to read the Torah in order to receive *zekhut*—it is enough to wash the floor on which the man who does read the Torah will stand. Providing ritual meals (*seudot mitzvah*) on, for example, anniversaries of deaths, involves the women in the life of the synagogue and gives them an opportunity to work for God. The meals please God, and so the cooking and serving are a type of *avodat Ha-Shem* (worship).

Conclusion

The ordering of sacred space says something about the ordering of society and ideology. The fact that women sit on the sidelines in synagogue is part of a cultural constellation that defines women as marginal. The fact that Jewish women of oriental origin, rather than visiting friends and singing women's songs (as they did in the Old Country), now sit in a balcony in the otherwise masculine synagogue, cannot be understood as mitigating that marginality. Yet, the women themselves believe that they are fortunate to be able to attend synagogue. They see their synagogue attendance as symbolic of their new-found knowledge of (male) normative, halakhic, literate, Israeli Judaism (as opposed to traditional nonliterate, non-halakhic, local, women's traditions). Whether women gain or lose through modernization and westernization, whether women's position is better or worse in highly sexually segregated cultures, is unclear. What is clear, however, is that in adopting male religious rituals, women have somehow moved from the center of the sidelines to the sidelines of the center. It remains to be seen whether, in the long run, that is to women's advantage.

Notes

1. Edmund Leach, *Culture and Communication* (Cambridge: Cambridge University Press, 1976), 33–36.
2. I have not included the ritual bath on the list of holy places because the women of this study have been post-menopausal for several decades.
3. Any of the informants' comments that appear in quotation marks are my translation of the Hebrew words of a particular woman. When I summarize comments made by several women, I do not use quotation marks.
4. For more information on women visiting tombs, see my articles, "Rachel's Tomb and the Milk Grotto of the Virgin Mary: Two Women's Shrines in Bethlehem," *Journal of Feminist Studies in Religion,* 2:2 (Fall 1986): 7–22, and "Rachel's Tomb: Societal Liminality and the Revitalization of a Shrine," *Religion* 19, 27–40.
5. Yael Katzir, *The Effects of Resettlement on the Status and Role of Yemini Women: The Case of Ramat Oranim, Israel* (Ph.D. diss., University of California, Berkeley, 1976), 143.
6. A. Brauer, *Jews of Kurdistan* (in Hebrew) (Jerusalem: HaMaarav Press, 1947), 215.
7. Ibid., 246ff.
8. Ibid., 217–25.
9. Yonah Sabar, "*Lel-Huza:* Story and History in a Cycle of Lamentations for the Ninth of Ab in the Jewish Neo-Aramaic Dialect of Zakho," *Journal of Semitic Studies* 21 (1976): 138–62.

10. Debbi Friedhaber, *From the Dance Customs of Kurdish Jews* (Jewish Dance Archives, 1974).

11. Nina Dubler Katz, "Culturally Determined Dichotomy in the Musical Practice of the Yemenite Jews." Paper given at the American Anthropological Association 70th Annual Meeting, November 1971, New York City.

12. For a fascinating description of Eastern European Jewish women's family protection rituals, *see* Isaac Bashevis Singer, "The Washerwoman," in *In My Father's Court* (New York: New American Library, 1967), esp. p. 31.

13. Donna Shai, *Neighborhood Relations in an Immigrant Quarter* (Jerusalem: Henrietta Szold Institute Research Report No. 149, Publication No. 499, April 1970), 13–14.

14. It is unusual for young women to come, and that is why this informant noted it. Furthermore, as she herself is in her eighties, she uses the term "young women" to include women up to about age 65.

Bibliography

Brauer, A. *Jews of Kurdistan* (in Hebrew). Jerusalem: HaMaarav Press, 1947.

Friedhaber, Debbi. *From the Dance Customs of Kurdish Jews.* Jewish Dance Archives, 1974.

Garnett, Lucy. *The Women of Turkey and their Folklore.* London: David Nutt, 1893.

Gilad, Lisa. *Yemini Jewish Women.* Ph.D. diss., University of Cambridge, England, 1982.

Israel Museum. *Jews of Kurdistan: Lifestyle, Tradition, and Art.* Summer-Winter 1981–1982, Publication No. 216.

Katz, Nina Dubler. "Culturally Determined Dichotomy in the Musical Practice of the Yemenite Jews." Paper given at the American Anthropological Association 70th Annual Meeting, Nov. 1971, New York City.

Katzir, Yael. *The Effects of Resettlement on the Status and Role of Yemini Women: The Case of Ramat Oranim, Israel.* Ph.D. diss., University of California, Berkeley, 1976.

Leach, Edmund. *Culture and Communication.* Cambridge, England: Cambridge University Press, 1976.

Rice, C. *Persian Women and Their Ways.* London: Seeley, Service and Co., 1923.

Sabar, Yona. "*Lel-Huza:* Story and History in a Cycle of Lamentations for the Ninth of Ab in the Jewish Neo-Aramaic Dialect of Zakho." *Journal of Semitic Studies* 21 (1976): 138–62.

Shai, Donna. *Neighborhood Relations in an Immigrant Quarter.* Henrietta Szold Institute Research Report No. 149, Publication No. 499, April 1970, Jerusalem.

Singer, Isaac Bashevis. "The Washerwoman," in *In My Father's Court.* New York: New American Library, 1967.

Zenner, Walter. "Saints and Piecemeal Supernaturalism Among the Jerusalem Sephardim." *Anthropological Quarterly,* 38:4 (Oct. 1965): 201–17.

Susan Grossman
Rivka Haut

FROM PERSIA TO NEW YORK: AN INTERVIEW WITH THREE GENERATIONS OF IRANIAN WOMEN

During the last decade, the Khoubian family has emigrated to the United States from Iran. The Editors interviewed three generations of women in this family to explore the role of women in the Iranian synagogue.

The maternal grandmother, Iran Ravaghi (80 years old), and her daughter (the Mother), Vaghar Khoubian (60 years old), grew up in Gulpaigan, a city in Southwestern Iran. Both eventually moved to Teheran. Parvin Khoubian, the granddaughter, was born in cosmopolitan Teheran and began attending college there before emigrating to the United States in 1976. Parvin served as translator for her mother and grandmother, who do not speak English.

PARVIN: My grandmother's father was a doctor. My grandmother was an herbalist. This type of education was passed down from one generation to the next. They came from Gulpaigan in the center of Iran. There was a large Jewish community there, like a ghetto. The Jews had their own area, separate from the Moslems. It was a wealthy area. There were 300 Jewish families there, 300 Jewish homes in that city. Now there are only three Jewish families left. There were four synagogues there. My mother tells about her grandfather's synagogue. He built it, and my Mom learned there and taught there. Grandma went to that *shul** also.

Grandma lived there for thirty years and left that city fifty years ago. Mom grew up there and left when she was eighteen. I never saw it.

EDITORS: How often did women go to synagogue?

GRANDMOTHER: Everybody went to synagogue Monday and Thursday mornings, women and men both. Each morning, before sunrise, for forty days before Yom Kippur, everyone went to synagogue and fasted too.[1] They went to hear the *shofar.* Girls sat with their mothers, even from the time they were very little.

MOTHER: In my time, if a father wanted to take a girl to sit with him in the men's section, it wasn't a problem.

EDITORS: Did women go to *shul* all year on Mondays and Thursdays?

PARVIN: Yes. When they read the Torah the women would come and listen to the Torah. After they would bring back the Torah to the *aron kodesh* [the ark containing the Torah scrolls], the women would leave. They came just to hear the Torah read.

EDITORS: Can you describe the synagogue in Iran?

GRANDMOTHER: In my time, the people didn't use chairs. The first floor belonged to the men, and it was full of beautiful rugs. The top floor was for women. It was a balcony and it had wooden separations (*meḥitzot*). The women had a parquet floor to sit on, bare, no rugs, no benches.

MOTHER: I also remember that.

EDITORS: Why were there no rugs upstairs for the women?

GRANDMOTHER: The reason was the men took off their shoes when they prayed. That's why they had little mats, little rugs, to sit on. But the women had to go upstairs to get to the balcony, so they needed their shoes. A rug needed to be cleaned all the time. The women couldn't leave their shoes on the steps, because then others couldn't pass, so they sat on the floor with their shoes on. There was a separate entrance for the women.

EDITORS: Was the women's section smaller than the men's?

GRANDMOTHER: It was smaller and more crowded because the chil-

*The granddaughter's use of the word *shul*, a Yiddish term for synagogue, indicates that she is absorbing some aspects of the dominant American Jewish culture, which is Ashkenazic.

dren also went upstairs. When the Torah was brought out, the women stood. All other times, they sat.

EDITORS: Tell us about the *meḥitzah.*

MOTHER: It was large, but later they made the wood in front of the balcony shorter. The wood was very beautiful, thick, nicely worked wood, not plain and ugly wood. The women could see completely what was going on because it had holes in it, and they could hear.

EDITORS: How many women would come on a regular Shabbat?

GRANDMOTHER: Everyone. Every man had his women there. If a man wasn't in the city, if he went on a trip, his wife would come, even if her husband was away. It was like a religious duty, women had to go, even if their husbands weren't there.

Menstruation

EDITORS: Did the women ever go into the men's section? Did they ever go near the Torah?

GRANDMOTHER: If a man was in the synagogue they were not allowed to go into the men's section. If it was early in the morning, and nobody was there yet, then they would go and they could clean around the *aron kodesh.* The women had to go to the *mikveh* first and be very clean before they could clean around the *aron.* When a woman wanted to go to synagogue, she had to be careful not to have her period. If she had her period, she had to wait seven days, then go to bathe, and then go to synagogue.

EDITORS: If a woman had her period she couldn't go to synagogue?

GRANDMOTHER AND MOTHER: She couldn't go.

EDITORS: On Rosh Hashanah and Yom Kippur, if a woman had her period, could she go to synagogue?

GRANDMOTHER: No.

MOTHER: In my time, on a regular Shabbat, no. Only on those times [the High Holidays] she could.

EDITORS: Could a woman pray when she had her period?

GRANDMOTHER AND MOTHER: She could say *Shema.*[2]

EDITORS: After giving birth, could a woman go to synagogue?

GRANDMOTHER AND MOTHER: For a boy, forty days after. For a girl, eighty days after.[3] Before that, she couldn't go to synagogue.

EDITORS: Did men go to the *mikveh* before going to the synagogue?

GRANDMOTHER AND MOTHER: If he had sex with his wife, he should go. Both of them, if they had sex, they should go.

EDITORS: How did women feel when they had their periods and they weren't allowed to go to synagogue?

GRANDMOTHER AND MOTHER: When a woman had her period she was completely separate from her whole family. She could not sit on the same rug as her husband; she had a special place to sit. She had separate dishes. She had to wear a special dress, not the regular dress that she always wore. She had a special bed, apart.

EDITORS: Could she cook for her family?

GRANDMOTHER: She couldn't do anything. She was like a dead mouse.

MOTHER: When I had my period, before I was married, my grandmother used to tell me to put my dishes upside down in a corner, so nobody would touch them. Women could clean the house, and whatever they were using for themselves, but they could not cook for the family.

PARVIN: Grandma is upset that in the women's prayer group that I once brought her to, the women didn't check if a woman is *niddah* (a menstruant).

EDITORS: Parvin, when you were growing up, did anyone tell you not to enter a synagogue if you had your period?

PARVIN: Mom used to tell me.

EDITORS: In Teheran, did women go to synagogue if they had their periods?

PARVIN: It was mixed up. My cousin, who is younger than I am, does not go to *shul* when she has her period, even here in the United States. In Teheran, the women were told that the Torah is too clean to have anything make it unclean. The rabbis told the women this; they wanted them to come to *shul*.

Cleaning the Ark and Making Candles

EDITORS: You mentioned that women would clean the ark. Why?

GRANDMOTHER AND MOTHER: A woman would ask God to give her something special, for example, if her child was sick, she wanted the child to get better, or if her husband was away, she wanted him to come home safely. If she got what she wanted, she was responsible to clean the *aron kodesh* because she had said if I get that, I will go and clean it.

GRANDMOTHER: I once cleaned the *aron kodesh*. I was 10 years old then. I still remember it. I went with my aunt and my cousins. It was in the old synagogue. Everyone believed that the Levi[4] who built that synagogue was very close to God. That synagogue had a special place in the community, so the women liked to clean the ark. It gave me a kind of happy feeling; I felt good about it. I never went there alone. The women would go together. We were afraid to go alone.

EDITORS: In order to clean around the *aron*, did a woman have to go to *mikveh*?

GRANDMOTHER: Yes.

EDITORS: Did you want to touch the Torah?

GRANDMOTHER: I wanted to, but I didn't. They told me it's not right for a woman to touch it.

MOTHER: When I was twelve, and also when I was fourteen, I went and cleaned the ark. Also, I once touched the Torah. They had a small Torah in our synagogue that was my father's. When I was six, I went with my father to synagogue and sat with him. When my father was called to the Torah, he wanted that Torah, the small one, when he said the blessing. That was the Torah I wanted to see, the small one. I told the rabbi that I wanted to see that Torah. The rabbi took me, and he opened it because he wanted to check it. The rabbi told me I could touch it, and I did.

EDITORS: Did cleaning the ark mean dusting it?

GRANDMOTHER AND MOTHER: Yes. Or bringing something special to cover the Torah, like a scarf. These are women's things to do.

Besides that, women were also responsible for making a candle for Yom Kippur. Women from one family would get together to make one big candle for the synagogue, so that each family had one candle there, a very tall, big candle. The women would make it from beeswax. They used to light the candle an hour before Yom Kippur started, and it was supposed to burn until the next day. If an accident happened and the candle went out, then they would say it would not be a good year for that family.

EDITORS: Where were the candles placed?

GRANDMOTHER AND MOTHER: Just in the men's section, not in the women's section. The synagogue had lights besides the candles. The candles were symbolic, each family brought their own light, and they could pray under that light.

EDITORS: In Teheran, did the women clean the ark or make candles?

GRANDMOTHER, MOTHER, AND PARVIN: No.

Holidays

EDITORS: Did women have any special holiday customs relating to the synagogue?

GRANDMOTHER: On Shavuot, the time of the giving of the Torah and also of springtime, the time of flowers, the women's responsibility was to pick flowers, as much as they could. During the day of Shavuot, when the Torah was taken out of the *aron,* the women—in the women's section— threw these flowers and candy, usually made especially for a bride, on the Torah, as if they were bringing out a bride. They would dance upstairs, but they had no Torah upstairs. In Arab countries they make a sound when they bring a bride out [ululating], like they do here at weddings when the bride is brought out. In my time they made that sound when the Torah was brought out on that day.

MOTHER: Also in my time. The men did not do that, only the women.

EDITORS: What about Simḥat Torah?

GRANDMOTHER: On the last two days of Sukkot, the whole synagogue was covered with beautiful cloths. Women donated those cloths. The women who wanted to donate scarves to cover the Torah would give them on those days.

EDITORS: Did women sing and dance on Simḥat Torah also?

GRANDMOTHER: Women danced at home, not in synagogue. The men went to synagogue, the women stayed at home. They would get together in someone's house and dance. When they wanted to watch the men dance, they would go to synagogue. The [extended] families of women, the same group that would make the candles, would get together and dance at home.

EDITORS: What do Iranian women do in the United States on Simḥat Torah?

PARVIN: The same thing as everyone else. I never saw anything different. [*Editors: In most Orthodox synagogues women watch the men dance. They themselves do not usually dance either at home or in the synagogue.*]

EDITORS: Did the women have special *Rosh Ḥodesh* celebrations?

GRANDMOTHER, MOTHER: No.

Prayers

EDITORS: Did most women know how to pray?

GRANDMOTHER: Yes. Only men had a *siddur* (prayer book). When the men read, the women would repeat after them. The women memorized the prayers; they could not read Hebrew.

MOTHER: The women who could read would bring their own *siddur,* those who couldn't read would listen to the men. The women read to themselves, not aloud. I learned from the rabbi how to read. Then he asked me to teach the others, and I did.

EDITORS: Were there any special prayers the women said?

GRANDMOTHER: For anything special, they would read the *tefillah* (prayer) of Hannah.[5] It was in our *siddur* before "*Elohai neshamah.*"[6] When Hannah wanted a child, she prayed that prayer. So, every woman would read Hannah's prayer. Only the women prayed that prayer.

Women also used to read *Tehillim* (Psalms), if they asked God for something. Men and women would both say *Tehillim.* The women would not say *Tehillim* in a crowd. They would invite the men to read for them.

MOTHER: In my day the women would read for themselves. They needed ten men to be there when they read. They would sit separately, but the women would read it themselves too.

Female Shammash

EDITORS: Did women have any role in the running of the synagogue?

GRANDMOTHER AND MOTHER: The one who did all the cleaning, turning on the lights, everything related to the synagogue was a woman, not a man. She was called a *shammash.* She had to be a good woman, clean on the inside, pure.

EDITORS: Was it an honorable job, or was it like being a janitor?

GRANDMOTHER: The woman was most religious and the people believed that she was very honest. She was responsible for opening the synagogue in the morning, and before *minḥah* (afternoon prayers), and for opening the lights so the men could come in. She was responsible for seeing that nothing was lost, that everything was OK in the synagogue. The men could not do the job that a woman could do. She was doing all of the cleaning and taking care in the way that a woman can take care of her own house. But because this place was higher than a house, it was a woman's job to do it, because she could do this kind of job best. Especially since she was very religious; she had more feeling.

MOTHER: All the synagogues in my town had a woman *shammash*.

EDITORS: Was she paid?

GRANDMOTHER: No, she was not paid. It was an honor.

EDITORS: Was this woman important?

GRANDMOTHER: The women were too shy to ask the rabbi about many questions relating to women. She spent most of her time in the synagogue, so she knew more about these things than other women. Women felt comfortable asking her many of these questions.

EDITORS: Was the rabbi's wife anyone special?

GRANDMOTHER AND MOTHER: No.

EDITORS: How was the *shammash* chosen?

GRANDMOTHER: She would say, "I would like to take care of the synagogue." The people would ask the rabbi if she was a good person. The rabbi and the people had to approve her. The men decided, not the women. If she was honorable enough to do that, they would accept her.

EDITORS: Could an unmarried woman be the *shammash?*

GRANDMOTHER: They were mostly widowed, older women, someone who had no other responsibilities.

EDITORS: Did this role exist in Teheran, also?

GRANDMOTHER AND MOTHER: No.

EDITORS: Are women as important to God as men?

MOTHER: No. A woman is looked down on in the Torah. In Jewish society, a woman is less than a man. She is less important.

EDITORS: Would you have liked to have been a man?

GRANDMOTHER: Yes.

MOTHER: Sure.

PARVIN: Until I came to the United States, I didn't want to be a woman. I think women have more sensitivity than men. Now I also see that I am as strong as a man, maybe sometimes stronger.

EDITORS: What does the synagogue mean to you?

GRANDMOTHER: It is the cleanest place. I feel comfortable because when I go there I feel free to pray to God and talk to God.

Notes

1. In Sephardic communities, people go to the synagogue forty days before Rosh Hashanah to hear the *shofar*. Ashkenazim go for thirty days.

2. This is the central prayer of Judaism: "Hear O Israel. . . . "

3. These numbers correspond to the biblical proscription of a parturient's attendance at the Tabernacle.

4. A Levi is a Jew who traces his ancestry to the Israelite tribe of Levi, a son of Jacob. The levites served as functionaries in the Temple and still retain certain ritual privileges.

5. Cf. I Sam. 2:1–11.

6. Part of the early morning prayers.

Rela Geffen Monson

THE IMPACT OF THE JEWISH WOMEN'S MOVEMENT ON THE AMERICAN SYNAGOGUE: 1972–1985

In 1963, a relatively unkown Jewish woman named Betty Friedan launched what became the contemporary feminist movement with the publication of *The Feminine Mystique*.[1] The National Organization for Women was formed in 1966 on a platform of political and social change. It was organized around small consciousness-raising groups, largely in response to Friedan's articulation of "the problem that has no name." Friedan wrote about college educated women who suffered from depression and general malaise even though, as wives of professional men and mothers of healthy children, they should have been happy. The root of their unhappiness lay, according to Friedan, in how society structured the role of women, encouraging higher education before their marriage but, once married, limiting their options for intellectual and professional satisfaction.

In 1972, the organized Jewish women's movement began when *Ezrat Nashim*, the fledgling Jewish women's study group turned consciousness-raising group, took on an activist orientation.[2] There had been some move toward including women in ritual and communal life prior to that time. One example of this is the 1956 responsum of the Rabbinical Assembly Law Committee, written by Rabbi Aaron Blumenthal, which permitted women to be called to the Torah, and thus allowed the institutionalization of the *Bat Mitzvah*. It was undoubtedly the involvement in and exposure to the civil rights movement and the American feminist movement, however, that motivated a small group of highly educated, traditional Jewish women to push for equality within the Jewish community.[3] Precisely because they were traditional, they chose the synagogue, the central institution of Jewish life, as the major arena in which to fight for women's rights.

Jewish women understood well that the synagogue was more than a house of worship, and that to be public persons within the synagogue, whether in the ritual or secular sphere, was symbolic of full citizenship. Even women who were not particularly observant began to attend synagogue meetings and to express what roles they wanted for themselves and their daughters. Some of them were accused of being hypocritical, because they seemed motivated to participate in synagogue life only because of this issue. Some of their critics said, "Let them come to services regularly, participate in all synagogue activities, and observe the Sabbath and dietary laws—then we will consider their 'bid' for full participation in synagogue ritual."

However, such women viewed their protest as a political as well as a religious act, even though it took place within the framework of a religious institution. At the same time that they were fighting to be counted in the *minyan* (quorum for worship), to have Torah honors, and to have *Bat Mitzvah* ceremonies for their daughters on Sabbath morning, they were also struggling for greater representation on synagogue boards and to be committee chairpeople and officers of congregations. They saw a link between the ritual and the secular roles within the synagogue. The exclusion of women from secular leadership roles was a direct derivative of their exclusion from ritual roles, for if the president of the synagogue sat on the *bimah* as a perquisite of his office, then a woman could not be president because she could not sit on the *bimah*. Whether or not the vast majority of women who fought for synagogue rights understood these links, they intuitively sensed that they existed.

In addition to nonreligious women, in the early and mid-1970s there were also women involved in the movement who were much more knowledgeable about Judaism and who fought from a different perspective. They sought recognition as full-fledged members of the congregation for reasons that came out of a deep commitment to the Jewish tradition and a desire to enhance the quality of their own lives as Jews. These women, a small group in comparison to the former group, were generally well educated and quite observant by the standards of the right wing of the Conservative Movement. They had studied classical Jewish sources, attended synagogue regularly, and observed many other ritual commandments. For these women, the prayer "May He Who blessed our fathers, Abraham, Isaac, and Jacob, bless the members of this holy congregation, them, their wives, their sons, their daughters, and all that belong to them. . . ," which was recited every Saturday morning in their synagogues, was taken as a personal challenge to their sense of belonging to the *kahal*—the congregation of Israel. Their crusade to count in the *minyan*, to have various Torah honors, and to be eligible to represent the congregation by leading it in prayer was serious and persistent. These women belonged to such organizations as the above-mentioned *Ezrat Nashim* in New York and *N'shay Hayil* in Philadelphia. They were established around the time of the first national Jewish women's conference sponsored by the North American Jewish Students Network in 1973.

Ezrat Nashim and *N'shay Hayil* remained active until 1980. Their activities evolved from study groups to community activism. They organized conferences, ran lecture bureaus, collected materials to create library resources on Jewish women, and wrote nonsexist Jewish children's stories and curricula for Jewish schools. Eventually, many of the women in these groups became recognized figures in Jewish life. At least four became professors of Jewish studies, one founded a magazine, one heads a day school, and another is executive director of a national Jewish organization. As many of the goals of these groups were attained, and they became part of the agenda of national Jewish organizations, their reason for existence was diminished. Similarly, the consciousness-raising groups of the beginning of the general women's movement disappeared as most charismatic cells became routinized into more traditional forms of organization.

Life Cycle Rituals

The power of the synagogue and of synagogue ritual as a rallying point for the Jewish feminist movement has been enhanced by the centrality of life cycle rituals for American Jews. Even those Jews who are quite removed from Jewish life on a day-to-day basis interact with the tradition and the community at times of birth, puberty, marriage, and death.

During these life cycle passages, the synagogue and its spiritual leader, the rabbi, become the arbiters of "the right thing to do." Many women who had not considered their own status in relation to the tradition became radicalized during the 1970s when they compared their changing status in the outside community with their experiences in the synagogue during these crucial life cycle events. For example, a woman who was respected in the work place might find herself shunted aside or ignored during the naming of her baby daughter. A woman physician might be pushed out of the room during the circumcision of her son because it wasn't "her place." A woman who was entering into an egalitarian relationship with her new husband, and who had "negotiated" all the aspects of her future married life, would discover that she was expected to be silent during the wedding ceremony on the synagogue's *bimah*. Some women found, to their chagrin, that when they lost a parent and wanted to say *Kaddish* they were made to feel like nonpersons within the confines of the synagogue. If a woman was the tenth person in the room, she might hear comments such as "There aren't enough people here for us to say *Kaddish*."

These women were strongly affected by the growth of the feminist movement in American society and their own professional success within that society. American Jewish women are, as a group, more highly educated than any other group of American women—including white Episcopalians, who are often held up as the group that has achieved the epitome of American success. In the United States, Jews generally outrank all other groups on the three classic measures of socioeconomic status: occupation, education, and income.[4] Jewish women, as well as Jewish men, are far more likely than non-Jews to have college and graduate degrees, to have achieved high occupational status in the professions and managerial positions, and to have high incomes. Although Jewish women have surpassed other women in these areas, they have not as yet equalled or surpassed Jewish or non-Jewish men.

Nevertheless, the discrepancy between their achievement in the outside world and within the Jewish community became more and more apparent as the 1970s unfolded. The compartmentalization they had adopted as a psychological device that enabled them to live their lives differently at some times than they did at others broke down. This compartmentalization was described in an article in the *New York Post*, in which Jewish historian and *Ezrat Nashim* member Paula Hyman was quoted as saying that her activism stemmed in part as the result of prodding from professors at Columbia University, who asked her why she turned into a different person on the weekends.[5]

The 1970s and the beginning of the 1980s was a time for evolution and revolution for many women. More and more women came to believe that their status as full members of the Jewish community had to be verified by their being eligible to participate in synagogue and political life. The following examples demonstrate the impact this growing awareness had on synagogue life in Judaism's various movements.

Social scientists consider a change of ten or fifteen percentage points in several decades significant. The percentage of Conservative synagogues granting *aliyot* (Torah honors) to women grew from seven percent in 1972 to fifty percent by 1976—a truly extraordinary phenomenon by any sociological measure.[6]

The Orthodox Movement

When analyzing the impact of the Jewish women's movement on Orthodox synagogues, it is necessary to look at different measures than we would in examining Conservative or Reform synagogues. Nevertheless, life cycle rituals provide a useful way to look at changes common to all of the movements. The introduction of ceremonies welcoming Jewish baby girls into the world (*simḥat bat*) is one of the impacts of the Jewish women's movement that has been felt in the Orthodox community. In addition, celebration of the *Bat Mitzvah*, which previously had been identified with non-Orthodox movements, became incorporated into the normative fabric of modern Orthodox life. In the United States, especially, it had been avoided so as not to associate Orthodoxy with the innovations of Mordecai Kaplan. Today, women who themselves never celebrated their Jewish coming of age arrange elaborate teas and other celebrations for their 12-year-old daughters. These ceremonies go beyond the social, often including delivery of a learned speech by the young girl. Sometimes the occasion of the *Bat Mitzvah* is publicly announced in the synagogue, and, in the girl's honor, the father and brothers of the *Bat Mitzvah* are given Torah honors. Although the performance of the girl does not take place in the context of a synagogue service, the occasion is still one that is connected to synagogue ritual. In a few synagogues, the *dvar Torah* (sermon) may be given by the *Bat Mitzvah* at the close of the service in the sanctuary. In others, a woman's prayer group provides the context for the *Bat Mitzvah* (see Penkowers, pp. 265ff.).[7]

Examples of the more direct involvement of Orthodox Jewish women in synagogue ritual include such innovations as giving a Torah to women to dance with on Simḥat Torah; passing the Torah, or marching with the Torah, to the women's section in the processions prior to and just after the reading on Sabbath morning; and designing synagogues with greater thought given to the placement and design of the women's section.[8] In addition, women's prayer (*tefillah*) groups, which meet regularly on the Sabbath (sometimes in synagogues) or monthly on the New Moon, traditionally considered a women's holiday, have also affected synagogue life. These groups are on the cutting edge of the Jewish women's movement within Orthodoxy.

In 1984, a controversial rabbinic responsum banning women's prayer groups was issued by five rabbis from Yeshiva University (the rabbinic seminary for modern Orthodoxy).[9] The consternation, disappointment, and anger of the women who were involved in *tefillah* groups led to the formation of a "Women's *Tefillah* Network" in the winter of 1985.

Contributing to their consternation was the fact that several Orthodox rabbis in New York were sponsoring women's prayer groups and personally guiding them so that their mode of prayer would be according to *halakhah* (*see* R. Haut, pp. 135ff.). The controversy even spilled over to Israel, where an acrimonious debate over the legitimacy of the responsum took place in the "Letters to the Editor" section of *The Jerusalem Post*.

Women's prayer groups continue to grow in size and number. From the sociological point of view, these groups are a functional alternative, serving as a safety valve, holding back a demand for greater equality within the context of the Orthodox *minyan*, while allowing the participants to expand their religious experience within an halakhic framework.

One cannot predict at this point the ultimate effect of the conflict surrounding prayer groups on Orthodox synagogue life. For some women, it may be the final push toward leaving the Orthodox framework of prayer, while for others it may strengthen their determination to effect change within their congregations.

A few individual Orthodox women have chosen publicly to display their commitment to positive, time-bound commandments within the synagogue by wearing prayer shawls in the women's section. While these individual actions do not change the structure of the synagogue or its service, they do, by their public nature, have an effect on the consciousness of all the men and women who are present. A similar function was performed earlier by those women within Orthodox synagogues who stood and said the *Kaddish* prayer aloud when they were in mourning, even though they were not required to do so. Today, a woman saying *Kaddish* is no longer an aberration that is met with resistance. Saying the *Kaddish* is both a verbal and physical symbol in synagogues, during the time when only the mourners stand. Wearing a prayer shawl is also a physical symbol that cannot be ignored by the rest of the congregation.

The impact of the women's movement on the Orthodox synagogue is an ongoing one that should be carefully monitored. Although these changes are less sweeping than those in other movements, they are not to be taken lightly. In Orthodox synagogues where some of the changes in the context of prayer have not taken place, others outside that context have occurred. For instance, it is much more likely now than it was a decade ago to find Orthodox synagogues in which women are considered members of the congregation, can vote at synagogue meetings, and are eligible to serve on committees and be officers of the congregation. In fact, in some Orthodox synagogues women were officially granted these other rights to demonstrate that Orthodoxy is not inherently discriminatory, but, rather, that there are halakhic matters that are immutable. However, where there is no halakhic barrier, the tradition may be made egalitarian.

The Conservative Movement

Within Conservative synagogues the impact of the Jewish feminist movement has been more dramatic and is apparent to even a casual observer. Where previously no women were on the *bimah,* is is now common to see them. Where before no women participated in the Torah service, it is now normative in many congregations to see them functioning in all its aspects. In June 1985, the first woman rabbi graduated from the Jewish Theological Seminary, and women graduates from other rabbinic institutions have served in Conservative synagogues for almost a decade. It is hard to believe that the ten women of *Ezrat Nashim* had such an impact on the largest religious movement within American Jewish life—an impact most evident within the synagogue. Women who were not even considered members of the congregation in many Conservative synagogues during the 1940s and 1950s are now leaders within their own synagogues and in regional and national synagogue organizations. They serve as committee chairpeople and officers of their congregations, and they have even, in some cases, attained the two most difficult and prestigious positions: synagogue president and chairperson of the ritual committee.

To be sure, these changes, and particularly the controversy over the ordination of women, have sparked a backlash in the form of the Union for Traditional Conservative Judaism. This well-organized group, centered around the senior Talmud faculty of the Jewish Theological Seminary, about ten percent of the membership of the Rabbinical Assembly (the Conservative rabbinic association), and some wealthy and influential lay people, has championed the cause of traditional roles for women within the Conservative Movement. While individual observance of the dietary laws and the Sabbath have also been foci of the organization, it was conceived and organized around opposition to the growing consensus on egalitarianism that threatened to "read out" the right wing of the movement. The actual power and influence of this group has yet to be analyzed since it is so new. However, the egalitarian movement is so normative at this point that, with the exception of civil law pertaining to women's roles (e.g., witnessing and acting as judges), the focus of this faction appears to be turning to other issues such as patrilineal descent, strict enforcement of the laws of personal status, maintenance of a *kashrut* "hot line" for questions concerning the dietary laws, and determination of the legitimacy of the new Rabbinical Assembly prayer book.

In sum, the Conservative Movement, as of this writing, still holds to some aspects of Jewish law that differentiate between men and women. These include the right to be a witness, judge, or the initiator in a divorce. However, within the synagogue as an institution, egalitarianism has taken root and flourished in the majority of congregations.

The Reform Movement

Within the Reform Movement one would have thought that egalitarianism would have been the norm from its inception, as it was in the Reconstructionist Movement. In fact, Reform temples were male turf as surely as were Orthodox synagogues. Hegemony of men within the Reform Movement was based on social custom, which was reinforced by the traditional past of many of the leaders of the movement. However, when American society began to change in the 1970s, the Reform Movement was quick to respond to the call for egalitarianism in the synagogue. This change did not evolve without difficulty, however, because the power of precedent can be as strong as law. Women in the Reform Movement had to fight hard to gain positions of power in the secular aspects of synagogue life and in the Union of American Hebrew Congregations on the regional and national levels. They also had to fight to be allowed on the *bimah* along with men. In the Reform Movement, there was not much lay participation in services in general, public ritual having been relegated almost entirely to professionals. However, the entry of women into the Reform cantorate and rabbinate has changed the public image of the service, at the same time that lay participation has increased. Nevertheless, the forces of social custom persist. Many women rabbis in the Reform Movement still meet resistance at certain life cycle functions, particularly funerals. Others are finding it difficult to move into larger congregations as senior rabbis.

The impact of the women's movement on the Reform synagogue is now also being felt in a move toward changes in the English liturgy of the prayer service. For over a decade the movement has been at work on the revision of its various prayer books for the cycle of the year. At the same time, a committee has been working on the abolition of male dominated terminology when referring to the congregation of Israel, whether it be in the Passover *Haggadah* or in the *Maḥzor*, the special prayer book for the High Holidays. An attempt is also being made to refer to God in neuter rather than masculine terms. This work will eventually have a profound influence on Reform synagogue life (*see* Daum, pp. 183ff.).

Summary and Conclusion

The relative deprivation that was felt by Jewish women when they compared themselves, as Jews, to men within the synagogue led to profound changes in synagogue life during the years 1972 to 1985. A close look at the American synagogue—whether Reform, Conservative, or Orthodox—reveals structural changes as well as changes in the content of ritual and prayer that may be traced directly to the influence of the Jewish women's movement. The impact of the activities of the women who were involved in this social change was enhanced by the growth and acceptance of the feminist movement in American society at large. At the same time, the change in American mores heightened the sense of relative deprivation felt by many Jewish women. High achievers in the non-Jewish world of their everyday life, they felt at an even greater disadvantage when they entered the male turf of the synagogue. The centrality of life cycle rituals for a majority of American Jews made the quest for equality more broadly based than it would have been if only those who were committed to tradition had been involved. The interface of life cycle events and the life of the synagogue led a large group of American Jewish women to actively push for change or to support it when it was proposed, during the decade of the 1970s. Changes in synagogue life are continuing as a result of the ongoing agenda and political organization of the Jewish women's movement.

The personal vignettes that follow typify the tenor of the times and the evolution that thousands of women have experienced. These poignant experiences of individual women give reality and substance to the dynamic movement that is occurring.

Notes

1. Virginia Sapiro, *Women in American Society* (Palo Alto, Calif.: Mayfield Publishing Co., 1986), 465.

2. Martha Ackelsberg, "Introduction," in *The Jewish Women*, ed. Elizabeth Koltun (New York: Schocken, 1976), xiii.

3. Anne Lapidus Lerner, "Who Hast Not Made Me a Man," in *American Jewish Year Book* (New York: American Jewish Committee, 1977), 256–57.

4. Steven M. Cohen, *American Modernity and Jewish Identity* (New York: Tavistock Publications, 1983), 76.

5. Barbara Trecker, "10 Religious Feminists to Confront the Rabbis," *New York Post* 14 March 1972, 71.

6. Rela Geffen Monson, Unpublished survey of Rabbinical Assembly members (Sponsored by *Ezrat Nashim* through the Rabbinical Assembly Newsletter, 1972); and Daniel Elazar and Rela Geffen Monson, "Women in the Synagogue Today," *Midstream* vol. 27 (April 1981): 25.

7. Most of this information comes from a personal collection of Orthodox *Bat Mitzvah* invitations, interviews with Orthodox women, and other, as yet unpublished, material.

8. *See* Elazar and Monson, "Women in the Synagogue Today,"; and Saul Berman, "The State of Women in Halachic Judaism," *Tradition*, 14:2 (Fall 1973), 5–28.

9. Larry Kohler, "Orthodox Rabbis' Responsa Condemns Women's Prayer Groups," 14; 37, *Long Island Jewish World* (15–21 Feb. 1985).

PERSONAL
VIGNETTES

The personal vignettes that follow represent a wide range of perspectives on women's place in normative Judaism. We begin with two women discussing very different communities, who find value and satisfaction in the traditional roles they fill. Shoshana Gelerenter-Liebowitz tells of the value placed on women's prayer and candlelighting in the Lubavitch Ḥasidic community in which she was raised. In that community, both men and women place a high value on the spiritual efficacy of women's religious functions. She also introduces a motif that recurs in a number of other vignettes: that of a young girl whose budding maturity means that she is no longer permitted to sit with her father in the men's section. Gelerenter did not resent this experience and accepted it as part of a natural process.

Beverly Lebeau, a rebbetzin for many years in Conservative synagogues, also writes of the satisfaction she feels in that traditional role. For generations, the rebbetzin was seen as an adjunct to the rabbi: listening, advising, becoming involved with the community's concerns. In the last two decades, expectations of the spouse of a rabbi (which now includes husbands as well as wives) have been changing, as spouses are no longer as readily available to devote their time to the congregation. Lebeau's vignette reflects this sense of change.

We chose to include these two articles because we wish to present a variety of voices. These two vignettes show that there are significant numbers of women who are happy with their traditional role as Jewish women.

Shoshana Gelerenter-Liebowitz

GROWING UP LUBAVITCH

When I was very young I loved to go to *shul* with my father. One of the many privileges I enjoyed as the oldest child was having my father to myself on our long walks to and from 770 (the headquarters and main synagogue of the Lubavitch Movement). My parents came from Poland and became Lubavitch when they arrived in the United States. I am therefore a first generation American and Lubavitcher.

On our walks to and from *shul* my father spoke to me quite freely of his parents who had died in the Holocaust. In Hrubishov, Poland, his mother was the *foreleiner* in *shul*. She was the woman who was able to read the prayers. She would say the prayers, word for word, and the other women would recite right after her. This meant my grandmother was a literate woman, which was atypical, as most women could not read or understand Hebrew. My father would talk about his mother with great pride. (*See* Taitz for more information on *foreleiners,* also called *firzogerin,* pp. 66ff.)

When I was little, I was allowed to enter the men's section with my father. Some other fathers brought in girls older than myself. When a little girl looked a little too old to be in the men's section, around ten years old, the men would become very agitated. Sometimes someone would say something to admonish her, and the big little girl would understand that she was too old to be with the men. Nobody had to explain why girls can not sit with their fathers in *shul* past age ten or why boys and girls don't pray together. Boys and girls don't do anything together. Nobody questions this. The separation of the sexes is accepted throughout the society. Boys and girls are never together. During my childhood, if a girl played with boys outside of *shul* she was called a *Ḥamor eizel,* a donkey. It was very frowned upon.

I don't remember ever feeling upset that I couldn't pray with the men anymore. The men's section was not a pleasant place in which to pray. It didn't feel peaceful because it was always crowded and hot and there was no room to sit.

Lubavitch women don't ever feel secondary or deprived. Their lives are as busy as the men's. There is always so much activity. An equal responsibility for performing *mitzvot* rests with with the males and females. All children are soldiers in *HaShem's* army. The boys encourage non-observant men to wear *tefillin;* the girls ask women to light candles: equal roles.

When girls start lighting candles on Friday nights, at three years old, their womanhood really begins. They light and their brothers don't. Candlelighting is stressed very much. Although little boys at age three get their first haircut, receive their first set of *tzitzit* (ritual fringes), and begin to always wear a *yarmulke* (skullcap), the *mitzvot* of *tallit* and *tefillin* only begin at a later developmental stage for boys. Girls do not feel at all like second-class citizens; little girls do not envy boys because there are *mitzvot* for both to observe.

Mothers don't usually go to *shul* on Friday night because they are home with their children. (*Editor's note: Observant Jews do not carry or wheel baby carriages outside on the Sabbath.*) My mother had her children closely spaced so she couldn't go to *shul,* but she davened at home every Shabbes. As I started to learn *tefillos* (prayers) in school, I began to daven at home every Shabbes morning and on Friday nights. My mother would say to my sisters and me, "Let's daven *Kabbalas Shabbes*" (the Friday evening prayers) and we would do so together. As we got older, each of my sisters would take a *siddur* and daven separately, though at the same time.

During the week, I had to say the beginning prayers before I came to breakfast. The rest of the morning prayers were recited in school. On days when there was no school, I was expected to complete the prayers at home after breakfast. My mother would remind me to daven, the same way she would remind me to get dressed in the morning. This was a normal part of the day's routine. At one point, I went through a little phase of davening *Minḥah* and *Maʿariv* (afternoon and evening prayers) of my own volition, and my parents were very pleased. They viewed it as a sort of charming thing. I remember when any of us exceeded their spiritual expectations of us, my parents smiled and my father was very proud of his daughters.

In my family, and, I think, in all Lubavitch families, women's prayers are taken very seriously. The power of a woman's prayers was often stressed as being the most valuable to God when granting blessings of help and health.

Every Shabbes my mother said all of *Tehillim* (Psalms), and she added specific verses to her daily prayers. My mother used to do this as a European custom, but now everyone does this. When someone is sick, there is a lot of focus on praying and saying *Tehillim*. I remember in my girls' school they would often announce on the loudspeaker that so and so, the daughter or son of so and so, is sick, and the children should have *kavannah* (intention) to pray for a *refuah sheleimah* (complete recovery). Girls were repeatedly told that their prayers are very important and that good things happen because of the *zekhut* (merit) of women.

Teenage girls go to *shul* on Friday night. Partly they go to *shul* to daven and partly for the social ambiance. They don't say "I am going to *shul*." They say "I am going to 770." All their friends go to *shul*. They don't talk in *shul*, but once they leave *shul*, they chitchat. There is no mingling between the sexes. The men stand on their side, and the woman on their side, socializing after *shul*. The women start walking, and their husbands usually catch up to them.

On *Yom Tov* (holiday), when baby carriages may be wheeled to *shul*, there is a noticeable increase in the number of women and children present. An entire area outside the *shul* is filled with women, with prayer books or *Tehillim* in their hands, rocking their baby carriages and praying at the same time.

Most married women also go to *shul*. However, some women don't go to 770 because they find that the social aspect of getting dressed, putting on their *sheitels* (the wigs that married women wear), and seeing and talking to friends might be a distraction to their *kavannah* (intention in prayer). Lubavitchers, compared to other kinds of Jews, however, do not dress up to a point that might be considered vain. Social standards are quite subtle though, for vanity can often be a woman's Achilles' heel when it comes to her observance of *mitzvot*.

Part of the focal point of going to 770 is really to see "The Rebbe."

That is special in Lubavitch life. The people want to get a glimpse of "The Rebbe." Women daven quietly because, if there is any noise, they can't hear the Torah reading or the *baʿal tefillah* (prayer leader). It is a gigantic place, 770. The downstairs (men's) section is very large. The women's section is built over it. There is a dark-tinted glass partition. The women can see through, but the men can't see in. The window opening is chest high, so women have to bend their heads in order to see down. There are only a limited number of seats in the front row, the only row from which one can see. Usually the young girls come early and get those front seats. When older women see this monopolization, they sometimes fight over seats, because everyone wants the privilege of seeing "The Rebbe."

In *shul,* the women never sing aloud. They only whisper "amen" and the sections that the entire congregation chants aloud. If hundreds of women started to say "Amen," in unison, nobody would hear what was going on. Also, in terms of *tzniut* (modesty) this would be inappropriate. However, in school, when the girls daven, they do daven out loud. They are led by a *ḥazzanit* (prayer leader). There is no Torah reading. Also, women never sing *zemiros* (Sabbath songs) out loud at home. However, Lubavitch has a girl's choir that sings only for women. They put on plays, always with a Lubavitch theme, such as celebrating the previous Rebbe's release from prison.

Women are supposed to go to *shul* to hear the *shofar* blown on Rosh Hashanah and to hear the *Megillah* read on Purim. They go to the little *shuls* for that. There are many small synagogues in Crown Heights, which serve many kinds of Jews. Now Lubavitchers are the only Jews in the area, and they do their best to maintain these *shteiblakh* (small *shuls*).

Women's responsibility to participate in all the *mitzvot* that are possible is taken very seriously by the women themselves and by the men. If a woman cannot get to *shul,* someone will come to her home to blow the *shofar* or read the *Megillah* for her. If anyone is in the hospital, arrangements will be made for her. Sometimes her husband will do it, or, if he cannot, someone else will.

Women never say *Kaddish.* If there is no male relative, then someone else is given that responsibility. Women do participate in many fundraising activities for the synagogue and many charities.

"The Rebbe" is a role model for both men and women. There are special *farbrengen* (gatherings to hear "The Rebbe" teach) for women several times a year. "The Rebbe's" wife was a mysterious figure in Crown Heights.

It is rather unusual that the rebbetzin of the community was so anonymous. Nobody knew anything about her. She did not have a special place in the *shul* where everyone davens (770) but stayed in a private room in the building.

The Rebbe" is a transcendental figure, very elevated and spiritually capable of guiding his followers in their personal decisions. Men and women share a respectful reverence toward him. Women and men share a desire to be in "The Rebbe's" presence, often pushing themselves to their physical limits to stay up at *farbrengens* until the early hours of the morning. He activates everybody. Women and men basically have the same role in their relationship to him.

Beverly A. Lebeau

ON BEING A *REBBETZIN*

Sharing in the glorious moment of childbirth with an encouraging husband and an enthusiastic obstetrician is more common today for women than it was sixteen years ago, when our fourth child was born and the hospital, for the first time, gave my husband, Bill, permission to be present in the delivery room.

When Bill, who has devoted himself to teaching his congregants to search for God's Presence in that which is ordinary, encountered God in the singular ecstasy of our daughter's birth, he was indelibly struck by it. Being there during the moment when our seconds-old infant, blue and motionless, inhaled her first breath and was transformed into a pink, healthy being was a sacred experience. In the last sixteen years, Bill has described that moment to thousands of people from the pulpit and in the classroom, as an integral part of his personal relationship with God.

When asked to write of my experiences as a rebbetzin, the delivery room scene came to mind first. It symbolized to me the evolution I had undergone from being a very private person, to accepting the public nature of my husband's profession, and finally to being openly comfortable in my relationship with our congregation.

The most public of moments for me was sitting in the congregation on

Shabbat morning listening to Bill guiding, interpreting, and preaching. It is hard work for a day of rest. Perhaps it was the contrast with the intensity of the mornings that made the privacy of our family Shabbat afternoons especially sweet and beautiful. It was this delicate balance between the private and public aspects of our lives that enriched our Shabbat and our weekdays.

My husband's rabbinate allowed me the privilege of sharing in the lives of our congregants. There is always the question of "What does a rebbetzin do?" What I "did" was make myself available to listen to people—at a *kiddush,* in the doctor's waiting room, in the supermarket aisle. From them I learned about dimensions of the human spirit with which I was unfamiliar.

I have seen them at their best, at times of their greatest happiness. I have observed their ability to enjoy those moments. I have seen them in their deepest sorrow. From them I have learned the power of the care and concern of one human being for another.

I have gained tremendous strength from my relationship with congregants. It is this strength that has enabled me to be comfortable as a rebbetzin and to be left with feelings of warmth and enthusiasm for the years of my husband's rabbinate.

Can it really be that all I did was "listen"? My congregational activities varied. What I did at age twenty-five was not the same as what I did at forty-five. Though my involvement varied, I did not at any age participate to satisfy congregational expectations. I took part in activities in which I was interested, for which I had time, and to which I could apply my strengths.

When I was twenty-five, Bill and I found ourselves in East Setauket, N.Y., a small Long Island community with an active congregation of eighty member families. I volunteered to organize the synagogue's library and to participate in the formation of the congregation's first nursery school. I had been a research assistant with Project Head Start's nursery school program. Preschool education was very much a concern of mine. The ordering, reading, and reviewing of books required by the library position was also work of special interest to me.

I had come to this community with a one-year-old son, and Bill and I were blessed with four more children during the next ten years. During those years, in which both the congregation and our family grew rapidly, my synagogue activities were enjoyable and intellectually stimulating.

Twelve years later, our now expanded family, ranging in ages from two to fourteen years, moved to a new and thriving synagogue community. I had not worked in a paid position outside the home since my first child was born, nor was I sorry for a moment of the time devoted to raising the children. College fees loomed ahead, however, and with them the inescapable reality that I needed to return to work outside the home. Shortly after arriving in Highland Park, a suburb of Chicago, I began a four-year juggling act, taking classes part-time toward a Master of Science Degree in Accounting, squeezing in study time between *Bar* and *Bat Mitzvahs,* weddings, and car pools. Since graduating, I have continued to work four days a week in tax accounting.

Needless to say, with this kind of schedule there was no time for the active congregational committee work I engaged in with the previous community. My interest in and respect for the accomplishments of the lay people of each of our two congregations was the same. My ability to participate actively with them is what changed.

Weekday pursuits may have changed over time, but the experience of sharing Shabbat with our community was always a welcome constant. My most vivid memories are of praying and studying together with our congregants on Shabbat, week after week. Raised in an Orthodox home, I have been satisfied with the traditional women's role in the synagogue. My three daughters have helped me come to understand the beautiful meaning that active participation in synagogue ritual has for them. Likewise, being in a profession that until recently has been mostly male, I can empathize with the struggle of women rabbis as they strive for acceptance in their chosen field.

Through the years of my husband's rabbinate, we have both given of ourselves to our community, and in return we have received. The enthusiasm and fondness we have for our two congregations will remain as a continuing blessing for us.

The Ḥavurah Movement helped bring about the equal involvement of women and men in leading services and participating in prayer. Although this movement of lay leaders was, from its inception, dedicated to the ideal of equality, it was an equality in which all men were created equal. Merle Feld reveals that equal treatment of women was not part of the original plan and did not occur until precipitated by the women themselves. She documents the internal processes from which changes developed. Her message is clear: change must begin from within.

Merle Feld

EGALITARIANISM AND THE *ḤAVURAH* MOVEMENT

I felt a certain personal irony when I was asked to contribute to a book on women and the synagogue, in part because until I was in my second or third year of college, I had almost never been in a synagogue. What excluded me is rather easy to explain: My family was assimilated and non-observant; even if we had some interest in "joining," our constant economic struggles kept the doors firmly closed. I guess you could say the first time I began going to *shul* was the first time I could get in for free—at Brooklyn College Hillel.

Quite simply, Hillel, and its director, Rabbi Norman Frimer, changed my life. Worlds of meaning opened to me—Jewish texts, the rhythms of Shabbat, holiday celebrations, the discipline of *kashrut,* the sense that a holy community was created between one human being and another. Then, in my senior year of college, I met a 24-year-old rabbinical student about to be ordained at the Jewish Theological Seminary. Very quickly we came to love each other. A girl who had heard of neither Sukkot nor Shavuot until she was 18 was on her way to becoming a rebbetzin at 20.

My fiancé, Eddie Feld, along with his friends, had had a difficult time of it at the Seminary. They longed for a religious environment that could provide community, serious text study, social action, and spiritual intensity. They decided to found a new seminary informed by all those ideals and to locate it in the Boston area, where some of the central players already lived. Their vision was radical, daring. Their dream was nothing less than the restructuring and rebirth of the American Jewish community. I joined them, primarily because I was in love and didn't want to be separated from Eddie. (I mention how I came to join them because it seems to me that how and why individual group members come to affiliate with a group has a lot to do with how they expect to participate in that group. Before the advent of the women's liberation movement, I suspect many women found themselves in groups for what were originally affiliative reasons and that we all failed to see the significance of that.)

Seven men were the founders and teachers of Ḥavurat Shalom, begun in Cambridge in the summer of 1968. There were about fifteen formally enrolled students, also all men. One of the important guiding principles of this new seminary community was to break down or minimize the distinctions between faculty and students. For example, decisions were not imposed from above by the faculty; rather, faculty and students all gathered at weekly community meetings and either everyone voted or together reached consensus.

The ethos of equality was powerful; in fact, there was serious discussion about faculty members also paying the annual $500 tuition. What was finally agreed upon was that students would pay, and faculty members would teach without salary. That selflessness and idealism moves me even more today than it did twenty years ago.

The only women who were associated with Ḥavurat Shalom at its inception were the wives and girlfriends of the faculty and students—we were adjuncts. We women were free to take courses with the students, although most of us were otherwise occupied. We participated in communal meals, in davening, and in group discussions. We could speak out at community meetings, but we did not have a vote.

We were included, and yet we weren't included. We were valued for our company, our insights, and our cooking. Yet there was a silent wall that held us back. Our ignorance? Our timidity? The insensitivity or prejudice of the men? Our peripheral status, our totally unclear role in the life of the community? To be fair all around, neither the young men nor the young women who participated in the founding of Ḥavurat Shalom, the cornerstone of Ḥavurah Judaism, had any role models for the equal participation of women in the Jewish community.

The popular subject of study at Ḥavurat Shalom was of Ḥasidism, of Buber and Rosenzweig. Both the Ḥasidic and the German Jewish writers celebrated direct, unmediated spiritual experience; both cultures questioned the authority of the Talmud and the rabbis. They promulgated revolutionary attitudes, which valued the spiritual life of the common [man], which dared to suggest that the uninitiated could also study biblical texts. I wonder now what the subliminal effect of that study was on us: Did it empower the students, did it empower the women, to think of themselves and each other as equals to their teachers?

What was the role of the women in Shabbat services, a centrally important group activity? I honestly don't remember if we were counted in the *minyan* or not. The room was always full and we didn't seem ever to need to wait for a *minyan*. Did the women lead parts of the service? Little or not at all, as I recall—it would have been difficult to gather together a more impressive, more intimidating group of men, and we women were either lacking in a Jewish education, temperamentally reserved, or both. I'm sure I wasn't the only one who felt awed simply to be in the room. Like most women in 1968, my consciousness was yet to be raised. The very factors that kept us, as women, on the periphery of the community were the issues we were just beginning to explore as nascent feminists. They came, as all human truths do, through the mundane, the everyday.

We were all away together on retreat, had eaten a big meal, and although most people helped to clear the table, the men then rushed into the meeting room for whatever deep spiritual discussion we were in the midst of. Faced with a cleanup for over twenty people, I exploded at the two least threatening students in the group. Hadn't everyone eaten? Who were we women, the servants? I think that, most importantly, this incident reminds me of how women and men at that time were still learning together what sexism was, were thinking with a sudden urgency that old patterns and attitudes might undermine a contemporary Jewish utopia.

It's easy to see in hindsight that to radicalize and empower a passive, rabbi-centered American Jewish community also implied breaking down the hierarchies that sexism imposed, but I think neither the men nor the women of Havurat Shalom realized that at the beginning. All of this is by way of saying that Havurat Shalom, arguably the most serious and ambitious of the groups that launched the Havurah Movement, was not feminist in its origins. It sought to reshape the American Jewish community, to educate and democratize it, to shatter the complacency of materialistic congregations, to fill the spiritual void we perceived, and to create a vital new participatory order. To make a revolution. We just didn't see at the outset that that revolution needed to include the way in which women were viewed and treated.

Yet, although feminist concerns were not on the agenda at the inception of Havurat Shalom, an openness to those concerns gradually developed as they became felt and were articulated. One example: In the middle of the year one student broke up with his girlfriend, and she then applied for independent student status in the group. Since he had been the one originally accepted, there was discussion of whether or not her continued presence would make him uncomfortable. When it seemed that that wasn't a problem, she was then accepted.

The first time a woman was called up for an *aliyah* at Ḥavurat Shalom (May 1969) was as a part of a couple—one of the students was about to be married and so he and his wife-to-be were honored at *their aufruf.* We did it that way because it seemed like the most natural way to celebrate together. It had never before occurred to any of us that the women were being excluded from having *aliyot.* Once having done it though, there was no going back—it suddenly seemed obvious that women should be honored with *aliyot,* and not only as part of a couple and not only to celebrate an impending marriage. We were quite young; we made changes as we went along, as fallible men and women honestly confronting themselves, each other, and the Jewish tradition they saw themselves bringing to new life. The story of the women of Ḥavurat Shalom in that first year is the story of women everywhere at the onset of the feminist movement. What we had to conquer before any of the external work of liberation could begin was the deeply ingrained self-image of being less than the men we loved and with whom we worked. Our liberation had to begin with our own questioning of the status quo, with our own assertion of our dignity and worth.

Time passes. Since the founding of Ḥavurat Shalom in the summer of 1968, deep and wide changes have been wrought in the American Jewish community. The Ḥavurah movement has played a crucial part in that. In some ways we've done less than we had hoped for back then; in some ways we've done more. In Ḥavurah communities across the country, men and women lead services, study together, celebrate the festival cycles and share their own life cycles. In mainstream American synagogues egalitarian ḥavurot have found homes and often form the heart of the larger congregation, challenging it to deeper and more substantial levels of spirituality, Jewish learning, and social justice. American Jewry has been revitalized and is in the process of becoming empowered. It seems natural and we take it all for granted.

A relatively recent crisis in the Ḥavurah Movement provides a telling conclusion to this evolution. The National Ḥavurah Committee, the umbrella organization for ḥavurot across the country, annually sponsors one or more intensive summer study institutes. In the summer of 1985, the local planning committee for the Los Angeles Institute announced to the National Ḥavurah Board that since it expected some of the California participants to be quite traditional, they were organizing a nonegalitarian service as one of the officially sanctioned options for davening. (There had sometimes in the past been an unofficial *"meḥitzah" minyan* at Ḥavurah Institutes to accommodate Orthodox participants.) An uproar ensued. The plan exposed an old old wound. Emergency meetings of the national board were convened, emotional speeches made, some board members were openly weeping at the thought that the Ḥavurah Movement might go back on its long-held and bitterly fought for status as an egalitarian model in the Jewish community. What was most painful was the argument on the other side—that traditional Jews unhappy with the nonegalitarian status of women in Orthodoxy and perhaps therefore open to some new alliances with egalitarian communities would feel unable to meet with us. We were caught in a terrible bind—wanting to be all-inclusive but at the same time feeling that more than any other value we stood for, we stood for the absolute right of women to be equal as Jews. While there was great pain and no pleasure taken in our "triumph" over the local planning committee, the principle of egalitarianism won out.

This incident raised a question that increasingly troubles those of us in the Ḥavurah Movement who have ongoing contact with the young Jews of today. Many young Jews today who are seekers of religious experience, as we were in the 1960s, look to Orthodoxy for their Jewish "shot of Adrenalin," and seem not to mind doing so with the young women a demure step or two behind the young men. We see some young Jewish women as turning their backs on our hard-won victories, not caring whether, as women, they are counted in the *minyan,* are permitted to lead davening, are asked to read from the Torah. I suppose they see us as they see all non-Orthodox, liberal Jews—as being somehow lazy, half-baked, hypocritical. They seem not to notice the intensity, the passion we had—and remarkably still have—which I think is not at all that different from their own.

While I believe that the Ḥavurah Movement has wrought sorely needed changes in the American Jewish community, helping to give it a renewed sense of collective purpose and vigor, I don't know how to make today's generation of young women care about the precious spiritual and political legacy their older counterparts want to share with them. Perhaps the lesson of feminism, the lesson of my early experience in Ḥavurat Shalom, is that the first liberation can come only from within.

Since 1972, when Sally Priesand became the first woman rabbi to be officially ordained, increasing numbers of women have entered the rabbinate and the cantorate. Despite the official endorsement by their movements, women who seek to enter these professions still experience difficulties. As Rabbi Emily Korzenick and Cantor Nancy Hausman show, congregants are often slow to accept women in roles traditionally reserved for men.

Hausman discusses the process by which women achieve professional equality: by dispelling male fears that the feminization of their profession would lower its status and by persisting in their efforts at communal acceptance. Hausman illustrates that discrimination often dissipates as congregants grow accustomed to women as leaders in the synagogue.

Korzenick details how women bring to the rabbinate special nurturing skills often acquired in their roles as mothers and wives. She is one of a growing number of rabbis who seek to re-establish the home as a focus of religious life. While in the Orthodox community religion was always centered both in the home and the synagogue, during the past century, non-Orthodox synagogues have supplanted the home as the loci for Jewish observance. The inclusion of women in the rabbinate has facilitated the process of integrating home and synagogue.

Emily Faust Korzenik

ON BEING A RABBI

I am one of the oldest women to become a rabbi in the United States, a fact that has significant implications for the way I have perceived my role in this profession. I took my own four children through *Bar* and *Bat*

Mitzvah ceremonies, and then had my own *Bat Mitzvah*, before I began to guide other families through that meaningful rite of passage. Most often, I guide mothers who, whether they work or not, usually bear the major responsibility for supervising their child's *Bar* or *Bat Mitzvah* preparation and for arranging the festive celebration.

Being older than most new rabbis also means that I had confronted the death of a loved one, a parent, before I began trying to assist others in the most painful hours of their lives. It also means that I graduated college and began my life as a wife and mother at a time when most middle-class women saw their primary function as serving their families.

Nurturing is good preparation for the rabbinate. For example, I enjoy inviting members of my congregation to my home for Shabbat dinner. I cook the meal as well as prepare a talk on a Jewish theme. This spring I invited my college bound youngsters for a Shabbat dinner and asked them to bring their college catalogues so that together we could look over the Jewish Studies courses available to them. Every Sukkot my very helpful and encouraging husband and some grown children build a *sukkah* in our yard, to which I invite some of the young couples I have married. They are beginning to come with their little ones. Passover is madness for me. I prepare and cook for my own big *seder* at home, and on the second evening I conduct my congregation's community *seder*. It is exhausting but I love it.

Coming to a rabbinical career as an older person and as a woman also means that I am not lonesome. Rabbinical colleagues, notably men, speak about the difficulty of making close friends, of being set apart, of having a religious and public role that complicates intimacy. Long before I became a rabbi, I had formed my cadre of close friends. Now I marry their children and can bring some special comfort, I believe, at sad times. I am first of all their friend, and, as a result, I intuitively approach my congregants as a friend who has a particular role. My way of being a rabbi has been shaped as much by my life as a wife and mother, a high school history teacher, and a social and political activist, as by rabbinical study and preparation itself.

People often ask me if I experience discrimination as a rabbi because I am a woman. From its inception, the Reconstructionist Movement accepted women as peers. Mordecai Kaplan performed the first *Bat Mitzvah* ceremony for his daughter in 1922. There was never any question about the role of women in the Reconstructionist congregation in White Plains, N.Y. to which my husband and I have belonged for thirty years. I read from the Torah, chanted the *haftarah* portion, was president of the synagogue, and even chairperson of the ritual committee. I was just one of many studious, participating women. That was the milieu within which I began to form my desire to become a rabbi. It was a milieu that made discrimination against women elsewhere in the Jewish religious world seem incomprehensible and, therefore, something to be overcome.

There have been disquieting moments, of course. A young woman doctor asked me to officiate at her wedding, and then she discovered her Israeli fiancé and his family would not be comfortable with a woman rabbi. She asked if I would co-officiate with a man. I replied that if I was not rabbi enough to perform the ceremony, I preferred not to participate. She wanted to satisfy her fiancé but she meant to be kind. Didn't I understand that the "social customs" were different in Israel? I did not remind her that "social customs" had kept women from becoming doctors until not long before her own entry into that profession.

The most egregious example of discourtesy toward women in the synagogue that I experienced took place in Poland. In September of 1985, I participated in a Shabbat morning service in Cracow with a *Bar Mitzvah* boy and his family who are members of my congregation in Stamford, Connecticut. A gentleman, whose daughter I had married the year before, returned from a United Jewish Appeal-Federation mission to Poland and Israel with a request from a leader of the remnant of elderly Jews in Cracow. When the American visitors had asked what they could do to help, Maria Jakabowicz said, "Bring us some life. Bring us some youth. Bring us a *Bar Mitzvah*." One of my *Bar Mitzvah* students, his family, and I immediately responded to the request. I also invited a wonderful, traditional Jewish man, a survivor of Auschwitz, to come with us to daven *Shaharit,* as I was sensitive from the first to the probable preferences of the elderly Jews in Cracow; however, I did plan to participate in the service.

In Cracow, I stood upon the *bimah, tallit* in hand, to be with the *Bar Mitzvah* boy when he chanted his beautiful *haftarah* portion from Isaiah. I offered a brief commentary, despite the actions of an American rabbi, who pulled my *tallit* from me and attempted to prevent me from speaking.

The experience in the synagogue was not painful because the congregation's sympathy was with us. We had succeeded in bringing some joy to these old people who had suffered so much. We had fulfilled their request. We had handled ourselves with dignity and restraint. It was a triumphant day, the rabbi who had challenged me notwithstanding.

However, it was sad, so very sad, to know that leaders of the Orthodox community at home in the States had, in fact, asked the Jews of Cracow to rescind their invitation to us because, as non-Orthodox Jews, our use of the fifteenth-century Remu Synagogue would have been a desecration in their eyes. The Jews of Cracow responded by arranging to have the *Bar Mitzvah* held in the Templum, a nineteenth-century non-Orthodox synagogue. The day following the Sabbath ceremony, Ed Blonder, the survivor who had led the morning *Shaḥarit* service and chanted the Torah portion, took us through Auschwitz. The torturers and murderers of over three million Polish Jews had not differentiated between the Orthodox and the non-Orthodox. I remembered stinging words from a Sholem Aleichem story, "You know how we Jews are, if the world does not pinch us, we pinch each other."

I cannot, however, end on so sorrowful a note. It is wonderful to be a woman and a Jew in America at the close of the twentieth century. Without question, the new opportunities for women in the religious world had their impetus in America's open, democratic, secular society. I am blessed to be a rabbi when most Jews are proud to be themselves. And I am so eager to serve.

Nancy S. Hausman

ON BECOMING A CANTOR

My parents raised me to believe that I could do anything I wanted to do. Partway through my junior year in college I realized that the prelaw program I was taking was not for me. It was then that I considered going to cantorial school. My parents were very active Reform Jews. They were one of the founding families of our temple in Upper Nyack, New York, and I had sung in the temple choir from its inception, eventually becoming the soprano soloist. Cantorial school seemed just the right career for me, a person who loves Judaism and who also loves to sing.

I entered Hebrew Union College—Jewish Institute of Religion's School of Sacred Music in the fall of 1974. I was part of a class of three women and five men—there was a grand total of forty-five students in the School of Sacred Music.

When I think back on my time at the School of Sacred Music, I remember it fondly. Since my class was so small, we were like a family. Everyone knew what was going on in everyone else's life. We tried to support each other during times of stress and cheered each other on during the good times. Our professors, mostly cantors, were still not sure how to teach women the traditional *"nusah"* [1] so every class was an experimental one for both them and us. However, they were all very positive; no exclusionary practices took place.

I do, however, remember negative comments from some of the male students about the female students. Some of the men were afraid that the women would take all of the jobs, leaving them with no employment. Others complained that salaries would suffer because occupations considered "women's" jobs are traditionally underpaid in our society. These kinds of comments made me angry, but as far as I can ascertain, these fears were unjustified.

There are now more women than men entering cantorial school. The number of men applying to cantorial school has always been small; therefore, the current increase in class size is due to the number of women applying. The changing class profile does not seem to be discouraging congregations from applying for cantors. The need for good Jewish music seems to be transcending any latent bias toward women.

One of the teaching techniques used in cantorial school is on-the-job training, or student pulpits. When I was applying for such a position, some congregations specified that they did not want to consider women. Fortunately, it was and still is a policy of the School of Sacred Music that any temple requesting a student cantor has to audition whoever applies for the job, regardless of sex. As it happened, my student pulpit was with a congregation that originally did not want to hear women. However, after the interview process, they were interested in two students, both women.

I worked there for three very happy years. I heard that there were some members who objected so strongly to my being hired that they left the temple. I also learned that those members owed back dues when they left. This appears to be another case of people using women as scapegoats for other, totally unrelated problems.

I taught second and third graders when I was in my student pulpit. I remember once, when we were all together for an assembly, one little second grader said to me, "Cantor, where is the cantor who was here last year?" I responded, "He's working at another temple." A first grader, who had been silently listening to this conversation, blurted out, "A boy cantor? In all my life, I never heard of one!" I had become the role model for these children. They thought that all cantors were women, just as I had once thought that all cantors were men.

These encounters heightened my awareness of the prejudices against women, which exist in varying degrees. I had a fine relationship with the rabbi of my student pulpit; however, he and I had to establish some rules from the outset. When I began at the temple, the rabbi let me know how glad he was that I was there. He said that I could assist him in so many ways. Often, there were appointments he needed to make by phone, but he had no time to do this. He suggested that I could make these calls as well as write some notes for him. I immediately responded, "I won't have the time, and I don't know how to type." He never made a similar suggestion again, and I think we understood each other and had respect for each other as a result of that encounter.

In my last year at the seminary, I was under a great deal of pressure. I worried about where, and even if, I would be working the following year. Women were still in the minority as students in the school. We were still a relatively untested phenomenon.

There was one job-hunting experience that left a lasting impression on me. A large Southern congregation came to New York to interview cantors. About twenty cantors (both graduating cantors and those out in the field) auditioned. I was one of three cantors, the only woman, that the temple chose to invite to their town for extended interviews. It was a very intensive experience, and I was pretty "green," but I thought it went well. When I came back to New York, some of my professors who were close to people in that temple told me to pack my bags; however, I didn't get the job. I wondered why, but the job I took instead kept me too busy to ponder this for long.

I became Associate Cantor at Hebrew Union College in Jerusalem. While I was in Israel, a convention of the World Union for Progressive Judaism took place. Jews from all over the world attended. I was fairly visible as one of the College's cantors. A member of the Southern congregation where I had been interviewed introduced herself to me. She said she had been on the cantorial search committee the year before but had been out of town when I was interviewed. She had heard very nice reports about me and was disappointed that I had not been hired, but there had been controversy over hiring a woman cantor, so they had hired a man. I was angry about that for a long time. That temple, by the way, now has a woman cantor.

I came back to the States in the spring of 1980 and took a full-time position. I worked at that temple for two years. During my second year, after the High Holy Days, two long-time members (women) told me that at first they were not used to seeing me on the *bimah*, but that now my presence seemed very natural to them. It was interesting that they never said they did not like me; they said they were not used to me.

The next congregation for which I worked was in Florida. I stayed there for four years and left to come back up North. However, it is rewarding to realize that I was able to be a positive role model for so many young girls there. By being exposed to a female cantor, they were made aware of yet another possible occupational choice. After I was at that congregation for a few years, a congregant made an interesting observation. He said, "Your voice seems to have gotten lower." We both laughed and agreed that rather than my voice having changed registers, he had just gotten used to hearing a woman's voice on the *bimah*.

I now have two jobs, one as a cantor in a temple in New Jersey and the other as the placement administrator of a national cantorial association. Through the second job, I speak with many congregations that are considering hiring cantors. They have all kinds of questions and a wide variety of needs. Not one has said that it does not want to hire a woman. In fact, some specifically request a woman cantor. These congregations feel a woman would add an extra dimension to their temple family. I try to convey to them that sex should not be a factor in employment. Their questions should be, "Does this cantor have the right qualifications for our temple? Can he or she add personally to our congregation?" An interview can only reveal so much about an applicant. When trying to make a positive impression, none of us needs the extra burden of sexual prejudice weighing us down.

Note

1. The traditional musical modes to which certain parts of the liturgy are sung.

Taking on new roles is often emotionally difficult for the individual as well as the community, which tends to acclimate itself slowly to change. In the Orthodox community, women are expanding their ritual involvement. The most outstanding example of this is the growing number of women's prayer groups, mentioned earlier, that are spreading around the world. The following three articles focus on one of these groups, in Brooklyn, New York, which has been the focus of much of the controversy surrounding this issue.

Naomi Doron, a very traditional Orthodox woman, articulates her dissatisfaction with her community's treatment of women. In her article, we see again the recurrent motif of the exclusion of young girls from the men's section upon their entering adolescence. Unlike Gelerenter-Liebowitz, Doron expresses anger at this situation, an anger that led her to help found a women's prayer group. She discusses the process by which the women of her group developed the ritual skills necessary to conduct their own services.

Susan Aranoff, who often serves as ḥazzanit for her women's prayer group, describes the experience of leading prayers in a community that welcomes and values her participation. Her analysis of the responsibilities of a prayer leader shows the seriousness and dedication with which women are taking on what has traditionally been seen as a male role. She also makes the point that women are excluded from involvement in an Orthodox synagogue even in nonritual areas.

Yael Penkower and her two eldest daughters, Talya and Yonina, tell of their decisions to hold Bat Mitzvah ceremonies in a women's prayer group and of the obstacles, both within themselves and from their community, that they overcame. Rather than allow their daughters to be physically distanced from synagogue ritual at puberty, the Penkowers chose to celebrate their entry into adulthood by having them brought closer to Torah through a Bat Mitzvah ceremony. As evidenced in other vignettes, individuals often seek change only after becoming aware of alternative possibilities. For Yael, this is especially true, as it was her attendance at a niece's Bat Mitzvah that led her to consider one for her daughters. Talya, the eldest daughter, embraced this idea wholeheartedly. Yonina, on the other hand, discusses the very real pressure she received from her peers, who disapproved of her Bat Mitzvah.

The inner struggle experienced when taking on new ritual roles is not unique to Orthodoxy. Women across the denominational spectrum have also grappled with many of these same issues. However, women are learning to become more comfortable with active participation in religious ritual.

Naomi Doron

BUILDING SYNAGOGUE SKILLS

As a boy grows up in the very traditional Orthodox world, he is welcomed more and more into the rich spiritual life of the Jew. The small boy begins by learning the Hebrew alphabet and how to pray; then he learns Bible, Mishnah, and, eventually, Talmud. This process is paralleled by his initiation into synagogue life. The very young boy goes to synagogue with his father even before he can pray. As he learns to pray, the young boy prays alongside his father. Even before his *Bar Mitzvah,* he is called upon to lead certain prayers. When he finally reaches the age of *Bar Mitzvah,* he will be fully accepted in the synagogue. He will be counted in the quorum. He will be able to lead any and all prayers. He will be able to read the Torah for the congregation.

This is in sharp contrast to the girl's experience. As the girl grows, she is closed off more and more from the synagogue. The small girl goes to synagogue with her father. At some point, she will be told, either openly or in a subtle manner, that she does not belong with him on the men's side. She belongs on the other side of the wall, with the women. She will find, when she gets there, that she cannot hear or see what is going on as well as she could before. The girl who, as a child, was so eager to go to the synagogue is no longer enthusiastic. She stops praying, as she sees that the women around her are not praying. As they do, she talks instead. The women around her do not know enough Torah to talk about Torah, so they talk about what they do know: their husbands and children, their friends and neighbors, clothing, recipes, and so on. Their talk is at best frivolous and at worst *lashon ha-ra* (slander).

It seems to me that the reason most women talk, rather than pray, in synagogue is because they are made to feel that they are not active participants but passive observers. They feel that the men do not really want them in the synagogue. Even worse, the men may make them feel that God also does not want them or their prayers there.

I am one of a growing number of Orthodox women and girls who is not satisfied with the role that Orthodox society has forced upon us. This is why I became one of the founding members of the Flatbush Women's Davening Group in Brooklyn, N.Y. Our group was formed by a handful of women and girls who were interested in having a more active role in davening than is possible in the traditional Orthodox *shul*. Some of the women had left *yeshivah* a number of years before and still were interested in increasing their knowledge of Torah. Several of us met at various classes in higher Jewish learning. The prayer group we founded meets regularly to conduct Shabbat morning services. We are not a *minyan* and do not recite prayers for which a *minyan* is necessary. We do, however, have a complete Torah and *haftarah* reading. We obtained halakhic supervision from an Orthodox rabbi, who is available to answer any of our questions.

When we formed our group, none of us had any of the skills required for leading a prayer service or reading the Torah. There was a home we could meet in and we had the promise of a Torah scroll that we could borrow. We organized in the spring, planning to have our first service the following fall on *Shabbat B'reishit,* the first Sabbath after the High Holy Day period, which begins the yearly cycle of Torah readings with the first chapters of Genesis.

The women and girls who volunteered to read the Torah and the *haftarah* and lead the prayers spent the entire summer preparing. A male cantor volunteered to teach us how to chant the Torah and prayers in the traditional melodies. We met with him weekly. The rest of the time we prepared alone with the help of tapes. The girl who was to read the *haftarah* studied with her father the whole summer. My daughter, who was to read the third Torah portion during our first meeting, also studied with her father during the summer. She learned the Torah reading verse by verse, day by day, week by week.

At last came the Shabbat for which we had prepared. The handful of women who had initiated the group and who had spent the summer preparing were joined by other women who had heard about the group and shared our interests in the spiritual experience; an experience that had hitherto been denied us as women. I got great *naḥas* (joy) from hearing my daughter *lain* (chant) from the Torah, a Jewish *naḥas* usually derived only from sons. Although my daughter's *Bat Mitzvah* had already passed during that summer of preparation, to me, her *Bat Mitzvah parashah* (portion) will always be B'reishit.

When we realized that davening and *laining* were skills that could be acquired by any competent person who was willing to make the effort, more women were moved to learn these skills, I among them. We began the custom of having a different woman *lain* each *aliyah*, making it easier to prepare and to actively involve more people. The first time I *lained*, it took me a month to prepare twenty-six verses, and so it was with everyone else.

When we began, only three women could *lain*, one could chant the *haftarah*, and two women were able to lead the services. Now more than a dozen members can chant the Torah with the *trop* (cantillation), several women can chant *haftarah*, and several more can lead prayers. Women who have been participating for some time have improved their skills, so that it no longer takes them months, or even weeks, to prepare the service.

We try to involve as many people as possible, so that even those who do not have the technical skills to lead a part of the service can actively participate. Each month, a different woman presents a *dvar Torah* (a sermon on a Torah theme). Over the years, more women have begun to feel comfortable enough standing in front of the group to share their thoughts. Similarly, we try to give new faces the honor of being called to the Torah or opening the ark. At first, many women were reluctant and apprehensive to accept these honors. As time went on, the women have become comfortable approaching and handling the Torah scroll, which represents our connection to the Divine.

We are very supportive of our members. When someone makes a mistake in *laining* or *davening*, we do not shout corrections at her as often occurs in the synagogue. Rather, we try to correct her in a gentle and encouraging manner. Perhaps the difference in our reaction is due to the difference in upbringing between men and women. Or, perhaps, it is due to our recognition that we are all beginners when it comes to the skills of the synagogue.

There is also no talking during our services. We are all there because we want to pray. We are not sitting on the sidelines, unneeded and perhaps unwanted. We are the ones for whom the group exists.

We have been asked why, suddenly, women are no longer satisfied with the role that Orthodox Jewish society has assigned to us. It is only in fairly recent times that women and girls have received formal Jewish education, beginning about seventy years ago with the *Bais Yaakov* educational movement for girls that was started in Poland by Sara Schnirer. We have been told that we are trying to be like men, and that there must be something wrong with us. Women have always borne all the hardships of being Jewish but have not enjoyed the compensations. Women have suffered equally with men from pogroms and other anti-Jewish activities; however, the comforts of prayer and learning have been denied to women. We are punished by non-Jews for being Jewish and by Jews for being women.

Souls have no gender. Our souls have the same desire and need to get close to God and the Torah through prayer and learning as do men's souls. Women's prayer groups bring us one step nearer to God.

Susan Aranoff

ON BEING A *ḤAZZANIT*

Awe mixed with pleasure, a high voltage current passing through me, binding my hands with magnetic force to the *etzei ḥayyim* of the Torah;[1] my heart pounding with the thrill and apprehension of holding the Torah securely; these were the feelings that flowed through me as I lifted the Torah to the sound of the familiar melody of *"ve-zot ha-Torah asher sam Moshe lifnei Bnai Yisraʾel . . ."* (This is the Torah that Moses set before the People of Israel).[2]

Lifting the Torah is the most vivid, but not the only, memory I have of my first Shabbat davening with a women's group. The intimacy of the services, the closeness to the Torah and *bimah*, the high level of *kavannah* (intention/concentration) and *ruḥaniyut* (spirituality) that pervaded the group, and the decorum—all contributed to the uniqueness of that davening experience.

My first experience as an adult *ḥazzanit* (prayer leader) also took place that Shabbat. A friend, who knew I had a trained singing voice, had recruited me to daven *Musaf;*[3] however, the impact of serving as *ḥazzanit* was overshadowed by the overall spiritual lift I felt that morning.

More specific feelings about being a *ḥazzanit* began to sort themselves out during subsequent months as I continued to attend the davening group in Brooklyn, New York. My thoughts focused on two concerns: davening with *kavannah* while serving as *ḥazzanit* and conducting the service in a way that is inspiring and pleasing for those listening to the prayers.

Davening with *Kavannah*

Davening with *kavannah* is a topic that has occupied Jewish scholars throughout the ages. An individual must contend with noise, time pressures, questions about the liturgy and religious doctrine, irrelevant thoughts that invade one's mind, and other disturbances while davening. The *ḥazzanit* must contend with all these difficulties plus an additional complication—the difficulty of not allowing one's concern about various technical aspects of singing to profane the act of davening.

A basic technical aspect of singing that may detract from *kavannah* is the need to concentrate on syllabifying and phrasing words so that the prayer text fits the melody properly. This problem decreased as I developed greater familiarity with the fit between the melody and the prayer text. As time passed, the melody became so integrated with the words that rather than detracting from my *kavannah,* the melody enhanced my absorption in an appreciation of the text. Synergism occurred. The chanted prayer evoked deeper feelings in me than either the words or music alone could have.

Each opportunity to serve as *ḥazzanit* is a new challenge to chant the prayers with vocal excellence. The tension between singing in a technically correct fashion and maintaining *kavannah* can be resolved through the mystical link between music and human thoughts and emotions. A prayer leader should review the prayer text and ponder its meaning. Intense concentration on the meaning of the text produces the most beautiful singing. The voice soars on the wings of emotion. *Kavannah* and the effort to sing beautifully do not interfere with each other; they are in harmony with each other.

Leading the Congregation

The experience of seeing numerous congregants, both women and men, lapse into their own conversations during the *ḥazzan*'s repetition of the *Amidah* has made me feel strongly that a *ḥazzan* or *ḥazzanit* must be sensitive to the fact that *ḥazzanut* characterized by excessive repetition of phrases or too slow a pace often tries the attention span of the congregation. Beautiful *ḥazzanut* stirs emotions and adds to religious feelings when it holds the congregants' attention and deepens their involvement in the content of the liturgy.

Participating Fully as a Congregant

Experiencing the stirring spirituality and beauty of the prayer services has been my principal reason for belonging to the women's davening group; however, there are other reasons why I, as an Orthodox woman, have found membership in a women's davening group a more satisfying religious experience than membership in a traditional Orthodox synagogue.

Synagogues are centers for many activities other than prayer: information is shared, funds are raised, classes are held, and political action is planned. In many Orthodox synagogues, however, there are barriers preventing able women from actively participating even in these non-ritualistic areas of synagogue activity. Women who have talent and ideas to contribute in these areas, but who live in neighborhoods whose synagogues proscribe women's participation, can participate more fully in Jewish communal life through women's davening groups.

My personal experiences at an Orthodox synagogue in the Flatbush section of Brooklyn provide a vivid illustration of how difficult it can be for an Orthodox synagogue to provide suitable roles for women who are interested in playing a part in Jewish communal affairs.

I am deeply involved in Jewish community life. I am a member of the leadership of the New York UJA-Federation campaign and the board of HIAS (Hebrew Immigrant Aid Society) as well as other communal organizations. I attempted to apply my experience to benefit the synagogue our family attended.

After a fundraising appeal had taken place in the synagogue for one of the organizations I am involved with, I mentioned to the rabbi that the members of the synagogue had not been given enough information about the organization and, in some cases, had been seriously misinformed. Since the appeal was made annually, I urged him to convey the correct information to the members of the synagogue in his speech the following year. He failed to do this the following year and the year after that, despite the fact that each year we had the same discussion, during which he agreed with me that the congregation had many misconceptions about the organization. I had no practical way of reaching these people since there was no forum in which women were allowed to speak or write to the congregation.

During this time, I also became involved with the sisterhood. The sisterhood voted to sponsor a class for women on the first night of Shavuot, following the tradition of *Tikkun Leil Shavuot*.[4] Several women offered to prepare material to present, and others who were unable to prepare anything were excited at the prospect of having an opportunity to learn. One of the older women became emotional about being able to attend a class in Jewish studies, something she had yearned for for many years.

Within hours of our sisterhood meeting, the plans for our classes were canceled. The synagogue president had objected to our plans. In his sermon on the following Shabbat, the rabbi questioned the motivation and character of women who call for such programs as Shavuot night Jewish studies classes for women. He expressed strong opposition to the idea of men changing a diaper on Shavuot night in order to allow their wives an hour to learn. The average age of the congregants in that synagogue is sixty years or more, far beyond the diaper changing stage. The sermon would almost have been funny if it were not so sad.

These incidents made it difficult for me to feel that I was fully accepted as a member of that congregation. I am aware that there are Orthodox synagogues that are more liberal in the roles they allow women to play, but from what I have observed and heard from others, even these synagogues have a long way to go toward making women equal partners even in nonritualistic aspects of synagogue activity.

Hillel said, "If I am not for myself who will be for me? And if I am only for myself what am I?"[5] Orthodox women have acted to establish davening groups that provide a framework in which women's prayer, learning, and community activity are encouraged and supported, not impeded. However, these groups are not only for women's benefit. Women's davening groups enrich Orthodoxy as a whole by opening up new paths for women to contribute to Judaism.

Notes

1. The wooden handles of the Torah scroll.
2. This is recited when the Torah is lifted up for the congregation to see during services.

3. The additional service added on Sabbath and holiday mornings.
4. The custom of remaining awake to study religious texts the night of Shavuot.
5. Mish. Avot 1 : 14.

BAT MITZVAH:
COMING OF AGE IN BROOKLYN

Yael Penkower

A Mother's Reflections

On the morning of *Simḥat Torah* 5741, in October 1980, my three daughters and I attended a woman's *tefillah* (prayer) service with the women of Lincoln Square Synagogue, held in the Esplanade Hotel on New York City's Upper West Side. On that occasion, we also celebrated the *Bat Mitzvah* of my niece, Amanda B. Rosen. It was the first time that I had attended a women's *tefillah*, and the impact proved to be everlasting.[1]

When the *ḥazzanit* took the Torah out from the *aron kodesh*, she was flanked by her three daughters, who joined in proclaiming the *Shema Yisra'el*. At that moment, thoughts and associated emotions from our people's past history raced through me. Suddenly, I understood how Jewish women could and did die *"al kiddush HaShem,"* martyrs' deaths.

Later, as I danced with joy, holding the Torah, images of mothers in medieval cities, in pogroms, and in the Holocaust passed before my eyes. Indeed, just before the *Bat Mitzvah*, I had read *Elli*, an autobiographical memoir published that same year. In this volume, Livia E. Bitton Jackson recalls her travail during the Holocaust as a young Orthodox woman from Hungary. One passage, in particular, describing the deportation from a ghetto in the Carpathian mountains to, ultimately, Auschwitz, struck me:

The Torah scrolls! The fire is dancing a bizarre dance of death with one large scroll in the middle, clutching and twisting in an embrace of cruel passion. Aged folios of Jewish wisdom and faith tumble and explode into fiery particles. . . . Our identity. Our soul. Weightless speckles of ash rising, fleeing the flames into nothingness. . . .

I have seen the Torah scroll twist and turn in the flames before I have ever had the chance of touching it. How does the Torah feel to the touch? Will I ever know?[2]

Both in Israel and in the United States, I, too, had had no opportunity to look into a Torah scroll. From behind the *meḥitzah*, the Torah appeared far away. Nor had I ever held a scroll in my arms. With Amanda's *Bat Mitzvah*, this possibility finally became reality. Now I felt that the Torah was truly a part of me. I should not have been so distant from it for so long.

When the time drew near to my oldest daughter's *Bat Mitzvah* celebration, my daughters, Talya, Yonina, and Ayelet, and I were already well versed in *tefillah* and Torah reading from attendance at the Flatbush Women's Davening Group. My husband, Monty, and I wanted the three girls to know that growing into Jewish womanhood meant even more than such fundamentals as Torah study, Shabbat, and *kashrut*. Consequently, we chose to hold their *Bat Mitzvah* celebrations at the Flatbush group. Talya would be our pioneer.

Talya C. Penkower

A Daughter's Decision

For a full year I practiced. My father taught me from the very beginning. The lessons started a little before my eleventh birthday, in June 1984. Step by step, my father instructed me how to *lain*. He began with the *trop* (cantillation) for the *parashah* and that of the *haftarah*, as I intended to do both. For a full year I practiced, after homework, on Sundays, and whenever I got the chance. Often the house would resound with my protests, "*Abba* (Dad), stop!," as my brother had complained two years earlier. I also worked on preparing a lengthy *dvar Torah* (a talk on the Torah portion) about the *Mekoshesh Etzim* (Num. 15:32−36).

All the while, I was going to my friends' *Bat Mitzvah* parties. Some were held in fancy catering halls, but most were just like regular birthday parties at home, in restaurants, and even in rollerskating rinks. These were very nice parties, but I felt that they were missing the point. When a girl becomes a *Bat Mitzvah*, she reaches Jewish womanhood and accepts all the commandments of the Torah as an adult. To my mind, this was very special.

When a boy becomes a *Bar Mitzvah*, he usually *lains* his *parashah*. I thought it very appropriate that I do the same. Since, however, this practice is not yet fully accepted as halakhically valid in the Orthodox community, it was hardly the norm. I received very different reactions when the subject came up in my circle. Most people could not comprehend what I was doing and did not understand why or how I could commit myself to such an undertaking. Even after countless explanations, some of my friends would not be permitted to come to that part of my *simḥah* (celebration).

After much anxiety and difficult preparation, the weekend of my *Bat Mitzvah* finally arrived. Flowers adorned our home everywhere. The Friday night meal was celebrated with some of my close relatives, and I chanted the *kiddush*.

As my mother explained to the assembled, Jewish women must observe the negative commandments just as men. Shabbat is included, because the commandment of *"shamor et yom ha-Shabbat"* (keep the Sabbath day) represents this category; however, since *"zakhor et yom ha-Shabbat"* (remember the Sabbath day), one of the positive commandments, was uniquely uttered at the same time at Mt. Sinai, it, too, is obligatory for women. According to the Talmud, Pes. 106a, *"zakhrehu al ha-yayin be-khnisato,"* the Jew must declare the remembrance of the day at its entry by saying *kiddush*. In other words, this is a Divine commandment that a mature Jewish woman must fulfill: she can do so for herself and also thereby satisfy the obligation for other women present. (As for her satisfying the obligation for men, since this obligation is equally incumbent upon both sexes, rabbinic opinion is divided.)

This public recognition of my passage into Jewish feminine adulthood, being able for the first time to satisfy the religious obligation of other women with my blessing of the Shabbat wine, was followed by my father's declaration: *"barukh she-petarani me-onsha shel zo"* (Blessed be, that I am no longer responsible for her punishment). He had pronounced almost the identical words, but in the masculine form, when my brother completed his *Bar Mitzvah* reading of the Torah, in Jerusalem. My father could not do likewise at my own Torah reading, the next morning, since our group does not have the halakhic status of a *minyan*. (The reading of the Torah in our own group is a function of learning; it is not a matter of *"keriah be-tzibbur,"* communal Torah reading.) My father then chanted the *kiddush* to satisfy the religious obligation of those males present. The entire procedure was stirring for all of us.

The next morning, the Women's Davening Group met in my house. Many people came but only about seven of my friends from school. My grandfather, father, uncles, and cousins sat in a separate room in the back. They could not be present, since a woman may *lain* only if no man present can do so. We took out the Torah and finally came to that for which everyone had been waiting. Despite my fears and nervousness, I *lained* the *parashah* and chanted the *haftarah* without one mistake! We gave out *aliyot* to my relatives and to some of my friends. Following the *haftarah,* to the cries of *"mazel tov!,"* everyone threw candies at the *Bat Mitzvah* girl. "I can't believe it is over," I thought. "Thank God! And I did it well!"

The Davening Group then presented me with a *Tikkun la-Korim,* an aid for Torah readers. This volume has since helped me prepare for all subsequent times that I've *lained* for the group. We had a *kiddush,* then lunch for all my relatives and classmates (including those who came after the *tefillah*).

This wonderful experience made me feel close to God. I had done something extra special. My father was the first American to celebrate a *Bar Mitzvah* in the reborn State of Israel; to be the first to *lain* a *Bat Mitzvah parashah* for our davening group made me extremely proud. I am equally happy to know that others have since followed in my footsteps.

Yonina R. Penkower

A Sister's Struggle

I began learning to *lain* in *Parashat Shoftim* (Deut. 16:18–21:9) for my *Bat Mitzvah* just after my eleventh birthday. A lot of time had to be spent, since the *parashah* and *haftarah* were very long, and I needed to learn everything well. I argued a lot with my parents because I wanted the type of lavish *Bat Mitzvah* party then celebrated by my friends at school.

My classmates' reactions when I told them I was preparing to *lain* went from shock to amazement. The girls did not believe that I would actually go through with it. Many of their mothers would not allow them to attend, saying, "It was not right." I had already been told by my mother to expect such a reaction, because some of my older sister's friends and mothers had responded in the same way. I was not sure that I wanted this kind of treatment from my friends. I guess in my heart I really did not want to do anything that would make me stand out. In fact, very few of my classmates did come, but perhaps that was also due to the fact that the celebration was held during the summer vacation. (The August 1987 date offered one supreme bonus: my older brother, Avi, came in from his yeshiva-high school in Efrat, Israel, during the summer, and he stayed just long enough for the special event.) My teachers were skeptical, just as they had been with Talya two years earlier. One even asked: "Are you Conservative?"

We continued with the preparations. It was not to be a very fancy affair. The format would follow that of my sister's celebration: Friday night dinner at our home for the immediate family, with the davening group held on Shabbat morning. Members of the family and close friends conducted the *tefillah* and were assigned *aliyot*. Then it was time.

Knees shaking, I went to the Torah. With one last look at my father, peeking from behind the doors, I appealed to him: "What if I forget, or make a mistake?" He reassured me with a kiss and a nod in the direction of the Torah. The *parashah* was now open in front of me. I turned to my mother, standing alongside to check for any mistakes, and she squeezed my hand for encouragement. I chanted the blessing and started to read.

As I went on, relief flooded my body. "This is not so bad after all!" I thought. It went quickly. I then chanted the *haftarah* as well.

I followed this up with a *dvar Torah*, which had been prepared months in advance. I purposely chose the section on *eglah arufah* (the broken-necked calf, Deut. 21:1–9) because of its emphasis on *"kol Yisraʾel areivim zeh la-zeh"* (all Israel is responsible for one another). I reviewed different commentaries, including that of Professor Nechama Lebowitz, and also the Talmud, tractate Sotah, on this topic. I ended as follows:

In conclusion, the entire concept of *eglah arufah* is to show how all of *Bnei Yisraʾel* (the Children of Israel) are responsible for one another . . . and to demonstrate the preciousness of each and every human being.

Now that I am a *Bat Mitzvah*, I take upon myself all of my *mitzvot* and *aveirot* (transgressions). I must be able to show more responsibility, to demonstrate that I can be a member of *Bnot Yisra'el* (daughters of Israel). As I grow older and become one of *n'shei Yisra'el* (women of Israel), I hope that I will be able to fulfill my duties of kindness, respect, and responsibility to *HaShem* and toward others and to show what a true *Bat Yisra'el* (daughter of Israel) represents.

Notes

1. My mother-in-law, Lillian S. Penkower, described her reaction to this *Bat Mitzvah* in the article "Tradition without Tokenism," *American Mizrachi Woman,* (Oct./Nov. 1981): 14–15. My brother-in-law, Joseph C. Kaplan, wrote about his feelings in "From Behind the Mechitzah," *Sh'ma* (27 Nov. 1981):10.
2. Livia E. Bitton Jackson, *Elli: Coming of Age in the Holocaust* (New York: Times Books, 1980), 47; reprinted with permission.

Pnina Peli and Rivka Haut depict two models of women's prayer groups in Israel, a Simḥat Torah celebration for women and the first women's prayer group that was held at the Western Wall. Peli shows that Israeli women, similar to their American counterparts, experienced inner struggles as they became involved in activities for which there were no role models. These women were faced with having to overcome the emotional barriers erected by centuries-old customs that restricted women during their menstrual periods. The effects of these customs have been seen all over the world (see Cohen, p. 103, Sered, p. 212, and, Khoubian, p. 219). Through advanced study, the women in Peli's group realized that menstruation is not a factor to be taken into account.

In the accounts of both Peli and Haut, the women acted in a spirit of co-operation and concern for the sensibilities of all involved. The commitment to sisterhood was strong enough to overcome very real ideological differences. Haut describes how women representing every facet of Judaism placed the goal of group prayer above denominational differences. The result provided a model of Jewish unity during a period of intense dissension.

Pnina Peli

CELEBRATING *SIMḤAT TORAH* IN JERUSALEM

We gathered in two large office rooms in a building facing the eastern hills of Jerusalem and the Old City to celebrate Simḥat Torah. This was the highlight of our first years of gathering as women to daven and read the Torah portion.

In the Orthodox synagogue on Simḥat Torah, the normally somber atmosphere is transformed, and a spirit of gaiety reigns as all present focus their attention on the sacred and beloved Torah scrolls. However, the intense activity in the synagogue on that day, when all men are invited to participate, underscores the customary passivity of women in their place of worship behind the *meḥitzah*.

Often, many women would go beyond the accepted boundaries of the women's section on Simḥat Torah, taking up positions closer to the scene of action in which children, waving holiday flags, were also conspicuous as active celebrants among the privileged men carrying Torahs. However, many of us felt a sense of exclusion accompanied by growing stirrings of restlessness and dissatisfaction. This resentment at being relegated to the role of little more than emphathetic onlookers was usually suppressed and was accompanied by twinges of guilt, as we thought it sinful to even feel that way.

Once we had begun holding our regular women's services, we soon discovered that there were women who were capable of being fine Torah readers and congregational leaders. We realized, of course, that organizing a Simḥat Torah celebration would involve different factors. As preparations for our first Simḥat Torah celebration for women went into high gear, many things had to be considered for which there was no precedent in modern Israel.

Until this point, our services were usually held at home. For Simḥat Torah, however, we had to find a larger space in a location that would be least offensive to the more cautious members of the Jerusalem community. We needed more good Torah readers, which meant enlisting new talent to share in the task. We wished to respect, as much as possible, the various sensitivities among us regarding women's "right" to act as full-fledged Jews, qualified to perform *mitzvot* generally seen as belonging strictly to the men's domain. Most of us involved in making arrangements for this Simḥat Torah "first" in Jerusalem came from traditionally observant backgrounds and had received good Jewish educations. Our determination to hold Simḥat Torah festivities for women was tempered only by our fear of being caught doing what might be considered the wrong thing.

To the surprise of some of us, at least, one supposedly big obstacle that was thought to affect women's participation in services turned out to be a nonissue. This was the question of menstrual impurity, which was often assumed to limit women's ability to participate in Jewish worship.

There are probably still many who are under the impression that women should be denied access to Torah scrolls during the time they are halakhically *niddah*, according to Jewish law in a state of menstrual impurity. What we had not realized was that men are also subject to states of ritual impurity. This is because the ashes of the red heifer, which were used for sacred purification, are not available to release any of us—male or female—from our ritual impurities. As a result of this, centuries ago, rabbinic deliberation on the subject had led to their decision that the Torah scrolls could not be contaminated by any kind of human impurity. This meant that even the strictest among us need not be deterred from active participation on this score.

Another matter of major concern to all of us was how far we could go in assuming the formal responsibilities of public prayer, which had been dominated by men for so many centuries. Women's halakhic exemption from various obligations had caused them to be virtually excluded from performing certain *mitzvot*. Rabbinic source study posed a real conundrum, as we learned: women were declared to be exempt from certain *mitzvot* because, historically, their social status was mainly that of dependents on male authority figures. Yet, interestingly, rabbinic thought showed that exceptional circumstances endowed some women with a special status that qualified them for fuller participation in Jewish rituals. An *ishah ḥashuvah*, i.e., a woman of learning or a woman of means, by halakhic definition must lean sideways on a cushion during the Passover *seder*, though generally women were considered secondary participants in the *seder* (*see* TB Pes. 108a). There were other cases in which women's voluntary commitment to fulfill *mitzvot* from which they were originally considered exempt obligated them, thereafter, to observe them regularly (*see* TB RH 33a and *Tosafot,* s.v. *"ha-Rabbi Yehudah"*).

This is not the place to discuss all the complicated dynamics of the halakhic system. These examples suffice to show how, in some cases, religious performance is affected by socially conditioned roles and other considerations. Above all, we wanted, as much as possible, to avoid trampling on each other's deeply embedded convictions and to deal gently with troubling conflicts and strong ambivalences.

Obtaining Torah scrolls was, fortunately, no problem, due to the disintegration of a small family synagogue through natural causes. We then had to solve the question of where to hold our Simḥat Torah service and celebration. We decided that the mere fact of our being women stepping outside of a conventional traditional grouping should not automatically force us to step into extant liberal Jewish camps. Since we identified ourselves mainly as a group of observant Jewish women, we would have to set our own precedents in the absence of any kind of recent models for halakhically held services for women. The responsibility for what we did was to be our own and would not be to anyone else's credit or discredit. We were pleased to find suitable space in an office building.

Lastly, we wondered if women would choose to miss joining in community celebrations where men, women, and families attended the same synagogue. Would the single women among us forgo the opportunity to be in places where the young men were, dancing and displaying their Simḥat Torah best?

And what would the neighbors say? A large gathering would certainly attract attention, though we planned to avoid any hint of any exhibitionist display of ourselves praying and rejoicing. The fear of heaven played a role, too, though the love of Torah strengthened our conviction that we had a right to proceed.

Being able to rejoice in the traditional way on Simḥat Torah, something habitually denied to women, filled us all with exhilaration and moved us deeply. Only those who have had similar experiences can appreciate what celebrating Simḥat Torah meant to us in the awe-inspiring environs of old-new Jerusalem—across the street from the Chief Rabbinate of the State of Israel.

Rivka Haut

THE PRESENCE OF WOMEN

We had arrived in Israel at a time of crisis for the Jewish people. The entire Jewish world was embroiled in conflict over the "Who is a Jew" issue.[1] The ill will between the various denominations of Judaism had reached new heights. Newspapers and television screens the world over were daily focusing world attention on this bitter struggle, which was blocking the ability of the Israeli government to form a working coalition. It was at the height of this controversy in the winter of 1988 that the First International Conference of Jewish Feminists took place. It was just then, at that watershed in Jewish history, that we, as women, decided that we must set an example, provide a model for Jewish unity. We chose to act in the very same arena in which the men were fighting—the religious arena. We decided to conduct a united prayer service at the *Kotel,* the Western Wall. I set about organizing this service, complete with Torah reading, following the halakhic guidelines for women's *tefillah* groups (*see* R. Haut, pp. 135ff.).

In order for us to conduct a halakhic service in which Orthodox women could participate, the non-Orthodox women would have to make difficult and serious concessions. For example, at first Rabbi Helene Ferris, a Reform rabbi then at the Steven Wise Free Synagogue, was not enthusiastic at the idea of praying at the *Kotel.* Since Reform Jews oppose praying behind a *mehitzah,* many stay away from the *Kotel,* or pray in the plaza before it, only up to the point where the *mehitzah* begins. However, after deep and heartfelt discussions about the significance of the *Kotel,* Rabbi Ferris overcame her initial resistance to the idea, and agreed to join us. It was she, in fact, who arranged for the loan of the *Sefer Torah.*

In order for us to pray together, everyone agreed that we would not constitute a *minyan* (a prayer quorum), and therefore not recite those prayers for which a *minyan* is necessary, such as *Kedushah* and *Kaddish.* Women who philosophically oppose prayers that express the desire to reinstate animal sacrifices nonetheless agreed to use the traditional prayer book, which includes such references. The women, in a display of true sisterhood, graciously and with understanding, accepted *all* the limitations that an Orthodox, non*minyan* service implies.

Although the *Kotel* service was inspired by Orthodox women, it was organized so that women from all denominations participated equally. Francine Klagsbrun (Conservative) carried the Torah to and from the *Kotel*. Geela Raizl Robinson (Reconstructionist) led us in *psukei de-zimrah*, the introductory prayers. Reconstructionist Rabbi Deborah Brin led *Shaharit*. The Torah was opened by Dr. Phyllis Chesler, feminist author and psychologist, and read by Rabbi Ferris (Reform), Marian Krug (Orthodox), and Shulamit Magnus, then teaching at the Reconstructionist Rabbinical College. Blu Greenberg (Orthodox) was honored with the first *aliyah*. Many secular women participated as well. The women came from many countries, including Israel, but most were Americans.

At a meeting the night before the *tefillah,* some of the women expressed fears that violence would result. (Although these fears were not realized on that occasion, the women who have since continued to conduct prayer services at the *Kotel* have been physically attacked.) After careful consideration of many issues, we decided to continue as planned: to pray at the *Kotel,* with a *Sefer Torah.* Everyone agreed that we were to conduct a serious service, not a media event. Everyone concurred that, at the slightest hint of violence, the women would form a tight circle and protect the Torah with their bodies. This last suggestion came from Rabbi Ferris, who was very concerned about the safety of the *Sefer Torah.* (It is a sad commentary on the state of affairs that we had to be concerned that, in the name of "Torah," the Torah we would be carrying might be harmed.)

Early the next morning, we boarded the buses that took us to the *Kotel.* When we arrived, reporters, who had been alerted to our arrival, pressed around us. One of the women began singing *"Oseh Shalom,"* a prayer for peace. Forming a tight group, we all took up that song, ignored the reporters, and walked through the security checkpoint to the *Kotel* area.

I was powerfully aware of the significance of our action, coming to the *Kotel* to pray together as a group, and to read from a *Sefer Torah.* Not since the days of the Second Temple, when the Torah was read by the king once every seven years during the *Hakhel* ceremony and by the High Priest each year on Yom Kippur, had the Torah been read in the *Ezrat Nashim,* the women's section. (Although we were certainly not in the site where the *Ezrat Nashim* was, the symbolism was powerful, just the same, as the *Kotel* represents the destroyed Temple, being its retaining wall.) Even more significantly, we were to read the Torah for ourselves. Unlike the *tzov'ot*, the "women who gathered" at the door of the desert Tabernacle to pray (Exod. 38:8), we were no longer waiting at the door, silently listening. We were no longer going to stand at the *Kotel*, ears pressed to the *meḥitzah*, straining to hear the Torah read by the men, hoping that they might magnanimously raise their voices, so that we might hear. We would read the Torah by ourselves, for ourselves.

Overcome with emotion, I approached the *Kotel*, leaned against the ancient stones, and wept. Even though I was surrounded by the group, I was able to pray my own, private prayers, with a depth and feeling never before experienced. The sense of private prayer and group prayer merged completely for me at that moment.

The combined voices of the women, uplifted in prayer at that holy place, were beautiful. We had managed to overcome our differences and pray with one voice. The sacred singing continued, uninterrupted, until the time came to read the Torah. When we began the Torah reading, one woman, a habitual "resident" of the *Kotel*, began screaming at us and insisting that it is *asur*, forbidden, for women to read from a *Sefer Torah*. She ran to complain to the rabbi of the *Kotel*, Rabbi Getz, who informed her that what we were doing was not against *halakhah*, and we could continue. She returned, and was quiet. By this time, the men praying on their side of the *meḥitzah* had been made aware of our presence.

We were by now in the midst of our Torah reading. A group of men began screaming at us, rhythmically, cursing us, warning us, shouting *asur*—forbidden, pigs; and *tameh*—unclean. For them, the sight of women reading from the Torah was more than they could bear. I lifted my eyes from the words of the Torah for a moment to glance at them. They seemed garbed in darkness, in intolerance. I forced my eyes back to the Torah scroll, to the holy black letters suspended on the white parchment. We women assembled were like the letters of the Torah, each one individually different, yet creating meaning in our unity, surrounded by the whiteness of the ancient stones.

Despite the frenzied shrieking of the fanatics, who were by then shaking and banging the *meḥitzah* up and down, attempting to terrorize us, we heeded Rabbi Brin's plea to "focus, focus" on the prayers. We continued the Torah reading, correctly and with feeling. The women had already formed a tight protective circle around the Torah, so that no one could harm it or take it from us. By this time, however, Norma Baumel Joseph, who had been given the task of judging the mood of the people, decided that we should quickly conclude our service and leave. We rolled the Torah and finished *Shaḥarit*. Those who wished to form a *minyan* for the women who wanted to say *Kaddish* separated themselves briefly from the group, as had been planned, and said *Kaddish*. Maintaining a very tight circle, and again singing *"Oseh Shalom,"* we walked back to our buses and left. We had certainly made our presence, the presence of women, felt.

Since the first women's prayer service at the *Kotel* on December 1, 1988, a group of women in Israel has continued praying together at the *Kotel,* following the model we set. This group has become known as "The Women of the Wall." They call their prayer group "Shirah Ḥadashah."[2] It is an interdenominational group that includes Orthodox, Conservative, Reform, Reconstructionist, and unaffiliated women. The group follows the halakhic guidelines set up by Orthodox rabbis for the Women's *Tefillah* Network (*see* R. Haut, p. 135). The women pray together at the *Kotel* every Friday morning and every *Rosh Ḥodesh* (New Moon). On April 24, 1989 and March 25, 1990, they prayed *Minḥa* (the afternoon service) together at the *Kotel,* to coincide with other interdenominational groups of women all over the world praying together at that same time.

As of this writing, the "Women of the Wall" continue to be attacked, both verbally and physically. They have literally been dragged away from the *Kotel* area by female guards hired by the Religion Ministry for that purpose. Some of the women have been injured; one has been briefly hospitalized. They are literally putting their lives on the line each time they go to pray together as a group, even when they pray without wearing *tallitot* (prayer shawls) and without a *Sefer Torah*. As a direct result of their activities, the Rabbi of the *Kotel,* Rabbi Getz, has forbidden women to "sing" aloud, at the *Kotel*. The group has appealed to the Supreme Court of the State of Israel for protection as they assert the halakhic right of women to pray together at the *Kotel,* to wear *tallitot,* and to read from a *Sefer Torah*.

The case was heard by the Supreme Court of Israel on February 27, 1991. It was joined by a lawsuit brought on behalf of Jewish women in the Diaspora by the International Committee for Women at the *Kotel,* an organization formed for that purpose. The issue is now one of international concern, as Jews all over the world watch the unfolding of events.

The *Kotel* experience, as well as the opportunity to work and pray with women of other denominations in a spirit of mutual respect and friendship, has taught me a great deal. I feel that it is essential, and urgent, that we continue to work together. The energy generated by the *Kotel* prayer service has created sparks that are continuing to glow. These flames must be fanned and encouraged to burn brighter yet.

Perhaps, in times of crisis, it is a particular strength of women to provide creative alternatives, to lead the way to a different approach. To do this takes courage, the courage to withstand the criticism and misunderstanding that inevitably follow. The daughters of Zelophehad (Num. 27) did this, so long ago. By choosing to demand their rights as daughters to inherit the land, even before the Israelites had reached and conquered the land, they strengthened the flagging faith of the nation.[3] By our choosing to assert our rights to pray as a group and to read from the Torah, we are trying to demonstrate that it is possible to transcend differences in the greater interests of peace. Hopefully, the Jewish world will hear the message we send and see new possibilities for furthering Jewish unity. I hope that we, as women, will continue to work together toward this sacred goal.

Notes

1. The controversy revolves around whether converts to Judaism who have been converted by non-Orthodox rabbis, or whose status as Jews has been otherwise questioned by Israel's Orthodox rabbinate, would be recognized as Jews under Israel's Law of Return, which grants all Jews immediate Israeli citizenship.

2. This is adapted from the verse in Psalms 96:1, "Sing unto the Lord a new song." *Shirah Ḥadashah"* means "new song."

3. *Yalkut Shimoni,* Pinḥas 27. This *midrash* makes the point that the daughters of Zelophehad chose that time to demand their share of a land yet unconquered, in order to strengthen the men. The men were beginning to doubt their ability to prevail over the larger Canaanite nations, and therefore these women, by arguing for their rightful inheritance, demonstrated their strong faith that the Israelites would, indeed, conquer the land.

Part of the process of filling new ritual roles is the need to be comfortable using ritual objects that traditionally have been taboo to women. As in a number of the previous vignettes, Susan Alter describes the psychological barriers she had to overcome before accepting an aliyah *to the Torah. The motif of the adolescent girl being banished from the men's section recurs again as a formative experience in creating these barriers. Through the help of a supportive community, Alter gained the strength and knowledge that enabled her to overcome a fear of defiling the Torah scroll. This led her to decide to purchase a Torah scroll for her Orthodox women's prayer group so that the Torah would be more accessible to women.*

Dvora Weisberg, as a Conservative Jew, describes how her decision to wear tallit *and* tefillin *was part of her personal journey to become religiously observant. In response to criticisms from family and friends that her goal is to imitate men, Weisberg explains that her motive is to serve God by fulfilling the commandments, even where a women is not obligated to do so.*

Both Alter and Weisberg show the difficulties that women face in being the first generation of women to demand access to Judaism's sacred objects.

Susan D. Alter

THE *SEFER TORAH* COMES HOME

My relationship to a *Sefer Torah* (Torah scroll) was no different than that of others of my gender, especially back in the 1940s. As females, we were permitted little physical contact with the *Sefer Torah*. We could not hold it, dress or undress it and, certainly, not read from it.

When I was young, my family davened in the Clymer Street *shul* in Williamsburg, Brooklyn, which had an extremely large congregation. My father always made sure to sit in the back row near the exit, so that if he had to, he could hustle my younger brother, who was uninterested, restless, and mischievous, out the door. The women's seats were upstairs in a balcony that extended over the back of the *shul* but, as a youngster, I often joined my father and brother in the men's section, which was on the main floor. It was on those occasions, when the Torah was taken from the Ark, that I had an opportunity to kiss the Torah with my *siddur* as the *ḥazzan* carried it through the synagogue.

My father never took me up to the *bimah* with him when he was called to the Torah for an *aliyah,* although he did take my brother. He viewed the *aliyah* as a very special honor and it was with great awe that my father always approached the Torah. For him, the Torah was our most sacred possession. I remember him telling me how careful a man must be when he carried the Torah because if he dropped it, he would have to fast for forty days. I never knew whether the fasting was a penance or a punishment, but just thinking about it struck terror in my heart. My only consolation was that it could never happen to me because I could not imagine, as a woman, I would ever be allowed to hold a Torah. I understood, almost intuitively, from all the activities that went on in *shul*, that a woman and a *Sefer Torah* were totally incompatible. These feelings, of course, were underscored by the fact that women never participated in *shul* in any activities that involved a *Sefer Torah*.

As a young child, I sat next to my father or on his lap as he read from the *siddur* in the synagogue. As I grew older, a strange thing happened. The men who sat around my father would comment about how I was getting to be a young lady, almost a *"kallah moid"* (lit. child bride), and would soon have to leave the men's section. My father told me that when I turned twelve, I would no longer be allowed to sit with him downstairs, but that I would have to sit in the balcony with my mother. The ultimate achievement of my womanhood would carry with it my total exclusion from any further opportunity to be close to a *Sefer Torah*. From my place of banishment upstairs in the balcony, it was not even possible to kiss the *Sefer Torah*, as I had done as a young girl. What so confused me was that for my brother exactly the opposite was true. Being a mature adult, or "becoming a man," as it were, and assuming responsibilities for doing the *mitzvot*, brought with it an even closer identification with the Torah, not only in the spiritual sense, but also in a very real and physical way. The *Bar Mitzvah* celebration, if nothing else, occasions the first time that a young boy of thirteen reads from the *Sefer Torah* and is permitted to do so from then on as a reader of the Torah who may represent the congregation in this sacred service.

I became reacquainted with the Torah twenty-eight years after my brother's *Bar Mitzvah*, when I was honored by being called to the Torah for an *aliya* at a new Orthodox women's davening group that had been formed in the Flatbush section of Brooklyn by a number of courageous and learned women who felt that they were not enjoying the full benefits of Jewish traditional prayer. These women had come together not to break the law but to enhance it by their devoted participation in monthly study and prayer with a *Sefer Torah*, just as their male counterparts were doing every week. I remember being panic-stricken when my Hebrew name was called: Devorah bat Menaḥem Mendel ve-Leah. Obviously, I had never been honored with an *aliyah* before. I shook my head back and forth frantically, indicating that I did not want to participate and I kept mouthing the word "no," but to no avail. As I approached the Torah, the injunctions from my childhood about a woman being forbidden to be near a *Sefer Torah* caused me a great deal of consternation. Anxiety overtook me. The fear of defiling the Torah almost immobilized me. As I uttered the blessing, however, I felt myself moving through time and space into a new world.

Never again, I thought, should any female feel as uncomfortable or alien around the *Sefer Torah* as I did. The Torah is as much a sacred possession of Jewish females as it is of Jewish males, I assured myself. It was this realization that brought about my interest in buying a *Sefer Torah* and donating it to the Flatbush Women's Davening Group, which was having a great deal of difficulty in obtaining a Torah for their once-a-month services. After having my initial thought about being an equal heir with Jewish males to the Torah, it never left me. Somehow, I felt that this was Jewish history in the making. By buying the Torah, I would be permanently guaranteeing the right of Jewish women to have continuous access to a *Sefer Torah* from which they could pray and learn.

But how does one go about obtaining a *Sefer Torah?* The obvious answer was to ask a male, preferably a rabbi or someone who is connected with the religious activities of a synagogue.

I must admit however, that I never thought about the possibility of finding a Torah in a shop that sells religious articles. Nevertheless, I was introduced to just such a shop, which sells not only *tallitot, tefillin,* and *seforim* (holy books) but also Torahs that have been restored and renewed.

To have a new *Sefer Torah* written by a scribe would have cost thousands of dollars. Fortunately, I was able to obtain an old *Sefer Torah*, at reasonable cost, from a fragile, holy-looking man named Eisenbach on Essex Street in Manhattan, who recovered Torahs from synagogues no longer in use in the United States and Europe. Never in my wildest imagination could I have foreseen that one day I would be doing *ḥakirah* (investigation) into the Torah, not only to find deeper understandings of the text, but in a more practical sense, to ascertain the condition and quality of the Torah as a consumer item. The experience was fascinating. I marched around a small room in Eisenbach's shop carrying Torahs of different sizes in an attempt to determine the weight of a Torah that would be comfortable for most women. I examined the *klaf* (parchment), to see that the text was clear and that the *otiyot* (letters) were large enough and easy to read. It was explained to me that the *klaf*, which is made of the skin of a young calf, was strong and durable enough to be scraped with a knife so that the accumulation of dust could be removed from it, and yet was firm enough so that the letters that are inked into the scroll would be unaffected. I finally chose an old Torah that had been saved from the Holocaust. The *etzei ḥaim*, or poles around which the Torah scroll is rolled, were dried out and cracked and had to be replaced. Finally, I was to have the wonderful privilege of choosing a beautiful mantle (covering) upon which would be handsewn the names of my late husband, Dr. Aaron A. Alter, in whose memory I was dedicating this Torah, and my two daughters, Beth and Shira, as well as my own name.

On a Sunday in June 1985, accompanied by my two daughters, my mother, and two aunts, all of us dressed in white, I carried my Torah into the 18th Avenue Synagogue in Flatbush for a *Siyum ha-Sefer*, a dedication ceremony. As we entered the synagogue, women of all ages danced and sang before us, as they joyously embraced their new Torah. The Torah had finally come home to the other half of the Jewish people.

Dvora E. Weisberg

ON WEARING *TALLIT* AND *TEFILLIN*

When I was seventeen, I asked my grandfather where I could buy *tefillin*. He told me that "girls don't wear *tefillin*." When I persisted, saying that I already was wearing *tefillin*, he told me that I wouldn't be able to afford them. After I said I was prepared to spend my entire summer salary, my grandfather, convinced I was serious, bought me the *tefillin*. The next morning he was in *minyan*, bragging to the other men about his granddaughter, who was "so religious, she even puts on *tefillin*."

My decision to wear *tallit* and *tefillin* was not particularly well thought out. The camp where I worked listed them as optional equipment for women, and I was intrigued. Given my personality, I probably became more intrigued as various relatives protested. If I knew little about the halakhic issues surrounding women's observance of time-bound positive *mitzvot* in general, and of *tallit* and *tefillin* in particular, I learned quickly. I was constantly called upon to defend my decision halakhically. I also had to deal with people's claims that I was offending them by my actions, even if those actions were halakhically permissible. During my first month in college, a man offered to buy my *tefillin* to stop me from wearing them. I found most frustrating the fact that many people ascribed motives to my wearing *tallit* and *tefillin* without asking me what my intentions actually were.

When I daven in *tallit* and *tefillin*, I am not trying to make a feminist gesture or prove that I can "pray like a man." I began to observe these *mitzvot* out of a desire to serve God by fulfilling God's commandments. It never occurred to me that the need to be reminded of God's presence in regular, concrete ways was limited to men. I felt, and still feel, that every *mitzvah* I perform strengthens the bond between me and my Creator. The recitation of "And I shall betroth you to me forever . . . " as I bind *tefillin* on my arm, the awareness of being enveloped in a *tallit*, evoke very powerful feelings in me. I can no more consider discarding my *tefillin* than I could consider eating pork; I regard all the *mitzvot* I observe as obligatory.

I realize that wearing *tallit* and *tefillin* is a highly visible action and one that arouses strong emotions in other people. I know that what I intend to be my personal commitment becomes a public statement every time I enter a synagogue. While part of me responds to the opportunity to represent a change in women's patterns of observance, there is also a part that sometimes longs to be an unremarkable member of the congregation.

My grandfather died two years ago. I have put his *tefillin* away, to be given someday to my first child, his great grandchild. I like to think my grandfather would be no less pleased if the child is a daughter rather than a son. I want to believe that his acceptance of my observance was not only a grandfather's pride in his granddaughter but also a reflection of his ability to accept the idea that women can be as committed to *mitzvot* they have accepted out of religious conviction as they are to those they have observed for centuries. This is all I would ask or expect from him . . . or from anyone else.

The dynamic process of women's growing involvement in communal worship, includes the development of new rituals that reflect their special con-

cerns, recreate women's traditions, and celebrate major events in women's lives. The most popular are meetings for prayer and study on Rosh Ḥodesh *(the New Moon), traditionally considered a woman's semi-holiday.* Simḥat Bat, *a celebration marking the birth of a daughter, long common in the Sephardic world, is now gaining acceptance in Ashkenazi communities. Since the* Simḥat Bat *does not yet have an established form, each family creates its own ritual.**

Women are also creating new liturgies to sacralize life cycle events. Susan Grossman and Tikva Frymer-Kensky provide two such liturgies. Grossman explains how she came to compose a prayer for comfort after experiencing a miscarriage. Tikva Frymer-Kensky presents a new celebration to mark the beginning of pregnancy.

Ritual highlights transitions. When Grossman and Frymer-Kensky sought to mark significant events in their lives they discovered that there were no traditional models from which to draw. Biological events particular to women have been ignored in a Hebrew liturgical tradition created by men. Where in the past, as we have seen above, women's biological processes were often used to distance women from the sacred, Grossman and Frymer-Kensky both raise women's biology to the sacred dimensions of the relationship between God and woman. Both give insights into the rationales behind their liturgies, thereby providing guidance for other women's endeavors. They accomplish this by mining tradition and forming it into new patterns.

Susan Grossman

FINDING COMFORT AFTER A MISCARRIAGE

When I miscarried during my sixth week of pregnancy, I felt a great sense of pain and loss. As a committed Jew who lives her life around the Jewish calendar and steeped in Jewish ritual, I naturally sought to find comfort

---

*Examples of *Rosh Ḥodesh* and *Simḥat Bat* ceremonies are available from the National Jewish Women's Resource Center at the National Council of Jewish Women, New York Section, at 9 E. 69th Street, New York, NY.

in Jewish prayer and ritual. However, I felt myself abandoned by the tradition with which I normally feel so much at home. There are no traditional prayers to recite over a miscarriage. There is no funeral or mourning ritual to follow. After suffering a miscarriage, a woman does not even routinely recite the prayer said after coming safely through a dangerous experience, *birkat ha-gomel*, something all women can do after giving birth.

The rabbis who shaped our traditions certainly were aware of the frequent occurrence of miscarriages. Material about miscarriages can be found in the Bible, the Talmud, and in later codes. Yet that material is generally concerned with causality and culpability. For example, according to the text in Exod. 21:22:

When men fight, and one of them pushes a pregnant woman, and a miscarriage results, but no other damage (to the woman) ensues, the one responsible shall be fined according as the woman's husband may exact from him, the payment to be based on reckoning (as the judges determine).

This source shows no concern for the sense of loss experienced by the woman. Similarly, Talmudic and later rabbis were most often concerned with determining whether a miscarriage—caused by accident or induced to save the mother—should be considered murder and be punished as such and whether a fetus is considered a human being.[1] Such material laid the foundation for contemporary discussions on Judaism's attitude toward abortion and the rightful priority placed on protecting the woman's life and well-being. However, they do little to help the woman searching the tradition for sources from which to develop a compassionate ritual for mourning the unintentional loss of a fetus.

Why is there no such liturgy or ritual in the normative tradition? The answer only partially lies in the high probability of miscarriage and infant mortality in the premodern world and in the consequent fact that a fetus—or even an infant that dies before reaching thirty days old—is not defined as a person according to Jewish law, and the laws of mourning therefore do not apply to it.

I believe the answer more completely lies in the fact that our traditions were framed by men and consequently reflect male perspectives and concerns.

From my own experience, and that of a random anecdotal sampling, I have found that men and women react very differently to a miscarriage.[2]

For the husband, the miscarriage represents a loss from which he is somewhat distanced, a loss of something expected but not experienced. For the modern man these expectations may focus around the ideas of fatherhood, the financial concerns of having a larger family, and the joy of helping to bring into the world a new life, one's mark on the world, one's little bit of immortality. Certainly in earlier times the man would look forward to having an extra hand to contribute to the support of the household in the family business or farm. Removed somewhat from the experience of pregnancy, the husband's primary concern during a miscarriage is probably (and justifiably) for the health and speedy recovery of his wife, rather than for what she is carrying, which seems foreign to him.

For the woman, however, the loss is immediate. She can feel the embryo stirring inside her. Even in those first weeks, I was aware of the changes occurring in my body as it became adjusted to carrying this new life. Thanks to modern science, images of what the embryo looks like in each stage of pregnancy are printed in most prenatal books. I could therefore visualize my growing fetus inside my womb. I sent it love on the emotional level, just as on the physical level I expressed my love by slowing down my hectic schedule and taking better care of myself for its sake so that it would receive the nutrients it needed. If a woman suffers a miscarriage during her first pregnancy, especially if it is a much desired pregnancy and the woman feels she is nearing the end of her childbearing years, her fears about ever being able to have children are strengthened as well.

Until I had suffered a miscarriage, I had never understood what had motivated European women to seek all those amulets arrayed on exhibit in the Israel Museum in Jerusalem—amulets against the Evil Eye and the much maligned Lilith, amulets calling on various angels for protection of the mother and unborn child. Now I understand. The feeling of helplessness is overwhelming during and after a miscarriage. The actual miscarriage is terrifying. As the body begins to bleed uncontrollably, one fears—at least a little—for one's own health and life. After recovering physically, one is often left without answers to that fundamental question: Why did it happen? Even modern science often cannot point to a cause, so as to reassure the mother it will not happen again, although friends and scientific statistics both assure her that the next pregnancy should come to term and bring forth a healthy child.

My strong feelings led me to seek in liturgy a way to turn to God in my pain and fear and sense of helplessness, to seek comfort in the protection of God's grace. Yet, I found no prayer in the standard prayer books of any of the movements that seemed to meet my needs. If such prayers exist in the Yiddish *tehinot* literature (*see* Berger, p. 73ff), they are not easily accessible.

Below is the meditation I composed for myself to introduce my recitation of *birkat ha-gomel* after receiving an *aliyah* during the Torah reading in the synagogue. I found that, while not obligatory, the recitation of *birkat ha-gomel* after a miscarriage should be encouraged, because a miscarriage does pose a danger to a woman's health.[3]

If a woman is uncomfortable with such a public statement, she may prefer to recite the prayer in a smaller group, for example, among ten friends invited to her home,[4] or she may wish to recite this meditation following immersion in the *mikveh* after the miscarriage.

I translated the prayer so as to avoid gender specific God language, and I adjusted the Hebrew of the congregational response to refer to a woman. However, I leave the entire reformulation of the Hebrew to others (*see* Daum, p. 188).

This prayer is one of a number of new liturgies being composed by women rabbis, cantors, scholars, and lay people to encompass female perspectives and concerns within our liturgy (*see* Frymer-Kensky, p. 290). This is consistent with the history of Jewish liturgical development, which saw periods of liturgical creativity in which no one standardized version became dominant for many generations.[5] The process of creating is itself healing, though. As for the multiplicity of prayers, which I hope we will see bloom forth on all aspects of a woman's life—the happy times as well as the sad—all these are for the sake of heaven and seek to serve the work of the living God in this world by granting us comfort and filling us with ideals for just action.

Meditation After a Miscarriage

„כציץ יצא וימל ויברח כצל ולא יעמוד. . . . ״[איוב יד:ב] אם חרוצים ימיו מספר חדשיו אתך חקיו עשית ולא יעבר.״[על איוב יד:ה]

"Ke-tzitz yatza va-yimal, va-yivrah ka-tzel ve-lo ya'amod. . . . Im harutzim yamav mispar hadashav itakh hukav asita ve-lo ya'avor."

"He blossoms like a flower and withers; he vanishes like a shadow and does not endure" (Job 14:2).

"Seeing his days are determined, the number of his months are with You, You set him limits that he *could* not pass" (on Job 14:5).

אלוקים, הריני משיבה לידיך הנאמנות את החי הנוצר שהפקרת בי לזמן כה קצר.

O God, I commend back to Your safe keeping the potential life entrusted to me for so short a time.

For first pregnancies terminated before 40 days:

טרם מלאו לו ארבעים ימי יצירה, עובר זה לא פתח את רחמי, אין הוא בכורי, ובכל זאת בוכיה אני על עזיבתו את גופי המגן.

Not yet having reached 40 days of life, this fetus did not open my womb, it was not my *bakhor*,[7] still I grieve its passing out of the protection of my body.

For first pregnancies terminated after 40 days:

בהגיעו ל_____ שבועות יצירה, עובר זה היה בכורי, פתח את רחמי. בוכיה אני על עזיבתו את גופי המגן.

Having reached _____ weeks, this fetus was my *bakhor*, opening my womb. I grieve its passing out of the protection of my body.

If not first pregnancy:

בהגיעו ל_____ שבועות יצירה, עובר זה היה יכול להיות ילדי ה_____, בוכיה אני על עזיבתו את גופי המגן.

Having reached _____ weeks, this fetus would have been my (number) child. I grieve its passing out of the protection of my body.

"ידעת עת לדת יעלי סלע חלל אילות תשמור" [על איוב לט:א]

"Yadaʿta et ledet yaʾalei sala, ḥolell ayalot tishmor."

"You know when the wild goats of the rock give birth, You mark when the hinds calve" (on Job 39:1).

אתה בראת את נס הלידה ואת פלא הגוף המשגיח על אם וילדיה.

You created the miracle of birth and the wonder of the body that cares for mother and child.

דיין האמת, אתה הדואג ליצירי כפיך אף כאשר כוס התמרורים מלאה. מי אנו
שנבין דרכיך, לדעת מה עתיד היה להיות לי ולילדי זה לו נולד אחרי תשעה
ירחים?

Dayyan Ha-Emet, Righteous Judge, You care for Your creatures even when
such care tastes bitter.

Who are we to understand Your ways, to know what future would have
lain ahead for myself and my child had it come to term?

„אַךְ בְּשָׂר[ה] עָלֶי[ה] יִכְאָב, וְנַפְשָׁ[ה] עָלֶי[ה] תֶּאֱבָל״ [על איוב יד:כב]

"Akh bsar(ah) ale(ha) yikh'av, ve-nafsh(ah) ale(ha) te'eval."

"But her flesh upon her shall have pain and her soul within her shall mourn"
(adapted from Job 14:22).

הרחמן, רפא גופי ונשמתי; רפא רחמי עד כי אוכל ללדת נשמה בריאה, שאוכל
לשיר להלל ולפאר את שמך כאם בריאה שבניה יסובבוה בחצות ירושלים
בשלום.

Ha-Raḥaman, O Merciful One, heal my body and my soul; heal my womb so
that I may carry to term a healthy soul, that I may come to sing Your praises as
a happy mother surrounded by her children in the courtyards of a Jerusalem
at peace.

Recite *birkat ha-gomel*:

ברוך אתה ה״ אלקינו מלך העולם הגומל לחייבים טובות שגמלני כל טוב.

*Barukh Atah Adonai Eloheinu Melekh ha-olam ha-gomel le-ḥayavim tovot she-
g'malani kol tov.*

Blessed are You, Almighty God, Sovereign of the Universe, Who bestows
kindness on the undeserving, and has shown me every kindness.

Congregation responds:

מי שגמלך כל טוב, הוא יגמלך כל טוב סלע. אמן.

Mi she-g'malekh kol tov, Hu yigmalekh kol tov sela. Amen.

May the One who has shown you every kindness, ever show kindness to you,
sela. Amen.

Notes

1. For example, TB Sanh. 57b, 72b, cf. TB BK 83a. For a fuller discussion, *see* David
Feldman, *Birth Control in Jewish Law* (New York: New York University Press, 1968), 253–57.
The Talmud does mention miscarriages in other contexts, e.g., TB Pes. 3a, on sacrifices re-

quired after a miscarriage, but such material is still not concerned with the woman's perception of the event, largely because rabbinic literature is seldom concerned with the woman's perspective.

2. I would like to express my appreciation to my husband, David Boder, and my friends, colleagues, and professors who shared their experiences and wisdom with me. A number of good books are available to help in recovering from a miscarriage. One I found particularly helpful is Sherokee Ilse and Linda Hammer Burns, *Miscarriage: A Shattered Dream* (available from Wintergreen Press, P.O.B. 165, Long Lake, MN 55356), which also includes a detailed bibliography of other related works.

3. This in consultation with Rabbi Joel Roth, head of the Law and Standards Committee of the Rabbinical Assembly, the halakhic decision-making body for the Conservative Movement. As of this writing, the Committee had just accepted a *teshuvah* (rabbinic opinion) on appropriate rituals for marking a miscarriage.

4. Orthodox women may choose to attend a women's prayer group, or to invite any number of women and one man. (*See Mishnah Berurah: Birkhot Hodaot* 219:3, and Haut, p. 145.)

5. For example, this is one of the themes discussed by Lawrence Hoffman, *Canonization of the Synagogue Service* (Notre Dame: University of Notre Dame Press, 1979). Samples of other liturgies about miscarriages can be forwarded to the Resource Library of the Jewish Women's Resource Center, National Council of Jewish Women, New York Section, 9 East 69th Street, New York, NY.

6. Translated into the Hebrew by Yael, Ari, and Monty Penkower.

7. First born. The fetus of a first pregnancy miscarried after the fortieth day from conception (rather than the first day of the previous period, as modern doctors count the age of the fetus) would be considered the first born. A subsequent child born to the mother would not have a *pidyon ha-ben*, redemption of the first born, in which a token amount is given to a *kohen* to redeem the child of Israelites from being consecrated to God's service.

Tikva Frymer-Kensky

A RITUAL FOR AFFIRMING AND ACCEPTING PREGNANCY

In many respects, pregnancy and parenting are new phenomena. This sounds like a patently absurd statement until we consider the dramatic changes that have taken place surrounding the experience of having children in the last 200 years. Women no longer expect to die in childbirth. Where once perhaps half of all women died giving birth, the number of women who do so now is small enough that we do not consciously worry about this risk any longer. At the same time that the physical prospect of bearing children has become less frightening, the material costs of raising these children have become more daunting. With the changes in our economic system, children are not the economic assets they once were. On the contrary, raising the middle-class child involves the expenditure of an enormous amount of money and a reduction in most parents' standard of living. Recent scholarship has indicated that the "maternal instinct" is neither innate nor universal. Deciding to have children is a difficult personal choice that involves love, will, determination, and a readiness for self-sacrifice.

It is in that word "choice" that the great magnitude of the change in childbirth becomes apparent. Pregnancy is no longer inevitable for most people. With our improved knowledge of birth control, pregnancy can usually be scheduled or prevented. Even when prophylaxis fails and accidents happen, modern abortion techniques make it possible to terminate a pregnancy early, easily, and safely. Theoretically, since every pregnancy *can* be terminated, every pregnancy that has not been ended has been accepted and chosen. Every pregnancy is a volitional act, every child is a "wanted" child.

If pregnancy has become an act of volition rather than inevitability, of decision rather than destiny, it demands conscious thought, recognition, and sacralization. We need to recognize parenting, with all its difficulties and sacrifices, as the valuable and valiant work that it is and to appreciate pregnancy for the labor and effort that it involves. We should celebrate pregnancy as a major contribution to our communal life. That we have not done so is due to the "naturalness" of the task and to the fact that the organized community has thought mainly about affairs in which men are more immediately involved. All the major biological events of women's lives—menarche, sexual maturation, pregnancy, lactation, menopause—have been ignored by our religious traditions and thereby made into secular events. The androcentricity of our inherited religious and cultural traditions, however, as well as their lack of attention to biology, are not irrevocable and should not cause irremedial loss. Now that women have had greater access to learning and to participation in Jewish public life, now that we have found our own voices, it is time to turn our attention to the "female" (biological) aspects of women's existence. If pregnancy is a decision, it should be a spiritual and religious decision, and if childbearing is an important and sacred task, it needs to be affirmed and celebrated as such. For this, we need new prayers and rituals, and women in the last decade have been writing and performing new women-centered and women-acted liturgy.

Creating such liturgy is a challenge, for if we do not want to perpetuate an arbitrary and outmoded split between Jewish women's social and biological experiences, we must create liturgy that is distinctly Jewish. Otherwise, we might as well enact our rituals in a coven or an ashram (at both of which we are likely to be sharing with other Jewish women) as in a synagogue or a *Rosh Ḥodesh* group. We must attempt to expand Jewish thinking into new directions, while staying in harmony with the rest of the religion's teachings and practices. The way to do this is to delve into the sources and mine Jewish literature for those nuggets of insight that were written there, with no intention of being relevant to birth or other "female" concerns. These can be reinterpreted and recombined to bring female experiences into the sanctified realm of Judaism.

In considering childbearing, two Jewish themes seem to cry out for such reinterpretation. One is the biblical notion of covenants sealed in blood, both the blood of the covenant of circumcision, and the sprinkling of the people with the "blood of the covenant" as they accepted the covenant of Sinai (Exod. 24:7–8). Menstrual blood should also be seen as a sign of a covenant, the covenant between God and woman, by which women become and continue to be the bearers and shapers of new life. God affirms this covenant in the blood of menarche, and women affirm it as they undertake a pregnancy. In their willingness to bear the child, both the man and the woman become "partners in the work of creation." This is an old and significant concept, for Judaism considers the work of God's creation to be unfinished and it is part of humanity's task to continue this labor, to become *"shutafim le-maʿasay beʾreishit,"* "partners in the work of creation." We may do so liturgically, for "everyone who prays on Friday night and says '[And the heavens and the earth] were finished,' Scripture considers him to have become a partner of the Blessed Holy One in the works of creation" (TB Shab. 119b). And we may do so socially, by working to improve social justice and to repair society, for "every judge who judges a righteous judgment even once, Scripture considers to have become a partner of the Blessed Holy One in the works of creation" (TB Shab. 10a). And there is another, obvious way in which we can be partners of God in creation: by helping to create new lives.

The following ritual is an acceptance of this covenantal role, a declaration of willingness to be God's partners and to accept unstintingly whatever hardships and sacrifices this might entail. Even though the decision to bear children is a personal family choice, the setting of this ritual is in the synagogue rather than the home. As a Jewish people, we consider it our obligation to become parents, we welcome new lives, and we actively worry about our declining or static birth rate. As a Jewish community, we should affirm each couple's choice to have children, witness their acceptance of their duties, celebrate their decision, and offer communal support and encouragement for their endeavors. Every birth is an occasion for rejoicing, and every joyously accepted pregnancy sanctifies all of us.

Ritual for Affirming and Accepting Pregnancy

The parents (or the mother): [1]

הננו מוכנים ומזומנים ומזומנות (הנני מוכנה ומזומנת) לקים מצות "פרו ורבו" אשר צונו (צוני) ה' אלקנו ביום בוראנו וביום גואלנו ממי המבול. ולשם קיום מצוה זאת אנו באים (אני באה) להכנס לברית אשר כרת ה' עם כל בנות חוה.

We declare ourselves fully ready to fulfill the commandment "Be fruitful and multiply," which God commanded us [2] on the day that God created us and on the day that God rescued us from the waters of the flood. And in order to fulfill this commandment, we hereby come to enter the covenant that God has made with the daughters of Eve.

The mother:

For Eve first recognized this bond of creation, affirming it at the birth of her first son, when she stated "קניתי איש את ה'," "I have created a man with the Lord" (Gen. 4:1). [3] God who creates us has created in woman the power to continue and participate in God's creations on earth.

I come to affirm this partnership with God:
In my womb You form the child [4]
   in my womb, I nourish it.
There You form and number the limbs [5]
   there I contain and protect them.
You who can see the child in the depths of my innards, [6]
   I who can feel the kicks and the turns—
Together we count the months,
together we plan the future, [7]
flesh of my flesh
form of Your form [8]
   another human upon the earth;
   a home for God in this, our world. [9]

The mother continues:

> Knowing that it is not easy to be a partner to God, knowing that it is hard to be a member to a covenant, I am prepared to observe all the laws, commandments, and obligations of this covenant of childbirth.
>   1. As the mother of Samson before his birth (Judg. 13:4–5), I, too, will refrain from drinking all wine, beer, or other alcohol and from eating impure foods.
>   2. I will not smoke.
>   3. I will not use drugs.
>   4. I will not drink coffee or caffeine in any form.
>   5. I will not abuse my body, or the life I shelter within me.
> I declare that:
>   6. I will exercise.
>   7. I will sleep.
>   8. I will eat properly.
>   9. I will visit my doctor whenever I should.
>   10. I will learn about parenting.
> In all these acts, I will prepare to give my child a faithful home in Israel בית נאמן בישראל. And I will love this child with all my heart, learning even as it grows within me the depths of mother-love.

The other parent (if present):

> In the months to come and the years to follow, I will be mindful of the fact that I too am a partner in this act of creation. I will help my wife in these months of her great effort, and I will do everything that I can to enable her to observe these rules and obligations.
>
> Together we will prepare our home, together we will welcome our baby, together we will love, protect, instruct, and cherish the child we are creating.

The Parents:

> ועתה גם אתה תצק רוחך על זרענו ברכתך על צאצאנו.
>
> And now, You, for Your part, pour Your spirit on our seed, Your blessings on our offspring.[10]
>
> Grant our child health and strength, happiness and length of days. May he or she grow at peace with one's self and at peace with the world.[11]
>
> And let us continue to work together, we and You, to form a true righteous human, one who can walk with God, one who will say "I am the Lord's" and carry proudly the name Israel.[12]

כשם שנכנסנו (שנכנסתי) לברית, כן נזכה (אזכה) לגדלו או לגדלה לתורה
ולמצוה, לחפה, ולמעשים טובים. ונאמר אמן.

As we have entered this covenant, so may we be privileged to bring our child
to the Torah, to the commandments, to the wedding canopy, and to a righteous life. And let us say Amen.

The Congregation:

Amen.

The Rabbi offers the following "personal prayer" (*mi she-berakh*):

מי שברך אבותינו אברהם, יצחק ויעקב, שרה רבקה, רחל ולאה, בלהה וזלפה,
הוא יברך את האשה הזאת _____ בת _____ ואת האיש
הזה _____ בן _____ בעבור זה שנכנסו (שנכנסה) לברית
עם בוראנו. בשכר זה הקדוש ברוך הוא ימלא רחמים עליה להחלימה ולרפאותה
להחזיקה ולהחיותה. ואת הילד או הילדה תוציא מרחמה בשעה טובה ובמזל
טוב. כי אתה המשביר והמוליד. יהי רצון מלפניך שיזכו הוריה לגדל ילדים
לתורה ולחפה ולמעשים טובים. ונאמר אמן.

May the One Who blessed our ancestors Abraham, Isaac, and Jacob, Sarah,
Rebecca, Rachel, Leah, Bilhah, and Zilpah,[13] bless this woman _____
and this man _____ because they have entered this pact with our Creator. For this may the Holy Blessed One be full of mercy for her, to keep her
safe, alive, healthy, and well.[14] And may God bring forth the child from her
womb[15] at a good and propitious time.[16] For You bring on labor and bring on
birth.[17] May it be Your wish that her parents will be privileged to raise children
to the Torah, the wedding canopy, and to a righteous life.[18] And let us say,
Amen.

Congregation:

Amen.

(Congregation then sings):[19]

y'varekh'khem Ha-Shem mi-Tzion
u-ra'u be-tuv Yerushalayim
ye-varekh'khem Ha-Shem mi-Tzion
kol ye-mei, ye-mei ḥayyeikhem
u-ra'u banim le-vnaikhem
shalom al Yisra'el.

יברככם השם מציון
וראו בטוב ירושלים
יברככם השם מציון
כל ימי, ימי חייכם
וראו בנים לבניכם
שלום על ישראל.

Notes

1. I have written the ritual for both parents. In the event that the father is not involved in the pregnancy, or simply does not wish to be part of the ceremony, the ritual is for the mother alone. I have indicated the alternative verbal forms in the Hebrew but have left the reformulation of the English to the performers of the ritual.

2. Technically, the Jewish tradition has held that only the male is obligated by the commandment of "be fruitful and multiply."

3. Older translations say, "I have gotten a man from the Lord," but the biblical verb קָנִי, *kny,* means "to create" and is used in this sense for the creation of heaven and earth (Gen. 14:19) and the creation of human innards (Ps. 139:13).

4. Ps. 139:13.

5. Ps. 139:16.

6. Ps. 139:15.

7. Cf. Jer. 1:5, Isa. 49:5.

8. Gen. 1:26.

9. TB Yev. 64a.

10. Isa. 44:3.

11. From the *She-heḥeyanu* for the mother of a newborn, written by Jules Harlow for the Rabbinical Assembly Manual (NY: Rabbinical Assembly, 1965), 8.

12. Isa. 44:5.

13. Women have generally added Rachel and Leah and omitted Bilhah and Zilphah. To do so is to deny them their status as mothers of Israel simply because they were not full wives. It will not suffice to claim that the children of Zilphah and Bilhah were among the lost tribes. People from the North, including the children of Bilhah and Zilphah, fled South at the time of the Assyrian conquest. It is wrong to speak of "ten" lost tribes for another reason: Benjamin was exiled with the North as was much of Judah (*see* Jer. 31). If Bilhah and Zilphah are omitted because their tribes are "lost," then Rachel should also be left out, with only Leah remaining as mother of Israel.

14. This line is from the *mi she-berakh* for a woman who has just given birth.

15. Cf. Job 10:18, Ps. 22:9–11.

16. This line is from the *mi she-berakh* at the naming of a girl.

17. Cf. Isa. 66:9.

18. Also from the *mi she-berakh* at a naming.

19. This is a popular song often sung at *Bar* and *Bat Mitzvot.* The words, adapted from Ps. 128:5–6, mean:

May the Lord bless you from Zion
    May you see the good of Jerusalem
May the Lord bless you all the days of your life
And may you see your children's children, peace on Israel.

I have changed the Hebrew endings to address a plural (father and mother). If there is no father present, the song should be sung in the singular.

Paula E. Hyman

LOOKING TO
THE FUTURE:
CONCLUSIONS

In his insightful depiction and analysis of an American Orthodox synagogue of the early 1970s, the sociologist Samuel Heilman posits sexual
segregation as a "symbolic absolute" for an Orthodox synagogue. It is
men, he notes, who fulfill "public ritual requirements." Consequently,
"even the space . . . [of the synagogue] asserts public dependency of female upon male vis-à-vis religious responsibility." Heilman also points
out that "[w]hen the women occasionally shush the men in order to
better hear the service, they are usually ignored—the implication being
that it is not important for them to hear, for they are not legitimate participants in the house-of-prayer activity."[1]

Throughout Jewish history, the synagogue has been primarily the domain of men. Judaism has traditionally limited the role of women in the
areas of public religious activity and has proclaimed that women and men
have different religious responsibilities. Yet, that gender separation tells
only part of the story. Despite their marginality and secondary status
within the synagogue, in many Jewish societies women have exhibited a
profound attachment to the synagogue that transcends their exemption
from public communal prayer. From the Roman period when one Juliana
donated the mosaic floor for the prayer hall in a North African synagogue[2]

to the sixteenth century when Doña Gracia Mendes funded a synagogue in Salonika, which was named "Sinagoga de la Señora" in her honor,[3] women have helped to support and adorn the synagogue. While they generally did not attend the synagogue with the regularity of men, some women, particularly in Western Ashkenazi culture of the early modern period, were assiduous in their participation in public prayer in the "woman's *shul*." For example, Gluckel of Hameln, the clever and pious memoir writer of the late seventeenth and early eighteenth centuries, referred in passing to her daughter Esther's daily presence in *shul*.[4]

Women's role in the synagogue has changed with time and place. Recent analysis of archaeological and inscriptional evidence indicates, for example, that there may have been no separate women's gallery in ancient synagogues.[5] The women's section of the synagogue appears to have been a far more vibrant locale in medieval and early modern Western and Central Europe than it was in medieval and early modern Islamic countries (where there were no prayer leaders for women worshipers and, in some cases, no expectation that women attend the synagogue at all). In the nineteenth century, the Jewish confrontation with modern Western thought led to the integration of women into the main space of the non-Orthodox synagogue and, in our own time, to the acceptance of women, primarily in the United States, as religious leaders for the entire congregation.

Recent changes in the status of women in contemporary American society have influenced Jewish women of all religious backgrounds to explore the role of women in Judaism and to seek expanded opportunities for religious expression and leadership. The distinction made between the public and private spheres, which defines women's domain as the domestic one and is so common in traditional cultures, no longer reflects the social reality or values of the vast majority of American Jewish women. It is no surprise, then, that so many Jewish women have expressed a measure of discontent with a religious role that developed under vastly different patriarchal social conditions and that is based upon presumptions about women's lives and natures that are no longer valid.

This book is a product of a new social reality for women and of a changed female consciousness. In giving voice to women's experience in the synagogue throughout history and in contemporary settings, it reflects the seriousness with which women are now examining both our personal perceptions and our history. It also reflects the growing consensus that the study of women's behavior and social status is a valid subject for scholarly investigation. What is associated with women can no longer be dismissed as trivial and unworthy of scholarly interest, as was the case just a few years ago with such topics as women's Yiddish religious literature or immigrant Jewish women's political mobilization.

By introducing the analytic category of gender, the new field of Women's Studies has alerted scholars to the centrality of gender in ordering and analyzing human experience. It cannot simply be assumed that women's and men's historical experience have been essentially the same; nor can it be assumed that "male" is equivalent to "human." By implication, the scholarly studies of Judaism in the past and indeed the traditional learning of Torah have both been flawed because of their failure to incorporate the experience or the perspectives of women. In fact, including women within the purview of Judaism and Jewish history will inevitably force scholars to recast the way in which they interpret religious and historical phenomena. Chava Weissler's important work on *teḥines* (the collection of personal prayers written in Yiddish for and by women), for example, suggests that the scholarly presentation of traditional Judaism has focused too exclusively upon the elite rabbinical and philosophical literature of Judaism to the exclusion of how the religion was practiced by the majority of Jews.[6]

In drawing upon new research on Jewish women, this volume reveals the diversity of opinion throughout Jewish history concerning what was deemed appropriate behavior for women in the religious sphere. It is evident that the rigid segregation of women and men in contemporary strict Orthodoxy, or in some Jewish communities situated in countries where Islam holds sway, has not always been the rule. Even within modern Middle Eastern societies, custom has varied. For example, Jewish women in Kurdistan (Sered) did not frequent the synagogue, whereas Jewish women in nearby Iran did (*see* Grossman and Haut, p. 217). Such scholarly studies demonstrate a number of elements that are familiar to the academic student of Jewish history and culture. First, that Jewish communities have always interacted, to a greater or lesser degree, with the cultures in which they have been situated and have, therefore, been influenced by those cultures and by their common assumptions. Thus, early rabbinic Judaism displays the impact of Hellenism, medieval Ashkenazi Judaism reflects some influence from Christian practice, and contemporary Judaism has absorbed some of the aesthetic features and moral concerns of

Western modernity. Second, the development of Judaism occurs through the interplay between a revered tradition and a changing socioeconomic reality. That interplay meant that even within premodern traditional Judaism a variety of customs and attitudes toward women, on both the elite and popular level, coexisted. To give but one example: The great twelfth-century rabbinic scholar and philosopher, Maimonides, living in Cairo, endorsed the concept of limited wife-beating to encourage a woman to perform her domestic housekeeping duties, but most of his European colleagues reacted with horror to that position and dismissed it as without foundation in Jewish law.[7]

Besides illustrating the geographical and chronological diversity within Judaism and Jewish experience, the scholarly studies reveal the many ways in which Jewish women of the past reacted to their subordinate status, particularly within the public religious sphere, and created a female Jewish culture to meet their spiritual needs. In medieval Ashkenazi communities, they developed an intense personal piety, which was celebrated by the Crusade chroniclers of the twelfth century, who noted the devotion with which women accepted martyrdom and even slaughtered their own children in obedience to Jewish law.[8] In early modern Europe they developed their own liturgy to supplement the formal Hebrew prayers that they often could neither read nor understand, and they accepted the leadership of elite women to facilitate their public prayer in the synagogue (*see* Berger, p. 73 and Taitz, p. 66). With fewer religious precepts to follow than men, they were able to innovate in the realm of popular custom. Ashkenazi women, who felt themselves responsible for maintaining the family network, translated that responsibility into concern for both the dead and the living members of their families, and so they frequented the cemetery as an appropriate place for prayer. They gathered in small groups on Sabbath afternoons to read aloud from the *Tsena u-R'enah,* the Yiddish collection of Bible stories and Midrash (rabbinic interpretation) arranged according to the portion of the week. They also gathered in groups to prepare memorial candles for Yom Kippur.[9] As a number of articles in this volume mention, in the countries of the Middle East, women developed symbolic gestures such as blowing kisses toward the Torah or performing acts such as cleaning the ark. In all Jewish communities, they donated covers for Torah scrolls to express their sense of connectedness to this most sacred of Jewish symbols—from which they were kept apart. This longing for Torah finds concrete expression today in women's study of Torah, their ritual reading of Torah in Conservative, Reconstructionist, and Reform synagogues, their formation of Orthodox women's prayer groups, and their assumption of the mantle of religious leadership in the rabbinate. This volume eloquently records not only how Jewish women expanded the role permitted to them in the public sacred space of the synagogue, but also how they created other sacred spaces—in their homes, in cemeteries, in philanthropic associations, and even in community centers.

As they were socialized into the highly gender-specific culture of traditional Judaism, Jewish women generally accepted their subordinate status as a divinely mandated one. Even today, as the testimony of Shoshana Gelerenter-Liebowitz demonstrates, subordination and segregation can be perceived as equality when reinforced by religious ideology. In the case of the laws of family purity, however, the ritual acts of separation and avoidance were so internalized by women as a mark of their periodic impurity that, as Shaye Cohen demonstrates, they extended their ritual disabilities and absence from synagogue beyond what the rabbis deemed necessary or legitimate. Was this behavior on the part of women a manifestation of their ignorance of *halakhah*, an assertion of their desire to define the nature of female piety in their own way, or a sign of profound self-loathing engendered by Judaism's ritual construction of menstruation?

If most premodern women seem to have accepted their position within traditional Judaism with equanimity and found means within it for expression of their sense of the sacred, such is not the case in our own contemporary society, in which new concepts of equality, combined with improvements in the socioeconomic status of women, have given expression to both dissatisfaction and strategies for change. Jewish women have assumed upon themselves those commandments from which they are exempted by *halakhah*. They have begun to assert their right to spiritual self-expression and to a public voice within the Jewish community.

Their strategies for enhancing the position of women within the public religious sphere of Jewish life have varied according to their attitude toward *halakhah* and the impact of feminism upon their lives. All Jewish women seeking to expand women's role within the synagogue look to the diversity of opinion within rabbinic literature on the subject of women's obligations and rights as well as to the variety of women's historical experience within the Jewish community. Unwilling to exceed the limits of halakhic consensus, Orthodox women have made innovation within the confines of tradition. In their women's prayer groups (*see* R. Haut, p. 135 and Alter, p. 279) they have discovered the delights of Torah experienced directly rather than vicariously, and they have literally set free their voices in prayer. They have acquired skills in leading religious services, in study, and in chanting of the Torah, skills that were scarcely known to women in the past (*see* Aranoff, p. 261, Doron, p. 258, and Penkowers p. 265). Accepting the gender division mandated by Jewish tradition, they have used it to move from the margins toward the center in terms of public worship and to experience the bonds of female solidarity. Yet, to stay within halakhic standards, they have refrained from asserting the equality of their prayer groups to regularly constituted male *minyanim*.

With fewer constraints imposed upon them, non-Orthodox women have sought access to all sectors of the sacred. Their way was facilitated by the precedent of mixed seating of women and men within the non-Orthodox synagogue, a practice initiated by Reform, Conservative, and Reconstructionist congregations in the nineteenth and twentieth centuries. The introduction of mixed seating opened up the "sacred space" of the synagogue to all Jews. Once that step had been taken, it became easier to make the argument that it was unethical to deny women the right to appear on the *bimah,* first for the honor of opening the ark, then for *aliyot* and reading the Torah, and ultimately to serve as *shliḥot tzibbur* (leaders of the congregation in prayer). The demand for equal access—loudly proclaimed once feminism had sensitized Jewish women and men to the idea that discrimination against women was unjust—culminated in the ordination of women as rabbis. Twenty years ago there were no female rabbis—there are now more than 200 in the United States.

Within all the denominations of Judaism, Jewish women seeking the full recognition of their spiritual needs and intellectual talents have appealed to two ideals of Judaism to subvert the Jewish tradition's relegation of women to a subordinate status. They have pointed to the concept of "in the image of God," that is, the equality of all human beings irrespective of gender, which is found in the creation story;[10] and they have posited the expansion of possibilities for women in study, public prayer, and religious leadership as a form of *tikkun olam* (repair of the imperfections of the world).

Feminist ideology has led some Jewish women to go beyond the recognition of women's social and intellectual equality with men and beyond the call for equal access to the spheres of Torah study, public prayer, and spiritual leadership. On the basis of their experience of exclusion and subordination, and under the impact of feminist literary and philosophical theory, many Jewish feminist intellectuals have offered a critique of Judaism that has questioned the fundamentals of language, liturgy, and theology.[11] Can a traditional liturgy, created exclusively by men and replete with masculine imagery for God, express the religious sensibilities of women? How can Jews incorporate women into a tradition that has marginalized them? What are the limits of the ongoing reinterpretation of classical Jewish texts that are at the heart of the perpetuation of Judaism? These questions, raised only recently, provide an agenda for serious reflection in the Jewish community during the coming decades. In many ways they constitute the latest in a series of challenges posed by modernity to Judaism. Just as the Enlightenment spurred Jewish philosophical and theological creativity, so does feminism promise to do likewise.

Jewish feminists have also developed a more comprehensive program for the full integration of women within Judaism that includes more than just equal access. They have called for the empowerment of women as interpreters of Jewish texts, as legitimate creators of *midrash*. Ideally, women's *midrash* would take its place alongside classical *midrash* and serve as a source of insight for the entire Jewish people. Women's experience and sensibility would be valued; their differences would become not a sign of ignorance but a symbol of the fullness of God's creation.

Finally, some Jewish feminists have questioned the reconcilability of women's experience with the halakhic process itself.[12] It is not only that halakhic authorities have treated women as objects and systematically excluded them from the special knowledge necessary for participation in halakhic decision making. More importantly, the *halakhah* presumes a hierarchical structure of society that contradicts women's experience of relatedness as the glue that holds together human social relations.[13] Some have argued, therefore, that women cannot be integrated into Judaism while the system of *halakhah* is left essentially unchanged.

This volume has suggested the excitement, both scholarly and personal, that attends Jewish women's discovery of our very selves and our rightful appropriation of the sacred—of sacred texts, of sacred history, and of sacred space. It suggests that within the historical experience of the Jewish people there has existed a variety of ways for women to relate to public worship. For some Jewish women and men, the legacy of the past may provide models for the future; others may acknowledge historical patterns but reject them as products of a patriarchal society and culture.

It is clear that there will be many paths toward the fuller integration of women into the life of the synagogue. One interesting question is whether women will be able to sustain experiments in gender-segregated prayer while continuing to argue for equal access. Limited and self-chosen segregation has provided women with opportunities for honing skills, for bonding, and for listening to their once hesitant voices. Will women be sufficiently persistent and powerful to bring into the synagogue their own cultural style, and will synagogue leadership be receptive to hearing the voices of women, even if they speak in tones not previously heard within the sanctuary?

Traditional Judaism declared that a woman's voice (heard publicly) was obscene, for it provoked licentious thoughts among men.[14] Contemporary Jewish women celebrate having found our voices; may our synagogues respond with our song.

Notes

1. Samuel C. Heilman, *Synagogue Life: A Study in Symbolic Interaction* (Chicago: University of Chicago Press, 1973), 69–73.

2. Bernadette J. Brooten, *Women Leaders in the Ancient Synagogue* (Chico, Calif.: Scholars Press, 1982), 128.

3. Cecil Roth, *The House of Nasi: Dona Gracia* (Philadelphia: JPS, 1948), 126–29.

4. *The Memoirs of Gluckel of Hameln*, trans. Marvin Lowenthal (New York: Schocken Books [repr.], 1977), 239–40.

5. Brooten, *Women Leaders*, 103–38.

6. Chava Weissler, "The Traditional Piety of Ashkenazic Women," in *Jewish Spirituality*, vol. 2, ed. Arthur Green (New York: Crossroads, 1987), 245–75; "The Religion of Traditional Ashkenazic Women: Some Methodological Issues," *Association of Jewish Studies Review*, 12:1 (Spring 1987): 73–94; and "Women in Paradise," *Tikkun*, 11:2, (1987): 43–46, 117–20. For a more extensive discussion of these issues, *see* my "Gender and Jewish History," *Tikkun*, 111:1 (1988): 35–38.

7. *See* Maimonides, *Mishneh Torah*, Hilkhot Ishut 21:10 and Rabad's commentary. For a brief survey of the halakhic opinions on wife-beating, *see* Rachel Biale, *Women and Jewish Law* (New York: Schocken Books, 1984), 93–96.

8. For a description of the behavor of women during the first Crusade, *see* Shlomo Eidelberg, ed., *The Jews and the Crusaders* (Madison: University of Wisconsin Press, 1977), 35, 37, 42, 111–13; Shlomo Noble, "The Jewish Woman in Medieval Martyrology," in *Studies in Jewish Bibliography, History and Literature in Honor of I. Edward Kiev*, ed. Charles Berl (New York: KTAV, 1971), 347–55; and Ivan Marcus, "Mothers, Martyrs, and Money-

makers: Some Jewish Women in Medieval Europe," *Conservative Judaism*, 38:3 (Spring 1986) 34–45.

9. For the social contexts of Ashkenazi women's spiritual expression, *see* Chava Weissler, "The Traditional Piety," 245–75, and "The Religion of Traditional Ashkenazic Women," 73–94, and Emily Taitz, "Kol Ishah—The Voice of Woman: Where Was It Heard in Medieval Europe," *Conservative Judaism*, 38:3 (Spring 1986): 46–59.

10. *See* Gen. 1:26, 27. For a feminist interpretation of the second creation story, *see* Phyllis Trible, *God and the Rhetoric of Sexuality* (Philadelphia: Fortress Press, 1978), 72–143.

11. *See* Judith Plaskow, "The Right Question is Theological," in *On Being a Jewish Feminist*, ed. Susannah Heschel (New York: Schocken Books, 1983), 223–33; "Standing at Sinai: Jewish Memory From a Feminist Perspective," *Response*, no. 44, (Spring 1983): 3–14; Ellen Umansky, "(Re)Imaging the Divine," *Response*, nos. 41–42 (Fall-Winter 1982): 110–19; and Judith Plaskow, *Standing Again at Sinai* (San Francisco: Harper & Row, 1990).

12. Judith Plaskow, "Halakha as a Feminist Issue," *The Melton Journal*, no. 22 (Fall 1987): 3–5, 25; Susannah Heschel, *On Being a Jewish Feminist*, "Introduction," pp. xxii–xxxi; and Rachel Adler, "I've Had Nothing Yet So I Can't Take More," *Moment*, 8:8 (September 1983), 22–26.

13. For one feminist statement of female psychology and perception of social reality, *see* Carol Gilligan, *In a Different Voice* (Cambridge: Harvard University Press, 1982).

14. TB Ber. 24a.

GLOSSARY

Agunah (pl. *agunot/agunas*): A "chained woman," unable to obtain a Jewish divorce (*get*) either because of the desertion, unproven death, or recalcitrance of her husband. She may not remarry (cf. *Get*).

Aleinu: One of the concluding prayers of the three daily prayer services.

Aliyah (pl. *aliyot*): The honor of being called up to the Torah. The person receiving an *aliyah* recites blessings before and after the reading of a section of the Torah portion (*see Parashah*).

Amidah: The central prayer of the three daily prayer services, also referred to as the "*Shemoneh Esreh,*" the Eighteen (actually nineteen) Blessings. The type of day (weekday, Sabbath, or holiday) determines the actual number of blessings recited.

Amora (pl. *Amoraim*): Sages of the Talmudic period who flourished in Israel and Babylon between the third and fifth centuries c.e.

Aron Kodesh: Lit. holy ark. Prominently located in the front of the synagogue, the *aron* houses the Torah scrolls. Consequently, it, too, has a degree of holiness.

Ashkenazim/Ashkenazic: Originally referring to Jews of German descent, the term now refers to all Jews of European background. European custom often differs from oriental or Spanish custom, (*see Sefardim*).

Babylonian Talmud: Commentary on the Mishnah compiled and edited in Babylon in the fifth century c.e. (Abbreviated in this text as TB.)

Baraita (pl. *baraitot*): A tannaitic teaching, many of which are not included in the Mishnah but are quoted in the Gemara and/or the Tosefta.

Bar/Bat Mitzvah (pl. *b'nei/b'not mitzvah* [children]; *bar/bat mitzvot* [ceremonies]): The age at which a child becomes responsible for observing all religious obligations, traditionally twelve years old for a girl and thirteen years old for a boy. This transition to adulthood is often marked by a celebration held in the synagogue.

Beit Midrash: House of study, often refers to the small chapel in a synagogue.

Beit Knesset: House of assembly, synagogue.

Bimah: The raised platform in the synagogue from which prayers are led and the Torah is read.

Daven/davening: Anglicized version of the Yiddish, meaning to pray or praying.

Days of Awe: See *High Holy Days.*

Dvar Torah (pl. *divrei Torah*): A sermon or lecture on a religious theme, often related to the weekly Torah portion (*see Parashah*). It is often delivered in the synagogue, from the *bimah* or pulpit, after completion of the Torah service.

Firzogerin: In Eastern Europe, a woman who led prayers for the other women in their section of the synagogue.

Gabbai: Person responsible for giving out synagogue honors (*see Torah honors*) and ensuring that the service flows smoothly.

Gemara: Commentary on the Mishnah (*see Talmud*).

Get: A writ of divorce. Under Jewish law, a civil divorce is not sufficient to allow remarriage; a religious divorce is necessary.

Haftarah: A portion from the Books of the Prophets (Joshua through Malakhai, according to the canon of Hebrew Scripture) chanted during Sabbath and holiday services after the Torah reading.

Haggadah: Perhaps the most popular of Jewish books, it contains the order of the Passover evening meal, the *seder.*

Halakhah/Halakhic: The system of Jewish law.

Hallah: The commandment of separating and burning a piece of dough when in the process of baking bread. This is one of the three commandments particularly directed to women (*see Niddah*).

Hallel: A collection of Psalms (113–118), with opening and closing benedictions, recited on festivals and New Moons.

Hanukkah: The eight-day winter festival, also known as the Festival of Lights in honor of the lighting of the menorah each night, commemorating the victory of the Maccabees over Antiochus IV Epiphanes (ruled 175–164 B.C.E.), the re-establishment of a Jewish independent nation, and the rededication of the Temple.

Hasidism/Hasidic: A movement originally founded in Eastern Europe in the late eighteenth century by Israel Baal Shem Tov. Today, there are many branches of Hasidism (e.g., Lubavitch), each following a rebbe, or charismatic leader. Hasidim follow strictly traditional Orthodox law and custom.

Ha-Shem: A euphemism for God, to avoid the careless use of God's name.

Havdalah: Ceremony marking the end of a Sabbath or holiday.

Havurah: A fellowship of Jews who come together for prayer and study, dedicated to the equal participation of women and men.

Ḥazzan: Professional cantor.

Ḥazzanit: Female prayer leader.

Ḥesed: (Deeds of) kindness.

High Holy Days: See Rosh Hashanah and *Yom Kippur.*

Ḥometz: Leaven, the eating or possession of which is prohibited on the eight days of Passover.

Kabbalah: Jewish mystical tradition (*see Zohar*).

Kabbalat Shabbat: Preliminary Friday night service welcoming the arrival of the Sabbath.

Kaddish: Prayers praising God, the best known of which is recited by mourners for eleven months following the death of a close relative.

Kahal, Kehillah: Congregation or community.

Kashrut: The dietary (kosher) laws.

Kiddush: Prayer over wine sanctifying the Sabbath and holidays. This term also refers to the gathering after services for refreshments.

Levites: Descendants of the tribe of Levi, who were assigned special duties in the Tabernacle and later in the Temple. Today, they are honored with the second *aliyah.*

Maḥzor: Special prayer book for the High Holy Days. *Maḥzorim* have also been published for the festivals.

Maimonides: The great medieval codist, philosopher, and physician who lived in Islamic Spain and Cairo (b. 1135–d. 1204). His best known works include his commentary to the Mishnah; his code of Jewish law, the *Mishneh Torah;* and his philosophical tract, *Guide to the Perplexed.*

Matriarchs: The foremothers Sarah, Rebecca, Rachel, and Leah.

Meḥitzah: Physical barrier separating the sexes in Orthodox synagogues.

Megillah: The *Book of Esther,* which is read on the holiday of Purim and celebrates the deliverance of the Jews of Persia. The *Megillah* (lit. scroll) is written on parchment similar to a *Sefer Torah.*

Mezuzah: Biblical verses written by a scribe on a small piece of parchment (usually housed in a decorative container) attached to the door posts of Jewish homes.

Midrash: Technically, a body of rabbinic literature containing sermons and legal and homiletic exegesis of biblical material based on a close reading of the text. In recent times, *midrash* has come to include creative interpretations, often using traditional texts as a starting point.

Mikveh: A ritual bath, immersion in which renders a person ritually pure. Traditionally, women must immerse one week after cessation of their menstrual flow before they can resume marital relations (*see Niddah*). Immersion is also required of women and men as part of their conversion to Judaism.

Minhag: Custom, as opposed to law. Certain customs attain the strength of laws.

Minyan: The quorum of ten required for group prayer: Traditionally, ten adult males, without which certain prayers (such as *Kaddish*) cannot be recited.

Mishkan: The desert Tabernacle, also referred to as the Tent of Meeting, which signified the Presence of God in the midst of the People. According to biblical tradition, it was the central shrine of the ancient Israelites.

Mishnah: Collection of rabbinic material from the tannaitic period, which, according to tradition was compiled by Rabbi Judah the Prince, c. 200 C.E. Together with the Gemara, it comprises the Talmud.

Mitzvah (pl. *mitzvot*): Commandment, obligation; colloquially, a good deed.

Musaf: Additional prayer (incorporating an *Amidah*) recited on Sabbaths, holidays, and New Moons.

Niddah: A menstruant. Also refers to the body of regulations restricting contact between husband and wife during the menstrual period; it is also called the "Laws of Family Purity." One of the three commandments particularly directed to women.

Ninth of Av (Tisha be-Av): The ninth day of the Hebrew month of Av, occurring in the summer, memorializing the tragedies of the Jewish people, particularly the destruction of the First and Second Temples, which tradition ascribes as having occurred on that day.

Palestinian (Jerusalem) Talmud: Commentary on the Mishnah edited in Palestine around the fourth century C.E. (Abbreviated in this text as TJ; *see Talmud*).

Parashah: Torah portion. The Torah is divided into weekly readings, to be read on each Sabbath.

Patriarchs: The three forefathers Abraham, Isaac, and Jacob.

Rabbinic Literature: An inclusive term referring to material written by rabbis from the Talmudic period to the present. In contemporary usage, rabbinic literature often refers to writings on topics of Jewish law.

Rashi: Rabbi Solomon ben Isaac (1040–1105 C.E., Troyes, France) the renowned biblical and Talmudic commentator, whose glosses appear in standard editions of these texts.

Responsum (pl. *responsa*): Legal decision written in response to a question on Jewish observance; in Hebrew: *teshuvah.*

Rosh Hashanah: The Jewish New Year, the beginning of the High Holy Day period, marked by intensive prayer and introspection.

Sefardim (Sefardic): Originally referring to Jews of Spanish descent, it now often includes reference to Jews from Arabic (Eastern) countries.

Sefer Torah: Torah scroll, containing the Five Books of Moses, the first five books of the Bible. Written by a scribe on parchment, it is Judaism's holiest object.

Shabbat: The Sabbath (Friday sundown to Saturday night). It is the day of rest, when religious Jews refrain from work.

Shaharit: Morning prayer service.

Shaliah Tzibbur (pl. *shlihei tzibbur*): Prayer leader.

Shavuot: The Festival of Weeks that occurs seven weeks after Passover. One of the three pilgrim festivals, when Jewish males were obligated to appear before the Lord with their families. Celebrating the giving of the Torah, it is often marked by all-night classes on religious topics.

Shema: "Hear O Israel," a central prayer of Judaism, consisting of three biblical paragraphs. It is considered the basic statement of faith, accepting the sovereignty of God.

Shemoneh Esreh: See Amidah.

Shtetl: Yiddish term for a small Jewish village or town.

Shtiebl (pl. *shteiblakh*): Yiddish word used to refer to a privately built synagogue, sometimes meeting in a house adapted for that purpose, often led by a Ḥasidic rabbi.

Shul: Yiddish term for synagogue.

Siddur: Hebrew term for prayer book.

Simḥat Bat: Celebration for the birth of a daughter. A growing practice in the Ashkenazic world; some Sefardic cultures have had some celebration for the birth of a daughter (as well as of a son) for generations.

Simḥat Torah: The last day of the festival of Sukkot, marked by joyous dancing with the Torah scrolls in seven *hakafot* (processions) around the synagogue.

Sukkot: One of the three pilgrim festivals. This holiday is observed by eating in a small booth (*sukkah*) for a week, and waving the palm branch and citron (*lulav* and *etrog*).

Tabernacle: See Mishkan.

Tallit (pl. *tallitot*): Prayer shawl. A four-cornered shawl with ritual fringes (*tzitzit*) worn by Jews during morning prayers.

Talmud (pl. *Talmudim*): Second only to the Bible as the central text of Judaism. It includes both the Mishnah and the Gemara. There are two versions, the *Babylonian Talmud* (TB) and the *Palestinian (Jerusalem) Talmud* (TJ). Generally the term is used to refer to the *Babylonian Talmud*, which has been considered the authoritative version since the early Middle Ages.

Tanna (pl. *Tannaim*): Sages of the Mishnaic period, ending with Rabbi Judah the Prince in c. 200 C.E.

Tefillah: Lit. prayer, it also is the term used in Talmudic literature for the *Amidah.*

Tefillin: Phylacteries. Small black leather boxes containing biblical verses that religious Jews wrap on their arms and place on their foreheads each morning, except for Sabbaths, holidays, and fast days.

Temple: The house of God in Jerusalem. The First Temple was built by Solomon and destroyed by the Babylonians in 586 B.C.E. The Second Temple, construction of which began approximately seventy years later, was remodeled by Herod in the first century B.C.E. It was destroyed by the Romans in 70 C.E.

Tetragrammaton: Greek for the four letter name of God, commonly translated as "Lord," which was pronounced only once a year, on Yom Kippur, by the High Priest when he entered the Holy of Holies in the Temple. Today, we no longer know how to pronounce it.

Tisha be-Av: See Ninth of Av.

Torah: The first five books of the Bible, known as the Five Books of Moses. The holiest document in Judaism, representing God's revelation to the Jewish people. *See also Sefer Torah.* The term is sometimes broadly used to refer to all Jewish learning, as in *Dvar Torah.*

Torah Honors: During synagogue services, honors that are distributed among congregants, such as *aliyot* and the opening and closing of the *aron.*

Tosafot: Compilation of commentaries by medieval rabbis from France and Germany, printed in the standard edition of the Talmud. The best known of the Tosafists is Rabbenu Tam, the grandson of Rashi.

Tosefta: Collection of extra-Mishnaic tannaitic material.

Yeshivah (**pl.** *yeshivot*)**:** Religious school, from the elementary level to institutions of higher learning. Traditionally, study focused on Talmud and rabbinic literature. Today most American *yeshivot* include secular studies as well.

Yizkor: Memorial service held on festivals and Yom Kippur. Prayers for the departed—close relatives and martyrs of the Jewish people—are chanted.

Yom Kippur: The Day of Atonement, the culmination of a period of introspection and repentance beginning with Rosh Hashanah, when Jews beseech God to forgive their sins and grant them a good year. The day is marked by fasting and day-long prayer.

Zohar: Kabbalistic text, attributed to Rabbi Simeon bar Yoḥai, containing mystical commentary on the Bible and esoteric subjects.

CONTRIBUTORS

SUSAN D. ALTER, an elected member of the Council of the City of New York for over twelve years, is active in women's rights issues. She has been a member of the Committee on Women of the New York City Council and is also a founding member of *Agunah,* which aids women who are having difficulty freeing themselves from unwanted marriages. She is a director of the International Committee for Women at the Kotel. She was the wife of the late Dr. Aaron A. Alter, the father of her two daughters. In 1985, Mrs. Alter married Rabbi Gilbert Klaperman, Esq.

SUSAN B. ARANOFF is a leader in the UJA-Federation New York Campaign and many other Jewish communal organizations. She is a director of *Agunah* and of the International Committee for Women at the Kotel. She is an assistant professor of Economics and Business at Kingsborough Community College of the City University of New York. She lives in Brooklyn with her husband and six children.

SHULAMITH Z. BERGER catalogued the Joffe Collection of rare Yiddish books at the Library of the Jewish Theological Seminary of America. She is presently a cataloguer and assistant archivist at the Mendel Gottesman Library of Yeshiva University. She holds two Master of Science degrees, one in Modern Jewish History and another in Library Science.

SHAYE J. D. COHEN is Ungerleider Professor of Judaic Studies at Brown University and author of *From the Maccabees to the Mishnah* (Philadelphia: Westminster Press, 1987). He is currently working on a history of conversion to Judaism.

ANNETTE DAUM was Director of the Department of Inter-religious Affairs of the Union of American Hebrew Congregations and Associate Director, Commission on Social Action of Reform Judaism. She edited all the publications of the Task Force on Equality of Women in Judaism and was a founder of "Feminists of Faith." Annette passed away in December 1988.

NAOMI DORON is a founding member of the Flatbush Women's Davening Group in Brooklyn, New York. She lectures to women on Jewish topics and works as a paramedic. She lives in Brooklyn with her husband and six children.

MERLE FELD is a playwright, poet, teacher, and editor. She has been the recipient of a New Jersey State Council on the Arts fellowship and is a member of the Dramatists' Guild. She is an active Jewish feminist and serves on the board of the National Ḥavurah Committee. Merle lives in Princeton, New Jersey, with her husband, daughter, and son.

TIKVA FRYMER-KENSKY teaches Bible at the Reconstructionist Rabbinical College. She has written *In the Wake of the Goddesses* (New York: Free Press, 1992).

SHOSHANA GELERENTER-LIEBOWITZ is a special education teacher specializing in working with the deaf. She also teaches Hebrew school and works with developmentally disabled children.

SUSAN GROSSMAN is a rabbi at Genesis Agudas Achim Congregation in Westchester, New York. She is one of the first women to be ordained by the Jewish Theological Seminary of America, where she is a doctoral candidate in Ancient Judaism. She has authored numerous articles on women and Judaism and Jewish ethics and spirituality.

JUDITH HAUPTMAN is an Associate Professor in Talmud and Rabbinics at the Jewish Theological Seminary of America. Long active in Jewish feminist causes, she has written and lectured extensively on the status of women in Judaism. Her first book is entitled *Development of the Talmudic Sugya* (Lanham: University Press of America, 1988).

NANCY S. HAUSMAN is cantor of Temple Shalom in River Edge, New Jersey and Placement Administrator of the American Conference of Cantors. She graduated from the Reform Movement's Hebrew Union College-Jewish Institute of Religion's School of Sacred Music in 1979.

IRWIN H. HAUT is an Orthodox rabbi and a practicing attorney in New York City. He is the author of two books, *Divorce in Jewish Law and Life* (New York: Sepher-Hermon Press, 1983), and *The Talmud as Law or Literature* (New York: Bet Sha'ar Press, 1982). He has also written numerous articles on secular and Jewish law in American and Israeli law and rabbinical journals.

RIVKA HAUT is an Orthodox activist. She is a founder of the Women's *Tefillah* Network and the Flatbush Women's Davening Group. She organized the first women's prayer service at the *Kotel* and is a director of *Agunah*, an organization that helps women unable to obtain religious divorces. She is a director of the International Committee for Women at the Kotel. She writes and lectures on issues relating to women and tradition and teaches Talmud and Midrash.

PAULA E. HYMAN is the Lucy Moses Professor of Modern Jewish History at Yale University. Co-author of *The Jewish Woman in America* (New York: Dial Press, 1976), she has published widely in the fields of European and American Jewish history. Her most recent book is *The Jewish Family: Myths and Reality* (co-edited with Steven M. Cohen) (New York: Holmes & Meier, 1986). Her book on the Jews of Alsace (tentatively entitled *Country Jews, City Jews*) will be published in 1991 by Yale University Press, and she is currently working on a book on gender and assimilation in modern Jewish history.

NORMA BAUMEL JOSEPH is a lecturer at Concordia University in Montreal, Canada. Her teaching specialties are women and religion and women and Judaism. She is completing her doctoral thesis on Rabbi Moses Feinstein's responsa. She is an Orthodox activist and was influential in the passage of the Canadian Get Amendment. She is a director of the International Committee for Women at the Kotel. She lives in Montreal with her husband, Rabbi Howard Joseph, and their four children.

EMILY FAUST KORZENIK, a rabbi in Stamford, Connecticut, is a member of the Reconstructionist Rabbinical Association. She lectures to religious, secular, and interfaith groups.

BEVERLY A. LEBEAU is a staff accountant with BDO/Seidman in New York City. She holds a Master of Science degree from Roosevelt University. She is married to Rabbi William Lebeau and has had twenty-three years of experience as a rebbetzin and as a mother of five children.

RELA GEFFEN MONSON is currently Professor of Sociology and Dean of Academic Affairs at Gratz College in Philadelphia. She is also a Fellow of the Center for Jewish Community Studies. Two of her most recent publications are *Jewish Women on the Way Up* and *Jewish Campus Life.* She is vice president of the board of the Association for Jewish Studies.

PNINA PELI, born and raised in New York City, has lived in Jerusalem since she made *aliyah* in 1952. A writer and lecturer on contemporary issues in Judaism, and a member of the Rainbow Circle for Interfaith Theological Exchange, she has directed the Shabbat Yaḥad Retreat Program since 1974. She was chairperson of the First Jerusalem International Conference on *Halakhah* and the Jewish Woman in December 1986; a founder of the Jewish Women's Minyan; and a founder and past President of the Mitzvah organization, which is committed to justice for women in Israeli rabbinical courts.

TALYA PENKOWER was a junior in the Shulamith High School for Girls when she wrote her piece.

YAEL PENKOWER holds a Bachelor of Arts degree from the Hebrew University in Jerusalem, a Masters degree in Jewish Studies from Brooklyn College, and a Master in Library Science degree from SUNY-Albany. She worked as a librarian in Stern College and then in YIVO. She is presently the Reference Librarian of the Jewish Theological Seminary in New York City. She lives in Flatbush, Brooklyn, New York, with her husband Monty and their five children.

YONINA PENKOWER was a Freshman in the Shulamith High School for Girls when she wrote her piece.

SARA REGUER, chairperson of the Department of Judaic Studies, Brooklyn College, is an Associate Professor of Judaic Studies. She has recently completed a manuscript on *The Jordan River: a Contemporary History of the Politics of Water,* and has published on topics relating to the Middle East and Jewish women.

HANNAH SAFRAI, Director of the Judith Lieberman Institute for learning for women in Ramat Shapira, Jerusalem, lectures and writes on women and Jewish tradition. Presently affiliated with the K.T.U.A. in Amsterdam, she is lecturing and researching Jewish tradition in Jesus' time.

SUSAN STARR SERED is a lecturer in the Department of Sociology and Anthropology at Bar Ilan University in Israel. She lives in Jerusalem with her husband and four children. She is the author of *Women as Ritual Experts: The Religious Lives of Elderly Jewish Women in Jerusalem* (forthcoming: Oxford University Press).

EMILY TAITZ is co-author (with Sondra Henry) of *Written Out Of History: Our Jewish Foremothers,* (3rd. rev. ed., Sunnyside, New York: Biblio Press, 1988); *One Woman's Power: The Biography of Gloria Steinem* (Minneapolis: Dillon Press, 1987); and *Israel: The Sacred Land* (Minneapolis: Dillon Press, 1987), which is a children's book on Israel. She is presently working on her dissertation on "The Social and Economic History of the Jews of Champagne Until 1306," at the Jewish Theological Seminary of America under a partial grant from the Memorial Foundation for Jewish Culture.

DVORA E. WEISBERG is a doctoral candidate at the Jewish Theological Seminary of America, where she has lectured in Mishnah, Talmud, and Halakhah.

KEY SOURCES

These are some of the important sources that are cited several times in this volume, with the page numbers where they appear. This is not meant to be an exhaustive list; it is to aid those readers who wish to research further the issue of women and the synagogue.

BIBLICAL SOURCES

Exodus 15:20, 21. Miriam.

Grossman: p. 31, n. 19; p. 32, n. 26.
Berger: pp. 78, 79.
Baumel Joseph: p. 131, n. 2.

R. Haut: p. 144; p. 155, n. 37.
Daum: p. 192.

Exodus 38:8. Women who assembled at the Tabernacle.

Grossman: p. 18; p. 33, n. 50.

R. Haut: p. 155, n. 37; p. 276.

Deuteronomy 31:10–12. Hakhel.

Grossman: p. 31, n. 16.
Safrai: p. 46.
Baumel Joseph: p. 131, n. 3.

Hauptman: p. 163.
R. Haut: p. 275.

Judges 4, 5. Deborah.

Grossman, Haut: p. 5.
Grossman: p. 18; p. 31, n. 15.
Taitz: p. 60.

Baumel Joseph: p. 131, n. 2.
R. Haut: p. 137; p. 156, n. 40.
Daum: p. 187.

I Samuel 1, 2 : 1–11. BT. Ber. 31a,b. Hannah.

Grossman: p. 17.
Safrai: p. 47.
Berger: p. 76.
I. Haut: p. 92; p. 100, n. 6.

Baumel Joseph: p. 131, n. 2.
R. Haut: p. 137; p. 153, n. 6.
Khoubian: p. 223.

TALMUDIC REFERENCES

Mish. Ber. 3 : 3. Women's obligations in mitzvot.

Safrai: p. 44; p. 48, n. 36.
Taitz: p. 62.

I. Haut: p. 92.
Hauptman: pp. 162, 173.

Mish. Suk. 5 : 2, TB Suk. 51 a,b–52a, and TJ Suk. 55b. Women's Balcony.

Grossman: p. 23 f.; p. 28.

Baumel Joseph: p. 119; p. 121.

Mish. Mid. 2 : 5,6. Women's Court.

Grossman: pp. 22, 23, 34, n. 61 f.; p. 35.

Baumel Joseph: p. 119; p. 122.

TB. Ber. 24a. Kol Ishah (Women's Voices).

Taitz: p. 61.
R. Haut: p. 137; p. 153, n. 13.

Hauptman: p. 181, n. 46.
Hyman: p. 304, 305, n. 14.

Ber. 45b. Women saying Grace.

Taitz: pp. 62, 63.
R. Haut: p. 145.

Hauptman: p. 162.

TB Meg. 23a. Kavod Hatzibbur (Honor of the Congregation).

Safrai: p. 43; p. 48, n. 26.
Taitz: p. 64.

R. Haut: p. 138.
Hauptman: p. 163.

R. Meir of Rothenberg [cited in Sefer Abudarham (Jerusalem: Usha, 1962), 130.] Aliyot for women.

Taitz: p. 64.

R. Haut: p. 153, n. 17.

Hag. 16b. Semikhah.

Grossman: pp. 20, 23, 25.
Taitz: p. 70, n. 20.
Baumel Joseph: p. 131, n. 3.

R. Haut: p. 151.
Hauptman: p. 170.

RH 33a (and commentary of Rabbenu Tam). Women performing optional mitzvot.

Taitz: pp. 63, 64; p. 70, n. 21.
I. Haut: p. 97; p. 98; p. 101, nn. 35, 45.
R. Haut: p. 141.

Hauptman: p. 170.
Peli: p. 273.

Sefer Abudarham (Jerusalem: Usha, 1962) p. 25. Wives' obligations to husbands.

Taitz: p. 60; p. 69, n. 3.
R. Haut: p. 153, n. 9.

Hauptman: p. 169; p. 180, n. 23.

INDEX

Kabbalat Shabbat service, origins of, 185
Kaddish prayer, 97, 98, 185
  acceptance of by women, 233
  as Aramaic, 186
  at Kotel, 277
  origins of, 185
  women's prayer groups and, 140, 154*n*
  women in synagogue and, 154*n*, 230
Kagan, R. Israel Meir ha-Kohen. *See* Ḥafetz
  Ḥayyim
Kalut rosh (frivolity), as reason for
  meḥitzah, 23, 29, 118, 119, 124
Kaplan, Mordecai
  equality of women emphasized by, 251
  Orthodox *Bat Mitzvah* and, 231
Karaites of Spain, menstruant/parturient
  separation and, 114*n*
Karina (al-Wuḥsha the Broker), 55
Karo, R. Joseph
  on ejaculant restrictions, 107
  on separation of menstruants, 103, 109
  on Torah and impurity, 103, 104
  on *tzitzit*, 166
Kashrut, as sacred activity, 206, 207
Kavod ha-tzibbur. See "Honor of the
  congregation"
Khadima, in medieval Cairo synagogues,
  54, 57*n*
Khoubian family stories, 203–204,
  217–225
Kiddush
  elderly oriental women and, 212
  as women's obligation, 267
  as women's role, 6
Kimḥit, xxiii
Kitchen as sacred space, for oriental
  women, 206
Klagsbrun, Francine, at *Kotel*, 275
Kohanim, 64, 70*n*. *See also* Priests,
  women as
  reinterpretation of law for, 170
  city of, 64, 153–154*n*
Kol Haneshamah, 199, 200
Kol ishah. See Voices of women
Kol Nidre service, 97
Korban ha-Edah (David ben Naftali Hirsch
  Fraenkel), xxiii
Kotel. *See* Women of the Wall
Krug, Marian, at *Kotel*, 275

Kurdistani women, sacred spaces of, 203,
  205–216
Kuzari (ha-Levi), 51

Labor, as donation, 6
Landau, R. Jacob, on menstruant prohibi-
  tion, 111
Language of liturgy. *See* Liturgy
Law. *See* Halakhah
"*Lel-Huza*" lament, 209
Levine, M. Hershel, 69*n*
Life cycle events
  feminist push for change in, 229–231
  new rituals for, 284–296
  in women's prayer groups, 142, 143
Light, women as source of, 5
Lightheadedness. *See Kalut rosh*
Liturgy, 183–202
  See also Prayer(s); Prayer books; *Teḥinot*
  Conservative changes in, 186, 189,
    190–192, 193
  creativity in, 186–187, 287
    miscarriage ritual, 284–290
    pregnancy ritual, 290–296
  language of, 186
    as masculine-based, 187–188,
      190–191
    references to God, 189, 192, 193–196,
      198, 200–201
    shift toward equality in, 188–189
    slowness of change in, 199, 200, 201
  men's prayer of thanks, 189–190
  origins of, 184–187
  prayers offensive to women, 189–193
  Reform changes in, 185, 186, 189
  translations, 196–198
    changes in meaning by, 186
Litvin, Baruch
  attitude toward women of, 130
  mixed seating suit by, 129
  on separation for prayer, 121, 122, 131*n*
Lubavitch life-style, described, 238–242
Lulav obligation, women and, 101*n*, 141
Lydia, at sermon by Paul, 46

Magen Avraham, on self-imposed *mitzvah*,
  174
Magnus, Shulamit, at *Kotel*, 275
Maharam. *See* Meir, R. of Rothenberg

precedents for, 144–145, 155–156n
reactions to, 135, 143, 145–148,
151–152n, 155n, 156n
sense of community in, 143–144
women's participation in
growth of, 150–151, 233
motivation and, 133n

Pagan religious practices, in Greco-Roman
period, 24, 27, 35n, 37n
Palestinian synagogue, female beadle in,
54, 57n
Palestinian tradition, Ashkenazic rite and,
185
Parturients
See also Childbirth, prayers after
purity rules for, 108, 109, 110
in Iran, 219, 225n
Paschal sacrifices, 32n–33n
Passover *seder*
Greek symposia and, 37n
women's obligations at, 91
women's participation in, 32n, 131n
Paul
on women at prayer meetings, 45, 46
on women in synagogue, 39
Personal prayers. *See Tehinot (tehines)*
Pharisees, influence of Temple and, 15–16
Philippi, prayer meetings in, 45, 46
Philo
on pagan festivals, 35n
on prayer assemblies, 39–40, 48n
Phocaea, women in synagogue of, 41, 42
Physical labor. *See* Labor
Pilgrimages
to holy tombs, by elderly oriental
women, 208, 209
paschal, 32–33n
women on, 20, 165, 179n
Poheah, women at Torah reading and,
43, 161
Poland
education for girls in, 261
women's prayer groups in, 67
Portugal, expulsions from, 70n
Prayer(s), 73–82
See also Tehinot (tehines)
central role of, 183–184
compassion concept and, 92, 99, 100n
essential elements of, 94, 97

group nature of, 160–161
women cantors and, 176
Hannah's influence on, 47, 92, 137, 223
leadership of, 160, 161
See also Rabbis; *Shaliah tzibbur*
as forbidden to women, 137
kavannah in, 262
by Lubavitch women, 239–240, 241
new imagery for, 201
ritual impurity and, 104, 105, 106–107,
109, 114n, 219, 220
as sacrifice substitute, 30n, 106, 184–187
separation of women for, 131n. *See also*
Mehitzah
as "service of the heart," 93
translations of by women, 66
types of, 91–92
women writers of
in European synagogues, 65–66, 67
in prayer groups, 142
Prayer books
See also Liturgy
central role of, 183
early compilations, 185
feminist alternatives to, 194, 200
as forbidden to menstruant, 105, 108,
109
by individual congregations, 200
of Orthodox women's prayer groups, 143
translations of, 186
Prayer groups
ancient, 160–161
minyanim vs., 140–141, 154n
women's participation in, 45
women-led, 4, 135, 139–152, 154–157
See also Women's *Tefillah* Network;
Women of the Wall
achievements of, 149–151
Bat Mitzvah in, 142, 150, 257,
265–270
demand for, 9
described, 140–144, 259–261
feminist non-Orthodox, 193–194
history of, 4, 6–7, 144, 155n
in Middle Ages, 64–68, 144
need for, 139–140, 263–264
network of, 148–149
precedents for, 144–145, 155–156n
reactions to, 135, 143, 145–148,
151–152n, 155n, 156n

Temple Israel

Minneapolis, Minnesota

```
            IN MEMORY OF
          FREDA SHAPIRO
               FROM
      DR. & MRS. NOLAN SEGAL
```